Predicting Adjustment in Marriage:

A COMPARISON OF A DIVORCED
AND A HAPPILY MARRIED GROUP

Predicting Adjustment in Marriage: *A COMPARISON OF A DIVORCED AND A HAPPILY MARRIED GROUP*

HARVEY J. LOCKE

GREENWOOD PRESS, PUBLISHERS
NEW YORK   1968

To the pioneers in the study of adjustment in marriage and to those who in the future make the science of predicting adjustment in marriage more exact

PREFACE

THE PURPOSE of the present study is to contribute to an understanding of human adjustment through an analysis of factors associated with marital adjustment and maladjustment. Specifically, the study is a comparison of relatively large samples of divorced and happily married persons in a single county in Indiana. These two groups are compared with reference to a large number of items. Conclusions on marital adjustment from this and other studies should assist in understanding the problem of adjustments in other types of situations.

All of the data were collected through direct contact and interviews with persons in the general population. Specific names and addresses of divorced and happily married persons were secured and these persons were visited and persuaded to participate in the study. Also, it was decided to obtain independent reports from both husband and wife on each marriage studied. It would have been very much easier, of course, to get volunteer subjects and to obtain information from only one spouse. However, the author had the conviction that a *representative* sample of the *general population* should be studied, and also that it would be valuable in given cases to analyze the similarities and differences in the way the two spouses look at their marriage.

It is almost impossible for one adequately to express his indebtedness to those whose prior studies form a part of the body of knowledge on any particular subject, or to express appreciation to all those who have given assistance in an investigation. Scattered throughout the volume are references to various studies, which only in part give credit to the contributions of other investigations.

The 929 persons who participated in the study by answering the questionnaires and by making informal statements about their personal marital experiences deserve particular mention. They received no financial remuneration for their time, and, on the whole, willingly cooperated with the hope that their individual experiences would be of value to other married persons as well as to young people considering marriage. The names of those participating in the study have been omitted from life-history documents, and, where names are used, they are fictitious.

The collection and recording of the data involved the assistance of several persons. Some helped by getting the names and addresses of divorced persons from the courthouse files and the names and addresses of the happily married persons from a random sample of married persons. A few advanced assistants secured part of the interviews. Still others spent long hours in carefully recording and checking the data on holerith cards. While the author expresses his appreciation to all of these, he feels a particular indebtedness to Floyd Ohlin, Karl Schuessler, Frances Butts, and Betty Calpha Cloyd. The last named made a special contribution in that she was the original stimulus in getting the study started; she not only helped in perfecting the questionnaire but also spent several months in interviewing divorced subjects.

In the analysis of the data the author was likewise assisted by several persons, of whom William Klausner, Richard Nugent, and Henry Clay Franklin made the greatest contribution. These three helped in tabulating the data and computed literally hundreds of critical ratios, chi squares, contingency correlations, and other statistics. They also gave critical suggestions as to the meaning of associations between given items and marital adjustment.

Several social scientists gave counsel and advice during the twelve years the study was in progress. Of these only three will be mentioned. Ernest W. Burgess made valuable suggestions for the construction of the questionnaire, for the method of securing the happily-married sample, and for the interpretation of a limited number of the findings. J. P. Guilford generously gave the author the benefit of his expert statistical knowledge. Many hours of technical assistance were made available by Howard Wilson.

The manuscript was read by Dennie Briggs and Helen P. Beem. The latter read the entire manuscript twice, finding many errors and making many constructive suggestions, helped write parts of the text, and read all of the galley proof. Jelly Büchli assisted in the preparation of the index.

Finally, the author expresses his appreciation for the patience and the understanding consideration given by his family—Evelyn Saxton Locke, Arla Mae, and David—during the course of the study.

Financial assistance was given the project by a grant-in-aid from the Social Science Research Council, by grants from the Graduate Research Committee of Indiana University, and by the University of Southern California. Both Indiana University and the University of Southern California took a certain number of units off of the author's teaching load semester after semester, thus enabling him to spend more time in interviewing happily married and divorced persons, in analyzing the data, and in writing up the conclusions of the study. The author also expresses his appreciation to Uppsala University, Sweden, for the very light teaching load given him as visiting professor in 1950–51. This greatly facilitated the completion of the final chapter and the reading of the proofs.

H.J.L.

Uppsala, Sweden
March 15, 1951

CONTENTS

PAGE

1. FOCAL VIEWPOINTS OF THE INQUIRY   1

Unique Features of the Study, The Selection of the
Criteria, The Nature of the Prediction Procedure, The
Use of Life-History Documents, Measurements of the
Degree of Difference between Groups, The Integrity of
the Subjects' Responses, The Role of Values in Predic-
tion, An Objective, Nonmoralistic Viewpoint, Predict-
ing Adjustment before and also during Marriage, Some
Devices Used in the Text, The Utility of Tentative
Knowledge.

2. THE NATURE OF THE SAMPLE   13

A Representative Sample: *Unrepresentative Samples of
Previous Studies, Representative Sample of Present
Study;* Gathering the Data: *Construction of the Ques-
tionnaire, Interviewing the Subjects;* Composition of
the Samples: *The Divorced Sample, The Happily Mar-
ried Sample;* Type of Marriage: *Forced Marriages,
Married-more-than-once, Married-only-once;* Date and
Length of Marriage: *Year of Marriage, Agreement on
Year When Married, Length of Marriage, Remarriage
of Divorced Persons;* Social Characteristics: *Education,
Education of Parents, Nationality, Religion, Date of
Birth, Economic Factors;* Place of Residence: *Place of
Birth, Rural-urban Background, Dispersion of the Di-
vorced after Separation, Mobility or Stability of Resi-*

dence; Limitations of the Study: *Factors Decreasing Representativeness of the Sample, The Use of Different Interviewers, Cross-sectional rather than Longitudinal Study, Responses Modified by the Experience of Divorce, Degree of Generality of Conclusions;* Summary.

3. MEASURING ADJUSTMENT IN MARRIAGE 42

Constructing the Adjustment Test: *Assignment of Weights, The Marital-Adjustment Test;* Validity of Marital-Adjustment Criteria: *Mean Adjustment-Test Score of Men and of Women, Mean Combined Adjustment-Test Score of Spouses, Overlapping Divorced and Married Scores;* Comparison of Adjustment Scores of Spouses; Modification of the Marital-Adjustment Test; Summary.

4. MARITAL DISAGREEMENTS AND CONFLICTS 67

Agreements and Disagreements: *On Basic Interests and Activities, Who Gives In When Disagreements Arise,* Marital Conflicts: *Things Mate Does the Spouse Doesn't Like, Things Which Annoy You about Your Marriage, Number and Kind of Marital Difficulties, Feeling about Marital Difficulties, Times Left Mate Because of Conflict, Talking with Third Party about Marital Difficulties;* Summary.

5. COURTSHIP AND ENGAGEMENT 86

Getting Acquainted: *Place of First Meeting with Future Mate, Length of Acquaintance, Frequency of Seeing Mate during Courtship;* Length of Engagement: *Forced Marriages, Those with a Previous Marriage, Married-only-once;* Conflict and Affection: *Conflict before Marriage, Affection before Marriage;* Reasons for Marrying: *The General Pattern, The Two Most Important Reasons;* Age Variables: *Age at Time of Mar-*

PAGE

riage, Difference in Age of Husband and Wife; Summary.

6. PARENTAL INFLUENCES ON MARITAL ADJUSTMENT 106

Parent-Child Attachments and Conflicts: *Happiness of Childhood, Attachment to and Conflict with Parents before Marriage, Discipline in the Parental Home;* Attachments and Conflicts between Parents: *Pattern of Divorce among Relatives, Happiness of Parents' Marriage, Conflict between Parents;* Relationships with In-laws: *Attitude of Parents toward Prospective Mate, Living with Parents during Marriage, Attitude toward Living with In-laws, Propinquity of Residence to That of Parents;* Summary.

7. SEXUAL BEHAVIOR 125

Conclusions of Other Studies: *Davis, Hamilton, Landis and Landis, Kinsey, Burgess and Cottrell, Terman;* Premarital Sex Behavior: *Number of Persons, Understatement on Frequency of Premarital Intercourse, Variations by Year of Birth, Judgment on Premarital Relations of Spouse;* Marital Sex Behavior: *Mate Overmodest toward Sex, Sex Interest in Comparison to That of Mate, Use of Birth Control, Fear of Pregnancy and Sex Enjoyment, Sex Satisfaction, Refusal of Intercourse when Desired by Mate;* Extramarital Sex Behavior: *Desire for Intercourse with Someone Other than Mate, Number of Persons, Judgment on Mate's Intercourse with Others during Marriage, Jealousy;* Summary.

8. CHILDREN AND MARITAL ADJUSTMENT 158

Presence of Children: *Conclusions of Various Studies, Sample Unmatched for Duration of Marriage, Sample Matched for Duration of Marriage;* Size of Family: *Sample Unmatched for Duration of Marriage, Sample*

PAGE

*Matched for Duration of Marriage, Mean Adjustment
Scores for Different Sizes of Family;* Desire for Children: *Burgess-Cottrell Conclusions, Where Children
Were Present, Childless Families, Comparison of Men's
and Women's Responses;* Summary.

9. PERSONALITY TRAITS (I)   171

*Directorial Ability: Assumes Responsibility Readily,
Strictness with Children, Leadership in the Community,
Ability to Make Decisions Readily, Determination,
Easily Influenced by Others;* Adaptability: *"Giving In"
in Arguments, Dominating—Pressing Opinions and
Ideas on Others, Speed of Getting Angry, Getting over
Anger Quickly;* Summary.

10. PERSONALITY TRAITS (II)   206

Affectionateness: *Presence of Affection, Demonstration
of Affection;* Sociability: *Making Friends Easily, Enjoyment in Belonging to Organizations, Cares What
People Say and Think, Sense of Humor;* Comparison
of Self- and Mate-ratings; Personality Traits of Parents; Summary.

11. GENERAL PERSONALITY PATTERNS   229

Sociability: *Conclusions of Other Studies, Friends before
Marriage, Friends after Marriage, Friends in Common
during Marriage;* Conventionality: *Conclusions of
Other Studies, Place of Marriage, Attendance at Sun-
day School, Affiliation with a Church, Frequency of
Church Attendance;* Summary.

12. THE COMPANIONSHIP FAMILY   245

Intimacy of Communication: *Presence of Face-to-face
Communication, Loss of Unity through Decline in Com-
munication, Sympathetic Understanding, Frequency of
Kissing, Talking Things over Together, Engaging in*

Outside Interests Together; Equality of Husband and
Wife: *Feelings of Equality toward Mate, Intelligence
of Self and Mate;* Shared or Individual Enjoyment of
Activities: *Mutual Enjoyment of Activities, Individual-
ism, Toleration of Activities, Indifference, Conflict over
Activities;* Democratic and Individualistic Behavior:
*Equality in Taking the Lead, Lead Taken by One
Spouse More than the Other, Comparison of the Re-
ports of Husbands with Those of Wives;* Summary.

13. ECONOMIC FACTORS   268

Conclusions of Other Studies: *Negative Findings, Positive Correlations;* Type of Occupation: *Occupation of
Father, Occupations of Men at Marriage, Occupations
of Women at Marriage, Occupations of Men during
Marriage, Occupations of Women during Marriage;*
Economic Level: *Rent and Home Ownership, Life Insurance, Savings, Utilities and Other Home "Necessities," Items Owned by the Family, Borrowing on
Credit, Adequacy of Income, Efficiency of Home Management;* Employment of Husband: *Regularity of Employment, Longest Period of Employment, Husband's
Efforts to Provide;* Employment of Wife: *Extent of
Employment of the Wife, Marital-Adjustment Scores,
Husband's Attitude toward Wife's Working;* Summary.

14. ADJUSTMENT IN SUBSEQUENT MAR-
RIAGES   298

Adjustment of Bereaved Persons Who Have Remarried;
Divorced Persons in Subsequent Marriages: *The Evi-
dence from the Present Study, The Evidence from the
Locke-Klausner Study;* Summary.

PAGE

15. CONCLUSIONS AND PROBLEMS FOR RE-
    SEARCH   310

        Longitudinal Studies of Marital Adjustment: *Predict-
        ing Divorce and Permanence of Marriage, Predicting
        Marital Adjustment from Adjustment in Engagement;*
        Marital-Prediction Items; Nondifferentiating Items; In-
        dependent Criteria of Adjustment and of Prediction;
        The Findings of Different Studies; General Conclu-
        sions; Research Problems.

APPENDIX I: Marriage and Divorce Questionnaire   364

APPENDIX   II: Personality Traits of Parents   384

APPENDIX   III: Research   Investigations   (in   the
        Chronological Order of Collecting the Samples)   388

INDEX   393

TABLES

1. Number and Per Cent of Divorced Cases Completed, and
   One-side-only Cases Secured, in Specified Years   22
2. Happily Married Cases by Number and Per Cent Secured in
   Different Years   23
3. Length of Marriage of Happily Married and Divorced
   Couples, Married only once, by Per Cents   28
4. Per Cent of Happily-Married and Divorced Born in Given
   Periods   31
5. Per Cent of Happily-Married and Divorced Born in Indiana 32
6. Marital-Adjustment Items and Weights for Men and Women
                                                        48–52
7. Per Cent of Happily Married and Divorced Couples Whose
   Average Combined Marital-Adjustment Scores Fell in Specified Intervals   54

PAGE

8. Difference in Scores of Happily Married and Divorced
   Spouses, by Per Cent   59

9. Contingency Correlations of Marital-Adjustment Items Differentiating Happily-Married and Divorced, in Rank Order
   for Husbands   62–64

10. Per Cent of Happily Married and Divorced *Men* Reporting
    Degrees of Agreement or Disagreement with Mate on Given
    Items, with Chi Squares   68

11. Per Cent of Happily Married and Divorced *Women* Report-
    ing Degrees of Agreement or Disagreement with Mate on
    Given Items, with Chi Squares   69

12. Per Cent of Happily-Married and Divorced Checking Items
    as Serious Marital Difficulties, with Critical Ratios of the Dif-
    ference of Per Cents   75–76

13. Length of Premarital Acquaintance of Happily-Married and
    Divorced for Given Months of Acquaintance, by Per Cent   89

14. Length of Engagement of Happily-Married and Divorced by
    Per Cent   94

15. Per Cent of Happily-Married and Divorced Checking Given
    Reasons for Marrying, with Critical Ratios of the Difference
    of Per Cents   98

16. Per Cent of Happily-Married and Divorced for Given Degrees
    of Happiness of Parents' Marriage, with Critical Ratios of
    the Difference of Per Cents   113

17. Per Cent of Happily-Married and Divorced Reporting Vari-
    ous Parental Attitudes toward Prospective Mate, with Critical
    Ratios of the Difference of Per Cents   119

18. Per Cent of Happily Married and Divorced Women Having
    Premarital Intercourse, as Reported by Women and by Men 134

19. Per Cent of Terman's Subjects Born before 1890 and in 1910
    or later, Having Premarital Intercourse with Spouse and with
    Others   135

20. Per Cent of Happily-Married and Divorced, by Period of
    Birth, Reporting Premarital Intercourse with One or More
    Persons   136

21. Per Cent of Happily-Married and Divorced, by Period of
    Birth, Reporting Premarital Intercourse with Mate   137

PAGE

22. Per Cent of Happily-Married and Divorced, Reporting Various Degrees of Sex Satisfaction with Mate, with Critical Ratios of the Difference of Per Cents   145

23. Per Cent of Divorced Women Who Frequently and Never Refused Intercourse with Mate, with Their Reports of Various Degrees of Sex Interest   147

24. Per Cent of Happily-Married and Divorced, Reporting Extramarital Intercourse, and Per Cent Reporting Belief, Knowledge, or Suspicion of Infidelity   152

25. Number and Per Cent of Happily-Married and Divorced Who Had and Desired Children, with Critical Ratios of the Difference of Per Cents   168

26. Number and Per Cent of Childless Happily-Married and Divorced Who Desired Children, with Critical Ratios of the Difference of Per Cents   168

27. Assumes Responsibility Readily: Per Cent of Happily-Married and Divorced, with Critical Ratios of the Difference of Per Cents   177

28. Strictness with Children: Per Cent of Happily-Married and Divorced, with Critical Ratios of the Difference of Per Cents   180

29. Leadership in the Community: Per Cent of Happily-Married and Divorced, with Critical Ratios of the Difference of Per Cents   182

30. Ability to Make Decisions Readily: Per Cent of Happily-Married and Divorced, with Critical Ratios of the Difference of Per Cents   185

31. Determination: Per Cent of Happily-Married and Divorced, with Critical Ratios of the Difference of Per Cents   187

32. Easily Influenced by Others: Per Cent of Happily-Married and Divorced, with Critical Ratios of the Difference of Per Cents   190

33. "Giving In" in Arguments: Per Cent of Happily-Married and Divorced, with Critical Ratios of the Difference of Per Cents   194

34. Dominating—Pressing Opinions and Ideas on Others: Per Cent of Happily-Married and Divorced, with Critical Ratios of the Difference of Per Cents   196

35. Getting Angry Easily: Per Cent of Happily-Married and Divorced, with Critical Ratios of the Difference of Per Cents   200

PAGE

36. Getting Over Anger Quickly: Per Cent of Happily-Married and Divorced, with Critical Ratios of the Difference of Per Cents   203

37. Affectionateness: Per Cent of Happily-Married and Divorced, with Critical Ratios of the Difference of Per Cents   208

38. Demonstrativeness: Per Cent of Happily-Married and Divorced, with Critical Ratios of the Differences of Per Cents 210

39. Sociability—Makes Friends Easily: Per Cent of Happily-Married and Divorced, with Critical Ratios of the Difference of Per Cents   213

40. Likes Belonging to Organizations: Per Cent of Happily-Married and Divorced, with Critical Ratios of the Difference of Per Cents   216

41. Cares What People Say and Think: Per Cent of Happily-Married and Divorced, with Critical Ratios of the Difference of Per Cents   218

42. Sense of Humor: Per Cent of Happily-Married and Divorced, with Critical Ratios of the Difference of Per Cents   223

43. Per Cent of Happily-Married and Divorced Married in a Given Place or by a Given Person   238

44. Per Cent of Happily-Married and Divorced Who Attended Sunday School at Given Ages   239

45. Regularity of Church Attendance of the Happily-Married and Divorced during the First Half of Marriage, by Per Cent, with Critical Ratios of the Difference of Per Cents   241

46. Regularity of Church Attendance of the Happily-Married and Divorced during Last Half of Marriage, by Per Cent, with Critical Ratios of the Difference of Per Cents   241

47. Per Cent of Happily-Married and Divorced Reporting the Mutual Enjoyment of Given Activities, with Critical Ratios of the Difference of Per Cents   257

48. Per Cent of Happily-Married and Divorced Reporting Democratic Relationships in Given Situations, with Critical Ratios of the Difference of Per Cents   263

49. Per Cent of Happily-Married and Divorced Who during Marriage Had Certain Utilities and Other Home "Necessities," with Critical Ratios of the Difference of Per Cents   278

PAGE

50. Per Cent of Happily-Married and Divorced Who during Marriage Owned Certain Things, with Critical Ratios of the Difference of Per Cents   279

51. Per Cent of Happily-Married and Divorced Who Reported Wife Gainfully Employed, for First and Last Half of Marriage   289

52. Ratings of Marital Happiness of Present Marriages by Persons Whose Prior Marriage Had Ended in Divorce   302

53. Mean Adjustment, Prediction, and Sex-Adjustment Scores of Broken and Unbroken Marriages, with Critical Ratios of the Difference of the Mean Scores   313

54. Significant Marital-Prediction Items, with Assigned Weights for the Various Categories   319–337

55. A Comparison of Findings of Marital-Prediction Studies: Items Favorable to Adjustment in Marriage, and Items Having No Relationship   342–357

CHARTS

1. Divorces per 1,000 Married Couples According to Size of Family, United States, 1948   161

2. Divorce Rate for Married Couples with and without Children under Age 18, First 40 Years of Marriage, United States, 1948   162

3. Per Cent of Divorced Families without Children under 21 Years of Age, by Number of Years Married, 1948   165

1

FOCAL VIEWPOINTS OF THE INQUIRY

INTEREST in success or failure in marriage has had a long history, but scientific inquiries into the factors involved in marital adjustment or maladjustment are of recent origin. The purpose of the present study is to add to this growing body of knowledge in the area of marital adjustment by comparing a divorced and a happily married group with respect to a wide variety of items.

Unique Features of the Study. The study has two distinct features which differentiate it from other marital-prediction studies. It is a comparison of marriages ending in divorce with those judged by relatives, friends, and acquaintances as the most happily married known to them, and the subjects are representative of the general population of a county in Indiana. Previous studies, for the most part, have merely taken a married sample and divided it into two groups, those adjusted and those maladjusted as determined by a marital-adjustment test, and the subjects have been highly selected segments of the population.

The desirability of using a divorced group as the unhappily married sample and comparing such cases with a happily married sample was recognized by Ernest W. Burgess in 1937 and 1938, when the author conferred with him on certain problems involved in setting up the study, as well as by Lewis M. Terman in 1939 in the following statement which he included in a memorandum to the National Council on Fam-

1

ily Relations: [1] "I would emphasize the need of research with divorced couples. It is relatively costly in time and labor, but has distinct advantages. The comparison of happily-married with divorced has the effect of holding constant certain aspects of personality which act as disturbing variables in comparisons of happily-married with unhappily-married."

The other distinct feature of the present study, that of securing a representative sample of the general population, is also rather costly and time-consuming. It is relatively easy to get students in a class to fill out questionnaires or even to get persons in the general population to do so if one is not interested in the representativeness of the sample. By contrast, it is very difficult to get specific persons at specific addresses. If a couple has moved, then one has to locate them at their new address, or if they are not at home, one has to go back until he finds them at home, or if they are not inclined to cooperate, one has to return time after time until he secures their confidence and cooperation. These procedures were followed in the present study.

The Selection of the Criteria. Divorce and happiness in marriage were selected as criteria of marital maladjustment and adjustment because significant differences are more likely to be revealed when the extremes of a continuum of behavior are compared. It was assumed that adjustment in marriage varies along a continuum from those few couples who approach 100-per cent adjustment to those few couples who are almost completely maladjusted. It also was assumed that the divorced would be on the lower end of the continuum, whereas those judged by an outsider to be happily married would be on the other end. If the two criteria represent the extremes of marital adjustment, then a comparison of the two groups on a series of items would reveal those items which are neutral as far as marital adjustment is concerned, those which are important for adjustment, and those which are highly associated

[1] In a mimeographed statement presented to the conference.

with maladjustment. Of the items which are significantly related to marital adjustment and maladjustment, some, of course, are much more discriminative than are others. There are very few persons who would deny that divorce is a criterion of marital maladjustment. The crucial question is whether or not happiness in marriage, as judged by an outsider, is a criterion of marital adjustment. Some believe that it is impossible for an outsider to know whether or not a couple are happily married, for the couple may put up a front to outsiders and engage in behavior which is expected of happily married couples, whereas in the privacy of the family they have disagreements, engage in quarreling, and act at cross-purposes with each other.

Two answers are available to the question of the adequacy of "happiness in marriage as judged by an outsider" as a criterion of marital adjustment. The first was provided by Burgess and Cottrell who, in their study of success or failure in marriage, found that an outsider who is fairly well acquainted with a married couple will rate the happiness of this marriage about the same as a member of the couple will rate the happiness of the marriage.[2] They compared 272 paired ratings of happiness of given marriages, with one rating by a member of the couple and the other by an outsider who was more or less acquainted with the marriage. The ratings were under conditions which made it impossible for the raters to collaborate. The ratings were on a five fold scale: very happy, happy, average, unhappy, and very unhappy. The outsiders and the members of the couples agreed in 48.5 per cent of the ratings, agreed within the range of one category in 42.7 per cent, and disagreed by two or more categories in 8.8 per cent. This seems to indicate that happiness in marriage, as judged by an outsider, is a fairly good index of marital adjustment.

The second answer to the question is provided by the present study. A later chapter on "Measuring Adjustment in Mar-

[2] Ernest W. Burgess and Leonard S. Cottrell, *Predicting Success or Failure in Marriage*, New York, Prentice-Hall, 1939, pp. 40–41.

riage" [3] gives a detailed discussion of a marital-adjustment test given to the two groups to see if the happily-married got high scores on the test and if the divorced secured low scores. The fact that this was discovered to be the case justifies the use of divorce as a criterion of marital maladjustment, and of "happiness in marriage as judged by an outsider" as the criterion of marital adjustment.

The Nature of the Prediction Procedure. The distinctive feature of the prediction procedure as used in this study is the analysis of those factors associated with the success or failure of persons in some activity, such as school achievement, and then the use of this information for the prediction of the success or failure of other persons in that activity. The prediction procedure is analogous to the method used by physicians for predicting the course of an illness. Doctors have studied the origin, development, and outcome of a particular disease, have collected the histories of many cases of this illness, and have organized information on what will probably occur under given conditions at any particular stage of its development. They then apply their knowledge to other cases of the illness.

The prediction procedure has been applied to various activities, such as to success or failure in school or in vocations, to supervision in a work situation, to criminal recidivism, to various types of service in the armed forces, and to adjustment and maladjustment in marriage. The procedure is to discover a series of items which separate those who are succeeding from those who are failing in the activity. Weights are then assigned to the various answers or categories given in each of the items. For example, one item in the marital-prediction test might be the question of how many friends a person has, and the categories could be: almost none, a few, several, and many. It might be found that the following weights should be given for these categories: [4] 8 for many, 6 for several, 5 for a few, and 2

[3] Chap. 3.
[4] Procedures for determining weights is described on pp. 46–47.

for almost none. By adding up the weights assigned to a person for each of the series of items, one gets a prediction score for his probable success or failure in the given activity. As will be indicated in detail in the chapter on "Measuring Adjustment in Marriage," this simply indicates the *probability* that a person will succeed or fail in the activity, but a particular person may get a poor score and succeed, or a good score and fail. Prediction is always in an actuarial frame of reference.

In prediction the emphasis is on the *combining* of a number of items into a total prediction test. This, of course, means that no one item, nor even a few, can be taken and used for predicting the success or failure of a person in a given activity. The author is aware that some of the items presented in the following chapters will be abstracted from their context and presented with the implication or the actual statement that by conforming to these ways of behavior a person will be happy in marriage. For example, persons interested in religion may take those religious items which are found more frequently in the happily married than in the divorced group, and present them with the implication or statement that it has been scientifically demonstrated that a person will be happy in marriage if he is affiliated with a church, goes to church with a certain frequency, continues in Sunday school up to a certain age, and the like. The author, however, emphasizes that such items assist in the prediction of adjustment or happiness in marriage *only* when they are combined with many other items.

A physician differentiates between the symptoms of a disease and the factors involved in its origin. So, likewise, the trained investigator knows that the predictive items are only indices of marital adjustment and maladjustment and are symptoms of more fundamental and basic satisfactions or difficulties. Those working in the field of marital prediction constantly keep in mind the fact that predictive items show whether or not marital adjustment *will be present* and do not indicate the conditions and relationships which *produce* adjustment in marriage.

The Use of Life-History Documents. Some social scientists feel that prediction should include data secured both from questionnaires and from life-history documents. In the present study life-history materials were collected in the informal interviews, but not systematically. The excerpts from the actual statements of the happily-married and the divorced, while presented only as illustrations, give insight into the meaning of marital adjustment and maladjustment through the eyes of those who have undergone or are undergoing the experience of marital happiness or unhappiness.

Measurements of the Degree of Difference between Groups. The investigator generally wants to know whether or not given differences between two or more groups might be due to chance. Simple statistical procedures are available which provide an answer to this question of whether or not a difference would disappear if a new sample were taken from the same population. The two most frequently used in the present study are the critical ratio and chi square.

An investigator arbitrarily decides the level of risk he is willing to assume on the probability that differences will or will not disappear in a new sample. The author chose to be conservative in that he arbitrarily decided to accept a difference between the happily-married and the divorced as significant if there were only 5 chances or less in 100 that it might disappear in a new sample. A critical ratio or CR * of 2.0 gives this level of risk, and the larger the critical ratio the greater the probability that a difference is real and not due to chance. Likewise, the greater the size of a chi square the greater the likelihood that the difference is actually present and will not disappear if new samples are secured. But it should be remembered that there is always a *chance* that the difference is due to chance. Later chapters reveal many items on which the happily-married and divorced differed on the level of significance selected for the study.

* CR is used throughout this study to indicate "critical ratio."

Often it is as important to discover that two groups do not differ significantly on given items as to discover that differences do exist. For example, persons have been in the habit of saying that various things are associated with marital success or adjustment. If it can be discovered that happily-married and divorced do not differ significantly on some of these, a real contribution to knowledge will be made. Later chapters reveal items that have been commonly assumed to be related to marital adjustment on which no significant differences were discovered between the present samples of happily-married and divorced.

The Integrity of the Subjects' Responses. Can one trust the happily-married and the divorced to give accurate answers to questions relative to subjective feelings and the more private and intimate phases of marital relationships? Will honest replies be given to questions about behavior which frequently receives a negative reaction from others? If one is happy in a situation, will he not look at that situation through rose-colored glasses, and if he is unhappy, will he not be likely to take a "dim view" of the situation? Such questions disturb those who are not familiar with the nature of prediction. In a prediction study one is searching for symptoms which will indicate the probable future development and outcome of an activity. Consequently, the *actual replies* may very well be more important indices for prediction than the *actual situations* which exist.

The present study and others have shown that, even though subjects try to be honest in reporting actual experiences, some of their replies indicate differences from that which actually happened. For example, when happily married and divorced men and women were asked to rate their mates on a personality trait or on some other behavior, the tendency of the happily-married was to give "good" ratings to the mate, while the tendency of the divorced was to be derogatory toward the mate. The important thing is not whether the reported behavior actually occurred, but the meaning of the behavior for the subject. For prediction purposes it is very important to know whether a person thinks of the mate as stingy or simply thrifty, irresponsible or just having hard luck, being too easily influenced by others or merely being considerate of others, and being grouchy or behaving like a little boy when irritated. The integrity of the subjects' responses should be thought of in terms of whether or not they assist in predicting the probable future behavior of the person in a given activity—in the present case adjustment or maladjustment in marriage.

The Role of Values in Prediction. If one had adequate information on the values of an individual or a group and on the degree to which these values are being satisfied, one could predict the behavior of the individual or group with a high degree of accuracy. Throughout the volume the author has frequently interpreted the differences in responses of the happily-married and divorced in terms of divergent values, or in terms of differential satisfaction of values. The responses subjects gave to a particular question often were clues to their values. For example, the statement of a person that the mate has many friends may or may not be exactly correct, but it may be an index of the value a person places on the sociability of the mate. Also, the statement that the couple went to church at least once a week during marriage again may or may not be an exact statement of the frequency of church attendance, but may be simply an index of the value a person places on conformity to community norms. The author feels that the present study has made only a beginning in the analysis of the relation of values to the prediction of marital adjustment, and that future studies will deal with this in a much more systematic manner.

An Objective, Nonmoralistic Viewpoint. All forms of normal and deviant behavior are considered by the social scientist to be natural in that they have an understandable origin.

Granted that various persons may desire to modify some of the deviant behavior, still, the scientist has to free himself from feelings of the goodness or badness of any activity. This was the spirit in which the study of marital happiness and divorce was made. The author, over a period of years, developed an objective, nonmoralistic viewpoint toward various forms of behavior. In training his assistants, this attitude was emphasized. It was found that divorced persons frequently expected the interviewer to have a negative attitude toward divorce and, even though they were willing to cooperate at the beginning of the interview, they became even more willing when they discovered that the interviewer not only did not have a negative attitude, but expressed a sympathetic, understanding attitude toward the problems of the divorced. Also, this was true for subjects who had engaged in behavior which was defined negatively in the culture. An objective, nonmoralistic viewpoint is a prerequisite to securing full cooperation of such subjects.

Predicting Adjustment before and also during Marriage. The present study and those of certain other investigators, particularly Burgess and Cottrell, differ in some basic assumptions. The difference revolves around the question whether the prediction of marital adjustment is limited to the premarital period or whether it is applicable at one time in a marriage to a future time of the marriage. In a recent volume published by the Social Science Research Council on *The Prediction of Personal Adjustment*,[5] the authors insist that the predictive factors should be those found to exist before participation in the activity. Another example of this view is that of Burgess and Cottrell, who assume that behavior tendencies existing in the persons before marriage determine whether or not they will be adjusted in their marriage.[6] These authors

---

[5] Paul Horst, editor, *The Prediction of Personal Adjustment*, New York, Social Science Research Council, 1941, particularly pp. 42–48.
[6] *Op. cit.*, chaps. 7 and 14.

pay little attention to the "new" behavior tendencies which develop during the marriage. They are inclined to hold that, if a trained observer had sharp enough instruments of perception, he could discover at the time of marriage practically all behavior which would be manifested during marriage. They tend to emphasize the psychiatric view that the foundation of later behavior is laid during the first few months or years of life. Therefore, they assume that prediction can be limited to premarital behavior.

The present investigator assumes that much of the marital behavior is the direct expression of behavior tendencies developed prior to marriage, but he also assumes that much marital behavior is the reflection of experiences which the persons have during marriage. It is assumed that behavior tendencies are modified and developed as the result of communication between persons within the marriage relationship and with outsiders. Thus, the behavior of the husband, wife, and children may be somewhat different year by year. The position has been taken, therefore, that one can secure a more perfect prediction of the success or failure of a marriage by taking into account not only the premarital behavior, but also marital experiences. One may be interested in predicting the future marital adjustment of persons already married.

Marriage, in most cases, is an activity extending over a long period of years. If one is interested in predicting the behavior of persons in the first years of marriage, then, of course, there may be disadvantages in using responses which have been modified by many years of marital experiences and made by subjects whose memories are undoubtedly faulty. If one is interested in predicting adjustment during the first few months of marriage, then possibly it would be desirable to secure a group of engaged persons and predict marital adjustment on the basis of premarital experiences, as Ernest W. Burgess and Paul Wallin have been able to do.[7] However, if one is inter-

---

[7] Ernest W. Burgess and Paul Wallin, *Engagement and Marriage*, New York, Harcourt, Brace and Co., to be published in 1951.

ested in predicting adjustment of persons three years after marriage, possibly one should not limit the sample to engaged persons, but should secure a sample of subjects who have had two years of marital experience and see if a prediction can be made of how adjusted the subjects will be a year later. In general, one would assume that, if one is interested in predicting the behavior of persons at a particular stage of marriage, then greater accuracy of prediction will be secured by including in the sample people who have had marital experience up to or near that stage of marriage.

This difference in basic assumptions—that prediction data should be limited to the premarital period in contrast with the view that marital data should also be included—is one of degree, for Burgess and Cottrell and others do not completely ignore marital experiences.

Some Devices Used in the Text. Two devices used in presenting the materials need a word of clarification. Occasionally it was desirable or necessary to combine two or more possible answers into a single category. Where this is done, "and" is placed in italics. For example, a significantly larger per cent of happily married men and women than divorced had "several" *and* "many" friends. This device enables the reader to know immediately when two or more answers are combined into a single category.

Another device is the use of the questions given to the happily-married, when specific questions are included in the text, without rewording them for the divorced. It would be cumbersome to include the way the question was phrased both for the happily-married and for the divorced. For example, one question might be phrased, "How many friends do (did) you and your mate (former mate) have in common during marriage?" Consequently, it was decided to use only the phrasing of the questions given to the happily-married, knowing that the reader will assume that appropriate rephrasing was made for the divorced.

The Utility of Tentative Knowledge. The author, although he is keenly aware of certain limitations of the present study, is also aware of the desire and need for scientific knowledge by persons who are engaged in premarital or marital counseling and are faced with the immediate rather than the ultimate application of knowledge. He assumes the position that a social practitioner, such as a minister, social worker, or counselor, has to use the most nearly adequate information which is available, although some of the information may be shown by later studies to be incorrect. He therefore expects that such persons, as well as those who are experiencing personal problems, will receive some assistance from the information included in the following chapters. He urges that the information be used with caution and be accepted as only tentatively correct. He fully expects that future studies will necessitate the revision of some of the conclusions derived from the present investigation.

2

THE NATURE OF THE SAMPLE

Most investigations of human behavior have been made by university professors on university and college students. It is often assumed that such information is applicable to the general population. An increasing number of social scientists have become highly critical of this type of study and are insisting that, if the conclusions of a study are going to be applied to the general population, then the sample must be from the general population.

This chapter describes the method used in the present study to secure a representative sample of two groups in the general population of a midwestern county in Indiana, the procedures used in collecting the data, the composition of the sample, the types of marriages investigated, the date and length of marriage, the social characteristics of the happily-married and divorced subjects, the place of residence, and the limitations of the study.

A REPRESENTATIVE SAMPLE

Only recently have social scientists given attention to the problem of securing a representative sample. In the past, and to a great extent even today, investigators have adopted the relatively easy method of obtaining cases by getting volunteers. This was the method employed by Alfred Kinsey in his study of human sex behavior and by Burgess and Cottrell and Terman in their marriage studies.[1]

[1] Alfred C. Kinsey, Wardell B. Pomeroy, and Clyde E. Martin, *Sexual Behavior in the Human Male*, Philadelphia, W. B. Sanders, 1948. Ernest W. Bur-

Unrepresentative Samples of Previous Studies. The difficulty encountered by students of family behavior in securing representative samples was described nearly two decades ago by Bernard as follows: [2]

Studies of normal families, depending, as they must, upon voluntary cooperation, will probably always select an exceptionally intelligent, well-educated group. Average people can seldom mobilize their intelligence and emotions sufficiently to cooperate in a study of family relations, dealing, as such studies so frequently do, with emotional sore spots.

Bernard was discussing the kind of samples ordinarily used in social-science studies and not the kind that can be secured. Obviously a sample will be highly selective if questionnaires are distributed through graduate and undergraduate students,[3] or through family-relations conferences, women's clubs, and other organizations interested in uplift activities.[4]

The unrepresentative character of the two previous marital-prediction studies is indicated by the fact that 52.5 per cent of husbands in the Burgess-Cottrell group were engaged in professional, semiprofessional, or upper-business activities, and 56.5 per cent of husbands in the Terman study held professional, business-executive, or managerial positions. The income level of the subjects of both studies was relatively high. Also, 58.3 per cent of Burgress-Cottrell subjects and 73.3 per cent of Terman subjects had one or more years of education beyond high school, with 16.2 per cent and 27.7 per cent, respectively, having one or more years of graduate work.[5]

gess and Leonard S. Cottrell, *Predicting Success or Failure in Marriage,* New York, Prentice-Hall, 1939. Lewis M. Terman, *et al., Psychological Factors in Marital Happiness,* New York, McGraw-Hill, 1938.

[2] Jessie Bernard, "Factors in the Distribution of Success in Marriage," *American Journal of Sociology,* XL, 1934, p. 52.

[3] Ernest W. Burgess and Leonard S. Cottrell, *op. cit.,* pp. 18–20.

[4] Lewis M. Terman, *et al., op. cit.,* pp. 40–41.

[5] Ernest W. Burgess and Leonard S. Cottrell, *op. cit.,* pp. 24–27. Lewis M. Terman, *et al., op. cit.,* pp. 41–43.

Representative Sample of Present Study. Rather than depending on the voluntary cooperation of selective groups, an attempt was made to secure a representative sample of divorced persons and of happily married persons from the general population of a single county in Indiana. The cooperation of given persons in these two groups was secured through personal contact by the author or by a person under his supervision.

The sample of divorced persons was obtained by getting from the courthouse files the names of all the couples divorced in the years immediately preceding the time of interviewing, and contacting every one of these that could be located.[6] A few additional names were secured from divorced persons, who occasionally volunteered names and addresses of other divorced persons. To be included in the study, couples either must have secured their divorces in the county or must have lived there at the time of the interview.

Over half of the divorced sample, 51.6 per cent, secured their divorces between 1938 and 1944. Only 4.0 per cent of the cases secured their divorces before 1930; 16.7 per cent between 1930 and 1934; and 27.7 between 1935 and 1937. Thus, four out of five of the cases in the divorced sample had secured their divorces in the ten-year period 1935–1944.

A couple was judged to be happily married if they were recommended by some relative, friend, or acquaintance as one of the most happily married couples known by the person making the recommendation.[7] It was decided to try to match each divorced case with a happily married couple suggested by one of the partners of the divorced case. This decision was made several months after the study was initiated and, consequently, a letter was sent to those divorced persons who had been interviewed asking for names of happily married couples. This brought but few responses. About a third of the

---

[6] At first we went back as far as 1929 for names of divorced persons. See footnote 11.

[7] No unmarried person's recommendations were used.

happily married couples were recommended by divorced persons.

The names of the remainder of the cases were secured from recommendations of a random sample of married persons in the county. These names were obtained in the following manner: every other street in the city was selected and the occupants were contacted in the first house of the first block on one side of the street, the second house in the second block on the other side of the street, and the third house in the third block, etc. When no one answered the door, the next house in that block was contacted.

The map below shows the distribution of those cases in the city where the husband and wife were both secured. An "o" is the symbol for a divorced case [8] and " • " for a married

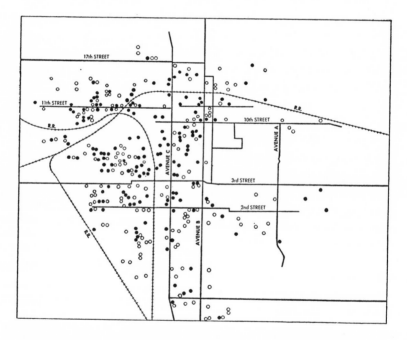

[8] The address of the divorced was the one at the time of the divorce, and the address of the happily-married was where the couple resided at the time of the interview. The map does not include cases outside the city.

case. Toward the end of getting the interviews an attempt was made to distribute divorced and married cases evenly in the different districts of the city and county.

It was very much more difficult and time-consuming, of course, to reach specific persons at particular addresses than it would have been to get the cooperation of volunteers. This was especially true in connection with the mate of a divorced person, for often the mate had moved out of the neighborhood or out of the county. However, it was felt that representativeness of the sample was essential, for, if the sample were biased, the generalizations would be biased. The representativeness of the sample was also safeguarded by interviewing only one couple of those supplied by a given person making recommendations.

The section later in the chapter on "limitations of the study" gives some of the factors affecting the representative nature of the divorced and happily married samples. The section on "social characteristics" indicates the kind of persons secured and the degree to which they were representative of the general population of the area.

GATHERING THE DATA

Gathering the data included various kinds of activities. Here the discussion will be limited to the construction of the questionnaire and to the problems involved in interviewing.

Construction of the Questionnaire. The first step in constructing the questionnaire was to formulate common-sense questions that seemed logically related to the problem being studied. This was done by a committee of three advanced students and the author in weekly conferences over a period of three months. These questions were added to and modified in the light of questions used in other marital-prediction studies. The questionnaire was then submitted to Ernest W. Burgess, who generously consented to criticize it. Certain revisions of the questions were found necessary from two pretests in the general population to which the questionnaire was to be applied. The final result was a schedule of 108 questions which could be completed in about a two-hour interview.

Inasmuch as each case was secured by a personal interview, supplementary information was obtained through informal conversation. Although occasionally this life-history material was recorded during the interview, generally it was written up immediately afterwards.

Interviewing the Subjects. Because the study did not depend upon volunteers but upon the rank and file of the general population, techniques of persuasion had to be developed. In general, the confidence and cooperation of subjects could be secured by a statement like the following:

I am from the university and would like your cooperation in a study which we are making. (While saying this the interviewer would make a slight bodily gesture of entering the house.) Men have written a lot on the family, but their ideas came out of their minds without their going out and finding what the facts are. We hope to help young people in selecting a partner and in their marriages by getting people like yourself to give information on the basis of their own experiences. You can be of great help to us and to these young people by answering a few questions for us. Your name, of course, will never be used.

The interviews, although somewhat standardized, were adjusted to the kind of person that was being interviewed and the kind of situation in which one found himself. When a subject was contacted, the immediate task was to "size him up" and to adjust the interview to his probable educational level, social status, and reactions. If a person was well educated, there was included the idea that social scientists have only recently developed a scientific approach, whereas physicists and chemists have been practicing careful experimentation for a long time. The study was presented as an attempt to arrive at scientific knowledge of the factors involved in marital adjustment by going out into the laboratory of the community and getting the experiences of people. On the other hand, if the subject was of low educational attainment or an illiterate, an appeal was made to his kindness of heart and his interest in the welfare of people. If the subject expressed strong religious sentiments, the interviewer would show a sympathetic attitude toward religious values.

The situations in which interviews were conducted varied greatly. Sometimes the subject lived in a one-, two-, or three-room house. The persons in the house were manipulated so as to isolate the one interviewed as far as possible from other persons in the house. Sometimes the interview took place in a bedroom; at other times it was in the interviewer's car or at the office. One divorced man was located in a tavern, and was induced to go to the university. Then he was talked to until he was relatively sober, when it was possible to check him on previous answers to questions and to secure additional information. Two were interviewed in prison and two were questioned in the woods with the subject sitting on one stump and the author on another. The author played rummy with one man to get him into the spirit of cooperating. Another man was shearing sheep, and the interview was carried on in this situation. The following excerpts from the life-history materials on a divorced case, which was secured by a trained woman interviewer, gives a concrete picture of the way interviews were adjusted to the type of subject and situation: [9]

When we got to the house we found the man all greasy and dirty from working on his car. We told him we were from the University and mentioned the letter which had been sent him asking for his cooperation in a study.[10]
"Is it about my divorce?"
"Yes."

[9] Case no. 10.
[10] After a few months the introductory letter was discontinued. It was as easy to get into a home without the letter as with it.

"I was afraid of that. I am awful busy right now. If you want me to answer the questions, you will have to read them to me, for I have to get under the car."

Finally he apparently got a little worried about us and got out from under the car. He told us, "Go into the house while I wash up and we'll see what we can do about this."

He was washing his shoulders when I went in. All the time we were there, he kept going into the next room, closing the door, and then would come back out with renewed willingness to co-operate. Apparently he felt the need of stimulation.

Once he stopped, and said, "You'll try to see my wife. I don't want any of this to reflect on my little girl. She will be eight in July. You will go out to see my wife and she will give me hell. Never saw such damned questions in my life."

It was difficult to secure the cooperation of the wife of the case presented above. The interviewer, who had handled the husband's case, was unable to persuade his wife to co-operate. Later another interviewer secured the case by getting acquainted with her "boy friend" and inducing him to per-suade her to help in the study. The following is a report of the efforts of the first interviewer to get the case:

Had made about eight trips there and each time she would be at one of three places—working, getting her hair fixed, or out riding with her boy friend. Have been going there about one and a half months at least. Had talked to her mother and to her younger sister. The entire family was very congenial and friendly toward me.

About the second time before the last, the mother told me, "Beatrice knows what you're coming after. She got your letter. She wanted me to tell you, you needn't come no more; she just isn't interested." I insisted I must see her—that I had instructions from the professor to contact each person personally. "Well, there isn't much use. Beatrice is all through with that now and she just isn't interested." I got her to tell me a time when Beatrice would be home—between 9:00 and 10:00 in the morning.

Today is the first time I have seen Beatrice. She is much different from what I had expected. In her late twenties or early thirties, nice looking, appears very conservative, and seems the type to cooperate. However, she did not.

"Are you Beatrice Brown?"

"Yes, I am. I know what you want, and I told Mother to tell you I wasn't interested, but she said you wouldn't take 'no' for an answer. I don't want to have anything to do with it."

"Well, do you understand it fully? I'd like for you just to read it over. Just answer a part of it."

I kept this up continually, putting heart and soul into a convincing speech, bringing in Dorothy Dix as nonscientific and that we were going at this thing scientifically. She listened with a rather defiant expression as though nothing I said would please her. It didn't. She was embroidering on the porch; her little girl was there, too; and the family was listening in the house.

"I just don't have much time. I work practically all the time, and what little time I am here at home, I like to rest. I know what those are like. You say they won't be published, but they will be. Things like that always are. Then they'll be read in class. That's what they're for. No, I'm just not interested. I don't care to do it."

I couldn't budge her.

A completely standardized approach to interviewing either the husband or wife of the above case would have been impossible. If one had a highly homogeneous group of subjects and were able to bring them into the same room, one might adopt a rather uniform approach. However, when interviews are with a representative sample of the general population in the situations where people are willing to be interviewed, modifications in the standardized approach have to be made.

COMPOSITION OF THE SAMPLES

The Divorced Sample. The divorced sample includes 201 persons with their respective mates,[11] plus 123 persons where

---

[11] An actual divorce had not been secured in 15 of the 201 couples, but in these cases either an application for divorce had been made or was contemplated. The schedules of nine couples were discarded for the following reasons: (1)

only one side of the case was secured; [12] of these, 50 were men and 73 were women. The reasons for not securing the respective spouses were as follows: The largest single group, 71, either could not be located or had to be discarded because they were too far away. The next largest group, 38, refused to cooperate in the study. A few, 11, might have been secured if the goal of 200 completed cases had not been attained. In 3 cases the mates had died.

The collection of divorced cases began in June of 1939 and ended in March of 1944. Table 1 shows that about three fourths of the cases were secured in three years—1940, 1941, and 1942.

TABLE 1

Number and Per Cent of Divorced Cases Completed, and One-side-only Cases Secured, in Specified Years *

Year	Completed		One-side-only	
	Number	Per Cent	Number	Per Cent
1939	24	11.9	19	15.4
1940	50	24.9	33	26.8
1941	61	30.3	45	36.6
1942	44	21.9	12	9.8
1943	1	0.5	0	0.0
1944	21	10.5	14	11.4
	201	100.0	123	100.0

* A case was considered completed when the respective mate had been secured.

It was decided to confine the sample to whites as the number of colored families in the county was very limited. In 1940 only 441 or 1.2 per cent of the population of the county were colored. Before this decision was made, three colored couples had been secured. (2) After the study was under way, it was decided to include those cases which had already been secured back through 1929 and to include thereafter only those who had secured divorces in 1933 and later. Five couples had secured divorces prior to 1929, and these were discarded. (3) The other couple was discarded because a check raised the question whether the man and woman had been husband and wife.

[12] Only 2 of the 123 one-side-only cases were separated rather than divorced persons. Sixteen unpaired cases were discarded because the divorces had been secured prior to 1929.

The Happily Married Sample. The married sample is composed of 200 persons with their respective mates, plus four cases where only one side was secured. The names of 76 of these were secured from divorced persons and the names of the remaining 128 from married persons. Sixteen of the latter were recommended by two different persons. Of the 76 secured from divorced cases 21 were either recommended by a second divorced person or recommended by one or more of the married persons.

Table 2 gives the number and per cent of the 200 happily married couples secured in different years. The collection of cases began in June of 1941 and was completed in March of 1944. The table shows that 82 per cent of the cases were secured in 1942.

TABLE 2

Happily Married Cases by Number and Per Cent Secured in Different Years

Year	Number	Per Cent
1941	10	5.0
1942	164	82.0
1943	20	10.0
1944	6	3.0
	200	100.0

TYPE OF MARRIAGE

It was felt that differences might exist between cases married only once, married more than once, and marriages which were due to pregnancy. Consequently, the divorced cases were divided into three samples: married-only-once, married-more-than-once, and marriages in which one or both spouses reported that pregnancy was the cause of marriage. There were only two or three cases in the happily married group in which pregnancy was given as the cause of marriage, and they were not put into a separate sample, but were included with the other happily married cases.

Forced Marriages. The marriage-caused-by-pregnancy sample is composed of 32 divorced couples, plus 9 cases (4 women and 5 men) where information was secured for only one side of the marriage. Thus 41 marriages ending in divorce are represented in this sample.

Married-more-than-once. This sample is composed of cases where either spouse was married prior to the marriage under investigation, but excludes such cases if pregnancy was the cause of the marriage. Among the married-more-than-once cases were 26 happily married men, the same number of happily married women, 50 divorced men, and 52 divorced women.[13]

The divorced sample did not include many persons married and divorced several times, for multiple divorce is not common in the population from which the samples were drawn. Of all divorced men and women the respective per cents having only one divorce were 86.5 and 87.5, and the respective per cents with more than two divorces were 3.2 and 2.6. For the happily-married 5.0 per cent of the men and 4.5 per cent of the women had had a prior marriage ending in divorce.

Happily married and divorced men and women who had had a prior marriage were asked to give the length of the longest prior marriage. The average length of this marriage in years was as follows: divorced men, 14.6; divorced women, 14.5; married men, 15.6; and married women, 13.0. Thus, if a person had been married prior to the marriage investigated, it was for a relatively long period. It is to be assumed that this long period in a prior marriage would affect the adjustment in the later marriage. Moreover, there was a considerable pe-

[13] The married sample included 7 men and 7 women in which only one spouse had been married more than once.

riod between the termination of the prior marriage and re-marriage.[14] It seemed advisable, therefore, to separate such marriages from those married only once, which would make the latter a more homogeneous group.

Married-only-once. The analysis in the following chapters is for the most part limited to those happily married and divorced cases married only once. As indicated above, this excludes cases where either the husband or the wife had been married more than once prior to the marriage under investigation, and the marriages due to pregnancy. The sample includes 173 happily married men, 171 happily married women, 164 divorced men, and 186 divorced women.[15] It will be recalled that information was not secured on the mates of 123 divorced and 4 happily married cases. This accounts for the difference in the number of men and women.

DATE AND LENGTH OF MARRIAGE

Were there differences in the per cents of the happily-married and divorced who married in given years? If there were differences, did marital-adjustment scores differ between those who married in the different periods? How long had happily married and divorced couples been married and what was the range of years married? These questions will be treated below.

Year of Marriage. The two samples differed in the proportion married in the different periods. As compared with the divorced sample, there was a larger per cent of the married, 37.4 and 29.7, married before 1923; a smaller per cent, 14.6 and 25.8, married in the period 1923–1929; a smaller per cent, 30.8 and 41.7, married between 1930–1938, and a larger per cent, 17.2 and 2.8, married in 1939–1943.[16]

14 For the married, the average years were 3.6 for men, and 3.5 for women.
15 The married-only-once divorce sample includes 4 men and 6 women who were married and divorced after the marriage being investigated.
16 The analysis is for married-only-once and those married more than once. It will be recalled that most of the married were interviewed after the majority

Marital-adjustment scores [17] did not differ very much for those who were married in the different periods. This is shown by the mean adjustment scores of married men, married women, divorced men, and divorced women in each of the four periods: before 1923, 1923–1929, 1930–1938, and 1939–1943. In the last period the number of divorced cases was too small (4 men and 7 women) to compute mean scores. The mean adjustment scores for married men in the four periods were respectively 138.9, 142.4, 136.8, and 137.5; and for married women, 136.4, 135.4, 137.7 and 139.8. The mean scores for the first three periods for divorced men were 98.1, 100.8, and 101.6; and for divorced women, 102.1, 101.1, and 103.6. With the exception of married men who married in 1923–1929 and those who married in 1930–1938,[18] there were no significant differences between the mean adjustment scores of the different periods of marriage. This was true for both married and divorced and for both men and women. Those getting married in one period, for instance during the depression, did not get adjustment scores significantly lower or higher than those marrying at other times.

Agreement on Year When Married. On many items there was greater agreement between the answers given by happily married men and women than between the divorced. One probable reason is that divorced men and women tended to justify the divorce by saying that the mate engaged in culturally unacceptable ways of behavior. On such a matter-of-fact item as the year of marriage it seems that there would be no reason for not agreeing on the date if it were known. It was found, however, that a decidedly larger per cent of happily

---

of the divorced sample had been secured. This accounts for part of the difference in the proportion of these two groups married in the 1930–1938 and 1939–1943 periods.

[17] See pp. 46–47 for a discussion of the way in which marital-adjustment scores were computed.

[18] CR 2.0.

married husbands and wives than divorced agreed on the year of marriage.[19] Does this mean that happily married couples had more communication between themselves than the divorced? Possibly it means that the divorced, having gotten out and away from the marriage under investigation, actually had forgotten some things about the marriage.

Length of Marriage. It was to be expected that marriages ending in divorce would be shorter than marriages of the happily married group. Not only would a terminated marriage be naturally shorter than one that continued, but the happily-married were interviewed after a large part of the divorced had been interviewed. This added to the length of the marriage of the happily-married, for the comparison was between the length of the marriage up to the time of interviewing and the length of marriage between the year of marriage and the year of divorce, including the period of separation prior to the actual divorce.

For persons married only once, the average length of marriage of the divorced and the happily-married was respectively 11.4 and 16.7 years; [20] for persons married more than once, it was 7.5 and 11.6 years; and for divorced persons where pregnancy was the reason for marrying, it was 9.3 years. In analyzing certain items the length of marriage of the happily-married and divorced was matched.

Table 3 gives the per cent of divorced and happily married persons married only once for different lengths of marriage. It will be observed that a very small per cent of both groups were married less than a year, that in terms of five-year periods a larger per cent of divorced than happily-married were in each period up to and including 16–20, and that a larger per cent of married than divorced were in each period beginning with 21–25.

[19] Per cents: 91.5 and 74.7, CR 4.6. This was for married-only-once and married-more-than-once marriages combined. There were only 72 per cent of the divorced who agreed on the year when the divorce occurred.
[20] CR 4.7.

TABLE 3

Length of Marriage of Happily Married and Divorced,
Married Only Once, by Per Cents

Years	Married N = 172	Divorced * N = 220
Less than 1	2.3	1.4
1	4.1	1.8
2	5.2	7.7
3	3.5	4.6
4	4.6	5.9
5	4.1	5.9
0–5	23.8	27.3
6–10	15.1	29.1
11–15	14.5	16.8
16–20	9.9	11.8
21–25	11.1	7.3
26–30	10.5	3.6
31–35	7.6	1.8
36–40	2.3	1.8
41–45	2.9	0.5
46–50	2.3	0.0
	100.0	100.0

* One-side-only cases account for the size of the divorced N.

Remarriage of Divorced Persons.[21] A large number of divorced persons had married again by the time of the interview. The time between the divorce and the remarriage was about two years for both men and women.[22] Of course, the time between the actual separation and the remarriage was considerably longer than two years, for several months generally elapsed between separation and divorce.

A significantly larger per cent of men than women had remarried, the ratio respectively being about 4 in 10 to 3 in 10.[23] The mean number of years between this new marriage and

21 Sample includes married-only-once and married-more-than-once.
22 Years: 1.9 and 2.0 respectively.
23 Per cents: 40.4 and 30.6, CR 2.0.

the time of the interview was 2.9 for men and 2.6 for women.[24] Experiences after separation and experiences where a new marriage had occurred may have affected the way divorced persons thought of their prior marriages.

SOCIAL CHARACTERISTICS

The social characteristics of the happily-married and divorced show that, by and large, they are similar to persons in the general population from which they were drawn, as contrasted with the highly selected samples of previous studies.[25] Five items will be presented to give an idea of the nature of the sample of the present study: educational level, nationality, date of birth, religious preference, and economic level.

Education. The similarity of the educational level of the persons who participated in the study with that of the general population is one of the best indices of the representative character of the sample of the present study. For the total sample, including married-only-once, married-more-than-once, and forced marriages, the median grade of husbands and wives combined was 8.9 for the divorced and 9.5 for the married, compared with 8.6 for the United States in 1940 and 8.7 for Indiana. It is known that the median education of the population varies with age. The average age of the happily-married at the time of interviewing was approximately 38 for women and 40 for men, and that of the divorced, 36½ for women and 39 for men. In Indiana in 1940, the median education of the age group 35–39, was 8.9 years. Thus, the persons in our study had approximately the same amount of education as that of the general population.

Inasmuch as the married-only-once is the basic group on which most of the analysis will be made, it is interesting to note that the grade level was only a little higher than when

24 N is 69 for men and 60 for women.
25 See p. 14.

forced marriages of young people and married-more-than-once marriages of older people were included. The median grades of husbands and wives combined was 9.9 for the married and 9.5 for the divorced.

In terms of per cents in different grade levels, it was found that for the married-only-once sample the respective per cents of married and divorced husbands and wives combined were as follows: eighth grade and under 40.0 and 43.1; one to four years of high school, 39.4 and 44.2; and above high school, 20.5 and 12.7. This is decidedly different from the educational level of the Burgess-Cottrell subjects or the subjects of the Terman study. Thus, the education of persons in the present sample approximates that of the general population.

Education of Parents. The parents of the happily-married and the divorced did not differ in the level of their education. The respective medians of education of the fathers of married men, divorced men, married women, and divorced women were 7.8, 8.0, 7.8, and 7.9. The respective medians for the mothers were 7.9, 7.8, 7.9, and 7.7. Thus, in so far as education is an index of cultural background, the happily-married and divorced were exposed to very similar cultural influences in their homes.

Nationality. In 1940 the county from which all of the cases of the present study were drawn had a population of which 99.4 per cent were native born. The happily married and divorced samples likewise were almost exclusively native born. Moreover, over 95 per cent were native born of native-born parents.

Religion. Central Indiana, in which the selected county is located, is almost exclusively Protestant. Likewise the happily-married and divorced were almost exclusively Protestant or had a Protestant background. There were no Jewish families in either group and the per cent reporting Catholic was, respectively, only 1.8 and 2.4 for married men and women and 0.6 and 3.8 for divorced men and women.

Date of birth. It is known that cultural patterns differ somewhat from period to period. Persons born before 1890 were subjected to different cultural influences from those born in later decades. This factor was held fairly constant in the present study in that approximately the same per cent of married and divorced men and married and divorced women were born in the same period. This is shown in Table 4 which gives the per cents of married and divorced born before 1890, 1890–1909, and 1910 and later.

TABLE 4

Per Cent of Happily-Married and Divorced Born in Given Periods

Period of Birth	Men		Women	
	Married	Divorced	Married	Divorced
Before 1890	23.5	20.5	16.9	13.2
1890–1909	47.8	50.3	44.7	45.7
1910 and later	28.7	29.2	38.4	41.1
	100.0	100.0	100.0	100.0

Economic Factors. In Chapter 13 economic factors are treated in detail. The discussion there shows that the economic characteristics of the subjects of the present study were much more representative of the general population than were the subjects of Burgess and Cottrell or Terman. The happily-married and divorced had similar economic activities, with the exception that the happily married group had more professional and semiprofessional persons than did the divorced. Nine out of ten happily married and divorced men at marriage were engaged in nonprofessional work, with about two thirds in unskilled and skilled work, or in farming. Three fourths of the fathers of the subjects were unskilled or semiskilled, or farmers. About a fourth of the wives worked during marriage, with the per cent being larger for the divorced than for the married. Both the happily-married and divorced had low incomes as indicated by the low rents they paid and the inexpensive houses they bought.

PLACE OF RESIDENCE

It is generally agreed that some of a person's behavior is the result of his place of residence during his formative years, and of the mobility or stability of his residence. This section describes the extent to which the happily-married and divorced differed or were alike in the general place of birth, in rural or urban background during childhood and adolescence, and in mobility or stability of residence before and during marriage.

Place of Birth.[26] One hypothesis of the study was that the divorced sample would include more persons born in other states than Indiana, particularly in the border state of Kentucky, than the happily married sample. This hypothesis grew out of the assumption that family disorganization is related to living in a "low level" of culture, such as that of the "hill" people of Kentucky. Table 5 shows that there were no significant differences between happily-married and divorced with respect to the state in which they were born.

TABLE 5

Per Cent of Happily-Married and Divorced Born in Indiana

	Men		Women	
	Married	Divorced	Married	Divorced
Self	85.3	89.2	83.8	84.6
Mother	79.6	80.6	77.0	78.7
Father	75.4	77.0	75.4	73.6

[26] The analysis was for the total sample, which includes married-only-once, married-more-than-once, and forced marriages.

The table shows that about 85 per cent of the men and women in both the happily married and divorced groups were born in Indiana and around 75 per cent of their mothers and fathers were born there. As far as Kentucky is concerned, only 3.8 per cent of divorced men and women and only 2.6 per cent of the married were born there.

Rural-Urban Background. Very similar proportions of the happily-married and divorced spent their childhood and adolescence in the country, in villages, and in cities.[27] Of happily married and divorced men, about half (48.8 and 50.6, respectively) spent their childhood and adolescence in the country, about 40 per cent (39.5 and 38.0) in a city of 2,500 or over, and about 11 per cent (11.6 and 11.4) in villages. Slightly less than half of happily married and divorced women (45.8 and 42.8) spent their childhood and adolescence in the country, about a third (33.9 and 37.8) lived in cities of a population of 2,500 or over, and about a fifth (20.2 and 19.4) lived in a village or small town.

At the time of marriage about the same per cent of happily married as divorced men and women lived in cities, villages, or the open country. Over 80 per cent of the happily-married and divorced men and women reported living in cities and small towns.

A comparison of the size of the place in which the happily-married and divorced resided during the first and the last half of marriage showed but slight differences. Throughout marriage about three fourths of both groups lived in a city of 2,500 or more population,[28] and another 12 per cent lived in a place of 1,000 to 2,500 population.[29]

[27] This is different from what one would expect from the conclusion of Burgess and Cottrell that the mean adjustment scores of men and women reared in the country and in small towns were significantly higher than the mean scores of men and women reared in cities. *Op. cit.*, pp. 85–86.

[28] Per cents of married and divorced men: first half, 76.2 and 68.7; last half, 80.4 and 73.3. For women: first half, 69.4 and 70.9; last half, 75.3 and 78.2.

[29] Per cents of married and divorced men: first half, 11.9 and 12.0; last half, 10.1 and 10.7. For women: first half, 15.9 and 9.5; last half, 15.3 and 7.7.

Dispersion of the Divorced after Separation. A comparison of the residence at the time of interviewing for the happily-married and at the time of divorce for the divorced, revealed that a significantly larger per cent of happily married men and women than divorced lived in the city where the study was centered: the respective per cents for men were 87.5 and 69.5,[30] and for women 88.9 and 76.1.[31]

The probable reason for this difference was the dispersion of divorced persons after the family had broken up. In the vast majority of cases, a period of several months' separation preceded the actual securing of the divorce. Generally, one or both returned to the parental home, which may have been in the country or in another city. Later one or both moved to a new location, thereby separating themselves from each other and from former friends. By moving to a new location the divorced person removed himself from objects and relationships which reminded him of the mate and other things associated with the marriage.

Mobility or Stability of Residence. Burgess and Cottrell found that those with poor adjustment differed significantly from those with good adjustment on their degree of mobility. Their conclusion was that the longer the length of residence in one place, the greater the marital adjustment.[32]

In the present study, mobility, as measured by questions on the number of states lived in before and during marriage, was not a significant factor in marital adjustment. The number of states lived in for at least six months before marriage was not significantly different for happily married and divorced men and women. More than two thirds lived only in Indiana.[33] During marriage more than four out of five happily married and divorced persons lived in no other state than

[30] CR 3.3.
[31] CR 2.7.
[32] *Op. cit.*, pp. 253–54.
[33] Per cents for happily married and divorced men: 67.8 and 67.6, respectively. For women: 79.3 and 72.3, CR only 1.4.

Indiana.[34] Also, neither the number of towns nor the number of counties lived in during marriage were significantly different for the happily-married and the divorced.

Thus, very much the same kind of cultural influences impinged upon the happily-married and the divorced. At least this is the conclusion as drawn from their living in a particular area at birth, living in a rural or urban area during childhood and adolescence, and stability of residence before and during marriage.

LIMITATIONS OF THE STUDY

The following questions indicate some possible limitations which were present in the current study: What factors were operating to decrease the representative character of the samples? Did the use of different interviewers result in differential responses by the subjects? What are the shortcomings of using the cross-sectional rather than the longitudinal approach? Would responses of divorced persons reflect situations in the marriage or the bitterness associated with securing the divorce? Do the conclusions of the study apply to the general population?

Factors Decreasing Representativeness of the Sample. Certain factors may have operated to decrease the representative character of the sample. Four of these are: refusals, movement away from the community, remarriage of some of the divorced persons, and the method of securing the sample.

A relatively few divorced and happily married persons, about 15 and 5 per cent respectively, refused to participate in the study.[35] In the early months of the study the per cent of

[34] Per cents for happily married and divorced men: 82.6 and 81.3. For women: 84.6 and 84.0. Married-only-once, married-more-than-once, and marriages caused by pregnancy were included in the count.

[35] Of 615 divorced cases which were contacted, 90, or 14.6 per cent refused to cooperate. Of the 432 married cases which were contacted, 16 couples or 32 cases refused to cooperate. In some of these couples, one partner was willing to

refusals was reduced by securing some of them through repeated contacts; later a refusal case was given up more readily in order to expedite the completion of the study. There were five primary reasons for refusing to cooperate: (1) the feeling that the information was too personal to give to an outsider; (2) a fear of not remaining anonymous; (3) the desire to forget the past; (4) the fact that the person had talked to another person who had been contacted by an interviewer and had made up his mind to refuse if contacted; and (5) a feeling that the study was unimportant.

The movement of persons so far away that it was too difficult to contact them may have been a selective factor in the divorced sample. It was decided not to attempt to get a case if it were known before contacting either the husband or the wife that one of them was more than 50 miles from the city chosen as the center of operations. This was not a factor in the married sample.

A few divorced persons had either remarried or were living together. Fifteen potential couples had to be discarded because they had gone back together. It is impossible to know the effect these cases would have had on the data if the information had been secured prior to their reunion. Also, it is possible that some of the cases that are included in the sample might subsequently have been reunited. However, in terms of the total number of cases, these reunited couples would be relatively few.

The method of securing names of couples to be interviewed was a fourth factor which may have decreased the representativeness of the sample. It will be recalled that, while most of the divorced sample was secured from the courthouse files, a few were obtained from names supplied by other divorced persons. Also, the happily married sample included couples recommended by divorced persons and couples recommended by married persons. A more uniform procedure of securing the

---

assist while the other refused. If we count all 32 persons as being refusals, the per cent of the total number contacted would be only 7.4.

names of divorced and happily married couples might have increased the representativeness of the sample.

The Use of Different Interviewers. Another limitation may have been the use of different interviewers. Care was taken to reduce the influence of this factor through giving interviewers preliminary training and by weekly staff conferences. The author and a trained assistant secured 63.8 per cent of the 525 divorced cases,[36] and the author and two trained assistants secured 77.8 per cent of the married sample. However, a third of the divorced and a quarter of the married were secured by several other interviewers.[37]

The question of the effect of using different interviewers is a particularly interesting methodological problem. An analysis of this problem was attempted by comparing the average marital-adjustment score of cases interviewed by the author or where he was present at the time of the interview with the average adjustment score of cases secured by his assistant interviewers.[38] The comparison was for married men, married women, divorced men, and divorced women. The average marital-adjustment scores of cases secured by the author and by others were respectively as follows: married men, 139.7 and 138.0; married women, 132.7 and 138.6; divorced men, 100.0 and 102.1; and divorced women, 100.4 and 102.7. The difference was not statistically significant in any of the four groups.[39] The conclusion is that the author and his assistants interviewed in a sufficiently uniform manner to secure approximately the same responses from subjects.

[36] The per cent secured by the author was 34.7 and by the assistant 29.1. Four sociology graduate students, engaged on a part-time basis, secured 22.8 per cent; 11 students enrolled in a course on the family got 13.4 per cent.

[37] The author secured 25.0 per cent of the married cases. One of the trained assistants, who was engaged on a full-time basis and who had several months of experience in interviewing in the Warren S. Thompson and P. K. Whelpton study of fertility in Indianapolis, secured 36.3 per cent. Three graduate and 11 undergraduate sociology students got 10.2 and 12.0 per cent respectively.

[38] See pp. 46–47 for discussion of the method of obtaining marital-adjustment test scores. The maximum for men was 157; for women 154.

[39] CRs were respectively 0.8, 1.8, 0.8, and 1.0.

Cross-sectional Rather than Longitudinal Study. A major limitation of this study, as of so many social science investigations, is that it is cross-sectional rather than longitudinal. Getting persons at a specific time to report their past experiences means, of course, some inaccuracies, for past experiences will be colored by those which occur later. Moreover, inasmuch as a longitudinal record would give sequences of behavior, it might reveal causative as well as predictive factors in marital adjustment. While a longitudinal study over a relatively long period through repeated interviews gives a more accurate report, it involves serious difficulties, such as expense and the loss of cases through mobility and death. Consequently, the cross-sectional approach was more practical.

Responses Modified by the Experience of Divorce. Another limitation closely related to that described above is that the answers of divorced persons to the various questions often reflected bitterness and resentment associated with the experience of divorce. Also, the answers, in part, may have been justifications of the divorce. In interpreting the differences between married and divorced on the various items, we constantly kept in mind the possibility that the responses from divorced persons might have been colored by the divorce experience rather than by the marital situation itself. The question is: Are the differences between the divorced and happily-married greater than those that might have been found between the same happily married group and a group on the brink of divorce, but who had not gone through the divorce process?

A partial solution to this problem was attempted by dividing each of the four groups—happily married men, happily married women, divorced men, and divorced women—into two parts on the basis of adjustment scores. A comparison was then made for certain items between the answers of persons with high marital-adjustment scores and those whose scores were low. This was done for personality traits. It is surprising that the items differentiated as well as they did between the more and the less adjusted of the happily-married and of the divorced.[40] Thus, the differences between the happily married and the divorced groups are only partly due to the tendency of the divorced to be derogatory toward their mates and to the tendency of the happily-married to be generous.

Terman likewise discovered that unhappy spouses tended to exaggerate certain relationships between themselves and their mates. He speaks of "the avidity with which unhappy spouses, especially unhappy husbands, avail themselves of the opportunity to express dissatisfaction with their mates." [41] He found high critical ratios between happy and unhappy spouses on complaints about sexual relationships with mate and held that the actual differences were not as great as the critical ratios would indicate. He felt that the high critical ratios were due to an irresistible inclination of the unhappily-married to account for their unhappiness in terms of almost anything that might be suggested. This was evidenced more in some of the items than in others and Terman illustrates one such item as follows: [42]

For example, the second complaint by husbands in Table 111, "vagina too large," is made more than two and a half times as frequently by unhappy as by happy husbands. One may well be skeptical as to whether actual measurement would show anatomical misfits bunched anything like so heavily among the maritally unhappy.

Rather than being a limitation, this tendency of the unhappily-married to exaggerate the difficulties in their marriage may prove to be a predictive item in marital adjustment. A derogatory attitude before marriage toward the intended mate or after marriage may indicate that the persons are not adjustable to the marital situation.

[40] See p. 173 for a definition of "the more" and "the less" adjusted.
[41] *Op. cit.*, p. 312.
[42] *Ibid.*, p. 314.

Degree of Generality of Conclusions. Finally, the sample
was drawn from a single county in a midwest state. The findings apply to the population from which the sample was drawn
and for the period in which the study was made. They may
apply to the more general population and to the current period. In so far as the findings agree with those of other studies
of marital adjustment, they may be considered to have greater
generality.

SUMMARY

The present study is unique in that happiness, as judged by
an outsider, and divorce were used as criteria of marital adjustment and maladjustment, and also in that subjects were from
the general population. Questionnaire data were secured
through personal interviews.

The divorced sample consisted of 201 husbands and their
wives, plus 123 cases where only a husband or a wife was secured. The happily married sample consisted of 200 husbands
and their wives, plus 4 cases where only one marital partner
was secured. Thus, the total sample consisted of 929 individuals. The happily married sample was divided into two sub-
groups: married-only-once and married-more-than-once. The
divorced sample was divided into three sub-groups: the above
two, plus persons who were forced to marry. The main analysis is on those cases married only once.

The length of marriage of the subjects ranged from a few
months to almost 50 years, although a relatively small per cent
was on either extreme. The average length for the married-
only-once was 11.4 years for the divorced and 16.7 for the married. The subjects were similar in education, nationality, religion, occupation, and income to the general population of the
area in which the study was made.

The following are possible limitations of the study: the subjects were not completely representative of the general population; different interviewers were used; the study was cross-

sectional rather than longitudinal; responses of subjects were colored by happiness in marriage and bitterness associated with conflicts in marriage or in securing the divorce; and the conclusions apply to a single county in Indiana in the early years of the 1940 decade.

3

MEASURING ADJUSTMENT IN MARRIAGE

MARITAL adjustment may be thought of as a continuum, ranging from complete adjustment to complete maladjustment. While probably no marriages are found at the extreme ends of the continuum, there are those which approximate 100-per cent adjustment or 100-per cent maladjustment.

The following excerpts from two cases illustrate the marital-adjustment continuum. One couple had a very high degree of marital adjustment and the other a very high degree of maladjustment. The excerpts reveal some of the items important for marital adjustment. The first is that of a happily married husband and wife whose marital-adjustment scores were in the upper three per cent of the happily married cases: [1]

Husband. "I think we are as well adjusted as any two persons in the present world confusion can be. We have known each other from childhood, and lived in adjoining rural communities. We come from rather strict church communities, and, when we were courting, going to church was our chief entertainment. This helped us adjust to each other. I think the world of my wife and there never have been any serious difficulties. While neither of us has stepped out, I think both husband and wife should be given a certain amount of freedom. I think a person might make a mistake and step the wrong way. I have told Mildred that if ever she should have an affair, she need not run away. I would expect

---

[1] Case no. 63. Adjustment score of husband 155.0; of wife 150.6. The maximum adjustment score for men is 157, and for women 154.

the same from her. There is no place for jealousy in marriage, if true love is present. I never have felt jealous of Mildred. If you love a person, you don't get jealous, but you may feel hurt inside. As long as a person is getting something that will make him happier, then it isn't jealousy that is felt. True love is the greatest of all feelings."

Wife. "We have been married eighteen years and we have had a wonderful time together. I have had no regret about my marriage to John and if I had my life to live over again I would take John—that is if he asked me, and the way he has acted during our marriage, I think he would ask me. We like to do the same things, always talk things over, and agree on practically everything. John and I have a kind of understanding about other people. I would not mind too much if he should go out with another woman. He feels the same about me. But there certainly is not much chance that such a thing will ever bother us."

Statement of Interviewer. Mrs. Patterson is a rather matronly woman, and has a beautiful smile, especially for her husband. Mr. Patterson also is pleasant and is neat and nicely dressed. The couple have no children and feel that this has been no particular handicap in their lives. Their present object of affection, besides each other, is a cat of which both are very fond. They have taught it all sorts of tricks and took great delight in showing the interviewer how well it performed. Every time one of them talked to the other, there was an endearing word. They did not hesitate to put their arms around each other when they stood at the door to tell the interviewer good-by.

The second case is that of a divorced couple where the marital-adjustment score of the husband was in the lower 15 per cent and where the wife's score was the lowest score attained by the women. The author had no difficulty in securing the cooperation of the husband, but had great difficulty in securing that of the wife. She was living with her parents and was very suspicious. Finally, he had to show her a university check he happened to have and other identification papers, and even then she was unwilling to fill out some questions,

Her mother kept peeping in at us from the other room, and finally the father came and sat in the room with us: [2]

Husband. "My wife is an only child and her parents spoiled her. She never would go to my folks and constantly wanted to visit her parents who live about 30 miles from here. One of the main difficulties in our marriage was the interference of her parents. In fact they were back of her getting the divorce. We had lots of other trouble, such as her attempt to control the way I spent money, constant bickering, her always wanting to be the boss, and her utter selfishness, but her parents were the main thing. You asked me if we agreed or disagreed on certain things. Well, we disagreed on practically everything. I came to the conclusion that our marriage wouldn't work out even though we went back together and so was willing to have it go through. My main worry is about my boy. Her parents are illiterate and he is going to grow up in that kind of a home. I would like to give him more advantages, particularly education. I have a feeling like the cards are stacked against him in her parents' home like they were stacked against our marriage."

Wife. "My husband used to come down and hunt and fish with my father, and then he just quit coming. We never did do much of anything together. I was content to stay at home and read true stories, but he always wanted to be on the go. He was as tight as could be on money matters. If I wanted a pair of shoes or a dress I would always have to go and ask him for the money." When her father stepped out of the room for a minute she was asked if her husband had paid attention to anyone else. With heat she replied: "Yes, he did, and that's why I separated from him. I just up and came home and then applied for divorce. My husband is a somewhat bossy person, and I am also that way, so I suppose that is part of our trouble. We were having lots of other trouble and so when I found that he had gone to bed with another woman I took our boy and came home."

It is apparent that the husband and wife in the first case were relatively well adjusted in marriage as compared with

---

[2] Case no. 920. Adjustment score of husband was 82.0; of wife 74.0.

the poor adjustment of the second couple. The first was in the group selected by the criterion of marital adjustment—happily married as judged by an outsider. The second was in the group selected by the criterion of marital maladjustment—divorce. A later section analyzes the validity of these two criteria of adjustment and maladjustment, as measured by differences in the average marital-adjustment test scores.

CONSTRUCTING THE ADJUSTMENT TEST

Marital adjustment is the process of adaptation of the husband and the wife in such a way as to avoid or resolve conflicts sufficiently so that the mates feel satisfied with the marriage and with each other, develop common interests and activities, and feel that the marriage is fulfilling their expectations. In the discussion that follows, marital adjustment will frequently be considered as that which is measured by the marital-adjustment test. Actually, the test measures the extent to which the husband and wife agree or disagree, are satisfied with the marriage and with each other, and have achieved common interests and activities.

To what extent do these two criteria "divorce" and "happiness in marriage as judged by an outsider," separate the well-adjusted from the poorly-adjusted? Provision was made to answer this question by including in the questionnaire items used by Burgess and Cottrell and others in marital-adjustment tests.

A marital-adjustment test gives the general level of adjustment of a given marriage, but it does not measure the actual adjustment of the *individual* marriage. The method of measuring marital adjustment is similar to the prediction procedures used by life insurance actuaries. Today life insurance companies, on the basis of such information as the occupation of a person, the length of life of his parents, and his age, determine the length of time he is expected to live, and insure him accordingly. The person may live for a longer or a shorter time than his life expectancy, but life insurance companies are confident that, on the whole, their predictions on length of life are accurate. So, likewise, a marriage with a given expectancy of adjustment may be more or less adjusted than the test indicates, but the work which has been done on marital-adjustment tests demonstrates that today one can measure the probability that a certain general level of marital adjustment will characterize a given marriage.

Assignment of Weights. In the present study, scores for each subject were secured by adding together the weights assigned the given answers to 29 adjustment items. Weights were determined by the degree of differences between the per cents of the happily-married and divorced giving the various answers to each question. For example, one of the questions was: "Do husband and wife engage in outside activities together?" There were four possible answers. These answers, the per cent of happily married and divorced men for each answer, and the assigned weights were as follows:

Answer	Per Cent of the Married	Per Cent of the Divorced	Weight Assigned
All	47.2	23.3	5
Some	45.6	43.7	4
Very few	5.1	26.2	2
None	2.1	6.8	2

The weight to each answer or category of a question was assigned by the method of graphical determination of weights, or an abac, constructed by J. P. Guilford.[3] The actual statistical procedure employed by him in the construction of the table of weights is complicated, but a general understanding of how the weights were assigned is possible without a thorough knowledge of the method of calculating the weights.

In the example given above a considerably larger per cent

[3] J. P. Guilford, *Fundamental Statistics in Psychology and Education,* New York, McGraw-Hill, 1950, p. 540. The amount of the weight was determined by a device of statistical analysis known as the phi coefficient.

of married than divorced men reported they engaged in "all" outside interests with their wives, practically the same per cents replied "some" of them, and a larger per cent of divorced than married said "very few" and "none" of them. A weight of 4 was given each category of a question which did not differentiate between the married and divorced; that is, about the same per cent of each group gave the same answer. Hence, "some" in the illustration above was given a weight of 4. If a given answer to a question was reported by a significantly larger per cent of married than divorced, it received a higher weight than 4. The higher weights were 5, 6, 7, or 8, depending on the *degree* of difference between the per cents of happily-married and divorced: in the example above "all" received 5 points. If a given answer was made by a significantly smaller per cent of married than divorced, then a number smaller than 4 (3, 2, 1, or 0) was given that category or answer: "very few" and "none" in the example received 2 points.

The Marital-Adjustment Test. Table 6 gives the 29 questions which constitute the test of the present study and the weights assigned to each of the possible answers to the items. The test includes 19 items from the Burgess-Cottrell marital-adjustment test,[4] 2 adaptations from Terman's items,[5] and 8 which were formulated by the author.

It will be observed from the table that men and women answered the questions somewhat differently. Consequently, some of the weights are slightly different for men and women. This was to be expected, for husbands and wives differ in their reactions to such things as type of parental home, amount of education, economic aspirations, personality characteristics, and to questions included in the marital-adjustment test. The highest possible score for the men was 157 and for the women 154.

[4] Ernest W. Burgess and Leonard S. Cottrell, *Predicting Success or Failure in Marriage*, New York, Prentice-Hall, 1939, pp. 59ff.

[5] Lewis M. Terman, *et al.*, *Psychological Factors in Marital Happiness*, New York, McGraw-Hill, 1938, p. 58.

TABLE 6

*Marital-Adjustment Items and Weights for
Men and Women*

	Men	Women
1. Have you ever wished you had not married?		
a. Frequently	2	2
a. Frequently	2	2
b. Occasionally	2	2
c. Rarely	6	5
2. If you had your life to live over again would you:		
a. Marry the same person?	7	7
b. Marry a different person?	1	1
c. Not marry at all?	1	1
3. Do husband and wife engage in outside activities together?		
a. All of them	5	5
b. Some of them	4	4
c. Few of them	2	2
d. None of them	2	2
4. In leisure time, which do you prefer?		
a. Both husband and wife to stay at home	6	6
b. Both to be on the go	3	4
c. One to be on the go and other to stay home	2	2
5. Do you and your mate generally talk things over together?		
a. Never	2	2
b. Now and then	2	2
c. Almost always	4	4
d. Always	5	5
6. How often do you kiss your mate?		
a. Every day	5	5
b. Now and then	3	3
c. Almost never	3	3
7. How happy would you rate your marriage?		
a. Very happy	6	6
b. Happy	4	5
c. Average	1	2

	Men	Women
d. Unhappy	1	2
e. Very unhappy	1	2

8. How happy would your mate rate your marriage?

	Men	Women
a. Very happy	6	6
b. Happy	5	5
c. Average	2	2
d. Unhappy	2	2
e. Very unhappy	2	2

9. Check any of the following items which you think have caused *serious* difficulties in your marriage (score is the number of items checked):

        Mate's attempt to control my spending money ____
        Other difficulties over money ____
        Religious differences ____
        Different amusement interests ____
        Lack of mutual friends ____
        Constant bickering ____
        Interference of in-laws ____
        Lack of mutual affection (no longer in love) ____
        Unsatisfying sex relations ____
        Selfishness and lack of cooperation ____
        Adultery ____
        Desire to have children ____
        Sterility of husband or wife ____
        Venereal diseases ____
        Mate paid attention to (became familiar with) another
          person ____
        Desertion ____
        Nonsupport ____
        Drunkenness ____
        Gambling ____
        Ill health ____
        Mate sent to jail ____
        Other reasons ____

	Men	Women
a. Nothing checked	6	6
b. One checked	6	6
c. Two checked	4	5
d. Three checked	4	4

	Men	Women
e. Four or five checked	2	3
f. Six or more checked	2	2

10. How many things does your mate do that you do not like?
    a. Nothing 6 6
    b. One thing 4 5
    c. Two things 3 3
    d. Three or more things 3 2

11. How many things seriously annoy you about your marriage?
    a. Nothing 6 6
    b. One thing 4 5
    c. Two things 3 3
    d. Three or more things 3 2

12. How many things satisfy you most about your marriage?
    a. Nothing 3 3
    b. One thing 3 3
    c. Two things 4 4
    d. Three or more 5 5

13. When disagreements arise they generally result in:
    a. Husband giving in 2 3
    b. Wife giving in 3 2
    c. Neither giving in 2 2
    d. Agreement by mutual give and take 6 6

14. What is the total number of times you left mate or mate left you because of conflict?
    a. No times 7 7
    b. One or more times 1 2

15. How frequently do you and your mate get on each other's nerves around the house?
    a. Never 5 5
    b. Almost never 5 4
    c. Occasionally 3 3
    d. Frequently 3 3
    e. Almost always 3 3
    f. Always 3 3

16. What are your feelings on sex relations between you and your mate?

	Men	Women
a. Very enjoyable	5	5
b. Enjoyable	4	5
c. Tolerable	2	2
d. Disgusting	2	2
e. Very disgusting	2	2

17. What are your mate's feelings on sex relations with you?

a. Very enjoyable	5	5
b. Enjoyable	4	3
c. Tolerable	3	3
d. Disgusting	3	3
e. Very disgusting	3	3

18. Did intercourse increase or decrease during marriage?

a. Increased greatly	4	4
b. Increased	4	4
c. Remained the same	4	4
d. Decreased some	5	4
e. Decreased greatly	3	3
f. Decreased entirely	3	3

State approximate extent of agreement or disagreement *during marriage* on the following items (where weights are different, score of women in parenthesis):

	Always Agree	Almost Always Agree	Occasionally Disagree	Frequently Disagree	Almost Always Disagree	Always Disagree
19. Handling family finances	5	5	2	2	2	2
20. Matters of recreation	5(4)	4	4(3)	3	3	3
21. Religious matters	4	4	3	3	3	3
22. Demonstration of affection	5	4	3	3	3	3
23. Friends	5	5	3(2)	2	2	2
24. Intimate relations (sex)	5	5(4)	2(3)	2(3)	2(3)	2(3)

	Always Agree	Almost Always Agree	Occa- sionally Disagree	Fre- quently Dis- agree	Almost Always Dis- agree	Always Dis- agree
25. Ways of dealing with in-laws	5	5	2(3)	2(3)	2(3)	2(3)
26. The amount of time that should be spent together	6(5)	4	2(3)	2	2	2
27. Table manners	4	4	3(4)	3(4)	3(4)	3(4)
28. Conventionality (good, right, and proper conduct) ..	5	5(4)	2	2	2	2
29. Aims, goals, and things believed to be important in life	6	4	2	2	2	2

VALIDITY OF MARITAL-ADJUSTMENT CRITERIA

Mean Adjustment-Test Score of Men and of Women. One way to test the validity of the categories "happily-married as recommended by an outsider," and "divorce," as criteria of marital adjustment and maladjustment is to compare the marital-adjustment test scores of the happily-married and divorced. As has been indicated, adjustment scores were computed for each divorced and each happily married man and woman.[6] The average score of married men was 138.5, compared with 100.8 for divorced men; for women the respective

[6] Not all persons answered all of the adjustment questions. It was decided that a case would be excluded from the marital-adjustment analysis if sufficient questions were not answered to make up one half of the maximum adjustment score. The scores for those who did not answer all of the questions were computed by getting the proportion that the sum of weights for questions answered was to the maximum score for these questions and multiplying by 157 for men and 154 for women. It was also decided to exclude forced marriages of the divorced sample.

scores were 137.4 and 102.4. The great differences between the average scores of the divorced and married [7] indicate that the two criteria have great validity, in that they separate the well-adjusted from the poorly-adjusted.

What would be the result if, rather than using the empirical weights derived from the answers of persons in the present study, the weights of the Burgess-Cottrell study were used? Adjustment scores derived from the weights used by these two authors constitute an independent criterion of marital adjustment for the subjects of the present study. These weights were derived from the answers of subjects who were highly educated, had relatively high incomes, and in other respects were quite different from the persons in the present study. It will be remembered that Burgess and Cottrell determined their weights by the degree of correlation between different answers and a fivefold, happiness scale—very unhappy, unhappy, average, happy, and very happy. Using only the 26 adjustment questions in the Burgess-Cottrell marital-adjustment test and their weights, marital-adjustment scores were computed for each person in the present study. The average score of married men was 167.3, compared with 110.7 for divorced men; for women the respective scores were 165.6 and 106.8.[8] It will be remembered that the maximum score of their marital-adjustment test was 194.

It did not make much difference whether adjustment scores were computed for the 29 questions used in the present study by the method described above or for the 26 Burgess-Cottrell questions and their weights. This is indicated by the high correlations between the scores derived by the two methods for married men, divorced men, married women, and divorced women. The correlations were as follows: .85 married men, .83 divorced men, .88 married women, and .87 divorced women. These high correlations might have been even higher if exactly the same questions had been used in both studies.

[7] CR for men: 24.0. For women: 28.4.
[8] CR for men: 19.3. For women: 22.0.

Mean Combined Adjustment-Test Score of Spouses. Another method of testing the validity of happily-married as judged by an outsider and divorce as criteria of marital adjustment is to compare the two groups in terms of the average of the combined scores of given husbands and their wives. In this case, scores were reduced to their per cent of the total possible score. Table 7 gives the per cents of happily married and divorced couples by five-point (5-per cent) intervals. The table

TABLE 7

Per Cent of Happily Married and Divorced Couples Whose Average Combined Marital-Adjustment Scores Fell in Specified Intervals

Score (Per Cent of Total Possible Score)	Married Couples N = 196	Divorced Couples N = 154
95–99	14.8	
90–94	34.2	
85–89	23.5	
80–84	14.3	3.3
75–79	8.2	5.8
70–74	3.0	15.6
65–69	2.0	26.6
60–64		22.7
55–59		18.8
50–54		6.5
45–49		0.7
	100.00	100.00

shows that the scores of 72.5 per cent of the married couples were higher than the highest scores of divorced couples, and the scores of 75.3 per cent of divorced couples were lower than the scores of all but 2.0 per cent of married couples. Of the happily-married 86.8 per cent had scores higher than all but 3.3 per cent of the divorced, and 90.9 per cent of the divorced had scores lower than all but 5.0 per cent of the married. The above indicates that the happily-married and divorced tended to be on the two extremes of the adjustment continuum, as measured by the adjustment test, and are valid criteria of marital adjustment and maladjustment.[9]

Overlapping Divorced and Married Scores. An interesting problem was raised by those divorced couples, about one fourth of the total, 24.7 per cent, whose average combined scores overlapped the scores of the married couples.[10] An investigation of the questionnaires revealed that these couples had gotten along well or fairly well in most things, which accounted for their relatively high adjustment scores, but had values so different on one or two kinds of behavior that the marriage was thrown out of adjustment. In 57.9 per cent of these cases, one or both reported that adultery was one of the major difficulties which led to divorce, with another 23.7 per cent reporting that the mate paid attention to another person, which statement was often used rather than the reference to adultery. Trouble with in-laws was given as a major difficulty by the remaining 18.4 per cent. Thus, these cases gave one or two principal factors as the basis of difficulties in the marriage.

[9] Burgess and Cottrell compared adjusted and maladjusted couples in terms of "poor" adjustment, 20–119 points; "fair" adjustment 120–159; and "good" adjustment, 160–194. By reducing these to per cents it is possible to find the proportion of the married and divorced couples who fell in the Burgess-Cottrell categories of poor (30.9 to 61.8 per cent), fair (61.9 to 82.3 per cent), and good (82.4–100.0 per cent). Table 7 shows that 3.3 per cent of divorced couples got average combined adjustment scores in the bottom of the good category, and no married couple got a score in the poor category.

[10] This excludes the 4 married cases which were eliminated because they were probably maladjusted. Examination of the questionnaires and the case-study material of the four couples whose scores constituted the lowest 2.0 per cent of the married scores revealed that these couples were not happily married. One husband was looking forward to getting a divorce when the children were grown. Another husband had left home for a period of six months and had talked to his wife about the advisability of getting a divorce. In the third case the husband had had three prior marriages—in the first the wife had died, and in the next two he had been divorced; his present wife had been married before and her first husband had died. In the fourth case, the first marriage of the husband had ended in divorce. The statements of friends that these couples were happily married were not borne out by the facts supplied by the couples nor by their scores on the marital-adjustment test. These 4 cases were eliminated from the happily married sample.

A clash on such things as adultery, familiarity with another person, and in-laws was so great that one or both could not or would not adjust to it.

This raises the question whether a marital-adjustment test based on questions similar to those of Burgess and Cottrell or Terman is an adequate device for measuring the adjustment of marriages which are thrown out of adjustment by one or two major breaches of desirable marital behavior, as judged by the husband or wife. It is interesting to note, however, that, whereas the average combined scores of a quarter of the divorced husbands and their wives overlapped the scores of the married couples, in 71.1 per cent of the divorced cases the score of either the husband or the wife was below the lowest score of married couples, and in all but two of the remaining cases either the husband or the wife had a score in the lowest interval (70–74) for married scores.

It is also interesting to note that, whereas the average combined scores of about one fourth (25.5 per cent) [11] of the happily married couples fell below the highest scores of divorced couples, in 48.0 per cent of these cases the scores of either the husband or the wife fell above the highest adjustment score of any divorced couple, and an additional 42.0 per cent fell in the top interval (80–84) of the divorced couples' scores. Thus, overlapping is greatly reduced if the highest score of either spouse of the married couples and the lowest score of either spouse of the divorced couples are considered.

The great differences between the average marital-adjustment scores of both happily married and divorced men and women and also between married and divorced couples justifies the use of happily-married as judged by an outsider and divorce as criteria of marital adjustment and maladjustment. Considering the radically different social characteristics of the subjects of the two studies, the application of the Burgess-Cottrell weights gave adjustment scores which differ-

11 This does not include the 4 cases which were eliminated from the married sample.

entiated the happily-married and divorced to a greater extent than might be expected. The analysis shows rather conclusively that the divorced sample represents the low end of the marital-adjustment continuum and that the happily married group represents the high end.

COMPARISON OF ADJUSTMENT SCORES
OF SPOUSES

How much correspondence is there between the adjustment scores of husbands and their respective wives? If an adjustment test actually measures the extent of success, or happiness, or adjustment in a marriage, should not the husband and wife approximately agree in their answers to the questions comprising the test? The first answer to this question was by Burgess and Cottrell and was a strong affirmative. The second, by Terman, was affirmative, but was considerably less emphatic. The third, that of the present study, is somewhat affirmative in the case of the happily married spouses, but negative in the case of divorced spouses. A fourth, by Harter, was somewhat affirmative for married spouses. He also found a correlation between scores from answers of parents and scores derived from answers by teen-age children to identical questions about parents' marital adjustment.

Burgess and Cottrell found a high correlation, .88, between the adjustment scores of 66 husbands and their respective wives, and they assumed that the subjects had met their request that the schedules be filled out independently.[12] This high correspondence between the adjustment scores of spouses, however, was probably due to collaboration, for unless the interviewer is present to control communication between husband and wife, they are likely to talk things over, with a consequent greater similarity of answers. At least the experience in the present study was that, even though an interviewer was present and the subjects were in different rooms, it was diffi-

[12] *Op. cit.*, pp. 70–71.

cult to keep a married subject from calling to the other spouse for the answers to some of the questions. Burgess, in a letter to the author, has the following to say on the similarity of adjustment scores of spouses in the Burgess-Cottrell study:

> We know our correlation of .88 is too high because we did not control the filling out of the schedule. Yours was lower than Terman's where the filling out of the schedules was apparently controlled. I think the correlation of our new study will be very little different from the one that you found.

Burgess and Wallin in the new study gave an adjustment test to 1,000 engaged couples, and then, three years after marriage, gave a marital-adjustment test to as many of these couples as could be contacted. They report that the correlation between the adjustment scores of men and women of engaged couples was .57 for the 1,000 couples. Three years after marriage the correlation between the marital-adjustment scores of 505 husbands and their wives was .41.[13]

Terman, who found a correlation of .59 between total happiness scores of husbands and wives, holds that it is unreasonable to expect spouses to be equally satisfied with one another and with the marriage. Extreme score divergence probably simply means that the attitudes of husband and wives are far from reciprocal.[14]

Terman and Oden, in their study of the marital adjustment of Terman's "genius" children, found a .52 correlation between the happiness scores of 556 husbands and the scores of their wives.[15]

The present study found some correspondence between the scores of the happily married spouses, but none between those

[13] Ernest W. Burgess and Paul Wallin, "Predicting Adjustment in Marriage from Adjustment in Engagement," *American Journal of Sociology*, 49, 1944, pp. 524–30.

[14] *Op. cit.*, pp. 80–83.

[15] Lewis M. Terman and Melita H. Oden, *The Gifted Child Grows up: Twenty-five Years' Follow-up of a Superior Group*, Stanford University Press, Stanford, 1947, pp. 241–42.

of divorced spouses. There was a correlation of .36 for the married spouses, but only .04 for the divorced. Using the Burgess-Cottrell questions and weights the correlation between the adjustment scores of married spouses was .38 and between the divorced .00.

Table 8 shows that the range of difference between the scores of happily-married was much less than the range between the scores of divorced couples. Almost half of the married as compared with about a fifth of the divorced spouses had less than 5 points divergence between their adjustment scores. Fifteen or more points divergence was found for 11.5 per cent of the happily married couples and for 37.0 per cent of the divorced couples.

TABLE 8

Difference in Scores * of Happily Married and Divorced Spouses, by Per Cent

Difference in Score	Married N = 196	Divorced N = 154
0–4	47.9	20.8
5–9	24.5	24.0
10–14	16.1	18.2
15–19	8.3	16.2
20–24	1.6	13.6
25–29	1.6	5.9
30–34	0.0	1.3
	100.0	100.0

* The score here was computed as the per cent which the actual score was of the total possible score.

Thus, the marital-adjustment scores of happily married spouses were much closer together than were the scores of divorced spouses. The degree of correspondence between the adjustment scores of spouses probably measures to some extent the degree of agreement between spouses rather than the validity of the adjustment test. This means that husbands and wives of both the divorced and the happily-married differed in their conception of the amount of agreement and disagreement in the marriage, in the extent of common interests and activities, demonstration of affection and confiding, and in expressions of satisfaction or dissatisfaction with the marriage, for these were the general types of items used in the construction of the adjustment test.

Harter secured marital-adjustment scores from 103 husbands and their wives and from a daughter or son of each family who was a senior in high school in a medium-sized city in Southern California.[16] Of the 103 families, 70 were unbroken by death, separation, or divorce. In these unbroken families there was an exactly equal number, 35, of sons and daughters. The correlation between the marital-adjustment scores of husbands and wives in these families was .65. The correlation between the marital-adjustment scores computed from answers of daughters to questions on the marital adjustment of parents and the scores made by mothers was .58, and with scores made by fathers, .48. The correlation between scores derived from answers of sons and the scores of the mothers was .56, and with those of fathers .56. Moreover, there were no significant differences between the mean adjustment scores computed from the answers of parents and the mean adjustment scores computed from the answers of their sons and daughters.

Thus, Harter presents data to support the hypothesis that there is considerable correspondence between the adjustment scores of husbands and wives and also the hypothesis that a high-school senior can give a fairly accurate picture of the degree of marital adjustment of his parents. Of course, different results might be secured from a sample in a different part of the country, in a different social or economic class, or even in a different high school in the same part of the country.

16 Aubrey B. Harter, *Adjustment of High-School Seniors and the Marital Adjustment of Their Parents in a Southern California City,* University of Southern California Library, 1950, pp. 65–71.

MODIFICATION OF THE MARITAL-ADJUSTMENT TEST

Modification of adjustment tests was the objective of a study by Wallace.[17] The goal was to restrict adjustment items to those which are most effective in separating well adjusted from poorly adjusted marriages. Wallace used 15 adjustment items which had proved most differentiating in previous studies. He weighted the different answers to each question and applied his test to a group of persons judged happy and well adjusted in marriage and to another group known to be maladjusted or recently divorced. Out of a maximum adjustment score of 158, the well adjusted group got a mean score of 135.9 and the maladjusted only 71.7, with a CR of 17.5. He concluded that it is possible to separate well adjusted from maladjusted marriages by using relatively few items.

Earlier in the chapter the 29 items used in the marital-adjustment test of the present study were listed, along with the weights assigned to given answers of each question. Here we are interested in discovering which items best differentiate the well-adjusted or happily-married from the maladjusted or the divorced. The items in Table 9 include all of those used by Burgess and Cottrell, some of those used by Terman, and a few constructed by the author. Contingency correlations between the answers given by the the happily-married and the divorced were computed for each item for both husbands and wives.[18] The table gives the order of importance of the adjustment items from the most to the least differentiating. Actually, the items are presented in rank order of contingency correlations for happily married and divorced husbands, but on the whole the order of importance of the items was about the same for wives. An asterisk has been placed before those items which might be eliminated from a new test.

[17] Karl M. Wallace, *Construction and Validation of Marital Adjustment and Prediction Scales,* University of Southern California Library, 1947, pp. 180–83.
[18] Contingency correlations were corrected for the number of possible answers to an item.

TABLE 9

Contingency Correlations of Marital-Adjustment Items Differentiating Happily-Married and Divorced, in Rank Order for Husbands

	Husbands	Wives
If you had your life to live over do you think you would marry the same person, marry a different person, not marry at all?	.65	.69
During marriage how many times did you leave mate or mate leave you because of conflict?	.60	.58
Check any of the following which caused *serious* difficulties in your marriage (list of 24 items included) . .	.59	.57
Have you ever wished you had not married: frequently, occasionally, rarely, never?	.53	.54
When disagreements have arisen, they usually have resulted in husband giving in, wife giving in, agreement by mutual give and take, neither giving in	.53	.54
In leisure time both husband and wife prefer to be "on the go," both prefer to stay at home, one prefers to be "on the go" and the other to stay at home	.52	.54
Extent of agreement on conventionality on six-fold scale: always agree, almost always agree, occasionally disagree, frequently disagree, almost always disagree, and always disagree	.51	.50
Extent of agreement on aims, goals, and things believed to be important in life (scale as for conventionality)	.50	.52
*Number of things mate does you do not like: nothing, one thing, two things, three or more things	.49	.43
Extent of agreement on amount of time that should be spent together (scale as for conventionality) . . .	.46	.43
*Number of things which annoy and dissatisfy you most about your marriage: nothing, one thing, two things, three or more things	.46	.50

	Husbands	Wives
Get on each other's nerves around the house: never, almost never, occasionally, frequently, almost always, always	·45	·43
Extent of agreement on friends (scale as for conventionality)	·45	·47
Extent of agreement on dealing with in-laws (scale as for conventionality)	·44	·37
Extent of agreement on finances (scale as for conventionality)	·43	·43
Extent of agreement on intimate (sex) relations (scale as for conventionality)	·41	·37
Generally talk things over with mate: almost never, now and then, almost always, always	·39	·47
Degree of sex satisfaction with mate: very enjoyable, enjoyable, tolerated, disgusting, very disgusting	·39	·42
*Increase or decrease of intercourse during marriage: increased greatly, increased, remained the same, decreased some, decreased greatly, ceased entirely	·38	.26
Extent of kissing mate: every day, now and then, almost never	·38	·38
Extent of engaging in outside interests together: all of them, some of them, very few of them, none of them	·35	·46
*Do you experience periods of lonesomeness? (yes or no)	·35	.25
Number of things in marriage which satisfy you most: nothing, one thing, two things, three or more things	·34	·41
Degree of sex satisfaction mate had with you: very enjoyable, enjoyable, tolerated, disgusting, very disgusting	·34	·32
Extent of agreement on demonstration of affection (scale as for conventionality)	·33	·31
Extent of agreement on recreation (scale as for conventionality)	·31	·33

	Husbands	Wives
*Extent of agreement on table manners (scale as for conventionality)	.27	.20
*Do you often feel just miserable? (yes or no) . . .	.25	.23
*Extent of agreement on religious matters (scale as for conventionality)	.21	.23
*Do you feel lonesome even when with other people? (yes or no)	.16	.30
*Are you usually even-tempered and happy in your outlook on life? (yes or no)	.12	.21
*Are you self-confident about your abilities? (yes or no)	.08	.12
*Does some particularly useless thought keep coming into your mind to bother you? (yes or no)	.06	.19
*Are you usually in good spirits? (yes or no)	.02	.20

Even though most of the items were statistically significant in differentiating between happily-married and divorced,[19] it would seem good procedure to use only the most differentiating. It is suggested that in a new marital-adjustment test those items in the above list with contingency correlations below .30 be arbitrarily eliminated. This would exclude the following items used in this or previous studies: degree of agreement on table manners and religious matters, and the seven so-called personality items—those dealing with lonesomeness, happiness, and self-confidence. On the item, "experience periods of lonesomeness," there was a correlation of .35 for husbands, but the interviews revealed that this was a function of the divorce situation, and consequently it should be eliminated as a measure of marital adjustment. The same is true for wives on "lonesome even when with other people." On the increase or decrease of intercourse during marriage, the contingency correlation was .38 for men and .26 for

[19] The last four items in the table are not statistically significant for men; for women, "self-confident" was the only item not statistically significant.

women, and it is suggested that this also be eliminated from a new test.

The interviews indicated that subjects gave about the same answers to each of the following three items: "check any of the following (24 items) which caused *serious* difficulties in your marriage," "things mate does which you do not like," and "things which annoy you most about the marriage." Consequently, it is suggested that the last two be eliminated and that the test include a list of items to be checked, for it has been found that the maritally-maladjusted seize upon all sorts of things as serious difficulties in their marriage, and the adjusted check practically nothing.

An additional item not in the above list has been found to differentiate between the adjusted and maladjusted in current studies. The following might be included in a new marital-adjustment test:

On the scale line below check the dot which best describes the degree of happiness, everything considered, of your present marriage. The middle point, "happy," represents the degree of happiness which most people get from marriage, and the scale gradually ranges on one side to those few who experience extreme joy in marriage and on the other to those few who are very unhappy in marriage.

·	·	·	·	·	·	·

Very Unhappy	Happy	Perfectly Happy

The inclusion of the items in Table 9 which do not have an asterisk and the item above would give a marital-adjustment test of 23 items. This should differentiate between those relatively adjusted and those relatively maladjusted in marriage.

SUMMARY

A marital-adjustment test does not measure the degree of adjustment of an individual marriage, but merely measures the probability that a given marriage will be characterized by a certain degree of adjustment.

The great difference between the mean adjustment scores of happily married and divorced men and happily married and divorced women, and also the difference in the mean combined scores of spouses of the two groups, indicate the validity of the criteria of "happily married as judged by an outsider" and "divorce" as measures of marital adjustment and maladjustment. The difference between mean scores of happily-married and divorced is so great that there is only one chance in several million that the difference could have been due to chance.

The maladjustment of divorced couples who got a fairly high score on the marital-adjustment test seems to be due to a clash on one or two things that were so important to the spouses that they could not or would not adjust to the situation.

Experimentation should be conducted with items in a marital-adjustment test so as to reduce to a minimum the number of items in the test and yet effectively distribute marriages along a continuum from good to poor adjustment.

4

MARITAL DISAGREEMENTS AND CONFLICTS

Marriage was defined some twenty-five years ago by Keyserling as a tragic state of tension.[1] Regardless of the accuracy of his definition, family members who experience major unsolved disagreements and conflicts think of the quarrels as tragic. Also, when the antagonisms become pervasive and strong, one or both spouses may begin to think of separation.

A major part of the marital-adjustment test presented in the previous chapter was composed of questions on the degree of agreement and disagreement on various items, and on certain aspects of conflict.[2] In the present chapter several of these items will be given detailed consideration and a few additional factors on conflict will be presented.

AGREEMENTS AND DISAGREEMENTS

On Basic Interests and Activities. The marital-adjustment test included 11 questions asking persons to indicate the degree of agreement or disagreement between self and mate on a sixfold scale: always agree, almost always agree, occasionally disagree, frequently disagree, almost always disagree, and al-

[1] Count Hermann Keyserling, *The Book of Marriage,* New York, Harcourt, Brace, and Co., 1926, pp. 47–48.

[2] Whenever reference is made to the marital-adjustment test, the samples include all cases except those divorced couples who were forced to marry. In the marital-adjustment test items, chi square rather than critical ratio will be used as the measure of the significance of difference.

TABLE 10

Per Cent of Happily Married and Divorced Men Reporting Degrees of Agreement or Disagreement with Mate on Given Items, with Chi Squares *

Items	Always Agree		Almost Always Agree		Occa-sionally Disagree		Frequently, Almost Al-ways, and Always Disagree		Chi Square
	Mar.	Div.	Mar.	Div.	Mar.	Div.	Mar.	Div.	
Handling Family Finances	50	25	40	25	8	21	2	29	81.4
Matters of Recreation	44	26	38	30	13	19	5	25	40.2
Religious Matters	69	63	24	21	6	5	1	11	14.9
Demonstration of Affection	58	37	30	27	9	16	3	20	42.4
Friends	51	20	33	20	12	21	4	39	93.8
Intimate Relations (Sex)	50	28	38	22	9	20	3	30	73.9
Ways of Dealing with In-laws	53	29	34	19	12	15	1	37	88.4
Amount of Time Spent Together	57	21	29	23	12	21	2	35	98.0
Table Manners	65	57	27	22	7	12	1	9	20.0
Conventionality	51	22	37	18	10	22	2	38	86.7
Aims, Goals, and Things Believed Important in Life	61	22	29	27	8	17	2	34	78.9

* Per cents were rounded for convenience. The number of cases varied slightly from item to item, but was about 190 for married and 210 for divorced.

ways disagree. Table 10 gives the per cent of happily married and divorced men and Table 11 the per cent of happily married and divorced women who reported varying degrees of agreement between self and mate on the various items. It will

TABLE 11

Per Cent of Happily Married and Divorced Women Reporting Degrees of Agreement or Disagreement with Mate on Given Items, with Chi Squares *

Items	Always Agree		Almost Always Agree		Occasionally Disagree		Frequently, Almost Always, and Always Disagree		Chi Square
	Mar.	Div.	Mar.	Div.	Mar.	Div.	Mar.	Div.	
Handling Family Finances	45	28	41	22	13	15	1	35	84.3
Matters of Recreation	41	29	42	29	15	19	2	23	45.5
Religious Matters	60	51	32	25	6	10	2	14	21.1
Demonstration of Affection	55	36	37	32	6	17	2	15	39.8
Friends	50	22	37	21	12	15	1	42	106.8
Intimate Relations (Sex)	45	26	41	30	12	17	2	27	59.2
Ways of Dealing with In-laws	49	31	37	23	12	17	2	29	58.8
Amount of Time Spent Together	55	24	32	24	10	17	3	35	84.1
Table Manners	51	52	36	28	10	9	3	11	11.0
Conventionality	52	17	35	30	12	15	1	38	89.4
Aims, Goals, and Things Believed Important in Life	56	18	38	27	5	15	1	40	102.2

* Per cents were rounded for convenience. The number of cases varied slightly from item to item, but was about 189 for married and 224 for divorced.

be noted that the first three categories are columns 1, 2, and 3, and that column 4 is the last three combined into a single category. This combining of three of the disagreement categories into one column makes it easier to see the much larger per cent of divorced than of happily-married who indicated relatively great disagreement between self and mate. For most of the items, the response, "occasionally disagree," also was made by a larger per cent of divorced than married, but the differences were not very great. It will be seen that the first column, "always agree," includes a very much larger per cent of happily-married than divorced. "Almost always agree" likewise indicates a larger per cent of happily-married than divorced. These two tables strikingly reveal the greater agreement reported between happily married than divorced couples.

The tables also give the size of the chi squares, which, of course, is a test of significance of the difference between the way the happily-married and divorced answered each of the 11 questions. In all of the items there was less than 1 chance in 100 that the difference could have been due to chance.[3] The very high chi squares show that the happily married men and women had much greater agreement with their mates than did the divorced on money, recreation, religion, the showing of affection, friends, sex relations, in-laws, spending time together, table manners, conventionality, and family objectives.

Who Gives in when Disagreements Arise. Immediately after the above 11 items, there was the following question in the marital-adjustment test:

When disagreements have arisen, they usually have resulted in: husband giving in _____*; wife giving in _____; agreement by mutual give and take _____; neither giving in _____.

The happily-married answered this question in a radically different way from the divorced.[4] The happily-married were

[3] This level of significance is present with a chi square of only 15.1, where the problem is similar to ours, that is, where two groups are compared on an item in which there are six possible answers. In the two items where the chi square was below 15.1, "religious matters" for men and "table manners" for women, the two groups were compared on four possible answers and a chi square of only 11.3 is needed for a one-per cent level of significance.

[4] Chi square for men: 125.2. For women: 136.8.

very much more inclined to reach agreement by "mutual give and take" than the divorced. About 8 in 10 happily married men and women gave this response as compared with about 3 in 10 divorced men and women.[5] "Husband gave in" was reported by about 3 in 10 divorced men, with 1 in 10 reporting the "wife gave in." [6] For divorced women, about 5 in 10 reported the "wife gave in," with 1 in 10 reporting the "husband gave in." [7] "Neither gave in" was reported by about 3 in 10 divorced men and 2 in 10 divorced women.[8]

MARITAL CONFLICTS

A typical process of marital conflict is revealed in the analysis of questionnaire and interview data. This process has certain sequences and, if carried to its logical conclusion, results in the disruption of the family. The sequences include some and often many of the following: development of difficulties and tensions between family members; debating the issues of the conflict with oneself; overt expressions of conflict; intermittent attempts to solve the marital difficulties; sleeping in different beds or different rooms; mentioning divorce as a possibility to the mate; spatial separation; reconciliation; making application for divorce; getting the application dismissed; reapplying for divorce; securing the divorce; seeing the former mate and possibly remarrying; if married again, securing a second divorce; efforts at emancipation from the mate; and adjustment to the crisis of divorce. Any stage in the above sequence may be omitted. Also, the process may be interrupted or permanently terminated at any stage.[9]

This process of alienation is illustrated in the case of a

[5] Per cents for happily-married: 84.9 and 82.3. For divorced: 30.8 and 25.5.
[6] Per cents: 31.3 and 10.4.
[7] Per cents: 46.3 and 9.1.
[8] Per cents: 27.5 and 19.0.
[9] This paragraph was adapted from the present study and used by Ernest W. Burgess and Harvey J. Locke in their book, *The Family: From Institution to Companionship*, New York, American Book Co., 1950, p. 638.

couple who had applied for divorce, who had the application dismissed, and who at the time of the interview were permanently separated. The wife, a dominant woman, had tried to take a hand in managing the husband's business which was on the road to bankruptcy. When the business was wiped out, the husband lost standing in her eyes and in his own. She "fussed" at him; he retaliated by eating away from home. During the menopause, she refused him intercourse; he retaliated again by leaving home. After the separation, she applied for divorce, only to have it dismissed. On his visits home he was given "the silent treatment." The cumulative alienation is described by the husband: [10]

"We were happy as could be for the first twenty years of our marriage. Then two things occurred which changed our marriage into unhappiness. I lost most of my business; second, my wife had the change of life. I would come home and would be worried about my business, and then she would argue and fuss and make me nervous, and I would have indigestion. So I got to staying down town and eating out.

"Then she became cold. We were very active sexually in our earlier life. Now she wouldn't have anything to do with me. I moved into another bed and then into another room. I told her that I would give her time to adjust to her change—four or five years. At the end of that time things were no better, so I packed up and left.

"Since I went away, I have been back occasionally. But when I go back for Christmas or Thanksgiving, she does not pay any attention to me. She talks and laughs with the others, but not with me. I may go out to the kitchen and try to wipe the dishes like I used to, but she says that she can get along all right by herself.

"A few weeks ago she suggested that I come back; we would live as man and wife; and I went over and talked with her. I found that the old trouble would still be there.

"Later, I went over and told her that I did not want to go to a prostitute and would like to come back, but she said that I would

[10] Case no. 895.

not find anything like that around there. In fact, when I was still at home, she suggested that I find someone else."

The paragraphs that follow deal with six general questions on marital conflict: things mate does the spouse does not like, things which are annoying in the marriage, the number and kind of marital difficulties, feelings during periods of difficulty, the number of times spouse left mate because of conflict, and, finally, talking over with an outsider critical problems of family life.

Things Mate Does the Spouse Doesn't Like. The marital-adjustment test included a question concerning "the number of things mate does you do not like." The number of complaints listed by the happily-married was decidedly smaller than the number listed by divorced men and women.[11] About half of the happily married men and a quarter of the happily married women reported that the mate did nothing they did not like,[12] whereas "nothing" was reported by only 1 in 20 divorced men and women.[13] Two or more things were listed by about 4 in 10 divorced men and 6 in 10 divorced women,[14] while this number was listed by only 1 in 10 happily married men and 2 in 10 happily married women.[15]

Things Which Annoy You about Your Marriage. A question similar to the above was on "the number of things which annoy you most about your marriage." Divorced men and women listed many more things which annoyed them about their marriages than did the happily-married.[16] "Nothing" was listed by 5 in 10 happily married men to 1 in ten divorced, and by 3 in 10 happily married women to 1 in 30 divorced.[17]

[11] Chi square for men: 59.9. For women: 53.9.
[12] Per cents: 49.0 and 23.5.
[13] Per cents: 5.7 and 4.5.
[14] Per cents: 44.3 and 63.0.
[15] Per cents: 12.9 and 24.7.
[16] Chi square for men: 54.5. For women: 74.0.
[17] Per cents for men: 48.7 and 9.5. For women: 32.0 and 3.3.

Two or more things were listed by 5 in 10 divorced men to 1 in 10 happily-married, and by 6 in 10 divorced women to 2 in 10 happily-married.[18]

Number and Kind of Marital Difficulties. The hypothesis was that couples experiencing marital adjustment or maladjustment will differ in the number and kind of serious marital difficulties. Twenty-four items were presented to happily married and divorced persons. The divorced were instructed to check those which "were the real causes of difficulties in your marriage which *led to your divorce*. These need not be legal grounds." The happily-married were instructed to check those which "have caused *serious* difficulties in your marriage."

The marital-adjustment test used one aspect of this question: the mere number of items checked. This gave an index of the prevalence of conflicts between spouses. It was found that happily married men and women had decidedly fewer conflicts than did the divorced.[19] The degree to which this was the case is shown by the fact that 63.7 per cent of happily married men checked none or only one of the items, while 64.0 per cent of the divorced checked 4 or more. For women, 55.3 per cent of the happily-married checked none or only one, while 69.4 per cent of the divorced checked 4 or more.

Table 12 lists the various items with the per cents of happily married and divorced men and women who checked each. It also gives the critical ratios of the differences of per cents of happily-married and divorced in those items where differences were significant.

The table shows that the happily-married and divorced differed greatly in the per cent who checked specific items and also in the kind of items which were checked. There was only one item which was checked by more than 20 per cent of happily married men, whereas 13 items were checked by more than 20 per cent of divorced men. For women, there were two

18 Per cents for men: 47.4 and 12.8. For women: 62.5 and 17.0.
19 Chi square for men: 170.4. For women: 176.2.

items checked by 20 per cent of the happily-married, whereas there were 15 items checked by more than 20 per cent of the divorced.

TABLE 12

Per Cent of Happily-Married and Divorced Checking Items as Serious Marital Difficulties, with Critical Ratios of the Difference of Per Cents

Item	Men			Women		
	Married N = 111	Divorced N = 123	CR	Married N = 125	Divorced N = 147	CR
A. Affectional and Sex Relationships.						
1. Mate paid attention to (became familiar with) another person	2.7	65.9	10.1	5.6	73.5	11.3
2. Lack of mutual affection (no longer in love)	4.5	60.2	9.0	1.6	61.2	10.3
3. Adultery	0.9	43.9	7.7	1.6	55.1	9.6
4. Unsatisfying sex relations	8.1	46.3	6.5	5.6	32.7	5.6
5. Venereal disease	0.0	1.6		0.8	12.2	3.7
6. Unsatisfied desire to have children	2.7	8.1	1.8	8.8	3.4	1.9
7. Sterility of husband or wife	0.9	3.3		4.8	0.7	2.1
B. Economic Difficulties.						
1. Mate's attempt to control my spending money	9.0	26.8	3.5	7.2	21.1	3.2
2. Other difficulties over money	14.4	34.1	3.5	19.2	38.1	3.4
3. Nonsupport	0.0	7.3	2.9	0.0	49.0	9.1
4. Desertion	0.0	20.3	5.0	0.0	27.2	6.3
C. Socially Disapproved Behavior.						
1. Drunkenness	2.7	26.0	5.0	1.6	56.5	9.7
2. Gambling	2.7	6.5		3.2	26.5	5.2
3. Mate sent to jail	0.0	4.9	2.4	0.0	16.3	4.7
D. Individualistic Behavior.						
1. Do not have mutual friends	10.8	38.2	4.8	6.4	25.2	4.2

Item	Men			Women		
	Married	Divorced	CR	Married	Divorced	CR
2. Selfishness and lack of cooperation	6.3	22.0	3.4	12.0	29.9	3.6
E. Miscellaneous Items.						
1. Interference of in-laws	17.1	52.8	5.7	20.0	29.9	1.9
2. Ill health	3.6	13.8	2.7	15.2	10.2	
3. Constant bickering ..	5.4	48.0	7.3	8.8	34.7	5.1
F. Undifferentiating Items.						
1. Different amusement interests	28.8	34.1		20.0	28.6	
2. Religious differences	6.3	8.1		4.8	7.5	
3. Cruelty to step-children	0.0	0.0		0.0	0.0	
4. Other reasons	6.3	12.2		15.2	19.0	
G. No difficulties at all	38.7	0.0	7.6	27.2	0.0	6.8

Items on which the happily-married and divorced differed significantly may be classified under five general categories: (1) affectional and sex relationships, (2) socially disapproved behavior, (3) economic problems, (4) individualism, and (5) miscellaneous difficulties.

Some of the greatest differences between happily-married and divorced were found in the area of affectional and sexual relationships. This area includes seven items: mate became familiar with another person, lack of love between the spouses, adultery, unsatisfying sex relations, venereal disease, unsatisfied desire to have children, and sterility. Both divorced men and women checked the first four of these as difficulties much more frequently than did the married. In fact they were among the very highest per cents checked by divorced persons. This seems to mean that the absence of these difficulties makes for marital adjustment and their presence makes for, or is indicative of, marital maladjustment.

Two of the above items, "unsatisfied desire to have children" and "sterility," were reported by a higher proportion of married than divorced women. Apparently the difficulty of satisfying the desire to have children due to such things as economic pressure or sterility of mate or self was not incompatible with happiness in marriage.

Economic difficulties included the attempt to control the spending of money by one spouse, other problems over money, nonsupport, and desertion. Nonsupport, of course, was a much more significant difficulty for the divorced than for the married, and for divorced women than divorced men. However, on all four items the divorced checked them more frequently than the married.

The table shows that difficulties over socially disapproved behavior were much more frequently reported by the divorced than by the happily-married. "Drunkenness" and "mate sent to jail" were checked more frequently by both divorced men and women than by married, and gambling was checked more frequently by divorced than by married women. All three were checked more frequently by divorced women than by men. It appears that women are more disturbed than men by socially disapproved behavior. For example, drunkenness was checked by 56.5 per cent of divorced women, or about as frequently as adultery, and only less frequently than 2 of the other 23 items listed in Table 12. By contrast, only 26.0 per cent of divorced men checked drunkenness as a serious difficulty in the marriage. The reaction of a divorced husband to the drunkenness of his wife is revealed in the following excerpt from a statement by his wife: [20]

"I think that if my husband had let me drink at home when I started and if he had not allowed me to have my own way about going out on parties with other persons including men, we would have gotten along. Drinking outside of the home at taverns, I got to be a drunkard, and running around made me want other men.

"He would stay at home and would not ask me any questions

[20] Case no. 214.

when I got home, even though I had stayed out all night. He was insanely jealous, but allowed me this freedom.

"I was at fault in that I did drink, went with other men, and got sent to prison on a charge of disturbing the peace."

A divorced man vividly describes his drunkenness as follows: [21]

"One of the main difficulties in our marriage was my drinking. I did not drink a bit during the first part of our marriage, possibly for the first five years. Then my wife and I began going with a crowd that drank and we both began to drink. I have seen my wife drunk a few times, but in my case I became drunk quite frequently. She threatened to divorce me, but I didn't think she would, and then one day she filed suit for divorce.

"Drinking is an awful habit; I would like to get over it. In fact, three or four weeks ago I went on a drunk and my landlady kept the empty bottles. When I sobered up after about a week of drinking, there was a whole bushel basket full of empty bottles. I figured up the cost, and it cost me about $22.50 for one week's drinking. I told myself then that I would quit, but I have told myself that so often that I really doubt whether I will quit."

Socially disapproved behavior, such as drunkenness, probably is symptomatic of underlying maladjustment in a marriage, or it may be an expression of basic personal needs which are not being satisfied. Whatever its cause, such behavior is predictive of marital disruption.

Individualism is not conducive to marital adjustment. This is revealed in the chapter "The Companionship Family," where it is shown that the divorced more than the married reported that only one spouse enjoyed certain activities, and where it is also shown that a larger per cent of divorced than married reported that one spouse more than the other took the lead in given situations.[22] Individualism on the part of the divorced more than of the married is also revealed in reports

[21] Case no. 21.
[22] See pp. 257–58, 264–65.

on difficulties in the marriage. This is true if the absence of mutual friends and selfishness and lack of cooperation are indices of individualism. Both divorced men and women checked these items much more frequently than did the married.

Constant bickering was checked by relatively few married men and women, but by about half of the divorced men and a third of the divorced women.

Table 12 also reveals certain differences between men as compared with differences between women. It shows that married and divorced men did not differ significantly on sterility, venereal disease, and gambling, whereas women did differ. The table also shows that married and divorced women did not differ significantly on interference of in-laws, but that the per cent of divorced men checking this item greatly exceeded that of the happily-married. "Ill health" was checked more frequently by divorced than by married men; by contrast more married than divorced women checked this as a difficulty, though the difference was not statistically significant. "Unsatisfied desire to have children" was checked more frequently by divorced than by happily married men and more by happily married than by divorced women.

On four items—religious differences, different amusement interests, cruelty to step-children, and difficulties other than those listed—there were no significant differences either between happily married and divorced men or between happily married and divorced women.[23]

Happily married men and women often reported that there were no serious difficulties in their marriage, whereas every divorced person checked at least one and usually several items. Four in ten happily married men, 38.7 per cent, and three in ten married women, 27.2 per cent, indicated that there were no serious difficulties in their marriage.

---

[23] Of course, on "cruelty to step-children" no checks were to be expected, for the above analysis is on couples married only once. Some subjects indicated that cruelty to their own children was a source of difficulty between them and their spouses.

The lack of serious difficulties in a large proportion of happily married couples is illustrated below by short excerpts from the case records of four happily married couples. In the first there were no serious difficulties, and the wife was inclined to laugh about their minor problems: [24]

After looking over the list of things that might cause serious difficulties, she sat back with an air of bewilderment and said, "My goodness! We never have any serious difficulties. The thing that annoys me slightly is that he is too even-tempered. That man is never elated or depressed over anything. I have to give vent to my emotions and I wish he would, too, sometimes." She chuckled over the question, "What does your mate do that you do not like?" Then she said, "Looking around while driving the car." After thinking a moment longer she said slowly, almost to herself, "There's another thing he does that I don't like: he puts things off and I can't stand that."

In the following case the marriage ceremony was simply an incident in the life of a busy farm couple, who had known each other for two or three years. There were no major difficulties, and the husband avoided the development of an argument by the simple device of walking away. The wife reported: [25]

"I thought maybe we ought to be married by a minister, but he was in a hurry to get another load of corn husked that day, so we just went to the justice of the peace.

"We never have any difficulties. He won't even talk back; just walks off. Guess that is the thing that he does that I don't like. I'd like it better if he would say something once in a while."

A happily married husband reported that disagreements between himself and his wife were kept from becoming difficulties by working out adjustments together: [26]

"Marriage is just what you make it. We don't believe in discussing our affairs outside of the family. But we have never had

24 Case no. 158.
25 Case no. 161.
26 Case no. 116.

any disagreements we couldn't work out ourselves. There are not enough differences to make us quarrel. We never let it get to that point. If one of us does not like what the other does, we just don't say anything about it at the time."

Over and over again happily married couples avoided saying anything which might be interpreted as uncomplimentary about the mate. The remarks of the wife and the husband in the following case illustrate the sympathetic understanding existing between many of these couples: [27]

Wife. "He is so gentle at all times, compared with other husbands whose wives have talked to me. He works so hard for what we have to show for. Sometimes he does things which I don't like, such as going fishing when I can't go; he chews tobacco and I don't like that; but everyone has a few faults."

Husband. "My wife is a pretty good 'side kick.' She is good to the children and we get along very, very well. I think a lot of her. Maybe she doesn't enjoy sex as much as I do, but she is a good woman."

The baby woke during the interview, and the husband took it up and talked to it in a loving way and then called his wife, saying that it needed her attention.

Feeling about Marital Difficulties. Couples differ not only on the number and kind of difficulties in their marriages, but in the intensity of feeling about the difficulties. Couples who are strongly attached to each other, who are secure about the permanence of the marriage, and who are considerate of each other even in times of disagreement, feel differently about marital problems and difficulties from those couples whose personal attachments are weaker, whose marriage is threatened with disruption, and who are inclined to hurt each other through angry, irritated, and critical reactions.

A specific question was devised to test the above hypothesis. Happily married and divorced persons were instructed to give

[27] Case no. 77.

the approximate degree of their feelings *during periods of difficulty* between them and their mates. Four alternate answers—very, somewhat, a little, and not at all—were given, and one of these was checked for each of the following ten feelings: lonely, miserable, irritated, angry, insecure, worried, hurt, inferior, self-confident, and critical of mate.

The happily-married and divorced differed decidedly in their responses to this question. The pattern was for the divorced to report "very" and the happily-married "not at all." The category of "a little" generally had a higher per cent of married than divorced.

In eight of the ten feelings, "very" was reported by a much larger per cent of divorced men and women than by the happily-married.[28] From the largest to the smallest statistically significant difference, the order for men and for women was as follows:

Men	CR	Women	CR
Critical of mate	6.4	Insecure	6.3
Irritated	5.5	Worried	6.0
Worried	5.4	Critical of mate	5.7
Angry	4.8	Miserable	4.5
Hurt	4.2	Lonely	4.1
Lonely	3.5	Hurt	4.0
Miserable	3.4	Irritated	3.5
Insecure	3.4	Angry	3.0

Thus, during periods of difficulty, the divorced had strong feelings of insecurity; were very angry, irritated, and critical of each other; were deeply hurt; and felt very lonely, miserable, and worried. Insecurity was a particularly strong feeling, for not only did a larger per cent of divorced than happily-

[28] "Self-confident" and "inferior" were not very differentiating. On "self-confident" a larger per cent of divorced than married men reported "very," 44.6 and 25.6, CR 2.6; a larger per cent of married than divorced reported "not at all," 32.3 and 17.9, CR 2.0. For women, a larger per cent of married than divorced reported "not at all," 39.0 and 26.1, CR 2.0. On "inferior" a larger per cent of happily married than divorced men reported "a little," 21.4 and 6.9, CR 2.5. For women, a larger per cent of divorced than married reported "somewhat," 23.5 and 9.6, CR 2.8.

married report "very," but also a significantly larger per cent reported "somewhat." [29]

By contrast, happily married men and women reported "not at all" or only "a little" to a much greater extent than did the divorced. From the largest to the smallest statistically significant difference, the order on "not at all" was as follows:

Men	CR		Women	CR
Insecure	4.2		Insecure	5.8
Critical of mate	3.8		Critical of mate	3.0
Angry	3.0		Miserable	2.5
Lonely	2.7		Worried	2.5
Miserable	2.6		Lonely	2.5
Worried	2.2		Self-confident	2.0
Self-confident	2.0			

The list of feelings for "a little" was as follows:

Men	CR		Women	CR
Angry	3.2		Worried	3.7
Inferior	2.5		Hurt	2.9
Irritated	2.2		Insecure	2.6
Hurt	2.2		Angry	2.2
			Lonely	2.1
			Critical of mate	2.1
			Irritated (a little and not at all)	2.3

Thus, during periods of difficulty the happily-married, as compared with the divorced, had very little or no feelings of insecurity, anger, loneliness, or miserableness; were not at all critical of mate; and were not worried as to the outcome of the difficulty. Of course, part of the differences between the married and divorced on such feelings as insecurity, loneliness, miserableness, and the like, may have been due to the fact that divorced persons were experiencing these feelings as divorced persons and were inclined to think of them as present in the marriage, even though they may have been absent.

[29] CR for men: 3.4. For women: 2.5.

Times Left Mate Because of Conflict. It is not uncommon in American culture for a husband or wife to leave the mate for varying lengths of time if marital conflicts become too intense, or if a person is unable to cope with them. An item on this was included in the marital-adjustment test and was phrased as follows:

During marriage how many times have you left your mate because of conflict _____; how many times has your mate left you _____.

It was to be expected that the divorced would have left the mate because of conflict much more frequently than the happily-married, but not to the extent that they actually did.[30] The most striking evidence of this is that 9 in 10 happily married men and women and only 3 in 10 divorced men and women indicated that they had never left the mate because of conflict.[31]

Once a person begins to walk out on the mate during a conflict, it is a signal that the conflict process is very far advanced and that the marriage may end in disruption.

Talking with Third Party about Marital Difficulties. Talking over marital difficulties with a third party is likewise, on the whole, a signal of a high degree of marital maladjustment. It is unfortunate that happily-married and divorced are not comparable on this item, for the happily-married were asked if they talked over difficulties, and the divorced if they talked over the advisability of securing a divorce. However, it is interesting to note that only 6.2 and 10.8 per cent of happily married men and women, respectively, had talked over marital difficulties with a third party, and that 54.0 and 48.6 per cent of divorced men and women, respectively, reported talking over with a third party the advisability of getting a divorce.

[30] Chi square for men: 117.0. For women: 114.8.
[31] Per cents for men: 92.2 and 29.5. For women: 89.4 and 25.8.

SUMMARY

This chapter has given additional evidence to that presented in the previous chapter on the importance for marital adjustment of (1) agreement between the mates on certain activities and (2) a relative lack of conflict between them. Specifically, the chapter revealed a positive association between the following and marital adjustment:

1. Always or almost always agree on handling finances, recreation, religion, demonstration of affection, sexual relations, ways of dealing with in-laws, amount of time spent together, table manners, conventionality, and aims or objectives of the family.

2. Agreements are reached by mutual give and take.

3. Relatively few things are annoying in the mate or in the marriage.

4. No feeling exists that there are serious difficulties in affectional and sexual relationships, or over money problems between family members.

5. Partners do not engage in socially disapproved behavior or in individualistic conduct.

6. Partners have a feeling of security, and are not inclined to become angry, irritated, and critical of the mate, nor inclined to be lonely, miserable, or worried.

7. Mates remain together during periods of conflict or great difficulty.

5

COURTSHIP AND ENGAGEMENT

THE CASE of a divorced couple is given below to illustrate the five general problems considered in the present chapter: (1) problems involved in getting acquainted, (2) length of engagement, (3) degree of conflict and affection before marriage, (4) reasons for marrying, and (5) differences in age: [1]

Wife. "I was going with a boy and was engaged to him, but my parents did not want me to marry him. My husband was on a thrashing crew and came to our house. My father said that if I married the other boy I couldn't set foot in the house again. My folks wanted me to marry the thrasher. I thought an awful lot of my folks and not enough of my own happiness, so I married him. I was only 15 and he was 14 years older than me. I really didn't know him when I married him, for I saw him only about two times a month. When my father and my husband brought home the license, I wanted to burn it up, but my mother wouldn't let me.

"As our difficulties grew, I got to thinking that I would separate from him as soon as our children were old enough. The final straw was when he refused to pay the last $600 on the mortgage and we lost our place. I told him, 'unless you take care of the mortgage, we'll lose the place, and if we lose it, I'll leave you as sure as you're alive.' Also, he drank a lot.

"When I would be going to church some of my friends would pick me up and my husband did not like that at all. If I went to

[1] Case no. 848.

86

see my folks, we'd have a racket the whole following week. So I quit going there, but kept going to church."

To the question whether the drinking of the husband was at all caused by unhappy sex life, which had been described as disgusting and as ceasing entirely, the wife responded, "Well, maybe. It might have been."

Husband. "I told her she couldn't serve the Lord on Saturday and Sunday, and the Devil the rest of the week. She would go to church on Saturday and Sunday, and then want to go to movies the rest of the week."

To the question, "Was pregnancy the reason for marrying?" the husband replied, "No, it wasn't. I will take that back. She was two months along. Later, she used something to keep from having children. I called it murder."

The interviewer raised the question as to how well the wife did in managing the home, and found that the husband was inclined to blame his wife for the loss of the home. "She was a very poor manager. I would tell her to save up and pay for the house, but she believed in putting on rags. Well, we had $2700 paid on the house and we owed only $500 more. I could have sold my mules and borrowed to save the house, but we let it go back."

The above is the case of a couple that had little or nothing in common. Before marriage they had known each other only a short time, they had no emotional attachments, their marriage was due to parental pressure—probably because of pregnancy, and they differed greatly in age.

Length of acquaintance, length of engagement, and age variables have been included in other studies, particularly those of Burgess and Cottrell and Terman. Conclusions from these other studies will be inserted in the appropriate places. On the whole, the answers to questions on courtship and engagement differentiated between the happily-married and the divorced.

The question arises whether the events relative to courtship and engagement can be remembered ten or fifteen years later: the average length of marriage of the happily-married was 16.7 years and of the divorced, 11.4 years. Inasmuch as the courtship experiences are generally "high points" in the individual's life, they probably are remembered with approximate accuracy. At any rate, as they were remembered, they differentiated between the happily married and the divorced group.

GETTING ACQUAINTED

Is marital adjustment related to such questions as where a couple meets, how long they know each other before marriage, and how frequently they see each other during courtship? Tentative conclusions on these three questions are presented in this section.

Place of First Meeting with Future Mate. The persons interviewed were asked to check one of the following general places to indicate where they first met the mate: home of a friend, home of a relative, place of business, school, church, casual meeting place ("pick-up"), travel, neighborhood, dance hall, or other place. Significant differences between the happily-married and divorced were found only where the meeting place was at the home of a friend or at a dance hall. A larger per cent of divorced men and women than married reported meeting their mates at the home of a friend,[2] and a larger per cent of divorced women than married women reported meeting their mates at a dance hall.[3]

The place of first meeting one's future mate, as far as the categories listed above are concerned, does not appear to be a very discriminating factor in marital adjustment. The per cent of the married who met in such conventional places as the home of a relative, in school, and in church was not significantly larger than the per cent of the divorced who met in such places. It appears that in our mobile culture one may first encounter his future mate in any of a variety of places without affecting the probability of marital adjustment.

[2] Per cents for men: 22.7 and 14.0, CR 2.1. For women: 22.4 and 11.1, CR 2.8.
[3] Per cents: 7.7 and 1.8, CR 2.6.

Length of Acquaintance. Previous studies have found a high correlation between length of acquaintance before marriage and marital adjustment. The data of Burgess and Cottrell show a consistent picture of the "direct positive relation of length of acquaintance with marital compatibility," two or more years being favorable for adjustment in marriage.[4] Terman, however, reports that the "most striking thing disclosed by our data is the almost negligible relationship between marital happiness and length of premarital acquaintance." [5] An analysis of his data, however, seems to indicate that a short period of acquaintance is somewhat unfavorable for husbands and wives, and that a period of three or more years is favorable.

TABLE 13

Length of Premarital Acquaintance of Happily-Married and Divorced for Given Months of Acquaintance, by Per Cent

Length in Months	Men		Women	
	Married N = 173	Divorced N = 163	Married N = 171	Divorced N = 184
6 or less	12.7	15.9	12.3	19.6
7–12	19.1	21.5	19.3	27.2
13–24	22.6	23.3	19.9	19.0
25–36	9.8	12.3	12.8	7.6
Over 36	35.8	27.0	35.7	26.6
	100.0	100.0	100.0	100.0

Table 13 shows that in the present study the per cent of happily married and divorced men for given lengths of acquaintance were about the same, whereas married and divorced women differed considerably. In none of the periods of acquaintance listed was the difference between happily mar-

[4] Ernest W. Burgess and Leonard S. Cottrell, *Predicting Success or Failure in Marriage,* New York, Prentice-Hall, 1939, pp. 164–66, 357.

[5] Lewis M. Terman, *et al., Psychological Factors in Marital Happiness,* New York, McGraw-Hill, 1938, pp. 197–98.

ried and divorced men statistically significant on the adopted level of significance. However, an acquaintance of over three years was reported by 35.8 per cent of happily married men and only 27.0 per cent of divorced men, and this difference is on the 8-per cent level of significance.[6]

For women, the married reported significantly longer premarital acquaintance than did the divorced. More than a year was reported by about 7 in 10 married as compared with 5 in 10 divorced.[7] This, of course, means that a year or less was reported by a significantly larger per cent of divorced than married women.[8] The difference remained very large when the married and divorced were compared for the period of over two years, 48.5 per cent of the married to 34.2 per cent of the divorced reporting this period of acquaintance.[9]

The above seems to indicate that length of acquaintance is not a very important item in marital adjustment of husbands, but for wives a year or less is very unfavorable, and over two years of acquaintance is decidedly favorable for marital adjustment.

Frequency of Seeing Mate during Courtship. It was thought that possibly the frequency of seeing each other during courtship might be related to marital adjustment. Consequently, the question was asked:

How frequently did you see mate during courtship: once a month _____; twice a month _____; once a week _____; twice a week _____; almost every day _____.

No statistically significant differences were found for either men or women. Consequently, on the basis of the answers given to the question, the conclusion is that the frequency of seeing each other in courtship is not closely associated with marital adjustment.

6 CR only 1.7.
7 Per cents: 68.4 and 53.2, CR 3.0.
8 Per cents: 46.8 and 31.6, CR 3.0.
9 CR 2.8.

The above, however, does not conclusively demonstrate that there is no relation between "frequency of seeing each other during courtship" and "marital adjustment." A relationship might be found if a comparison of marital-adjustment scores were made between those with infrequent contact during courtship and those who saw each other frequently. This was not attempted, for in the present study more than 80 per cent of the subjects questioned reported seeing each other two or more times a week.

LENGTH OF ENGAGEMENT

Our findings on length of engagement strongly support the findings of other studies that a long engagement is positively associated with the probability of a good marital adjustment. Burgess and Cottrell found that as duration of engagement increased the proportion of couples with "poor" adjustment declined from 50.0 per cent for under 3 months to 11.0 per cent for 24 months and over, and that the per cent with "good" adjustment increased from 25.7 for under 3 months to 62.6 for 24 months and over.[10] Terman reported that engagements of less than 6 months for husbands and of less than 3 months for wives were unfavorable for marital adjustment and that long engagements of 5 years and over had the highest average happiness score.[11]

In the present study, length of engagement of divorced subjects varied with three different groups in the divorced sample: cases in which (1) the marriage under investigation was the only marriage and had not been due to pregnancy; (2) there had been a prior marriage and the one in question was not due to pregnancy; and (3) the reason for marrying was pregnancy. A brief description of courtship in the latter two will be followed by a detailed analysis of the length of engagement of the first group.

[10] *Op. cit.*, pp. 167–68.
[11] *Op. cit.*, pp. 198–200.

Forced Marriages. The number of reported forced marriages among the married was too small—only three—to compare with the 41 forced marriages ending in divorce. Forced marriages ending in divorce generally occurred after casual contact and brief acquaintance; the average length of engagement as reported by the men was but 2.7 months and as reported by the women 3.1 months. The following excerpt from an interview with the husband of one of these forced marriages illustrates the type of courtship: [12]

"I hate to think of my first wife. She was just a streetwalker. I had known her just about two weeks. We were out on a drinking party. The first thing I knew, she said she was pregnant. I married her, but never lived with her. I was going with the girl I am now married to. I went down town a free man; the next time I went I was a married man. I did not get a divorce for four years. The same day I divorced this woman, I married my present wife."

Those with a Previous Marriage. In the second group of cases—those in which there had been a prior marriage—the happily-married reported a longer engagement than did the divorced: the average length as reported by happily married and divorced men was 9.5 and 3.5 months [13] and by women 11.1 and 5.4 months,[14] though the differences were not significant on the selected level.

In addition to differing somewhat on the duration of the engagement, the happily-married and divorced may have differed on the kind of courtship in the second marriage. The following excerpt is from an interview with a divorced woman who had lived 43 years with her first husband, and who after his death married a man who had been married six times (the first two wives died and the other marriages ended in divorce). While maladjustment in her second marriage was due, in part, to her idealized picture of her first husband, it was to some

[12] Case no. 404.
[13] CR only 1.5.
[14] CR only 1.4.

extent associated with her casual acquaintance with her second husband: [15]

"One day I was in the courthouse where a lot of old people visit, and Jim came up to me and said, 'Howdy-do.' I said, 'Howdy.' He said, 'I don't believe I know you.' I told him my name. He said, 'Are you a widow woman?' I said, 'I am.' He asked, 'Is your man dead?' I said, 'He is.' I saw him at the store and he made a date with me. He told me tall tales about his fine house and furniture. I went with Jim about six months, and then we were married. He came and lived in my house and paid the rent only two months.

"I would be awfully happy if I could just go home to my first husband. Hugh was always so good to me, and Jim was always so mean. After Jim and me were separated, he told some stories about me sleeping with another man. But as God is my judge I am innocent. Since my divorce from Jim, an old man has been coming to see me once a week. I don't want him around much. Men get on my nerves."

Married-only-once. Table 14 gives the per cent of married and divorced men and women for given lengths of engagement for the group married-only-once, and shows that the length of engagement is highly correlated with marital adjustment. A very short engagement was much more prevalent in divorced cases than in the happily-married, and a relatively long engagement was much more prevalent among the happily-married.

A reported engagement by men of under a month was very unfavorable,[16] of 1 to 11 months neutral, of 12 months and over favorable.[17] If the period "6 to 11 months" is included with the "12 months and over," the size of the critical ratio is increased,[18] which probably means that for men an engagement of 6 months or over is very highly associated with marital

[15] Case no. 762.
[16] CR 3.9.
[17] CR 2.3.
[18] CR 3.3.

adjustment. For women a reported engagement of under a month is unfavorable,[19] of 1 to 5 months unfavorable,[20] of these two combined—under a month and 1 to 5 months—very unfavorable,[21] of 6 to 11 months neutral, of 12 months and over very favorable,[22] and of 24 months and over favorable.[23]

TABLE 14

Length of Engagement of Happily-Married and Divorced by Per Cent

Length in Months	Men		Women	
	Married N = 167	Divorced N = 164	Married N = 169	Divorced N = 182
Under 1	12.0	29.3	12.4	22.5
1–5	24.5	25.0	20.1	33.5
6–11	26.3	20.1	22.5	21.4
12–23	21.0	15.2	23.1	11.6
24–35	9.0	5.5	11.8	5.5
36 and over	7.2	4.9	10.1	5.5
	100.0	100.0	100.0	100.0

The differences were more significant for women than for men. This probably means that women place a higher value on the length of engagement than do men.

In terms of average length, happily married men reported an engagement of 10.2 months as compared with 7.3 months for divorced men,[24] or a 40 per cent longer engagement. Married women reported an average engagement of 12.0 months as compared with 7.1 months for divorced women,[25] or a 69 per cent longer engagement.

It is interesting to note that, where interviews were secured with both the husband and the wife, happily married wives

[19] CR 2.5.
[20] CR 2.8.
[21] CR 4.3.
[22] CR 4.5.
[23] CR 2.8.
[24] CR 2.4.
[25] CR 4.3.

reported a somewhat longer average engagement than did their husbands, 11.9 and 10.4 months, respectively, whereas the average length of engagement as reported by identical divorced mates was about the same, 7.1 months for women and 7.6 months for men. The difference between the happily married men and women on reported lengths of engagement, while not large enough to be statistically significant,[26] might be statistically significant if the sample were larger.

Differences in the type of engagement of the divorced and of the happily-married are revealed in the two following excerpts from life-history materials. In the first, a divorced woman expresses regret for having married a man whom she had known when she was a little girl, but to whom she had been engaged but three days: [27]

"I had known this fellow when I was a little girl, but hadn't seen him for a long time. He had went away, and then he come back. I was 18 about then. He was there 3 days, and on the third day I married him. There wasn't no courtship or engagement. We were really just pals. He was back from the place where he was working and he says, 'Let's get married, and I won't go back, but will stay here.' I liked him all right, and it seemed the thing to do. So we got married. I don't think those kind of marriages are good. You didn't know no others or have any experience. I found out later that there wasn't really love like it should be. Even at that we would have done all right, if he hadn't met up with old friends and took to gambling again."

In the next case a happily married woman, who was engaged 6 months, describes the way her mother and brother entered into the courtship process: [28]

"From the time I started dating my husband, I knew that I wanted to marry him. I had had a few dates with him, and my brother wanted to meet him. So I asked my brother and my mother to go

26 CR only 1.2.
27 Case no. 809.
28 Case no. 99.

to church with us. On the way back I walked with my mother, and my brother walked with 'Smiles,' which was the nickname of my husband. When we were at breakfast the next morning, my brother told me what a fine boy he thought 'Smiles' was. He had asked him about his jobs, his family, and so on. So after that my mother didn't worry about it and began to like 'Smiles.' In six months we were married."

Investigators of family and marriage relationships have presented several hypotheses as possible explanations of the high relationship between long engagements and marital adjustment. The Burgess-Cottrell hypothesis is stated as follows: [29] "Companionship tested by time appears therefore to be a better basis for successful marriage than the emotional feeling of certainty inspired by short-lived romantic love." Additional hypotheses are that a long period of intimate association will enable the persons to test their temperamental and emotional compatibility; it leads to accommodation prior to marriage and thus takes some of the strain off relationships in the marriage; and it screens out some possible marriage failures through broken engagements.

CONFLICT AND AFFECTION

Conflict before Marriage. The amount of conflict a husband and wife had before marriage is associated with the degree of their marital adjustment. The happily-married reported decidedly less conflict between themselves and their mates before marriage than did the divorced.

The degree of conflict was measured on a fivefold scale: none, very little, moderate, a good deal, and very great. The respective per cents of happily married and divorced men who reported none *and* very little conflict were 95.6 and 75.0, respectively; the per cents for women were 88.4 and 72.2.[30] This means, of course, that moderate, a good deal, *and* very great

[29] *Op. cit.,* p. 168.
[30] CR for men, 4.7. For women, 3.3.

conflict between a husband and wife before marriage was unfavorable to marital adjustment.[31]

It should be emphasized again that this difference may have been due, in part, to the fact that it was based on the reported degree of conflict, which probably reflected conflict or absence of conflict *during* marriage. Also, in the case of divorced men and women, the reported premarital conflict may have been affected by conflict and bitterness associated with securing the divorce.

Affection before Marriage. Happily married men and women reported much more affection before marriage than did the divorced, as measured on a fivefold scale: none, very little, moderate, a good deal, and very great. Very great affection was reported by over two thirds of happily married men and women as compared with one third of divorced men and slightly under half of divorced women.[32] A significantly larger per cent of divorced than married men reported moderate affection.[33] None, a little, *and* moderate combined characterized the reports of a larger per cent of divorced than married women.[34]

The giving and receiving of affection tends to unite a couple, and, if part of the unification occurs before marriage, it is favorable to marital adjustment.

REASONS FOR MARRYING

At the beginning of the study it was assumed that happily married persons would marry for different reasons from those of the divorced. It was also assumed that the reported reasons for

[31] For men the following single categories were statistically significant, with the happily-married per cent given first: a little, 40.3 and 23.7, CR 2.5; moderate, 3.8 and 14.5, CR 3.0; a good deal, 0.6 and 7.9, CR 3.1. For women: a good deal, 2.4 and 10.3, CR 2.7; very great, 0.6 and 6.2, CR 2.7.

[32] Per cents for men: 71.1 and 33.8, CR 5.5. For women: 69.5 and 46.5, CR 3.7.

[33] Per cents: 33.8 and 7.8, CR 5.1.

[34] Per cents: 27.3 and 8.4, CR 4.1.

marrying would probably be the real reasons for marrying. However, it now appears that answers to this question were affected, in part, by the alienation process in marriages which terminated in divorce or by the divorce experience itself. If it were felt that one did not get from marriage some of the things included in the list of reasons for marriage, a person might be inclined not to check such items.

The General Pattern. Table 15 gives the per cents of happily married men, divorced men, happily married women, and divorced women, who checked items in a list of reasons for marrying. Persons were to check as many reasons as they thought applied to their marriage. The table shows that *the order* of reported reasons for marrying was about the same for married men, divorced men, married women, and divorced

TABLE 15

Per Cent of Happily-Married and Divorced Checking Given Reasons for Marrying, with Critical Ratios of the Difference of Per Cents

Item	Men			Women		
	Married N = 173	Divorced N = 155	CR	Married N = 171	Divorced N = 179	CR
Love	97.1	84.5	4.0	98.2	83.8	4.7
To have a home	74.0	60.6	2.6	66.1	51.4	2.8
Common interests	58.4	43.2	2.7	70.2	41.9	5.3
To have children	37.6	24.5	2.6	38.0	22.9	3.1
To satisfy sex interests	28.3	16.8	2.5	22.2	3.9	5.1
Loneliness	13.9	17.4		10.5	8.9	
Economic security	3.5	1.9		12.3	4.5	2.6
To escape own family	3.5	4.5		4.1	16.2	3.7

women, but that the per cents of the divorced were consistently lower than the per cents of the married who checked given items. The five most frequently checked items were "love," "to have a home," "common interests," "to have children," and "to satisfy sex desires."

There were three variations in the general pattern of reasons for marrying. One was that divorced women practically never checked "to satisfy sex desires," whereas the other three groups checked this rather frequently. Another was that married women gave "economic security" much more frequently than did the other three groups. The third variation was that divorced women checked "to escape own family" much more frequently than did married women, divorced men, or married men.

The Two Most Important Reasons. In addition to the above general question on reasons for marrying the mate, persons were asked to underline the two things in the list which were considered the most important reasons for marrying their mates. For men, the most important difference was on the item "love," which was underlined by 93.9 and 71.5 per cents of the married and divorced, respectively.[35] The only other significant difference was on "loneliness," which was given by a larger per cent of the divorced than of the married, 10.0 to 3.1.[36] For women, a larger per cent of the married than divorced, 90.6 to 77.7, likewise underlined "love" as one of the two most important reasons for marrying.[37] Also, a larger per cent of the married than divorced, 38.0 to 21.7, gave "common interests." [38] Finally, more divorced than married, 14.6 to 1.2, underlined "to escape own family" as one of the two principal reasons for marrying.[39]

The reported reasons for marrying may or may not correspond to the actual reasons. As has been suggested for other items, the reasons given by divorced persons might be associated with and colored by the alienation process. In any case they can be used as predictive factors in marital adjustment. At least it is certain that the first five items—love, to have a

[35] CR 5.2.
[36] CR 2.5.
[37] CR 3.2.
[38] CR 3.2.
[39] CR 3.4.

home, common interests, to have children, and to satisfy sex interests—differentiate between happily married men and women and divorced men and women, and the last two—economic security, and to escape own family—between married and divorced women.

AGE VARIABLES

What is the relationship between marital adjustment and age at marriage and between marital adjustment and differences between the ages of a couple? There are many common-sense opinions on these questions and some conclusions from studies of marital adjustment. This section presents the results of this and other studies on age at marriage and on age differences between husbands and wives.

Age at Time of Marriage. Burgess and Cottrell indicate that age may be an index of two related aspects of behavior—degree of maturity and degree of flexibility. One hypothesis is that a more flexible person adjusts more readily in marriage and that, inasmuch as one is more flexible in early than in later years of life, well adjusted persons are married at an earlier age than poorly-adjusted. The other hypothesis is that maturity is associated with adjustment in marriage and that, inasmuch as one matures with age, those who are older at marriage are better adjusted than those who are younger. Findings seem to support the latter hypothesis.

Burgess and Cottrell report that wives under 19 and husbands under 22 tend toward poor marital adjustment and that "in the great majority of cases there seems to be no doubt regarding the unfortunate effects of very early marriages." [40] Terman found that, except for wives who marry under 20 and possibly for husbands under 22, there is a negligible correlation between happiness and age at marriage.[41]

The present study found significant differences between

[40] *Op. cit.,* pp. 115–17.
[41] *Op. cit.,* pp. 180–83.

the mean age at marriage of (1) happily married and divorced persons married only once, (2) those married more than once and those married only once, and (3) those in the divorced sample who were forced to marry and those married only once.

For the sample married only once, the differences between the mean age at marriage of married and divorced women was very significant, 21.5 to 19.9 years.[42] Married and divorced men also differed significantly in the mean age at marriage, 24.1 to 23.2.[43]

The average age *at the time of the first marriage* of happily married women who were married two or more times was significantly younger than that of happily married women married only once.[44] Divorced women who had had one or more prior marriages were also significantly younger at the time of the first marriage than divorced women married only once.[45] No differences were found for men with prior marriages and men married only once.

A comparison of age at marriage of persons married only once with divorced persons who were forced to marry [46] revealed that the women of forced marriages were significantly younger at marriage than either happily married or other divorced women.[47] The average age at marriage for women of forced marriages was 18.0 years. Men of forced marriages did not differ significantly in their average age at marriage, 22.7, from that of other divorced men, but did differ significantly from that of happily married men.[48]

In terms of the per cent distribution of the married-only-once for different age periods, it was found that marriage before the age of 18 was very unfavorable for women: 15.6 and 37.8 per cent, respectively, of married and divorced women

[42] CR 3.6.
[43] CR 2.0.
[44] Means: 19.6 and 21.5, CR 2.5.
[45] Means: 17.9 and 19.9, CR 3.4.
[46] Married-more-than-once cases in which pregnancy was the cause of marriage were excluded.
[47] CR with happily-married, 9.6; with divorced, 3.5.
[48] CR 2.2.

married before 18.[49] For men, marriage before 21 was unfavorable: the respective per cents for married and divorced were 19.9 and 31.5.[50]

The optimum age of marriage for women was between 21 and 29. The respective per cents of married and divorced women marrying between 21 and 23 were 28.1 and 15.8, with a critical ratio of 2.8. The critical ratio was increased to 3.8 when the age group was extended to 29: the respective per cents of those who married in the age period 21–29 were 44.9 and 25.7. The optimum age of marriage for men was between 24 and 29. The respective per cents of married and divorced who married in this age period was 38.0 and 24.0.[51]

The above analysis of the difference between mean age at marriage and per cent marrying at different age periods strongly supports the hypothesis that early marriages are risky as compared with later marriage. Also, the present study supports the hypothesis that maturity at marriage, as measured by the age of 21–29 for women and 24–29 for men, is associated with marital adjustment.

The following excerpt from a divorced case makes plain the meaning of early marriage for the persons concerned. The rebelliousness of the divorced wife is revealed in her statement, and the husband's statement shows that he is "hoping against hope" that after she has had experience outside the family she will come back to him: [52]

Wife. "I married at the age of 15 to get away from home. Nobody paid any attention to me there. I guess any person that had come along would have done. I married the first bed I saw. He should have known better, for he was 21 at the time. I never did love him. I was sorry I married him almost from the beginning. I was too young to get married."

Husband. "I am about 7 years older than Dorothy. She was mar-

[49] CR 3.7.
[50] CR 2.5.
[51] CR 2.8.
[52] Case no. 868.

ried and had a child too young. She is just coming into her womanhood and is beginning to realize the things she missed that a young girl should have. I wanted to be on the go as much as she did, but I put all my money into the house, the car, clothing, and things for her. I loved her when I first saw her, I always have loved her, and I think I always will, no matter what she does. She married me to get away from home, but I did not know it at the time. I think and hope that after she gets out a little bit, and sees what it's like, she'll come back. If she did come back and live with me, I would live with her from now on and not ask her to have intercourse with me or anything else. I would just do things for her as I always have."

Difference in Age of Husband and Wife. Age differences between husbands and wives of the samples [53] conform to the traditional American folkway that the husband should be older, but not too much older, than the wife: 62.8 per cent of the married and 68.5 per cent of the divorced were the same age, or the husband was 1 to 5 years older. Wives were older in only 11.2 per cent of the married and in 10.0 per cent of the divorced cases, and were almost never more than 3 years older.

The findings of the present study and those of other studies on the relationship between differences of age and marital adjustment are inconclusive. Burgess and Cottrell found the highest marital adjustment when ages were equal or the husband was one to three years older. Terman found the highest happiness scores for husbands when they were older by three to five years and twelve years and over, and for wives when the husband was three to five years older and four to ten years younger.[54]

The present study found that approximate equality of age was favorable to marital adjustment, and that if men were 3 to 4 years older than their wives, the prospects of adjustment were unfavorable. The per cents of the married and the di-

[53] The comparison is for married only once cases. Data on differences of age are available in 170 of the married and 124 of the divorced cases.
[54] Ernest W. Burgess and Leonard S. Cottrell, *op. cit.,* pp. 161–64. Lewis M. Terman *et al., op. cit.,* pp. 183–87.

vorced cases where the spouses were of the same age or the wife was one year older were, respectively, 16.5 and 8.0, with a CR of 2.1. If husbands one or two years older than wives are added to this group, the per cents are, respectively, 45.3 and 34.6, with a CR of 1.8. Thus, there is some possibility that approximate equality of age is conducive to marital adjustment.

The per cent of married and divorced cases where husbands were 3 or 4 years older than wives were, respectively, 15.2 and 26.6, with a CR of 2.4. This was the highest critical ratio of any age comparison, but the number of cases was relatively small, 26 and 33 respectively.

From the above it is obvious that the age differences between husbands and wives was not a major factor in marital adjustment. The only relationship with sufficient cases to make the difference between happily-married and divorced reliable is approximate equality of the ages of husbands and wives.

Additional information on the significance of differences in ages of husbands and wives is secured from a comparison of the mean age at marriage of happily married men and women and divorced men and women. The difference between the mean age at marriage of happily married men and women was significantly less than the difference between the mean age of divorced men and women.[55] It will be recalled that the respective mean ages at marriage of happily married men and women were 24.1 and 21.5 with a 2.6 year difference, and that the mean ages of the divorced were 23.2 and 19.9 with a 3.3 year difference. While both of these differences were statistically significant,[56] the differential for the divorced was much greater than that of the married.[57] This seems to indicate that marital adjustment is better when wives are not too much younger than their husbands at the time of marriage.

[55] The analysis is for cases married only once.
[56] CR for married: 5.5. For divorced: 10.3.
[57] CR of the difference between CR of married and CR of divorced: 3.4. Formula is: $\frac{CR_1 - CR_2}{\sqrt{2}}$

SUMMARY

The conclusions on the association between marital adjustment and certain factors in courtship and engagement apply to the population from which the happily married and divorced samples were drawn. However, tentative conclusions of a more general nature will be presented, which possibly apply to other areas than that in which the people in the present study lived. It appears that marital adjustment is positively associated with the following items relating to length of acquaintance and engagement, conflict and affection before marriage, reasons for marriage, and age variables. Unless otherwise indicated, the correlations apply to both men and women.

1. A period of acquaintance for women of over a year and preferably of over two years.

2. An engagement of six months or over for men and of a year or over for women.

3. Little or no conflict with mate before marriage.

4. Very great affection between self and mate before marriage.

5. Marrying for love, to have a home, because of common interests, to have children, and to satisfy sex desires; also for economic security in the case of women.

6. Marriage between the ages of 21 to 29 for women and between 24 to 29 for men.

7. Approximate equality of the ages of husband and wife.

6

PARENTAL INFLUENCES ON MARITAL ADJUSTMENT

THE CLASSIC description of the importance of early parent-child attachments for later behavior, developed by Freud and others, has been widely accepted as providing the key to the understanding of all sorts of behavior, including marital maladjustment. Today, many marriage counselors, psychologists, ministers, and others have joined the psychoanalysts in interpreting and treating the behavior of men and women in the marriage situation in terms of early childhood emotional attachments to one or the other parent. In the last decade or two, investigators have raised the question whether systematic observation of actual behavior would support this psychoanalytic doctrine of the importance of early parent-child relationships.

The present investigation, while not oriented directly to testing the theory that early parent-child attachments determine the degree of marital adjustment, does throw light on this and related questions. Specifically, the present chapter inquires into three general types of parental influences as related to marital adjustment: (1) the home atmosphere revealed by parent-child attachments and conflicts, (2) the home atmosphere as revealed by attachments and conflicts between parents, and (3) the degree of emancipation of the new family from the parental families of the husband and wife, as revealed by relationships with in-laws.

PARENT-CHILD ATTACHMENTS
AND CONFLICTS

Is marital adjustment correlated with the degree of happiness in childhood, the amount of affection toward mother and father, the extent of conflict with mother and father, and the type of discipline in the parental home? The present study found significant differences between the happily-married and divorced on happiness of childhood, conflict with mother and father, and discipline, but no difference on the amount of affection toward parents.

Happiness of Childhood. Terman found that no item relative to background was more important for marital adjustment than was happiness in childhood. It far outweighed such items as adequacy of sex instruction, source of sex information, religious education, adolescent petting, and premarital intercourse.[1] Hill, in a study of adjustment to the crises of separation and reunion of 135 Iowa families in which the husband had been in the armed services, found a positive association between the childhood happiness of the wife and "good" adjustment to separation.[2]

In the present study the question on this item was phrased as follows:

My childhood on the whole was: very happy _____; happy _____; about averagely happy _____; unhappy _____; very unhappy _____.

A significantly larger per cent of both happily married men and women than divorced reported their childhood as happy *and* very happy. In this combined category there were about two thirds of the happily-married as compared to about half of

[1] Lewis M. Terman *et al., Psychological Factors in Marital Happiness,* New York, McGraw-Hill, 1938, pp. 225–28.
[2] Reuben Hill, *Families Under Stress,* New York, Harper and Brothers, 1949, p. 111.

the divorced.[3] This means, of course, that a significantly larger per cent of divorced than happily-married were in the combined category of average, unhappy, *and* very unhappy. For women, an unhappy *and* very unhappy childhood was reported by 1 in 7 divorced to 1 in 20 happily-married.[4]

There are several theories which might explain the relationship between the reported happiness of childhood and marital adjustment. A possible explanation is that one who is experiencing marital happiness may tend to see his childhood through rose-colored glasses, thus rating it happier than it really was. Another hypothesis is that one who experiences unhappiness in childhood and adolescence may have been less selective in the choice of a mate than would otherwise have been the case, with consequently increased chances of marital maladjustment. Later in the chapter an example of this is given in a case in which a divorced wife reported that one of the reasons for her marrying was that "my mother and I were having a great deal of conflict."

Attachment to and Conflict with Parents before Marriage. Previous studies have found that close attachment to the mother and father before marriage and little or no conflict with either parent are associated with marital adjustment. Burgess and Cottrell state their conclusions on parent-child attachments and conflicts and marital adjustment as follows: [5]

Closeness of attachment and absence of conflict in the association of parents and son show a consistent although small positive relation to marital adjustment.

No such consistent pattern appears in the association between parents and daughter, although "no" attachment to the father and "little" or "no" attachment to the mother appear to work against a high marital-adjustment score.

[3] Per cents for men: 65.2 and 54.0, CR 2.1. For women: 70.6 and 56.3, CR 2.8.
[4] Per cents: 13.7 and 4.7, CR 2.9.
[5] Ernest W. Burgess and Leonard S. Cottrell, *Predicting Success or Failure in Marriage*, New York, Prentice-Hall, 1939, p. 98.

Terman found correlations between marital adjustment and attachment to father, attachment to mother, lack of conflict with father, and lack of conflict with mother. He summarizes his findings as follows: [6]

The happiness of both spouses is positively correlated with attachment and also with lack of conflict. The correlations are highly reliable and are consistent in direction. . . . The highest means (happiness scores) are for subjects reporting greatest attachment or least conflict, and they drop with considerable regularity as attachment decreases or conflict increases. The critical ratios of these differences run high. The data justify the assignment of fairly heavy weights in the happiness prediction scale.

The findings of the present study are not strictly comparable with those of Burgess and Cottrell and Terman. In the first place, the categories were slightly different, and then in place of "attachment" the term "affection" was used. Keeping these differences in mind, it appears that the conclusions on harmonious and unharmonious relationships with parents are different from those of the previous studies. Affection toward parents appears unrelated to marital adjustment, whereas conflict with parents was related in the reverse order from that found in the other studies.

Degrees of affection and conflict between self and mother and self and father were measured on a fivefold scale: none, very little, moderate, a good deal, and very great.[7]

On reported affection of self for parents, no significant differences between the divorced and the married were found for either men or women.[8] "A good deal" *and* "very great" affection was reported by about three fourths of the married

---

[6] *Op. cit.*, p. 215.

[7] Subjects were asked whether they were an only child, the youngest, oldest, or not the oldest or youngest child. No differences were found between the happily-married and divorced on this item.

[8] One exception was that a significantly larger per cent of divorced than married men reported no affection between self and mother, 3.8 and 0.0, CR 2.5, but only six cases were involved.

and divorced for the mother and by about two thirds for the father.

The data indicate that "no conflict" between self and father is associated with marital maladjustment, whereas "a little" conflict is associated with marital adjustment. Both divorced men and women reported "none" much more frequently than did the happily-married. "No conflict" was reported by roughly two thirds of the divorced as compared to one half of the married.[9] A significantly larger per cent of happily married than divorced men reported "a little" conflict with father [10] and "moderate" conflict with mother.[11] For women, a significantly larger per cent of happily-married than divorced reported "a little" conflict with father [12] and also with mother.[13]

Thus, the report of "no conflict" with father was associated with marital maladjustment and "a little" conflict with adjustment. This may mean that the divorced felt that the failure of their marriage was not due to their home situations and minimized the conflict with parents; however, they did not report more affection than did the married. Another interpretation is that some emancipation from parents is an essential factor in marital adjustment and possibly "a little" conflict goes along with such emancipation. Also, no conflict at all may imply parental domination. This view is supported, in part, by the data on discipline in the parental home.

Discipline in the Parental Home. Terman found a relationship between type of discipline in childhood and marital adjustment. "Firm but not harsh" discipline was found to be

[9] Per cents for men: with father, 64.8 and 50.0, CR 2.7; with mother, 69.0 and 58.0, CR 2.0. For women: with father, 64.6 and 49.7, CR 2.8; with mother, 61.9 and 53.7, CR only 1.5.

[10] Per cents: 33.5 and 22.6, CR 2.2.

[11] Per cents: 11.5 and 3.8, CR 2.6. For men, "a good deal" of conflict with mother was reported by a small per cent of divorced men and practically no married: 4.4 and 0.6, CR 2.2.

[12] Per cents: 31.5 and 19.4, CR 2.6.

[13] Per cents: 32.1 and 21.0, CR 2.3.

the type most associated with marital adjustment.[14] The present study is not strictly comparable with the Terman study, for somewhat different categories were used. The subjects of this study were asked the following question on the kind of discipline experienced in the parental home:

Do you feel that in your parental home you: never had your own way about anything _____; usually had your own way _____; had your own way about everything _____.

A significantly larger per cent of both divorced men and women than of happily-married reported that they "never had own way" in their parental homes.[15] "Usually had own way" was reported by a significantly larger per cent of both happily married men and women than by the divorced.[16]

The above seems to indicate that the happily-married came from homes where the parents were considerate of the desires of the children, and that the divorced came from homes where the parents were inclined to dominate their children.

ATTACHMENTS AND CONFLICTS BETWEEN PARENTS

What is the relationship between marital adjustment and the pattern of divorce among close relatives, the degree of happiness of the parents' marriage, and the extent of conflict between the father and mother? These items give a rough indication of the type of home atmosphere in which the happily-married and divorced were reared. They will be analyzed in the following paragraphs.

Pattern of Divorce among Relatives. One hypothesis formed at the beginning of the study was that divorce would be more prevalent among those who had had the most experience with the pattern of divorce. More specifically, this

[14] *Op. cit.,* pp. 228–36.
[15] Per cents for men: 30.1 and 18.3, CR 2.5. For women: 33.5 and 18.8, CR 3.1.
[16] Per cents for men: 78.0 and 61.3, CR 3.3. For women: 75.8 and 59.8, CR 3.2.

hypothesis was that the pattern of divorce among relatives would be more prevalent for divorced than for the happily-married. Consequently, persons were asked for the total number of divorces among brothers, sisters, parents, aunts, and uncles.

Limited support is given to this hypothesis, particularly in the case of men. A significantly larger per cent of divorced than married men reported one or more divorces among these relatives.[17] For both men and women, a larger per cent of married than divorced reported no divorces among relatives. The differences in per cents were below the level of significance established for this study,[18] but both were in the same direction, which lends support to the probability that divorces were less frequent among relatives of the happily-married than among those of the divorced.

It seems likely that a person would be more willing to engage in the activities necessary in securing a divorce if he has had intimate contact with this general pattern of behavior. Of course, learning about divorce is not limited to contact with one's relatives, for, naturally, most persons have had friends who were divorced and have read of divorce cases in the newspapers. It would be desirable to secure a more sensitive method for measuring the learning of the divorce pattern than simply recording the number of divorces among relatives.

Happiness of Parents' Marriage. Both the Burgess-Cottrell study and that of Terman found a fairly high association between the ratings subjects gave their parents' marriages and the degree of marital adjustment of the subjects.[19]

Table 16 shows that the present study gives limited support to the earlier findings. On a five-point happiness scale—very happy, happy, average, unhappy, and very unhappy—a significantly larger per cent of married than divorced men rated

17 Per cents: 34.6 and 22.2, CR 2.4.
18 Per cents for men: 52.7 and 45.1, CR 1.4. For women: 52.1 and 44.1, CR 1.5.
19 Ernest W. Burgess and Leonard S. Cottrell, *op. cit.*, pp. 98–102. Lewis M. Terman, *et al.*, *op. cit.*, pp. 202–207.

their parents' marriage "very happy" and a significantly larger per cent of divorced rated their parents' marriage "average." For women a larger per cent of married than divorced gave ratings of "happy," though the difference was considerably below the selected level of significance. However, the fact that it was in the same direction as in the case of the men increases the likelihood that it represents a real difference.

TABLE 16

Per Cent of Happily-Married and Divorced for Given Degrees of Happiness of Parents' Marriage, with Critical Ratios of the Difference of Per Cents

Degrees of Happiness	Men			Women		
	Married N = 193	Divorced N = 202	CR	Married N = 194	Divorced N = 228	CR
Very happy	32.1	22.3	2.2	27.8	31.1	
Happy	31.6	31.7		30.4	23.7	1.6
Average	29.5	40.6	2.3	32.0	34.2	
Unhappy	4.2	3.0		5.7	8.8	
Very unhappy	2.6	2.4		4.1	2.2	
	100.0	100.0		100.0	100.0	

The conclusion is that there is a fair probability that persons in adjusted marriages come from happy homes more frequently than do persons in maladjusted marriages.

Conflict between Parents. It was felt that divorced persons would have been reared in homes where conflict was present between the parents to a greater extent than the happily-married.[20] This hypothesis was not supported by the data, for there were no statistically significant differences between the happily-married and divorced with respect to any single category —none, a little, moderate, a good deal, and very great—or any

[20] Conflict between parents, of course, may provide the motivation to work for a happy marriage. Where parents engage in quarreling and make family life unpleasant, a son or a daughter may determine not to allow the same situation to develop in his or her own family.

combination of categories.[21] If the selected level of significance is disregarded—5 in 100 due to chance—a larger per
cent of both divorced men and women than happily-married
reported no conflict between mother and father.[22] This seems
to contradict the finding on happiness of parents' marriage
and the adjustment of the children's marriage. However, possibly "some" conflict indicates the presence of a democratic
attitude toward the discussion of family and personal objectives and desires, which may be related to marital happiness.

RELATIONSHIPS WITH IN-LAWS

The folkways of the United States include the belief that the
stability of a new family is increased if parents have a direct or
indirect voice in the selection of a mate for a son or daughter,
that living with in-laws is inadvisable, and that living in the
same general area as that in which the in-laws live has little or
no effect on the happiness of the new family. To what extent
are these beliefs supported by empirical research?

The life-history documents throw some light on these and
similar questions. The following document was written for
the author by a rather well-educated woman of the divorced
sample. It shows how her parents disapproved of her fiancé,
thus indirectly causing her to break the engagement; how conflict with her mother was involved in marrying the second
man; and how the girl married without letting her parents
know her plans. The document also shows how the difficulties
in the marriage were largely, although not entirely, due to the
relations with her parents and with the mother of the husband.
There were three general sources of difficulty: the fact that the
husband's social status suffered in comparison with that of
the family of the wife; the wife's father and mother assumed
"paternalistic" attitudes toward the new family; and the

---

[21] There was one exception: a significantly larger per cent of married than
divorced women reported very great conflict between parents, but the per cents
were small: 6.1 and 1.1, CR 2.5.

[22] Per cents for men: 45.2 and 36.0, CR 1.7. For women: 43.3 and 34.1, CR 1.7.

mother-in-law not only disapproved of her son's marriage to this girl, but sided with the son against the wife during periods of difficulty. The document also shows how the wife returned to her home after the divorce, only to find that she was lonely in the old home relationships: [23]

"My father was a professional man and very prominent in the town where we lived. This entitled me to a high social position in the younger crowd. My family gave me everything I wanted.

"In my third year of high school, I started to have dates with a boy I had known for years, and fell very much in love with him. We became engaged after going together about three months. We were to be married when graduated, but the position Bob was to have did not materialize, so we postponed it. My family decided that I should go to a woman's college in the East, even though I preferred to go to the state university, which Bob was attending.

"Late in the summer I had a date with a fellow seven years my senior, whom I had known for ten years. A week before I was to leave for school, my fiancé came home from the university, and we went to my father, asking him if we could get married. He told us he would give us his answer on the week-end. The next night I went out with Dick. I suppose the reason he fascinated me was that he was older and had a steady income. By the week-end I was out of the notion of getting married. My family encouraged my going out with Dick, because they would have done anything to keep me from marrying Bob.

"I left for the eastern school still fascinated by Dick. During Christmas vacation I severed all relations with Bob. In February, Dick came to see me, and I found that some of the glamour had worn off. I saw him in relation to the people of my walk of life, and there were some things which were lacking.

"When I came home in the summer, I had a date with Dick every night. He was very jealous and would check up on me several times a day. I did not see Bob during this time, so I could rationalize very well with myself that Dick was much better for me.

"Several things happened at this time that made me decide that marriage was the best solution to my problems that looked so big

[23] Case no. 623.

to a girl of nineteen. First, my mother and I were having a great deal of conflict; second, I did not want to continue school; and, third, I wanted to spite Bob, for he hadn't even come to see me.

"One day in August we were invited to a friend's home in the southern part of the state, so we planned to be married on our way there. We secured our license and went to a Justice of the Peace (this seemed to go with an elopement) and went on to my friend's.

"We did not tell our families until the next evening. My father suggested that we take a trip and that they would announce our marriage after we had left. My family and Dick's father took it well enough, but Dick's mother became very upset over it. When we returned from our trip, we stayed with my family for a month until we could find an apartment.

"For the first three months, I was very happy. I was sure that it did not make any difference that Dick was 'from the other side of the tracks' so to speak. I thought I could teach him my mode of living, but it never quite worked out that way. And then came the period of adjustment. For two weeks there was constant conflict, and after that there was acquired an understanding and an adjustment to married life.

"All this time Dick had been working. With what he made, the money I had in the bank, and that which my family gave us, we lived very comfortably. As long as my family gave us things, we were under obligation to them, and that caused some conflict, too. But after five months, Dick lost his job and my father suggested we move into one of his apartments.

"The climax came one day when Dick and I had been fighting and I came back to the apartment to find his mother there. She, naturally, took his side, but the mere fact that she should interfere at all made me very angry, and I stayed away from her as much as possible.

"As the months went by, I became satisfied with my life, even though I did not love Dick. We had a nice companionship, and he would not go any place unless I could go also. I had completely broken away from my crowd and accepted Dick's friends as mine. The next six months were probably the happiest of my married life.

"Everything was just right up until Thanksgiving. Dick insisted that he had to work that day and would be out of town until Friday night. From that time on he always spent at least three nights a week out on the road. He became more and more indifferent, and even my family began to notice it. A few days before Christmas, he said that he was going to leave me, but I did not believe that he would. He did not come home for Christmas Eve, and did not arrive until late in the afternoon of Christmas day. New Year's Eve Dick was again out, and about ten o'clock the next night he came home and said he was leaving the next day, that I could get the divorce and he would pay for it.

"I had not told my family anything about the possibility of divorce, and was afraid they would not take it very well. However, the next morning I talked to my mother and she talked to Dick. My father promised me anything I wanted; that I could do anything I wanted to do. I moved home and rented my apartment. I started divorce proceedings at once.

"I thought that after I had my divorce I could start life over again, but it wasn't as easy as it sounded. There was a certain loneliness that I could not escape.

"I decided to go back to school—this time at the university. I felt more contented and escaped a little of the strain that had been placed on me at home, but I had grown very sensitive and people hurt me very easily. For one semester I battled with myself, and had almost decided to give up and go home, when I met a young man that was different from the rest. He reminded me very much of Bob, the first boy I loved, but he had some qualities that were much finer. Now after going with him for two years, I am completely cured. We are to be married in a short time."

The above life-history document gives an insight into the dynamic processes involved in the adjustments which usually have to take place between the new family and the in-laws. Often the parental family is a sort of closed corporation, structurally organized on the basis of interdependent attitudes and strong attachments. Upon marriage the son, daughter, or parents find difficulty in breaking off these attachments. The attempt may be made to incorporate the mate into the closed corporation; frequently this involves moving in with the in-laws. If the mate does not fit into the closed set of relationships and follow the practices which have become habitual to the parental family, irritation and conflict may ensue and may result in the departure of the mate, and finally divorce. Over and over again the men of the divorced sample said that, if they had their lives to live over again, they would marry the same girl, but would see to it that they did not move in with the in-laws.

Certain items were included in the questionnaire on relationships with in-laws. Did the parents before marriage approve or disapprove of the mate? Did the new family live with the parents during the last half of marriage? What was the attitude of the husband and wife toward living with in-laws? And, how far from the parental home did the new family live? These will be considered in the following paragraphs.

Attitude of Parents toward Prospective Mate. A man or woman does not merely marry another individual, but in a sense marries into the family of the spouse. Consequently, the question was raised whether parental approval or disapproval of the prospective mate is correlated with marital adjustment.

On the question of the attitude of the parents toward the prospective mate, four possible answers were available: parents approved, parents were indifferent, parents disapproved, and parents did not know the mate. Parental approval of the prospective mate was highly associated with marital adjustment, indifference was somewhat associated with marital maladjustment, and disapproval was highly associated with marital maladjustment. This item was more discriminating between married and divorced women than between married and divorced men.

Table 17 shows that more than three fourths of the happily married men and women reported that their parents approved their prospective mates, whereas only about half of the divorced reported parental approval. It also indicated that about 1 in 20 happily married men and women reported parental disapproval of their mates as compared with 1 in 5 divorced men and 1 in 3 divorced women. For both men and women, a significantly higher per cent of divorced than married reported that their parents were indifferent toward their prospective mate.

TABLE 17

Per Cent of Happily-Married and Divorced Reporting
Various Parental Attitudes toward Prospective Mate,
with Critical Ratios of the Difference of Per Cents

Parental Attitude	Men			Women		
	Married N = 168	Divorced N = 158	CR	Married N = 169	Divorced N = 182	CR
Approved	76.8	51.9	4.6	82.3	45.6	7.1
Were Indifferent	7.1	15.8	2.6	5.9	12.6	2.1
Disapproved	5.4	19.0	4.0	4.7	35.2	7.1
Did Not Know	10.7	13.3		7.1	6.6	
	100.0	100.0		100.0	100.0	

Living with Parents during Marriage. Common-sense knowledge includes the view that living with one's own parents or the parents of the mate is unfavorable to marital adjustment. Do empirical data support this conclusion? Happily married and divorced men and women were asked whether or not the family lived with the husband's or wife's parents during the last half of marriage.

A larger per cent of divorced than married reported living with husband's parents or wife's parents. However, the greatest differences were on living with the parents of the mate—the in-laws. On the per cent reporting living with the wife's parents, the difference between married and divorced women was not clearly significant,[24] whereas the difference between married and divorced men was very significant.[25] On living with the husband's parents, the difference between married

24 Per cents: 22.6 and 11.9, CR only 1.8.
25 Per cents: 26.5 and 11.6, CR 3.3.

and divorced men was not clearly significant,[26] whereas the difference between married and divorced women was very significant.[27]

Moreover, although married men and women did not differ in the per cent of those who reported living with the husband's parents as against those who reported living with the wife's parents, and although divorced men and women did not differ in the per cent of those who reported living with the wife's parents, a significantly larger per cent of divorced women than men reported living with the husband's parents: 35.2 as against 21.8.[28] This may mean that a short stay with the husband's parents was considered by divorced men as *visiting* his parents, while divorced women thought of it as *living* with in-laws.

From the above we would conclude that living with in-laws is unfavorable to marital adjustment, both in the case of the daughter-in-law and of the son-in-law.

The following excerpt from the case of a divorced man illustrates the problem of living with in-laws, particularly when it is over a long period: [29]

"I lived with my wife and her folks for six years before we separated. Her mother was a very dominating person. I got so I just couldn't stand it. Our boy visited my mother, and when it was near the time for school to start, my wife said it was about time for the boy to come back. I replied that maybe he would go to school there with his grandmother. She had a fit, and said that I had it all planned. But as God is my judge, it had just come into my mind as a possibility. She told me to get out, so I got out. I would not say anything against my wife. I think she is a fine person, and we would have gotten along if it had not been for living with her people."

Attitude toward Living with In-Laws. It was assumed that more divorced persons than happily-married would be

26 Per cents: 21.8 and 14.4, CR only 1.7.
27 Per cents: 35.2 and 16.0, CR 3.9.
28 CR 2.6.
29 Case no. 791.

found to have disliked living with in-laws. This was found to be the case. Happily married and divorced persons were asked what their own and their mate's attitude was toward living with in-laws, and the responses were classified in three general categories: disliked, did not mind, and enjoyed.

The married and the divorced, while they did not differ on judgments of their mates' attitude, differed on their own attitudes. For those who reported that they disliked living with in-laws, the per cents of divorced and married men were, respectively, 57.5 and 43.7,[30] and for the women, 70.4 and 44.6.[31] Happily married men reported more frequently than the divorced that they enjoyed living with in-laws, 28.7 as against 8.0,[32] and a larger per cent of married than divorced women reported that they did not mind it, 41.0 as against 20.3.[33]

The statistical analysis has shown that a favorable attitude of happily-married toward living with in-laws was not infrequent. The life-history materials, like those from which the following two short excerpts were taken, document this type of response.

The first is the case of a family who lived on a large farm in a big, comfortable house. The wife reported: [34]

"Yes, we lived with his parents, but they are dead now, and he runs the farm. Living with them was not much of a problem to us, for we both knew that some day the place would be ours."

In the second case, a wife indicated that she enjoyed living with her husband's parents, and referred to her mother-in-law as "Mom": [35]

"We have not been married very long, nor have we been living by ourselves long. We stayed with John's parents for some time after

[30] CR only 1.8.
[31] CR 3.7.
[32] CR 3.5.
[33] CR 3.2. The per cents for married and divorced men reporting "did not mind" were 27.6 and 34.5, respectively.
[34] Case no. 108.
[35] Case no. 167.

our marriage. I really like John's mother. Mom would do anything for me."

Probably part of the reaction of dislike shown by divorced persons toward living with in-laws was colored by unpleasant experiences which they had had with the in-laws in connection with marital difficulties or with the actual securing of the divorce.

Propinquity of Residence to That of Parents. It was thought that living near the residence of parents of the mate would be associated with marital maladjustment. The data did not support this hypothesis.

There were two questions on this item. The first asked for the number of miles or blocks the subject lived from the home of the mate's parents. The per cents of happily married and divorced men who reported they lived two and one half miles or less from their own parents' home were, respectively, 47.9 and 48.0, while 41.9 and 41.8 per cents reported living that distance from the home of the wife's parents. For women of the happily married and divorced groups, the per cents reporting two and one half miles or less from the husband's parents were, respectively, 42.0 and 51.9,[36] and from own parents' home, 39.5 and 43.2.

The second question on the location of the residence of the subjects relative to that of their own parents or of in-laws, gave five alternative answers: same neighborhood, same city, same county, same state, and different state. There were no statistically significant differences between happily married and divorced men on the proximity of their own parents' homes or of those of the parents of the mate, nor between married and divorced women on those of the parents of the mate, although in all three comparisons the per cent giving "same neighborhood" was higher for the divorced than for the married.[37] The one significant difference was that a smaller per

36 CR only 1.7.

37 Per cents for men: on own parents, 30.9 and 23.1; on mate's parents, 31.9 and 20.9. For women: on mate's parents, 28.4 and 21.1.

cent of divorced than married women reported living in the same neighborhood as that in which their parents lived.[38]

It is difficult to explain why fewer divorced than married women, but not fewer men, reported living in the same neighborhood as that of the wife's parents. The size of the critical ratio indicates that there are 5 chances in 100 that the difference could be due to chance, and it is probably due to chance. For one thing, a smaller per cent of divorced women than of divorced men reported living in the same neighborhood as that of the wife's parents.[39] Also, the difference disappears when "living in the same neighborhood" and "living in the same city" (all of the cities in the county in which the study was made are relatively small) were combined into a single category.[40] It is concluded, consequently, that the residences of happily married and divorced men and women were not significantly different with respect to proximity to residences of parents or in-laws.

SUMMARY

This chapter on the association between marital adjustment and parent-child attachments and conflicts, attachments and conflicts between a person's parents, and relationships with in-laws found the following items to be positively associated with marital adjustment:

1. A happy or very happy childhood.
2. Some, but not extreme, conflict with mother and father.
3. A history of being allowed usually, but not always, to have one's own way by parents.
4. A pattern of no divorce among relatives.
5. A rating of happy or very happy for the marriage of the parents.
6. Approval of the prospective mate by the parents.

[38] Per cents: 14.7 and 26.5, CR 2.2.
[39] Per cents: 14.7 and 31.9, CR 2.8.
[40] Per cents: 45.2 divorced, and 51.8 married.

7. Not living with own parents or parents of mate during marriage.

8. The reaction: "Would not mind living with in-laws" (Women); "would enjoy living with in-laws" (Men).

7

SEXUAL BEHAVIOR

In RECENT years much has been written on the relationship between sexual compatibility and marital adjustment. On the one hand, there are those who consider sexual adjustment the most determining factor in success in marriage, and on the other, there are those who minimize the importance of sex in marital adjustment. The current trend in the literature is to assign sex a role in marital adjustment equal, but not superior, to such other factors as personality traits, cultural background, and the sharing of values and attitudes.

This chapter summarizes the conclusions of other studies on the relationship between certain aspects of sexual behavior and marital adjustment, and gives a detailed presentation of the sexual items included in the present study.

CONCLUSIONS OF OTHER STUDIES

Davis.[1] This study, completed in 1929, compared married and unmarried women with reference to a variety of questions. The married were divided into two groups: 872 who gave an unqualified affirmative response that their married life was a happy one, and 116 who did not give an unqualified affirmative statement that their married life was happy. The study also includes a comparison of the 116 unhappily married

[1] Katherine Bement Davis, *Factors in the Sex Life of Twenty-Two Hundred Women*, New York, Harper and Brothers, 1929, particularly chap. 4.

women and 116 happily-married matched for identical age and education.[2]

Davis found statistically significant differences between the 116 unhappily-married and the total happily married sample of 872, and also between the unhappily-married and the matched sample of 116 happily-married. Her major conclusions were as follows: (1) Happiness in marriage was associated with some instruction in preparation for marriage. (2) Initial attraction to the way marital relations came into experience was more prevalent in the happily-married. (3) A larger proportion of happily-married found pleasure in marriage at the beginning of marriage and also throughout marriage. (4) The happily-married reported about the same intensity and frequency of sex desire of husbands and wives, while the unhappily-married reported the wife's intensity of interest and frequency of desire was greater than that of the husband. (5) Intercourse more than once a day in the early years of marriage was unfavorable, and one to three times a month, favorable. (6) Abortion was much more prevalent among the unhappily-married than among the happily-married. (7) There were no significant differences on the use of contraceptives. (8) There were no significant differences on intercourse during pregnancy.

Since the sample was selective, highly educated, and composed of an older age group, Davis cautions the reader that "it will be necessary to study numerous other groups before it will be safe to make any general application of our results."

Hamilton.[3] This study by a psychiatrist was the earliest study of marital adjustment to use the method of weighting answers to certain questions, thereby securing a "marital sat-

[2] Questionnaires were sent to a highly educated sample throughout the United States. Returns were secured from 11 per cent of those who received a preliminary letter asking for cooperation and from 47 per cent of those who expressed willingness to cooperate.

[3] G. V. Hamilton, *A Research in Marriage,* New York, Lear, 1948 edition, particularly chap. 22.

isfaction grade" or score for each person. It was begun in 1924 and completed in 1929. Hamilton spent from two to thirty hours with each of his 100 husbands and 100 wives. He used a standardized method of interviewing that was kept uniform for all persons of each sex, thereby securing approximately comparable data. Hamilton maintained throughout his investigation an attitude like that suggested in the following quotation from his preface: [4]

Never wander a hair's breadth from the facts of subjective experience in an impatient effort to make logical constructions gratify your urge to explain things. Sufficiently patient and prolonged observation may be expected to disclose, in time, various natural lines of cleavage within the total psycho-dynamic set-up of the individual, and when enough patients are studied in this spirit we or our successors shall come to know what particular types of events —both inner and outer—characteristically occur in recognizable constellation and sequence patterns.

The following conclusions on the relation of sex activities and marital satisfaction are presented by Hamilton as "suggestive explanatory possibilities": (1) Unless a woman is frigid, or at least very much under-sexed, marriage to a man with definitely low sex desire or capacity is not likely to be successful. (2) Men who rate the degree of their sex desire as about average or below average are more likely to have higher marital-satisfaction scores than those who rate themselves as above the average in sexual desire. (3) Husbands and wives who have intercourse more than four times a week during the first year of marriage are less likely to be satisfied in marriage than those who report a lower frequency. (4) Frequent masturbation during marriage is likely to be associated with dissatisfaction with marriage. (5) Those who report that they have not committed adultery are more likely to be satisfied in marriage than those who admit adultery. (6) Those who have complaints about the sexual adequacy of their mates are more

[4] *Ibid.*, pp. xii–xiii.

likely to be dissatisfied with the marriage than those who make no such complaints. (7) Unless the sex act ends in an orgasm of the woman in at least 20 per cent of copulations, the marriage is likely to be unsuccessful.

Of the 46 women who were inadequate as to orgasm capacity, almost half had been diagnosed at some time in their lives, by a psychiatrist other than Hamilton, as seriously psychoneurotic. Only one of the 54 women who had orgasms with reasonable frequency had ever been regarded as psychoneurotic. According to Hamilton, failure to achieve orgasm is due to psychological rather than to physiological factors.

Landis and Landis.[5] Landis and Landis instructed their subjects to rate the degree of their marital happiness on a threefold scale: very happy, happy, and average. Answers to certain items were then compared with this happiness rating.

On the length of time required for adjustment in sexual relations, in a sample of 409 couples, a rating of very happy was given by a larger per cent of those who felt that sex relations were satisfactory from the beginning or had been worked out within the first year, than of those who reported that adjustment was worked out after the first year. Those who said sexual adjustments had never been satisfactory rated their marriage as average in happiness much more frequently than did those who reported adjustment as satisfactory from the beginning.

On equality of sex desire, in a sample of 544 couples, it was found that 80 per cent of the spouses reporting equality in sex desire rated their marriages as very happy, as compared to 50 per cent who gave this happiness rating but who said the spouse was either too responsive or not responsive enough.

In the sample of 544 couples, a rating of very happy was given by 66 per cent of those who said that they always agreed in sex expression, by 31 per cent who agreed most of the time,

[5] Judson T. Landis and Mary G. Landis, *Building a Successful Marriage,* New York, Prentice-Hall, 1948, pp. 267, 276–77.

and by 13 per cent who agreed half or less than half of the time.

Kinsey.[6] In his book, *Sexual Behavior in the Human Male*, Kinsey presents some conclusions, in reality guesses, on the relationship between marital adjustment and sexual attitudes and behavior. He plans to publish a later volume on sexual behavior and marital adjustment. At present he gives his impressions from the case histories which have been collected. He thinks that sexual maladjustment contributes to perhaps three quarters of the separations and divorces of upper-level marriages and to a smaller per cent of broken marriages of lower-level couples.

Specifically, Kinsey holds that for upper-level marriages the following are the sexual factors which cause difficulty: (1) failure of the male to show skill in approach and technique, (2) failure of the female to participate with the abandon necessary for sexual consummation, and (3) inhibitions due to conceptions of the esthetic acceptability and moral decency of some types of sexual behavior. On the relationship between extramarital intercourse and marital adjustment Kinsey feels that extramarital intercourse results in greater difficulty in the lower-level than in the upper-level marriages, for in the upper-level cases it is generally unknown to anyone except to the persons immediately involved. Also, he feels that extramarital intercourse sometimes increases the marital adjustment of couples.

Kinsey's conclusions should be interpreted as hypotheses for future verification or negation, for, first, they are impressions from cases, and, second, his statistical analyses are subject to severe criticisms.[7]

[6] Alfred C. Kinsey, Wardell B. Pomeroy, and Clyde E. Martin, *Sexual Behavior in the Human Male*, Philadelphia, W. B. Saunders Co., 1948, pp. 544–46, 589–94.

[7] For an excellent critique of Kinsey's first volume see Lewis M. Terman, "Kinsey's 'Sexual Behavior in the Human Male': Some Comments and Criticisms," *Psychological Bulletin*, 45, No. 5, September 1948, pp. 443–59.

Burgess and Cottrell.[8] Items on sexual behavior were intentionally omitted by Burgess and Cottrell from their schedule with the plan of securing such information from interviews. Sexual material was collected through interviews or autobiographical documents from 100 cases. Of these only 49 contained sufficient data on sexual adjustment to be of use. The following tentative conclusions were drawn from an analysis of these 49 cases, supplemented by fragmentary data from the remaining 51 cases: (1) There is a wide variation from couple to couple in intensity of desire, kinds of acts which stimulate sexual desire, nature and extent of preliminary interstimulation before coitus, postures taken in coitus, height of feeling in the orgasm, time taken in the sex act, and intervals between coitus. (2) Marital adjustment is associated with adequate knowledge and skill in sexual activity. (3) Sexual malformations of an organic nature may be associated with marital adjustment, but the number of such cases is relatively few. (4) Most problems of sexual compatibility are due primarily to conscious or unconscious attitudes toward sexual behavior. (5) Sex adjustment is tied in with other factors which are associated with marital adjustment. These broad conclusions are not of much assistance in predicting adjustment in marriage.

Terman.[9] Terman included many sexual items in his schedule and dealt with sex and marital adjustment much more systematically than did Burgess and Cottrell. His general conclusion was that "the sex factors combined are far from being the one major determinant of success in marriage." [10] His conclusions will be summarized under three general points: items which are not correlated with marital adjustment, items which are positively associated with marital adjustment, and factors related to the failure of the wife to achieve orgasm.

[8] Ernest W. Burgess and Leonard S. Cottrell, *Predicting Success or Failure in Marriage,* New York, Prentice-Hall, 1939, chap. 12.
[9] Lewis M. Terman *et al., Psychological Factors in Marital Happiness,* New York, McGraw-Hill, 1938, particularly pp. 373–77, 407–408.
[10] *Ibid.,* p. 373.

There is little or no correlation between marital adjustment and either the reported or the preferred frequency of intercourse, control of ejaculation, methods of contraception, fear of pregnancy, pain at time of first intercourse, sex shock by wife, rhythm of wife's sexual desire, multiple orgasms, failure of husband to be as dominant as wife would like in initiating or demanding intercourse, and the sex techniques which are used.

Marital adjustment for the wife is correlated with the degree of pleasure experienced at first intercourse, and for the husband with the display of little or no prudishness or excessive modesty on the part of the wife. For both husbands and wives there are correlations between marital happiness and *symptoms* of sexual compatibility, such as few sexual complaints, a high degree of sexual satisfaction from intercourse, infrequent refusal of intercourse, an agreeable and considerate reaction of the spouse who is refused intercourse, and infrequent desire for extramarital intercourse. There is also a correlation with equality or near equality of sex drive, as measured by the ratio of the actual to the preferred number of copulations per month and by the spouses' ratings of their relative passionateness. The most important correlation found by Terman between marital adjustment and sexual items was on the orgasm-adequacy of the wife. This was correlated with the happiness scores of both wives and husbands.

The respective per cents of women in his sample who never, sometimes, usually, and always achieved orgasm were 8.3, 25.1, 44.5, and 22.1. A comparison of those who never achieved orgasm and those who sometimes achieved orgasm revealed no correlations with early emotional conditioning, sex techniques used, contraceptive methods, or attitudes and relationships with parents. He concluded that failure to achieve orgasm probably is biological rather than psychological in origin. This interpretation was based on correlations between failure to achieve orgasm and a goodly number of Bernreuter and Strong personality and interest items.

The present study included 17 sex items in the question-naire. In addition, certain information was secured in the informal interviews. Little or no difficulty was experienced in securing the cooperation of persons in answering questions on sexual behavior, although older persons were somewhat more hesitant than younger in answering the questions. It was found that, if the interviewer took a casual, natural approach in asking the sex questions, casual, natural, unembarrassed responses were secured.

In the first stages of the study, the various sex items were presented in the form of questions. This was soon modified for three of the items, so that rather than asking a question a statement of fact was made. Thus, the interviewer stated: "Before marriage you had intercourse with a few or many." If a person responded "none" or "one," the interviewer would use a questioning inflection of the voice and repeat "none?" or "one?" A second statement of fact was: "You had intercourse with mate before marriage." And the third was: "During marriage you had intercourse with one, a few, or many other persons than mate." It was felt that the assumption that the behavior had occurred would convey the idea that the interviewer had no moral scruples on sex behavior, and, consequently, that the subject might be willing to give a more accurate reply.

Conclusions will be presented under three general headings: premarital behavior, marital behavior, and extramarital behavior.

PREMARITAL SEX BEHAVIOR

Number of Persons.[11] Before marriage, most divorced and happily married men of the present study had experienced intercourse, and this had been with others than the mate, or with the mate and others. This is indicated by responses to the item which was stated in the questionnaire as follows:

11 Married-only-once sample.

Before marriage, with how many persons did you have sex intercourse: none _____; one _____; a few _____; many _____.

A significantly larger per cent of divorced than happily married men reported premarital intercourse. Intercourse with a few women was reported by half of the married men and by two thirds of the divorced,[12] while 1 in 20 married to 1 in 5 divorced reported many women.[13] Combining a few *and* many the respective per cents of happily-married and divorced were 56.6 and 85.4. Slightly more than a third of the married as compared with about a tenth of the divorced reported no intercourse with others before marriage.[14]

There were no significant differences between divorced and happily married women on *reported* intercourse before marriage: 88.4 per cent of the married and 85.3 per cent of the divorced reported no intercourse with others before marriage, while 8.8 and 12.4 per cent, respectively, reported intercourse with one person prior to marriage. The emphasis on *reported* intercourse is obvious from the discussion below.

Table 18, on the next page, shows that a larger per cent of happily married than divorced women and a larger per cent of divorced than happily married men reported premarital intercourse with the future spouse. However, neither of the differences in per cents was statistically significant.

Understatement on Frequency of Premarital Intercourse. The above per cents on frequency of intercourse before marriage may be understatements of the actual frequencies for men and are understatements for women. This is shown in Table 18, which gives the per cent of married and divorced women who reported having intercourse with one, a few, or many, the per cent of women reporting intercourse with mate before marriage, and the per cent of men reporting intercourse with mate prior to marriage. The table shows that the per

12 Per cents: 66.2 and 49.7, CR 2.9.
13 Per cents: 19.2 and 6.9, CR 3.1.
14 Per cents: 36.6 and 11.9, CR 5.0.

cent of married and divorced women reporting intercourse
with one or more men prior to marriage was decidedly
smaller than was the per cent of women who reported intercourse with mate prior to marriage, and this per cent in
turn was smaller than the per cent of men who reported
intercourse with mate prior to marriage.[15] Even the per cent
of premarital intercourse of women with mate as reported by
men was an understatement, if it is assumed that premarital

TABLE 18

*Per Cent of Happily Married and Divorced Women Having
Premarital Intercourse, as Reported by Women and by Men*

	By Women: One, a Few, Many	By Women: With Future Spouse	By Men: With Future Spouse	By One or Both Spouses: With Future Mate
Divorced	14.7	19.3	36.8	41.0
Married	11.6	24.0	28.7	35.2

intercourse of spouses occurred if one partner said it did and
the other said it did not. A comparison of *matched* husbands
and wives revealed that, as admitted by one or both of the
spouses, 35.2 per cent of the married and 41.0 per cent of the
divorced had had premarital intercourse.

Some of the understatement of premarital intercourse may
have been due to an unwillingness to report "irregular" sex
behavior if it were felt that it would reflect on the mate or that
the mate would not want it reported. This was the author's interpretation of the failure of the husband in the following
married case to report premarital intercourse with the wife,
whereas the wife casually admitted it: [16]

[15] It makes little difference whether the comparison is between men and
women or by matched husbands and wives. The respective per cents of reported
premarital intercourse for men and women and identical husbands and wives
were: for married men, 28.7 and 29.7; for divorced men, 36.8 and 32.4; for
married women, 24.0 and 23.4; for divorced women, 19.3 and 19.0.
[16] Case no. 93.

Husband. "No, I did not have sex with my wife before marriage. As far as I know, she has had sex only with me during marriage."

Wife. "Yes, I had intercourse with my husband before marriage. I have had an affair with one man during marriage." When asked if husband knew, she said, "Oh, yes, he knows all about it."

Interpretation. The interpretation of the difference here is that the husband thought that the wife might not want it known, for he had said on another point that he thought he would not answer it, because his wife might not want him to do so.

Variations by Year of Birth. Terman found that the extent of reported premarital intercourse was much greater for those born in 1910 or later than for those born in earlier decades. Table 19 compares those in his sample born in 1910 or later with those born before 1890. It shows that the per cent having intercourse only with spouse, with others than spouse, and with spouse plus others was much greater for younger than for older husbands and wives.

TABLE 19

*Per Cent of Terman's Subjects Born before 1890 and in 1910 or later, Having Premarital Intercourse with Spouse and with Others **

Had Intercourse	Born Before 1890		Born in 1910 or Later	
	Husbands	Wives	Husbands	Wives
Only with future spouse	4.6	8.7	31.9	45.0
Only with others than future spouse	35.6	1.9	13.6	3.3
Future spouse plus others	49.4	13.5	86.4	68.3

* Data from Lewis M. Terman *et al., Psychological Factors in Marital Happiness,* p. 321.

The question was raised in the present study whether the happily married and divorced husbands and wives would

follow the same general pattern of a higher reported incidence of premarital intercourse by younger as compared with
older persons. Consequently, the happily-married and divorced were divided into the four periods of birth used by
Terman: 1910 and later, 1900–1909, 1890–1899, and before
1890. Table 20 gives the per cent of husbands and wives in
each of the four periods who reported premarital intercourse
with one or more persons.[17]

TABLE 20

*Per Cent of Happily-Married and Divorced, by Period of
Birth, Reporting Premarital Intercourse with One or
More Persons*

| Period | Men | | Women | |
of Birth	Married	Divorced	Married	Divorced
1910 and later	71.4	89.9	22.7	34.3
1900–1909	72.0	95.1	18.0	18.6
1890–1899	60.0	87.5	0.0	13.9
Before 1890	52.9	76.2	4.5	20.0

The table shows that, for the most part, the per cent reporting premarital intercourse with one or more persons was not
very different for the first two birth periods and for the last
two, but that there was a difference between the youngest and
oldest for both the happily married and divorced husbands
and wives. The differences in per cent between those born in
1910 and later and before 1890 have relatively low critical
ratios, which, of course, is partly due to the small number of
cases.[18] Inasmuch as the differences are all in the same direction, we would conclude that the reported incidence of pre-

___

[17] This combines one, a few, and many into a single category. The remainder
of the one hundred per cent answered "none." The number of persons in the
sample of persons born in 1910 and later, 1900–1909, 1890–1899, and before 1890
was respectively: married men, 49, 50, 35, and 34; divorced men, 69, 81, 40, and
42; married women, 66, 50, 27, and 22; divorced women, 102, 70, 36, and 30.

[18] CR for married men, 1.7; divorced men, 2.0; married women, 1.9 and
divorced women, 1.5.

marital intercourse is significantly greater for younger than for older husbands and wives.

Persons reporting premarital relations with spouse were also distributed according to the four periods of birth. Table 21 gives for each period the per cent of happily-married and divorced who reported that they had intercourse with mate before marriage. It shows that the per cents for happily married and divorced husbands and wives born in 1910 or later were larger than those for persons born before 1890: the difference was statistically significant for married men, divorced men, and married women, with the younger reporting a greater incidence of premarital intercourse with mate.[19]

TABLE 21

Per Cent of Happily-Married and Divorced, by Period of Birth, Reporting Premarital Intercourse with Mate

Period of Birth	Men		Women	
	Married	Divorced	Married	Divorced
1910 and later	42.0	57.4	38.9	33.3
1900–1909	35.7	54.3	23.5	22.4
1890–1899	24.3	34.1	0.0	18.9
Before 1890	5.7	38.1	4.5	20.0

The greater *reported* incidence among younger than among older happily married and divorced persons probably was due both to an increase in premarital intercourse and to a greater willingness of younger than older persons to report and discuss sexual behavior.

Judgment on Premarital Relations of Spouse. Another question on premarital intercourse was whether it was believed, known, or suspected that the mate had had intercourse with others. The question was stated as follows:

Do you believe _____, know _____, suspect _____ your mate had sex intercourse with others *before marriage:* yes _____ no _____.

[19] Respective CRs were: 3.8, 2.0, and 3.1. For divorced women CR was 1.4.

A decidedly larger per cent of divorced than happily married men and women reported in the affirmative, that is they reported either yes, or that they believed, knew, or suspected that the mate had had intercourse with others before marriage.[20] For men, there was a significantly larger per cent of divorced than married in each of the three categories—believed, knew, and suspected.[21] For women, there was a significantly larger per cent of divorced than of married who knew or who suspected that mate had had intercourse with others before marriage.[22]

A companion question was whether or not a given subject thought that his mate believed, knew, or suspected him of having had intercourse with others before marriage. About two thirds of the divorced men as compared with one half of the happily-married reported that the mate believed, knew, or suspected them of having had intercourse with others before marriage.[23] There was a larger per cent of divorced than married men in both the "believed" and "knew" categories.[24] For women, the per cents of divorced and married who reported that the mate believed, knew, or suspected them of having had intercourse with others before marriage were almost identical: 13.0 and 11.4 respectively.

Interesting results were secured by comparing the per cent of happily married and divorced husbands and wives who said the mate had had premarital intercourse with others and the per cent of the mates who reported that the spouse believed, knew, or suspected them of premarital intercourse with others. The per cent of divorced men who thought the mate believed they had had intercourse before marriage was 66.4, whereas 70.4 per cent of divorced women thought their husbands had had intercourse with others before marriage. A

[20] Per cents for men: 41.0 and 11.0, CR 5.9. For women, 70.4 and 39.7, CR 5.5.
[21] Per cents: believed, 4.2 and 0.6, CR 2.1; knew, 22.2 and 3.2, CR 5.0; suspected, 9.0 and 3.2, CR 2.1.
[22] Per cents: knew, 34.0 and 16.6, CR 3.5; suspected, 11.1 and 4.6, CR 2.1.
[23] Per cents: 66.4 and 47.3, CR 3.3.
[24] Per cents: believed, 7.5 and 2.0, CR 2.2; knew, 36.3, and 25.7, CR 2.0.

larger per cent (47.3) of happily married men reported mates thought they had had intercourse with others before marriages than the per cent (39.7) of women who reported that they thought their mates had had intercourse with others. The differences, however, were not statistically significant either for the divorced or for the married men.

Of happily married women, 11.4 per cent reported that mates believed, knew, or suspected them of having had intercourse with others before marriage, and 11.0 per cent of the men reported that they thought mates had had intercourse with others before marriage. In the case of divorced women, there was a very significant difference between the 13.0 per cent who thought their mates believed they had had intercourse with others before marriage and the 41.0 per cent of divorced men who thought their mates had had intercourse with others.[25] Here there was either an unwillingness on the part of divorced women to admit that their mates thought they had engaged in intercourse before marriage, or there was an exaggeration on the part of divorced husbands, or there was a lack of communication between husbands and wives.

MARITAL SEX BEHAVIOR

Items on sex behavior within the marriage will be discussed under the following points: mate over-modest toward sex, interest in sex compared to that of mate, use of birth control, fear of pregnancy and sex enjoyment, sex satisfaction, and refusal of intercourse when desired by mate.

Mate Over-modest toward Sex. One hypothesis of the study was that marital maladjustment is associated with the husband's feeling that the wife is over-modest and shy in attitudes toward sex. The question to test this hypothesis was stated as follows:

[25] CR 5.4.

Do you feel that your mate is over-modest and shy in attitudes toward sex: very much _____; a good deal _____; some _____; very little _____; not at all _____.

The data gave limited support to the hypothesis. For both men and women, the happily-married had a significantly larger per cent in the combined category of "some" *and* "very little" than did the divorced.[26] A significantly larger per cent of divorced than married men and women reported their mates had "very much" *and* "a good deal" modesty and shyness in attitudes toward sex,[27] although in the case of men the difference was just below our level of significance. The above seems to indicate that having some but not great modesty in attitudes toward sex is related to marital adjustment for both husbands and wives.

In the following excerpt from a divorced case the husband reported great modesty on the part of his wife, while she reported great "carrying on" by her husband. Possibly the two were related: [28]

Husband. This man, during the first part of the interview, kept on busily painting. The questions were asked in the midst of people, cars, and dogs. When we got to the sex questions, he came down off the ladder. On the question of modesty, he said, "That was our whole trouble. You see, she was an old maid when I married her—she was thirty years old—and she just couldn't stand to have a man touch her. Naturally, if you live with someone like that, you want to get out with other women."

Wife. "Well, if you had had a husband that was carrying on the way mine was, you'd have gotten a divorce too. I told him, 'If you bring that woman here again, I'll stomp her in the ground.' Well, she professed to be a neighbor and a friend. Her husband lives right across the street there in that little white house. You ought to go and see him. He could tell you a lot about the divorce.

"He left me, and then three months later she left her husband.

[26] Per cents for men: 48.2 and 32.6, CR 2.9. For women: 33.8 and 21.4, CR 2.5.
[27] Per cents for men: 21.1 and 13.3, CR 1.9. For women: 10.0 and 3.7, CR 2.6.
[28] Case no. 59.

So you see that speaks for them. I don't reckon he did love me, for he left me for another woman."

Sex Interest in Comparison to That of Mate. The main hypothesis on this item was that equal interest in sex is associated with marital adjustment and unequal interest with marital maladjustment. A second hypothesis was that, if differences in sex interest exist, marital adjustment is associated with the husband having the greater interest. Data from the questionnaire supported the first hypothesis but not the second. The question was phrased as follows:

Do you feel that the strength of your sex interest, as compared with that of your mate is: very much greater _____; much greater _____; about the same _____; much less intense _____; very much less _____.

Happily married men and women reported "about the same" sex interest to a much greater extent than did divorced men and women. The respective proportions for men were 7 in 10 to 5 in 10,[29] and for women 6 in 10 to 4 in 10.[30] Significantly larger per cents of divorced than happily married men reported both more intense interest and less intense interest in sex than that of their mates.[31] Likewise, significantly larger per cents of divorced than happily married women reported both more and less intense interest in sex than that of their husbands.[32]

The informal material secured in the interviews reveals that husbands of the happily-married occasionally had a stronger desire for intercourse than that of their wives. Other things in the marriage seemed to compensate for the relatively low sex interest of the wife. Also, it will be noted in the last

[29] Per cents: 70.1 and 47.4, CR 4.1.
[30] Per cents: 61.7 and 39.2, CR 4.1.
[31] Per cents: very much greater *and* much greater, 40.1 and 27.5, CR 2.4; much less *and* very much less, 12.5 and 2.4, CR 3.4.
[32] Per cents: very much greater *and* much greater, 16.8 and 6.1, CR 3.0; much less *and* very much less, 44.0 and 32.1, CR 2.2.

of the following three excerpts that the husband adjusted "agreeably" to less intercourse than he desired: [33]

"The main thing I do not like about my marriage is that I like to love and have more sex play than my wife. She is an ideal wife in every other way. She cooperates and we work well together. But she does not like loving."

"My wife says that I would want to have her if I was on the border of death. I said, 'Yes, I would come to you if you wanted me to even though I had double-pneumonia.' We are very happy, but we would be happier if she was a little more interested in sex. She doesn't like it, and simply tolerates me."

"No, I never was very much on the kissing bug, and sex just doesn't bother me at all. Now, I do think that there are some women whom it does bother; they seem as passionate as men. But it doesn't bother me. I am so busy, and always have been, that I don't have time for such foolishness, especially now that we are getting older. If a woman raises a family, sews, keeps house, and cooks for them, she has enough on her mind, so that she doesn't let those thoughts enter her mind. My sister used to tease me, for she was a lot more affectionate than I was. She would come here and put her arms around George, and say, 'Don't you ever kiss George?' I'd say, 'Law, no, I don't have time for that stuff!' George took it in a joking manner, though, and it didn't cause any trouble. I think I have sort of cooled him off during the years, though, and that, along with the fact that we are getting older, has caused sex to take a less important place in our lives. He was always agreeable about it though, and at night, if I was tired, I would say, 'Now you turn over there and go to sleep, for I don't want to monkey with such foolishness.' And he wouldn't bother me any more. I just don't have any complaints about my husband. When he's here, he always helps me with the work. He empties the wash water, helps clean the house, and all such stuff as that. So you see, I just don't have a kick coming."

Use of Birth Control. The hypothesis on this item was that the use of birth control is associated with adjustment in mar-

[33] Respective case numbers: 184, 103, and 101.

riage. The question simply asked for a "yes" or "no" response on the use of birth control methods. A larger per cent of happily married women than divorced reported the use of birth control.[34] The same was true for men, though the difference was not statistically significant.[35]

Ignorance of birth control techniques and the problems involved in a farm family which did not have modern plumbing are indicated in the following excerpt from a divorced husband's case. The husband was married again. The interview took place in the woods with the subject sitting on one stump and the author on another: [36]

"Say, what is the best way of keeping from having children? I don't know much about sex. I try to withdraw, but if we are in doubt, then we use water. I have to hurry and build a fire and heat some water."

The next excerpt is from a happily married couple, where before marriage, the couple decided to limit the size of the family: [37]

"Me and my wife decided before we were married that we wasn't going to have no big family, 'cause we was older. We didn't expect to have this one. Since it happened, we are glad we got him. We don't intend to have no more, since we can hardly afford the things we want for ourselves."

Does the practice of birth control remove the fear of pregnancy and tend to increase the likelihood of sex enjoyment, and is this associated with marital adjustment? This is considered in the next item.

Fear of Pregnancy and Sex Enjoyment. Subjects were asked for a "yes" or "no" response on the question: "Does fear of

---

34 Per cents: 61.5 and 47.7, CR 2.5.
35 Per cents: 56.5 and 50.3, CR 1.1.
36 Case no. 802.
37 Case no. 132.

having children make sex less enjoyable?" An affirmative answer was given by a significantly larger per cent of both divorced men and women than by the happily-married.[38] This seems to mean that the use of birth control by the happily-married to a greater extent than by the divorced reduced the fear of pregnancy, and that this led to greater sex enjoyment. This is shown in the following excerpt from the case of a divorced woman: [39]

"I was scared all the time I'd get pregnant. I didn't like to have intercourse because I was scared. I had a child every year. My baby was two months old when I left him."

Sex Satisfaction. It will be recalled that the marital-adjustment test included two questions on sex satisfaction.[40] These questions dealt with the degree of satisfaction a person had with the mate and an estimate of the satisfaction of the mate. Five alternate answers were provided for these questions: very enjoyable, enjoyable, tolerated, disgusting, and very disgusting.

Happily married men and women reported much greater sex satisfaction with the mate than did the divorced. Table 22 on the opposite page gives the percentages of happily married and divorced men and women reporting various categories of sex satisfaction. The high critical ratios of the differences between the per cents of happily-married and divorced for given answers indicate that happily married and divorced men differed decidedly in four degrees of satisfaction: "very enjoyable" was reported by more of the happily-married, and "tolerated," "disgusting," and "very disgusting" by more of the divorced. Women differed very decidedly in all of the possible answers: more happily-married than divorced reported "very enjoyable" and also "enjoyable," with

[38] Per cents for men: 38.5 and 21.8, CR 3.2. For women: 31.4 and 19.8, CR 2.4.
[39] Case no. 780.
[40] The analysis of these questions used the total samples, excluding only the forced marriages from the divorced sample.

the reverse being true for "tolerated," "disgusting," and "very disgusting."

TABLE 22

Per Cent of Happily-Married and Divorced Reporting Various Degrees of Sex Satisfaction with Mate, with Critical Ratios of the Difference of Per Cents

Degree of Satisfaction	Men			Women		
	Married N = 180	Divorced N = 205	CR	Married N = 181	Divorced N = 210	CR
Very enjoyable	54.4	21.9	6.6	32.6	15.3	4.1
Enjoyable	38.9	46.3	1.3	58.0	38.1	3.9
Tolerated	6.1	17.1	3.3	8.2	20.0	3.3
Disgusting	0.6	9.3	3.8	0.6	15.2	5.4
Very disgusting	0.0	5.4	3.2	0.6	11.4	4.4
	100.0	100.0		100.0	100.0	

On the question of estimating the sex satisfaction of the mate, the happily-married and divorced differed in about the same respects as they did in rating their own satisfaction. For men, the categories in which there were significant differences were exactly the same.[41] For women, a larger per cent of married than divorced reported "very enjoyable," [42] with the reverse for "tolerated" [43] and "disgusting." [44]

Thus, on the whole, married men and women rated their own and estimated their mates' sex satisfaction as greater than did the divorced.

It is interesting to compare married men and women and divorced men and women on their own sex satisfaction and their mates' estimate of their sex satisfaction. This comparison revealed no significant differences between married men and

[41] Per cents for married and divorced: "very enjoyable," 46.9 and 21.9, CR 5.1; "tolerated," 11.2 and 19.9, CR 2.2; "disgusting," 1.1 and 8.4, CR 3.6; and "very disgusting," 0.6 and 7.0, CR 3.2.

[42] Per cents: 52.2 and 29.2, CR 4.6.

[43] Per cents: 1.1 and 10.1, CR 4.4.

[44] Per cents: 0.6 and 7.1, CR 3.2.

women, but significant differences between divorced men and women. The per cents of persons with self-ratings and ratings by mate in the combined category of "very enjoyable" *and* "enjoyable" were as follows: by married men and by women on their husbands, 93.3 and 98.3, respectively; by married women and by men on their wives, 90.6 and 87.1, respectively; by divorced men and by divorced women on their former husbands, 68.2 and 82.8, respectively; [45] and by divorced women and by divorced men on their former wives, 53.3 and 64.7, respectively.[46] This indicates that divorced men and women estimated the degree of sex satisfaction of their mates higher than either rated their own sex satisfaction.

Refusal of Intercourse when Desired by Mate. On the question whether a person refused intercourse when the mate desired it, four possible answers were provided: frequently, sometimes, rarely, and never. The hypothesis was that marital adjustment would be associated with never refusing the sexual desires of the mate. The assumption was that sexual frustration would be associated with refusal on the part of the mate, and that it would also be associated with marital maladjustment. The hypothesis was not supported by the data.

Never refusing the mate was reported by a significantly larger per cent of divorced than of happily married women,[47] and by a larger per cent, though not clearly significant, of divorced than married men.[48] Both married women and men reported "rarely" more frequently than did the divorced.[49] "Rarely" *and* "sometimes" combined was reported by three quarters of happily married women and by slightly less than half of the divorced.[50]

45 CR 3.5.
46 CR 2.5.
47 Per cents: 42.6 and 23.3, CR 3.7.
48 Per cents: 73.7 and 66.2, CR 1.5.
49 Per cents for men: 24.8 and 11.2, CR 3.1. For women: 30.7 and 13.6, CR 3.8.
50 Per cents: 71.2 and 47.9, CR 4.3. For men, sometimes refused was reported by a larger per cent of divorced than married, though the difference was not statistically significant: 12.5 and 7.0, CR 1.8.

What is the meaning of the greater per cent of divorced men and women who reported never refusing sex relations when desired by the mate, and the greater per cent of happily-married who reported refusing, though rarely? It seems that sexual adjustment involves mutual accommodation to sexual desires. If a wife rarely or sometimes refuses to have intercourse, the happily married husband apparently understands the moods of the wife and adjusts to them. The same is true if the husband rarely refuses.

Another interpretation is that the divorced exaggerated the degree to which they never refused intercourse, for never refusing was considered the mark of a good mate, and it was difficult to admit that the reason for the failure of the marriage was that one was not a good mate.

TABLE 23

Per Cent of Divorced Women Who Frequently and Never Refused Intercourse with Mate, with Their Reports of Various Degrees of Sex Interest

Sex Interest as Compared to That of Husband	Frequently Refused N = 17	Never Refused N = 70
Very much greater	5.9	8.6
Much greater	5.9	7.1
About the same	11.8	55.7
Much less intense	23.5	17.2
Very much less	52.9	11.4
	100.0	100.0

However, it appears that exaggeration was not the only factor. This is shown in Table 23, which compares divorced women who never refused with those who frequently refused in terms of the relative sex interest of the wife as compared to that of the husband. For divorced women, refusing intercourse was associated with the strength of their sex interest as compared with that of their husbands. One who had less interest in sex than her husband was inclined to refuse frequently. By contrast one who had the same or more interest in sex than the husband tended to report that she never refused to have intercourse.

Table 23 shows that 7 in 10 of those who never refused had the same sex interest as the husband, or more than he, while only 2 in 10 who frequently refused had this degree of sex interest.[51] This, of course, means that 8 in 10 who frequently refused had less sex interest than the husband, while only 3 in 10 who never refused had this lower degree of sex interest. Thus, never refusing intercourse was associated with the same sex interest as that of the husband, or more, and frequently refusing with less interest.

EXTRAMARITAL SEX BEHAVIOR

To what extent during marriage did happily-married and divorced differ in their desire for intercourse with someone other than the mate, in the number of persons with whom they had intercourse, in their belief, knowledge, or suspicion that the mate had relations with others, in their judgment that the mate believed, knew, or suspected them of extramarital relations, and in jealousy? These are the questions considered in this section.

Desire for Intercourse with Someone Other than Mate. The question on the desire for extramarital relations was phrased as follows:

During marriage have you desired sex intercourse with someone other than your mate: very frequently _____; frequently _____; sometimes _____; rarely _____; never _____.

Happily married and divorced women differed in that a larger per cent of happily-married than divorced responded

[51] Per cents: 71.4 and 23.6, CR 3.9.

"never," 96.3 and 88.0, respectively,[52] and a larger per cent of divorced than married responded "sometimes." [53] For men, half of the happily-married as compared with a third of the divorced answered "never." [54] A significantly larger per cent of divorced than married men desired intercourse with someone other than mate "sometimes" [55] and also "frequently." [56] Thus, the divorced reported a more frequent desire for intercourse with someone other than the mate than did the happily-married.

The above indicates that both happily married and divorced men reported a desire for intercourse with someone other than mate to a much greater extent than did women.

Number of Persons. Information was secured on the number of persons other than mate with whom subjects had had intercourse during marriage. The question was phrased as follows:

During marriage, with how many persons other than your mate have you had sex intercourse: none _____; one _____; a few _____; many _____.

Happily married men reported extramarital relations much less frequently than did the divorced. "None" was given by 83.1 per cent of the happily-married as compared with 52.9 per cent of the divorced.[57] Also, a much smaller per cent of happily-married than divorced reported "a few": 9.7 as against 37.3.[58] There were no significant differences in the replies of married and divorced women: 98.8 and 95.2 per cents, respectively, reported "none."

A comparison in terms of the period in which persons were

[52] CR 2.8.
[53] Per cents: 4.8 and 0.6, CR 2.3.
[54] Per cents: 50.6 and 35.5, CR 2.7.
[55] Per cents: 34.9 and 19.4, CR 3.1.
[56] Per cents: 7.9 and 2.5, CR 2.2.
[57] CR 5.7.
[58] CR 5.7.

born—before 1890, 1890–1899, 1900–1909, and 1910 and later—reveals that for women there were no differences between periods of birth and reported frequency of intercourse with others during marriage. For men, there was a significantly larger per cent of divorced born before 1890 than of those born in the periods 1890–1899 [59] and 1900–1909 [60] who reported no intercourse with others than mate: the per cents for the three periods were 70.7, 47.6, and 49.4, respectively. In the case of happily married men, there was a larger per cent of those born before 1890 than of those born in 1910 and later who reported no intercourse with others than mate.[61] This means that older men were either more conventional in their actual behavior than younger men or were more unwilling to report their extramarital behavior.

Judgment on Mate's Intercourse with Others during Marriage. To what extent do happily married and divorced men and women differ in their belief, knowledge, or suspicion that the mate had had intercourse with other persons during marriage? The question on this item was phrased as follows:

Do you believe _____, know _____, suspect _____ that your mate has had sexual intercourse with some other person *during your marriage:* yes _____; no _____.

Happily married and divorced men differed decidedly on the negative reply; the respective per cents who said they did not believe, know, or suspect that the mate had had intercourse with others during marriage were 98.6 and 43.9.[62] The same great difference was found between happily married and divorced women, the respective per cents being 90.9 and 24.8.[63]

Considering the first four possible answers to the question, there was a negligible per cent of married men and women for

[59] CR 2.1.
[60] CR 2.2.
[61] Per cents: 94.1 and 78.8, CR 1.94.
[62] CR 10.3.
[63] CR 11.9.

each. By contrast, the respective per cents of divorced men and women for these answers were as follows: "believe," 8.8 and 6.1; "know," 25.7 and 43.6; "suspect," 14.2 and 13.9; and "yes" without indicating whether they believed, knew, or suspected, 7.4 and 11.5.

Thus, divorced men and women had a much larger per cent than happily-married who felt that the mate had been unfaithful. Of course, the happily-married may have been unwilling to admit the mate had been unfaithful, whereas the divorced may have been quite willing to justify their divorce by imputing infidelity to the mate.

The divorced woman in the following case did not merely impute infidelity to her husband, for she had obvious evidence: [64]

"He lived with that other woman the last two years of our marriage, and then for about the five years we were separated. I reckon he did commit adultery. She had a baby, and she didn't get that by sitting in the water. He still lives with her, and isn't married to her."

Happily-married and divorced were also asked if they thought the mate believed, knew, or suspected that they had had intercourse with someone else during marriage. A decidedly larger per cent of divorced men than happily-married thought their mates believed, knew, or suspected them of infidelity; the respective per cents were 58.6 and 12.6.[65] The same was true for women, though the difference was not as great; the respective per cents were 17.4 and 5.2.[66] A larger per cent of divorced than happily married men reported in each of the three categories—believed, knew, and suspected,[67] whereas, for women, only the category "suspected" had a significantly larger per cent of divorced than married.[68]

[64] Case no. 39.
[65] CR 8.3.
[66] CR 3.3.
[67] Per cents: "believed," 6.2 and 1.3, CR 2.2; "knew," 14.5 and 2.6, CR 3.7; "suspected," 26.9 and 7.9, CR 4.3.
[68] Per cents: 11.1 and 0.0, CR 4.2.

The above discussion has presented data on (1) the number of extramarital experiences, (2) the question whether a person thought the mate believed, knew, or suspected him of having had intercourse with others, and (3) the report by the mate on whether or not he believed, knew, or suspected the spouse of having had extramarital relations with others. Table 24 gives the per cents for these three items.

TABLE 24

Per Cent of Happily-Married and Divorced, Reporting Extramarital Intercourse, and Per Cent Reporting Belief, Knowledge, or Suspicion of Infidelity

Group Reporting	Relations with One, a Few, or Many	Think Mate Believed, Knew, or Suspected	Mate's Report on Believed, Knew, or Suspected
Married men	16.9	12.6	9.1
Married women	1.2	5.2	1.4
Divorced men	47.1	58.6	75.2
Divorced women	4.8	17.4	56.1

The table shows that the per cents were very similar for happily married men and women. For divorced men and women there were great differences: the smallest per cent was on the report of actual intercourse with one, a few, or many persons other than the mate; the next smallest per cent was on the judgment of what the mate probably believed, knew, or suspected about the infidelity of the husband or wife; and the largest per cent was on the statement by the mate on the belief, knowledge, or suspicion that the husband or wife had been unfaithful.

Specifically, the table shows that a larger per cent of happily-married thought their mates believed, knew, or suspected them of being unfaithful than was actually reported by their spouses, though the differences were not statistically significant.[69] The reverse was true for divorced men and women. A

[69] CR for men: only 1.0. For women: only 1.8.

decidedly larger per cent of divorced women were considered by their husbands to have had intercourse with others than the per cent of divorced women who thought their husbands believed, knew, or suspected them of being unfaithful.[70] Also, a significantly larger per cent of divorced men were reported by wives to have had intercourse with others during marriage than the per cent of men who thought their wives believed, knew, or suspected them of being unfaithful.[71] Divorced persons, particularly women, either were unwilling to admit that their mates believed, knew or suspected that they had had intercourse with others during marriage, or the channels of communication between divorced men and women were not as open as in the case of the happily-married.

Jealousy. Persons were asked if the mate was inclined to be jealous if they danced, talked, or engaged in other kinds of association with those of the opposite sex. Jealousy was reported much less frequently by happily married than by divorced persons. The per cents of married and divorced men who reported that the mate was jealous were, respectively, 15.6 and 55.3, and for women, 12.7 and 45.3.[72] This is not surprising in view of the data given above and the large per cent of divorced who gave "mate paying attention to another" and "adultery" as serious difficulties in the marriage.[73]

Jealousy was a primary factor in the disruption of the couple in the following case. This couple was happy in the first years of marriage, but separated when the wife found that the husband was paying attention to another woman: [74]

"We were very happy in the first years of our marriage. We both engaged in the same professional work. I guess I was more interested in my profession than in my home. Even in these early

[70] CR 6.7.
[71] CR 3.3.
[72] CR for men: 7.5. For women: 6.6.
[73] See p. 75.
[74] Case no. 874.

years, I began to be skeptical of him. He took my savings, and said that in his marriage he was going to handle the money. Then, when his brother died and we were going through his things, I found a letter in which my husband had written him about a couple of women whom they had taken on a trip. About four years after our marriage, I found that he had gotten a girl pregnant, and we had to pay $500 to fix it up. But I thought that maybe he had been framed. The final thing was when I found that he was going out with another woman. After that, I would not have anything to do with him sexually. I took complete charge of the money; in fact I did not want to live with him. I wanted separation, but not divorce."

Interpretation. This is a case of gradual development of estrangement between the husband and wife. When the wife discovered a few "indiscretions," the reaction of the husband was a demonstration of more affection than formerly. But the wife's reaction was one of complete withdrawal. He felt that he could not live at home because of her psychological withdrawal. He secured the divorce, married again, got a job in his profession in another city, and is happier than formerly. The wife is still working, is lonesome and discouraged. Tears came into her eyes when she said that he was always so cheerful and fine around the home.

In contrast to the more or less restrained description of jealousy given above by a well-educated professional woman is that of the following by a woman who had less than an eighth-grade education, and whose husband could neither read nor write: [75]

"We never had no trouble until about three years before we divorced. He got insane jealous of me. I couldn't have went next door that he didn't accuse me of something. Once I went a few minutes to a neighbor's house, and he come out and met me half way back. Accused me of going there to meet a neighbor man. I couldn't look at a person that he didn't get jealous. But the funny thing about him was he'd have the very men he was most jealous of around all the time—invite them to the house and throw them at

[75] Case no. 842.

me. One man was nice to me. After our divorce I went with him, but he didn't mean nothing to me. I never loved him like I done my husband."

A woman of the happily married group indicates in the following excerpt that she would prefer to have her husband "run around" with a lot of women than to become attached to just one. She questions the double standard, but is responding in terms of it, and without much jealousy: [76]

"One thing I never understood was why men thought they could play around and were so opposed to women doing the same.

"You ask how I would act if I found that my husband had sex with another woman during marriage. Well I haven't thought much about it. I would not like it. If he ran around with a lot of women, I don't think I would make too much fuss. I would prefer that, of course, to his becoming attached to one and falling for one, even though it were for just a short time."

SUMMARY

Certain information which is not directly related to predicting marital adjustment is summarized below, and this is followed by an outline of the sexual factors which are associated with marital adjustment.

1. Happily married and divorced persons, particularly women, understated the frequency of their premarital intercourse.

2. Younger men and women reported more premarital intercourse than did older men and women.

3. A larger per cent of divorced men believed, knew, or suspected that the mate had had premarital sex relations than the per cent of divorced women who thought mate believed, knew, or suspected that they had had premarital sex relations.

4. Divorced persons estimated the sex enjoyment of their mates higher than the mates' self-ratings.

[76] Case no. 121.

5. Extramarital intercourse was reported more frequently by younger than by older men.

6. Fewer divorced men and women estimated that the mate believed, knew, or suspected that they had had extramarital relations than the number of mates who gave these views.

7. Both happily married and divorced men desired intercourse with others than mate to a much greater extent than did women.

The analysis in this chapter revealed that most of the sex questions included in the present study were related to marital adjustment or maladjustment. The results will be summarized by indicating the items which are positively associated with marital adjustment. The association is for both men and women, except in cases where (Men) or (Women) is placed after the item.

1. Report that no premarital intercourse was experienced. (Men)

2. No belief, knowledge, or suspicion that the mate had had intercourse with others before marriage.

3. The assumption that the mate did not believe, know, or suspect that the spouse had had premarital intercourse. (Men)

4. Some but not very much modesty and shyness on sex matters.

5. About the same degree of interest in sex.

6. The use of birth control methods. (Women)

7. No fear of pregnancy.

8. Rating of sex relations with mate as "very enjoyable" (Men); as "enjoyable." (Women)

9. Estimate that the mate would rate sex relations with spouse as "very enjoyable."

10. Rare or infrequent refusal of intercourse when mate desired it.

11. No desire for extramarital relations.

12. No intercourse during marriage with others than mate. (Men)

13. No belief, knowledge, or suspicion that mate has had intercourse with others during marriage.

14. The assumption that the mate did not believe, know, or suspect that the spouse had had intercourse with others during marriage.

15. No jealousy on the part of mate if one dances, talks, or associates with persons of the opposite sex.

8

CHILDREN AND MARITAL ADJUSTMENT

A POPULAR belief is that the presence of children in a family increases the chances of marital happiness. In fact, childless couples who are experiencing marital difficulties sometimes consider having a child or adopting one as a way of solving their marital problems. This popular belief that children make for the success of a marriage was frequently expressed by happily married persons. In the first of the two following excerpts, a wife responded as follows to the question whether she thought there was a possibility that her marriage would end in divorce: [1]

"I don't think so, but, of course, that's something no one knows. At least, I hope it never does. We think a lot of our baby. It is ten weeks old now, and I think that it will join us closer together."

In the second case, the husband believed that a marriage would last if the wife had a child to "settle the couple down": [2]

"If you want a marriage to stick, have a child to keep the woman in the house; at least have one within a year after marriage. I don't say have a whole 'slew' of them, but have at least one. By the time the child gets older, both the husband and the wife will settle down. My wife used to run around a lot uptown before our child was born, and we used to have a little argument about that. She didn't pay attention to other men or anything like that, just was on the go. Now, after the child, my wife is settled and never goes out."

[1] Case no. 153.
[2] Case no. 165.

Some authorities on the family believe that the popular view is correct and suggest that, since a considerable proportion of divorced families are childless, there must be a relationship between having children and marital adjustment. For instance, Nimkoff, while citing the evidence which seems to indicate no relation between the presence of children and marital happiness, suggests that, if the samples of such families had included divorced families, different results might have been secured.[3] If the couples who were unhappy because they were without children had already become divorced, then a random sample of married couples might show no relation between the absence of children and marital maladjustment. Explicitly, Nimkoff states this view as follows: [4] "In a less selective sample, the presence or absence of children might be more highly correlated with marital happiness, as the statistics of divorce suggest." Moreover, he holds that the size of the family is one of the most important considerations affecting the probability of divorce.

Is marital adjustment related to the *presence* of children in the family, to the *size* of the family, or to the *desire* to have children? Tentative answers to these three questions can be given on the basis of various investigations and the conclusions of the present study.[5] A summary will first be given of the evidence of other studies on the relationship between marital adjustment and the presence of children and between marital adjustment and the size of the family.

PRESENCE OF CHILDREN

Conclusions of Various Studies. Hamilton, in his study of 100 husbands and 100 wives, found nothing to suggest that the presence of children was associated with the degree of marital satisfaction among the highly educated group which consti-

---

[3] Myer F. Nimkoff, *Marriage and the Family*, Boston, Houghton Mifflin, 1947, pp. 494–96, 630–31.

[4] *Ibid.*, pp. 495–96.

[5] The analysis is on married-only-once cases, excluding persons married more than once and forced marriages of the divorced sample.

tuted his sample.[6] For those married five years or longer, Terman reported a zero correlation for the presence or absence of children with the happiness score of either the husband or the wife. Moreover, the mean scores of childless husbands and wives and of those with children were not significantly different.[7] He concludes that the presence of children is capable of affecting the happiness of a given marriage in either direction, and that the opposing influences may approximately balance each other in a relatively large sample. Bernard found no correlation between the success in marriage and the absence of children.[8] Hill, in his study of adjustment of 135 families to the crises of separation and reunion where the husband had been in the armed services, found a negative association between the number of children and adjustment to separation, and a slight negative association between the number of children and adjustment to reunion.[9]

Burgess and Cottrell found that the mean adjustment scores of couples with no children were significantly higher than for couples with two or more children.[10] An analysis of data included in the appendix of their book [11] revealed no significant differences between childless and nonchildless couples and poor, fair, or good adjustment. However, the per cent of couples with two or more children in the "good-adjustment" category alone was decidedly lower than the per cent with no children, and considerably lower than those with one child.[12] Landis and Landis in their study of 409 couples reported that those without children tended toward the extremes of either

[6] G. V. Hamilton, *A Research in Marriage*, New York, Lear, 1948 edition, p. 511.

[7] Lewis M. Terman, *et al.*, *Psychological Factors in Marital Happiness*, New York, McGraw-Hill, 1938, pp. 171–73.

[8] Jessie Bernard, "Factors in the Distribution of Success in Marriage," *American Journal of Sociology*, XL, 1934, p. 51.

[9] Reuben Hill, *Families Under Stress*, New York, Harper and Brothers, 1949, pp. 126–28.

[10] Ernest W. Burgess and Leonard S. Cottrell, *Predicting Success or Failure in Marriage*, New York, Prentice-Hall, 1939, pp. 258–61.

[11] *Ibid.*, p. 413.

[12] *Ibid.*, p. 259. The CR was 3.1 for no children; CR 2.6 for one child.

very happy or very unhappy, while those with children ap-
proached the average of happiness in marriage.[18]

A few studies have investigated the difference in the divorce rate of childless families and of those with children.
The most careful study for the United States is that of Jacobson. He summarizes his conclusions in Charts 1 and 2 and in
the extended statement given below.[14] Two studies for other
countries,[15] the Netherlands (Amsterdam) and Sweden, found

CHART 1

*Divorces per 1,000 Married Couples According to Size
of Family, United States, 1948* *

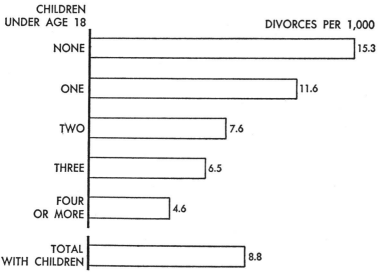

* From Paul H. Jacobson, "Differentials in Divorce by Duration of Marriage
and Size of Family," *American Sociological Review*, XV, 1950, p. 242. (Reproduced by courtesy of the Society.)

Note: Includes annulments. Rates are provisional.

[13] Judson T. Landis and Mary G. Landis, *Building a Successful Marriage*,
New York, Prentice-Hall, 1948, p. 434.
[14] Paul H. Jacobson, "Differentials in Divorce by Duration of Marriage and
Size of Family," *American Sociological Review*, XV, 1950, pp. 235–44.
[15] J. H. van Zanten and T. van den Brink, "Population Phenomena in Am-

that the divorce rate for childless families was respectively 2.0 and 2.2 times higher than that for families with children.

CHART 2

Divorce Rate for Married Couples with and without Children under Age 18, First 40 Years of Marriage, United States, 1948 *

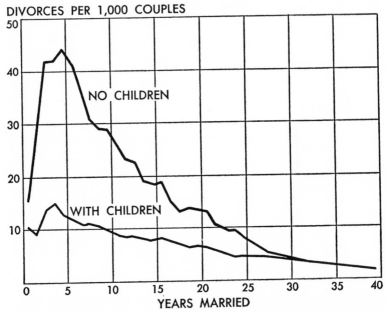

DIVORCES PER 1,000 COUPLES

NO CHILDREN

WITH CHILDREN

YEARS MARRIED

* From Paul H. Jacobson, "Differentials in Divorce by Duration of Marriage and Size of Family," *American Sociological Review*, XV, 1950, p. 242. (Reproduced by courtesy of the Society.)

Note: Includes annulments. Rates are provisional.

It is evident that the relative frequency of divorce varies inversely with the number of children in the family. For couples without children, the divorce rate in 1948 was 15.3 per 1,000 (married couples). Where one child was present, the estimated rate was 11.6

sterdam," *Population, The Journal of the International Union for the Scientific Investigation of Population Problems*, August, 1938, p. 30. (Rate for 1929–1932.) Carl-Erik Quensel, "Frequency of Divorce with Special Regard to the Number of Children," *Annex No. 6*, Statistical Institute of Lund, 1938, p. 202. (Rate for 1933.)

per 1,000. The figure thus continues to decrease, and in families with four or more children, it was 4.6. Altogether, the rate for couples with children was 8.8 per 1,000. In other words the rate for "childless" couples was almost double the rate for families with children. . . .

It is readily apparent (Chart 2) that the differential in the divorce rate between "childless" couples and those with children is not uniform throughout married life. Rather, divorce is much more frequent among those without children in the early years of marriage, and the differential diminishes rapidly thereafter. The divorce rate for parent-couples climbs to a maximum of 15 per 1,000 at duration 3–4 years, whereas the rate for couples without children reaches a peak of 44 per 1,000 one year later. The chances for divorce among the "childless" fall off so much more rapidly after the peak that the ratio between the rates for the two groups drops from about 3½ after four years of marriage, to 3 by the tenth year, and to 2 by the twentieth year. Indeed, after the thirtieth wedding anniversary, the two rates are practically identical.

Sample Unmatched for Duration of Marriage. In the present study a comparison was made in two general samples: those in which the married and divorced were not matched for length of marriage, and those in which they were matched. In the unmatched sample it was to be expected that, inasmuch as the married had had a longer period in which to have children, childlessness would be more prevalent among the divorced. However, there was no significant difference in childlessness between the married and divorced. The per cent of childlessness reported by divorced and happily married men was respectively 28.0 and 20.2.[16] For women the respective per cents reporting no children were 26.9 and 21.0.[17] Therefore, the conclusion is that there was no statistically significant difference between the happily-married and divorced on childlessness.

[16] CR 1.6.
[17] CR 1.3.

Sample Matched for Duration of Marriage. The married sample contained more couples who had been married 20 years or more than did the divorced sample. When the two groups were matched for exactly the same number of married and divorced cases for each of the first twenty years of marriage, almost identical per cents of married and divorced reported no children, 24.4 and 24.8, respectively.

The conclusion that there is no relationship between childlessness and being divorced or happily married is different from what one would expect from the reported proportion of divorced families which are childless. More than 60 per cent of divorced couples had no minor children in 1928, as reported by Cahen,[18] and in 1948, as reported by Jacobson.[19] However, these figures were estimates from data secured from only a few states, and even from some of these states the data were considered somewhat unreliable. The figures in the present study refer to all the children of a family regardless of whether or not they were minors, whereas Jacobson's study was on minor children. Chart 3 from his study reveals the increase in childlessness of divorced couples after 20 to 25 years of marriage. This probably reflects the departure of children from the home.

The relatively high proportion of childlessness in divorced families is not too different from the relatively high proportion of childlessness in all families. In 1949 about one half (48.0 per cent) of all families in the United States had no children of their own under 18 years of age living with them.[20]

The fact that our sample was from a semi-rural area may account for the low per cent of childlessness among both the happily-married and the divorced. Jacobson indicates that possibly the high per cent of childlessness among the divorced in

[18] Alfred Cahen, *Statistical Analysis of American Divorce,* New York, Columbia University Press, 1932, p. 112.

[19] *Op. cit.,* p. 241.

[20] United States Department of Commerce, Bureau of the Census, *Current Population Reports, Population Characteristics,* Series P-20, No. 26, January 27, 1950; p. 4.

CHART 3

*Per Cent of Divorced Families without Children
under 21 Years of Age, by Number of Years
Married, 1948* *

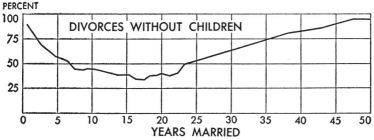

* From paper read before the American Sociological Society, December 29, 1949. (Reproduced by courtesy of the Society.)

the general population may be due to the relatively large proportion of divorces from urban areas which are characterized by low fertility rates. Quensel estimates that in Sweden the differential in divorce among childless families and among families with children would be cut in half by taking into account rural-urban differences and the period of separation prior to the divorce.[21]

SIZE OF FAMILY

Sample Unmatched for Duration of Marriage. In the unmatched sample, it was to be expected that the average number of children would be larger for the married than for the divorced, and this proved to be true. From the reports of married and divorced men, the mean number of children was, respectively, 2.26 and 1.68, and for the women, 2.27 and 1.85.[22]

Sample Matched for Duration of Marriage. When the two groups were matched by having exactly the same number of

[21] Quensel's conclusions summarized by Paul H. Jacobson, *op. cit.*, p. 244.
[22] CRs respectively 2.8 and 1.9.

married and divorced for each of the first 20 years of marriage, the mean number of children was almost identical, 1.34 and 1.35 respectively.[23] When those married 21 years and more were matched for exactly the same number of married and divorced cases for each year of marriage, the means were, respectively, 4.07 and 3.60, and the difference was not statistically significant.[24]

Mean Adjustment Scores for Different Sizes of Family. The question was raised whether the mean adjustment scores of persons would vary with the number of children in the family. Consequently, each of the four groups—married men, married women, divorced men, and divorced women—were compared for average adjustment scores of those with no, one, two, three, four, and five or more children. There were no significant differences within any of the four groups between the number of children and the mean adjustment score.

It was thought that possibly the small number of cases in each of the categories, when specific numbers of children were compared, might have accounted for the failure to find significant differences. Therefore, the mean adjustment scores of those with no or one child and those with two or more children were compared. Here again, no significant differences were found. The respective mean marital adjustment scores (in terms of the per cent the score was of the total possible score) of "small" families and of "large" families were as follows: married men, 88.3 and 88.6; married women, 89.4 and 88.6; divorced men, 66.0 and 63.7; and divorced women, 66.6 and 67.0.

Thus, when the two groups of the present study were matched for number of years of marriage, there was no difference between the happily-married and divorced on the presence or absence of children or on the average number of children in the family.

23 CR 0.2.
24 CR 1.0.

DESIRE FOR CHILDREN

Burgess-Cottrell Conclusions. Burgess and Cottrell felt that the presence or absence of children, or their number, might not be as important as the attitude of couples toward having them. They reported that their findings on this question showed a more marked relationship to marital adjustment than any other item included in the study. Couples having no children but desiring them had the highest marital-adjustment score, and those having one or more and desiring them had the next highest. The lowest marital adjustment was for marriages having unwanted children, and the next to the lowest was for couples having no children and not wanting any.[25]

The present study attempted to test the hypothesis of Burgess and Cottrell and, consequently, each person was asked the following questions:

Did the husband want the child or the children of the marriage in question: yes _____; no _____. Did wife want the child or the children: yes _____; no _____. If no children, did the husband want children: yes _____; no _____. Did the wife: yes_____; no _____.

Where Children Were Present. Table 25, on the next page, shows that, where children were already present, the desire for them was much more prevalent among the married than among the divorced. In families with children, a significantly larger per cent of both happily married men and women than divorced reported the mate desired children, but there were no significant differences in the per cent who reported that they themselves desired children. However, frequently in the informal interviews a happily married person would express sentiments similar to that of the following (by a happily married husband): "I would not take a million dollars for any one of my children, and I would not give a penny for another." [26]

25 *Op. cit.,* pp. 260–61.
26 Case no. 101.

TABLE 25

Number and Per Cent of Happily-Married and Divorced
Who Had and Desired Children, with Critical Ratios
of the Difference of Per Cents

Person Who Desired Children	Married		Divorced		
	No. of Cases	Per Cent	No. of Cases	Per Cent	CR
Reported by Men					
Self	114	95.0	102	91.1	
Mate	115	94.3	92	85.2	2.3
Reported by Women					
Self	120	96.8	121	93.8	
Mate	124	98.4	106	84.8	3.9

Childless Families. Table 26 shows that the desire for children was much stronger among childless happily-married than among the childless divorced. This was true both for statements on self and on mate. A desire for children by self and mate was expressed by almost 9 in 10 of the childless happily-married as compared with about 6 in 10 of the childless divorced who reported on self, and about 4 in 10 of those who reported on the desire of the spouse.

TABLE 26

Number and Per Cent of Childless Happily-Married and
Divorced Who Desired Children, with Critical Ratios
of the Difference of Per Cents

Person Who Desired Children	Married		Divorced		
	No. of Cases	Per Cent	No. of Cases	Per Cent	CR
Reported by Men					
Self	23	85.2	22	55.0	2.6
Mate	24	88.9	16	40.0	4.0
Reported by Women					
Self	24	88.9	25	62.5	2.4
Mate	24	88.9	15	37.5	4.2

Thus, the hypothesis that an affirmative attitude of husband and wife toward having children is associated with marital adjustment was supported where (1) children were present (in the reports on the mate's desire), and (2) families were childless (in statements about both self and mate).

Comparison of Men's and Women's Responses. Approximately the same per cent of both happily married men and women reported that self and mate desired children. By contrast, a significantly larger per cent of divorced women who had children [27] and also of those who did not have children [28] reported that self rather than mate desired children. The same tendencies were present for divorced men, but the differences in per cents were not statistically significant.

The above may have been due to better communication between happily married husbands and wives than between the divorced. In the case where children were present in families, it may mean that children were a source of conflict between the divorced, either during marriage or more likely in the divorce proceedings, and, consequently, both husband and wife claimed that it was their desire to have children more than that of the mate. The same attitude probably was present in childless families, because married persons are expected to desire children, and therefore the divorced were inclined to report that they desired children more than did the mate. Here again, the difference between self and mate ratings may have been due, in part, to the derogatory attitude of divorced persons toward the spouse.

SUMMARY

The findings of other studies on the relation of marital adjustment and the presence or absence of children are not conclusive. However, for the most part, these studies found that the

[27] CR 2.3.
[28] CR 2.2.

absence of children is not correlated with marital maladjustment. The conclusions of the present study on presence of
children, size of family, and desire for children are as follows:

1. When matched for duration of marriage, the happily-
married and divorced did not differ on either childlessness or
on size of family.

2. Where children were present, marital adjustment was
associated with the judgment that the mate desired children.

3. Where there were no children in the family, marital adjustment was associated with reports that both self and mate
desired children.

9

PERSONALITY TRAITS (I)

IN CONSIDERING marriage, a person measures possible partners against his conception of the ideal husband or wife. One's conception of an ideal mate includes a number of desired personality traits, which, of course, vary somewhat from person to person. If a possible partner falls too far short of the desired mate, hardly a second thought will be given to him. If he meets the ideal fairly well, the tendency is to emphasize those ways of behavior which are desirable, and to think of the other traits as simply a little less desirable.

In view of the great attention given to personality traits in mate selection, it is somewhat surprising that they have not been systematically analyzed in research studies of happiness in marriage or in studies of marital maladjustment. In the present investigation it was decided to compare happily married and divorced men and women on sixteen personality traits.

It was found that marital adjustment is associated with the presence in a person of such traits as sociability, a sense of responsibility, a sense of humor, and affectionateness, and the absence of such traits as dominating, having a hot temper, and being easily influenced by others. The evidence supporting this conclusion was derived from an analysis of judgments of persons on the degree to which they and their mates possessed certain personality traits. The conclusion was also supported by an analysis of the extent to which these traits discriminated between the *more-* and the *less-*adjusted, as measured by marital-adjustment scores, of (1) happily married men, (2) happily married women, (3) divorced men, and (4) divorced women.[1]

There is no standard definition of personality trait, and the term is often used without definition. In view of the looseness with which the term has been used, the desirability of calling our items by some other name, such as behavior pattern or conduct pattern, was considered. Inasmuch as other students of marital adjustment using similar items have adopted the term personality trait, it was decided to use this term and define its meaning in the current study. By trait is meant a distinctive way of behavior of a more or less permanent nature which ranges along a continuum from very little to very great.[2]

Our personality scale is a modification of one prepared by Ernest W. Burgess and Paul Wallin for their engagement study, and one prepared by Leonard S. Cottrell.[3] It includes items relative to such general patterns of behavior as directorial ability, adaptability, affectionateness, and sociability. The scale provides for five possible answers on the relative possession of a given trait: markedly, considerably, somewhat, a little, and not at all. Below are the sixteen personality traits in the order in which they differentiated between the judgments by happily married and divorced women of their husbands' traits.[4] This is also the approximate order in which the items differentiated between married and divorced men's judgments of their wives' traits. If the sixteen items are di-

[1] Cases included in the comparison of married and divorced were those married only once. Inasmuch as it was found that the discriminating value of personality traits appears to be relatively independent of the number of times married (see footnote 8, p. 174), the comparison of the more- or less-adjusted included cases married more than once. Pregnancy cases were excluded.

[2] See *Dictionary of Psychology*, Howard C. Warren (ed.), Boston, Houghton Mifflin Co., 1934, and Philip L. Harriman, *The New Dictionary of Psychology*, New York, Philosophical Library, 1947.

[3] The Burgess-Wallin scale contained 23 items and the Cottrell scale 14; 5 of our 16 items are almost identical with items only in the Burgess-Wallin scale, 6 with items only in the Cottrell scale, and 5 with items in both the Burgess-Wallin and Cottrell scales.

[4] As measured by chi square.

vided into four groups, the four items in each quarter have the same rank for both men and women.

1. Assumes responsibility readily
2. Is easily influenced by others
3. Gets angry easily
4. "Gives in" in arguments

5. Is a leader in the community
6. Has a sense of humor
7. Is dominating
8. Is affectionate

9. Gets over anger quickly
10. Is sociable
11. Makes decisions readily
12. Is strict with children

13. Likes belonging to organizations
14. Cares what people say and think
15. Is demonstrative
16. Is determined

Judgments on the mate's personality traits are more discriminating between adjusted and maladjusted marriages than are self-judgments. On *self-judgments* there were 9 items which discriminated between happily married and divorced men and 5 items for women.[5] On *judgments of mate* there were 14 items which clearly differentiated between happily married and divorced men and the same number for women.[6]

This chapter, as indicated above, includes an analysis of differences on personality traits between the *more*-adjusted and the *less*-adjusted. The more-adjusted are those with relatively high adjustment scores, and the less-adjusted are those with relatively low scores as measured by a marital-adjustment test.[7] The analysis of personality traits of the more- and the less-

[5] For men, 5 of the items had chi squares above the 1-per cent level of significance and 4 from the 1- to the 5-per cent level; for women, 2 were above the 1-per cent level and 3 were from the 1- to the 5-per cent level.

[6] For both men and women, 12 of the items had chi squares on better than the one-thousandth level of significance and 2 were on the 1-per cent level. On judgments of mate the differentiating items were the same for men and women with the exception of two: "demonstration of affection" was differentiating for men, but not for women, while "cares what people say and think" differentiated the women, but not the men.

[7] The separation of cases into a *more*-adjusted and a *less*-adjusted group was made on the basis of the Burgess-Cottrell questions and weights. The use of their questions and weights was due to the fact that this part of the study was

adjusted involved two judgments by four sub-groups: judgments of self and judgments of mate by happily married men,
happily married women, divorced men and divorced women.[8]
The number of personality traits on which the more- and the
less-adjusted of the four groups differed in self-judgments was,
respectively, 8, 6, 3, and 3, whereas the number on judgments
of mate was 13, 7, 7, and 8. Thus, judgments of mate were
much more differentiating than judgments of self.[9]

---

completed prior to the determination of empirical weights from the differences
in the answers of the happily-married and the divorced to the various questions
of the marital-adjustment test of the present study. It will be recalled that
there was a high correlation between the scores computed from the questions
and weights of Burgess-Cottrell and the scores computed from the questions
and empirical weights of the present study. (See p. 53.) This means that, if the
division had not been on the basis of the marital-adjustment test of Burgess and
Cottrell, but on the marital-adjustment test of the present study, about the
same persons would have been in the more and in the less adjusted groups. By
definition, the "more-adjusted" are those married persons who had adjustment
scores of 160 and above and 111 and above for the divorced; the "less-adjusted"
are those having scores of 159 and below for the married, and 110 and below
for the divorced. It will be remembered that when the Burgess-Cottrell questions and weights were used the mean adjustment score of married men was
167.3, of married women 165.6, of divorced men 110.7, and of divorced women
106.8.

[8] In the analysis of the more- and the less-adjusted, cases married more than
once were added to the cases married only once. To test the validity of this,
an analysis was made of the degree to which personality traits discriminated
between happily married and divorced persons married more than once. Inasmuch as the number of persons who had prior marriages to the marriage being
investigated was too small to compare separately, it was decided to add these
cases to those married only once. The assumption was that, if in the new
analysis of differences between happily-married and divorced a significant chi
square remained about the same size or an insignificant chi square became
significant, then happily married and divorced persons married more than
once differed in such personality traits. All items which discriminated between
happily married and divorced persons married only once also discriminated for
those married more than once with the following exceptions: on self-judgment,
"a sense of humor" became insignificant, and "speed of getting over anger"
became significant for men, and "gives in in arguments" and "cares what people
say and think" became significant for women; on judgments of mate, all sixteen
traits were significant for both men and women. Thus, regardless of the
number of times married, about the same personality traits of men and women
were associated with marital adjustment. Consequently, for the analysis of the
more- and the less-adjusted, all cases but those forced to marry were included
in the samples.

[9] In some of the personality items significant differences were found for given
categories as measured by critical ratios, even though the chi squares were not
significant.

The fact that judgments of mate are more differentiating than judgments of self may reflect attitudes of bitterness and resentment of divorced persons toward their mates.[10] On the other hand, this may be due to the greater likelihood that judgments about another person, who is known as intimately as is a marriage partner, approximate that person's behavior traits more closely than his own judgments. There is a natural tendency to feel that one possesses behavior patterns which are defined in the culture as desirable and that one does not possess behavior defined as undesirable. At least there is a tendency to minimize undesirable behavior in oneself. Consequently, judgments of the mate may be a more correct evaluation of one's behavior than self-judgments. Regardless of whether or not statements about self or about mate correspond with the actual behavior itself, they work as predictive items in the study of marital adjustment.

Significant differences in the per cents of given groups reporting ratings in the five answers sometimes involved a combination of categories, such as "markedly" and "considerably." To indicate such a combination "and" has been put in italics.

The 16 personality traits will be classified under the general headings of directorial ability, adaptability, affectionateness, and sociability. It will be apparent that some of the traits do not fit the given categories as logically as do others. Directorial ability and adaptability will be presented in this chapter; affectionateness and sociability will be considered in the next.

DIRECTORIAL ABILITY

We did not find the exact terms under which to classify the first group of traits. However, directorial ability, executive capacity, and managerial ability most nearly characterize the kind of person who assumes responsibility readily, engages in disciplining the children, is a leader, is able to make decisions

[10] For a discussion of this as a limitation of the study see pp. 38–39.

readily, has determination, and is not easily influenced by relatives, friends, and acquaintances. Marital adjustment is associated with these items, and may be associated with the type of
person who unobtrusively manipulates, works with, and directs the efforts of family members so that the goals and objectives of the family may be attained. "Directorial ability" was
selected as the term which best describes the six traits given
above.

Assumes Responsibility Readily. The degree of marital adjustment is associated with the degree to which responsibility
is assumed by the husband and the wife. The evidence indicates that the happily-married and those with high adjustment
scores rated themselves and their mates as more responsible
than did the divorced and those with low adjustment scores.[11]
Table 27 presents the evidence on the extent of the difference
in the self-ratings and ratings of mate on the assumption of
responsibility by happily married and divorced men and
women.

The table shows that on *self-ratings* a larger per cent of married than divorced men rated themselves as "somewhat," "considerably," *and* "markedly" responsible. However, there were
no differences between married and divorced women. Also, a
larger per cent of happily married men with marital-adjustment scores in the more adjusted group than those with scores
in the less adjusted group rated themselves as "markedly" responsible.[12]

In their *ratings of mate,* on the trait, assumes responsibility,
readily, there were decided differences between happily married and divorced men and women. Of the five categories—
markedly, considerably, somewhat, a little, and not at all—

[11] Significant chi squares between happily-married and divorced: self-ratings
of men, 8.4; ratings of mate by men, 69.6; by women, 128.5. Between upper and
lower half by adjustment scores: self-ratings by married men, 7.5, 3 degrees of
freedom; ratings of mate by married women, 8.2, 3 degrees of freedom; by
divorced men, 15.5; by divorced women, 10.0.

[12] Per cents: 50.4 and 28.0, CR 2.2.

TABLE 27

Assumes Responsibility Readily: Per Cent of Happily-Married and Divorced, with Critical Ratios of the Difference of Per Cents

| | Ratings on Self | | | | | |
| | Men | | | Women | | |
	Married N = 155	Divorced N = 137	CR	Married N = 154	Divorced N = 174	CR
Markedly	43.2	38.7		47.4	42.0	
Considerably	40.6	39.4	2.6	33.1	38.5	
Somewhat	12.9	10.9		16.9	13.8	
A little	3.3	7.3		2.0	4.6	
Not at all	0.0	3.7		0.6	1.1	
	100.0	100.0		100.0	100.0	

	Ratings on Mate					
Markedly	42.1	20.4	4.0	53.3	8.3	8.8
Considerably	34.9	18.3	3.2	34.9	22.6	2.4
Somewhat	17.8	15.3		7.2	15.5	2.3
A little	5.2	22.6	4.3	4.6	24.4	5.0
Not at all	0.0	23.4	6.5	0.0	29.2	7.3
	100.0	100.0		100.0	100.0	

men differed in four and women in all five. A larger per cent of both married men and women than divorced rated their mates in each of the two top categories—"considerably" and "markedly" responsible. There was a larger proportion of divorced than married husbands who reported that the mate was "a little" and also "not at all" responsible. More divorced than married wives rated their mates in each of the three lower categories—"somewhat," "a little," and "not at all." Married women, divorced men, and divorced women with higher adjustment scores rated their mates as more responsible than those with lower adjustment scores.[13]

13 Per cents of upper and lower half of marital-adjustment scores: married women for "markedly" responsible, 60.0 and 43.1, CR 2.0; "somewhat" *and*

A wife, who made the following statement about the irresponsibility of her husband as a major reason for divorcing him, rated herself in the questionnaire as "markedly" responsible and her husband as "not at all" responsible: [14]

"My husband seemed quite content to move in here with my folks. He earned pretty good money, but was always broke. He would buy a car, use it a little, and then sell it and buy another. He borrowed money at the bank, and twice he forged my name to a note at the bank. Moreover, he ran around all the time and never spent an evening at home. The thing I wanted was a home of my own, and when Bert wasn't at all interested, I lost interest in him."

The author, who interviewed both the wife and the husband, found that the couple had married at the age of sixteen, after an acquaintance of less than two months. They both checked unsatisfying sex relations as a serious difficulty in the marriage. The author, at the time of the interview, made the notation that, although the wife lived with her parents in one of the most deteriorated areas of the city, she had aspirations beyond the economic level of her background. While it was obvious from the interview that there were many factors involved in the break-up of this family, the wife focused on the irresponsibility of her husband as the major difficulty leading to the divorce.

The tendency is for those who are maladjusted in marriage to consider their mates as not assuming responsibility readily, and for the adjusted to think of their mates as assuming responsibility very readily. In addition, men who are adjusted in marriage more than those who are maladjusted think of themselves as assuming responsibility very readily, whereas women who are adjusted do not differ in self-ratings from the maladjusted. This fits the cultural pattern that decrees that

---

"a little," 8.4 and 19.6, CR 2.1. Divorced men and women for "markedly" responsible: men 25.0 and 11.2, CR 2.3; women, 14.1 and 5.8, CR 2.0. Divorced men for "not at all": 12.5 and 34.8, CR 3.4. Divorced women for "a little" *and* "not at all": 41.0 and 59.8, CR 2.6.

[14] Case no. 908.

husbands should assume more responsibility than wives. Failure to do this is associated with marital maladjustment. Of course, the reverse is likewise probable: the development of marital maladjustment occurs, and spouses then look for defects in themselves and in their mates on which they can blame the failure of the marriage, such as not assuming responsibility.

Strictness with Children. A tendency toward strictness in dealing with children is associated with marital adjustment, and a tendency toward leniency with maladjustment. The evidence indicates that married men and women reported both themselves and their mates as stricter with children than did the divorced.[15]

An analysis of *self-rating,* as revealed in Table 28, shows that when the upper three categories, "markedly," "considerably," *and* "somewhat," were combined, the differences between married and divorced men and women were very great: about 9 in 10 married men and 8 in 10 married women fell in these categories, whereas only a little over 6 in 10 divorced men and women rated themselves in these three categories. For men, the divorced had a larger per cent than the married in each of the lower two categories, "a little" and "not at all." For women, the divorced had a larger per cent than married for the rating "a little." There were no significant differences between the more- and the less-adjusted in self-ratings on strictness in dealing with children.

The table shows that happily married men and women also *rated their mates* as stricter with children than did the divorced. About half of the married men rated their wives as "markedly" *and* "considerably" strict with children, as compared with a third of the divorced. The difference for women was a little lower: a significantly larger per cent of married

---

[15] Significant chi squares: self-ratings by married and divorced men, 18.6; by women, 11.1; ratings of mate by married and divorced men, 26.2; by women, 17.9.

TABLE 28

Strictness with Children: Per Cent of Happily-Married and Divorced, with Critical Ratios of the Difference of Per Cents

| | Ratings on Self | | | | | |
| | Men | | | Women | | |
	Married N = 131	Divorced N = 122	CR	Married N = 125	Divorced N = 157	CR
Markedly	23.7	17.2 ⎫		16.8	14.0 ⎫	
Considerably	29.0	25.4 ⎬ 3.9		36.0	26.8 ⎬ 3.3	
Somewhat	34.4	23.8 ⎭		28.8	22.9 ⎭	
A little	11.4	21.3	2.1	12.8	24.2	
Not at all	1.5	12.3	3.4	5.6	12.1	
	100.0	100.0		100.0	100.0	

	Ratings on Mate					
Markedly	19.4	16.4 ⎫ 2.4		18.9	21.6	
Considerably	29.9	18.1 ⎭		26.0	18.3 ⎫ 3.8	
Somewhat	35.8	27.5		29.1	14.2 ⎭	
A little	13.4	19.0 ⎫ 4.2		17.3	25.0 ⎫ 3.4	
Not at all	1.5	19.0 ⎭		8.7	20.9 ⎭	
	100.0	100.0		100.0	100.0	

than divorced rated their mates as "considerably" *and* "somewhat" strict in dealing with children. Both divorced men and women rated their mates in the combined category of "a little" *and* "not at all" much more frequently than did the married.

Differences in ratings of mate by the more- and the less-adjusted were found only for divorced men. A larger per cent of the more-adjusted rated their mates "considerably," "somewhat," *and* "a little" strict,[16] whereas the less-adjusted reported their mates as "not at all" strict in dealing with children.[17]

[16] Per cents: 72.3 and 50.7, CR 2.6; "somewhat" *and* "a little," 53.8 and 36.0, CR 2.1.

[17] Per cents: 29.3 and 12.3, CR 2.5.

Just what the significance is of this tendency for the married to be stricter with children than the divorced is hard to say. It could mean that "making children mind" is a conventional pattern, and marital adjustment is associated with conventionality. It might mean that being strict with children is conducive to a more peaceful home life in which the adult members enjoy themselves and remain calm, while the reverse results in irritation with subsequent difficulties between the spouses. Another possibility is that marital maladjustment is related to complaints about the spouse. The maladjusted charge their mates with all sorts of deficiencies, including that of not making children mind. Finally, there is the point that married persons expect their mates to assume some responsibility in disciplining the children, and being somewhat strict with children is, therefore, appreciated. Regardless of the fundamental attitudes involved, there is a positive correlation between strictness in dealing with children, as revealed in self-judgments and in judgments of mate, and marital adjustment.

Leadership in the Community. Leadership is positively associated with marital adjustment, and its absence with marital maladjustment.[18] While leadership in itself is probably not the thing which is important, it may be indicative of personality characteristics or social situations which are associated with marital adjustment. Table 29, which gives the per cent of happily married and divorced men and women who rated themselves and their mates for various degrees of leadership, reveals again that ratings of the mate were much more differentiating than were self-ratings.

On *self-ratings,* 4 in 10 divorced persons in contrast with 2 in 10 married reported no leadership in the community whatever. A larger per cent of married than divorced men rated

18 Significant chi squares: self-rating of married and divorced men, 15.2; of women, 20.9; rating of mate by married and divorced men, 30.7; by women, 72.1; rating of mate by more and by less adjusted married men, 9.6; by divorced men, 20.5.

themselves "somewhat" a leader, and a larger per cent of married than divorced women rated themselves "markedly" a leader.

TABLE 29

Leadership in the Community: Per Cent of Happily-Married and Divorced, with Critical Ratios of the Difference of Per Cents

| | *Ratings on Self* | | | | | |
| | Men | | | Women | | |
	Married N = 151	Divorced N = 136	CR	Married N = 153	Divorced N = 165	CR
Markedly	11.3	7.4		11.8	3.6	2.8
Considerably	17.2	13.2		11.8	9.1	
Somewhat	31.1	16.9	2.8	30.0	22.4	
A little	17.2	22.8		22.9	19.4	
Not at all	23.2	39.7	3.0	23.5	45.5	4.1
	100.0	100.0		100.0	100.0	

	Ratings on Mate					
Markedly	14.7	5.8	2.5	14.7	3.1	3.6
Considerably	14.0	8.8		17.3	6.2	3.0
Somewhat	28.0	16.1	2.4	22.0	10.6	2.7
A little	21.3	16.8		22.7	20.5	
Not at all	22.0	52.5	5.4	23.3	59.6	6.5
	100.0	100.0		100.0	100.0	

Married men and women who were more adjusted reported a higher degree of leadership in themselves than did those who were less adjusted.[19]

In *rating mates* on leadership, the most significant difference for both men and women was in the lowest rating—"not at all." Half of the divorced and only 2 in 10 of the married gave this rating to their mates. While a larger per cent of married than divorced men and women was in each of the other

[19] Per cents for men: "markedly" *and* "considerably," 33.1 and 12.3, CR 2.8. For women: "markedly" *and* "considerably," 27.4 and 13.7, CR 2.0.

degrees of leadership, the differences were significant in only two categories for men, "markedly" and "somewhat," and three for women, "markedly," "considerably," and "somewhat." The differences were, on the whole, greater for women than for men.

The comparison of ratings of mate by persons with adjustment scores in the more-adjusted of a given group with those in the less-adjusted revealed differences in all four groups: married men, married women, divorced men, and divorced women. The pattern of response was essentially the same as that found in the comparison of happily married and divorced persons. Those having higher adjustment scores rated their mates as having a higher degree of leadership than did those with lower adjustment scores. A larger per cent of more adjusted married men and women rated their mates as "considerably" *and* "markedly" a leader,[20] while a larger per cent of women who were less adjusted rated their mates at the bottom of the scale.[21] A larger number of the more adjusted divorced men and women rated their mates in the middle categories,[22] while a larger per cent of the less adjusted men rated their mates in the "no leadership at all" category.[23]

The differences between the married and divorced on leadership may have been due, in part, to the method by which the samples were secured. It will be remembered that the married sample was composed of persons suggested by friends and acquaintances as the most happily married they knew, while the divorced sample was secured from persons whose names were in the divorce file at the courthouse. To some extent, persons recommended as happily married were in positions of leadership in the local communities.

[20] Per cents for men: "markedly," 16.5 and 4.1, CR 2.2; "markedly" *and* "considerably," 32.2 and 12.3, CR 2.7. For women: "considerably," 20.8 and 8.0, CR 2.0; "markedly" *and* "considerably," 37.5 and 16.0, CR 2.8.

[21] Per cents: 34.0 and 20.0, CR 2.0.

[22] Per cents for men: "considerably," 12.7 and 1.1, CR 3.0; "somewhat," 21.5 and 9.3, CR 2.2. For women: "considerably," "somewhat" *and* "a little," 46.1 and 29.1, CR 2.4; "somewhat" *and* "a little," 39.7 and 24.0, CR 2.3.

[23] Per cents: 72.1 and 40.5, CR 4.1.

The association of leadership with marital adjustment, and the lack of leadership with marital maladjustment, was not entirely due to the method of selecting the sample, for the same general pattern of differences was found in the comparison of the more- and less-adjusted of the divorced and of the married. Consequently, other factors, of which leadership is an index, probably were operating. For example, a leader is sociable, makes compromises, manipulates people, and directs the activities of the group so that goals and objectives may be attained; such characteristics probably are associated with marital success. Another hypothesis which may explain the association between leadership and marital adjustment is that a leader has a relatively high social status, and this results in a relatively high status for the family, which in turn may be related to marital adjustment.

Ability to Make Decisions Readily. The ability to make decisions quickly is associated with marital adjustment, and the reverse with maladjustment.[24] Table 30 shows that happily married men and women gave higher ratings both to their own and to the mate's ability to make decisions readily than did the divorced.

On *self-ratings* married men were inclined to report that they made decisions "markedly" *and* "considerably" fast, with divorced men saying that their readiness in making decisions was in the combined category of "somewhat," "a little," *and* "not at all." For women, about 9 in 10 married to 8 in 10 divorced reported themselves "somewhat," "considerably," *and* "markedly" quick in making decisions.

The comparison of persons with adjustment scores in the more adjusted group with those having scores in the less adjusted showed no differences on self-ratings.

On *ratings of mate* the pattern was similar to that found for

[24] Significant chi squares: self-ratings of married and divorced men, 8.2, 3 degrees of freedom; ratings of mate by married and divorced men, 25.9; by women, 18.9.

TABLE 30

*Ability to Make Decisions Readily: Per Cent of Happily-
Married and Divorced, with Critical Ratios of the
Difference of Per Cents*

| | Ratings on Self | | | | | |
| | Men | | | Women | | |
	Married N = 158	Divorced N = 141	CR	Married N = 155	Divorced N = 174	CR
Markedly	40.5	31.2 ⎫		25.8	19.0 ⎫	
Considerably	39.2	32.6 ⎬ 3.1		34.8	33.9 ⎬ 2.4	
Somewhat	15.2	22.0		26.5	24.1 ⎭	
A little	4.5	10.6		10.3	16.7	
Not at all	0.6	3.6		2.6	6.3	
	100.0	100.0		100.0	100.0	

	Ratings on Mate					
Markedly	33.8	25.8 ⎫		28.8	19.8 ⎫	
Considerably	38.9	25.0 ⎬ 4.9		39.2	32.0 ⎬ 3.0	
Somewhat	22.3	25.0		23.5	21.5	
A little	3.1	12.1 ⎫		6.5	19.2 ⎫	
Not at all	1.9	12.1 ⎬ 4.7		2.0	7.5 ⎬ 4.2	
	100.0	100.0		100.0	100.0	

self-ratings. A larger per cent of both happily married men
and women than divorced rated their mates' ability to make
decisions readily as "markedly" *and* "considerably." By contrast, divorced men and women much more frequently than
married, rated their mates' ability to make decisions readily
as "a little" *and* "not at all": 1 in 4 divorced men to 1 in 20
married gave these ratings, and for women the ratio was 1 in
4 divorced to 1 in 12 married.

On this trait of making decisions readily, married men who
were in the more adjusted group reported the rating of
"markedly" for their wives more frequently than did the less-
adjusted.[25]

[25] Per cents: 39.2 and 21.6, CR 2.2.

The evidence indicates that persons who are adjusted in marriage make decisions more readily than those who are mal-adjusted. What are the possible explanations of this differ-ence? One hypothesis may be stated in terms of fundamental characteristics of the successful executive or director. The suc-cessful director of an enterprise is one who is able to make deci-sions with dispatch, for he knows not only the objectives of the business and the available means of attaining them, but also the probable reactions of other persons involved in the enter-prise. So, likewise, the husband or wife who is being successful in the enterprise of marriage makes decisions readily, for he or she knows the objectives of the family, and has the ability to play the roles of other members, thereby knowing their prob-able reactions to any decision.

Another hypothesis is that ability to make decisions read-ily is an index of self-confidence. A certain amount of self-confidence is a prerequisite to the successful functioning of any group, including the family.

A third hypothesis is that persons *at the time of marriage* differ in the speed of making decisions, and that those who are quick in making decisions solve marital problems be-fore they disrupt intrafamily relationships, whereas problems tend to accumulate in marriages where the spouses are very slow in making decisions. It will be interesting to note whether Ernest W. Burgess and Paul Wallin in their study of one thou-sand engaged couples find that persons successful in marriage were able to make decisions before marriage with consider-able speed, while the unsuccessful were slow in making up their minds.[26]

Determination. The degree to which a person shows deter-mination, while not a very important predictive item, is asso-ciated with the degree of marital adjustment.[27] Little or no

[26] Ernest W. Burgess and Paul Wallin, *Engagement and Marriage,* New York, Harcourt Brace, to be published in 1951.

[27] Significant chi squares: self-ratings of married and divorced men, 11.4, 3 degrees of freedom; ratings of mate by more and less adjusted divorced men, 15.1.

determination appears to be associated with marital maladjustment.

Table 31 shows that on *self-ratings* married and divorced men differed in their answers to this item, but women did not. Married men had a greater degree of determination than the divorced, as indicated by a significantly larger per cent reporting themselves "markedly" *and* "considerably" determined, with the divorced having a larger per cent rating themselves "a little" *and* "not at all" determined.

TABLE 31

Determination: Per Cent of Happily-Married and Divorced, with Critical Ratios of the Difference of Per Cents

	Ratings on Self					
	Men			Women		
	Married N = 154	Divorced N = 136	CR	Married N = 154	Divorced N = 169	CR
Markedly	44.2	32.4 ⎫	2.9	34.4	29.0	
Considerably	37.0	33.8 ⎭		29.9	32.5	
Somewhat	13.6	18.4		23.4	22.5	
A little	4.6	9.5 ⎫	2.9	9.7	12.4	
Not at all	0.6	5.9 ⎭		2.6	3.6	
	100.0	100.0		100.0	100.0	
	Ratings on Mate					
Markedly	42.0	38.0		38.4	40.8	
Considerably	33.3	30.6		27.2	20.7	
Somewhat	19.3	19.0		24.5	20.7	
A little	4.0	9.5 ⎫	2.1	7.3	10.7 ⎫	2.0
Not at all	1.4	2.9 ⎭		2.6	7.1 ⎭	
	100.0	100.0		100.0	100.0	

The comparison of the more-adjusted with the less-adjusted revealed only one significant difference on self-ratings: divorced men with higher adjustment scores rated themselves "somewhat" determined more frequently than did those with lower scores.[28]

Divorced men and women *rated their mates* as less determined than did the married. For both men and women, there was a significantly larger per cent of divorced rating their mates in the lower two categories—"a little" *and* "not at all."

Divorced men with higher adjustment scores as compared with those with lower scores rated their mates more frequently in the three middle categories—"considerably," "somewhat," *and* "a little"; [29] those with low adjustment scores had a larger per cent who rated mates as "not at all" determined. Less adjusted happily married women reported that their mates were "considerably" determined more frequently than did the more-adjusted.[30]

One interpretation of the fact that the maladjusted appear to have less determination is that the objectives and goals of a family are not as likely to be attained by one with little determination. The fact that married and divorced men differed in self-ratings, whereas women did not, may mean that in American culture men are supposed to take the lead in the attainment of family goals and that, consequently, a man in a well-adjusted marriage is expected to have more determination than the woman. This hypothesis is supported in part by a comparison of self-ratings of men with the self-ratings of women. Married men and women differed decidedly in the rating of "markedly" *and* "considerably" determined, with men having the higher per cent,[31] whereas divorced men and women did not differ.[32] This seems to indicate that in the well-adjusted marriage the man has more determination than his wife, while in the poorly-adjusted, not only is there less deter-

[28] Per cents: 23.1 and 11.4, CR 2.0.
[29] Per cents: "considerably," "somewhat," *and* "a little," 71.6 and 50.6, CR 2.8; "somewhat" by itself, 27.2 and 11.5, CR 2.6; "not at all," 0.0 and 9.2, CR 2.8.
[30] Per cents: 42.9 and 24.0, CR 2.5.
[31] Per cents: 81.2 and 64.3, CR 3.3.
[32] Per cents: 66.2 and 61.5, CR only 0.8.

mination, but the man and his wife do not differ in the degree of their determination.

Determination, while it is a predictive item in marital adjustment, is not as discriminating as most of the other personality traits. It should be excluded in future studies of personality traits and marital adjustment.

Easily Influenced by Others. Marital maladjustment is highly associated with the trait of being easily influenced by others.[33] Self-ratings of men and ratings of mate by both men and women support this conclusion, as do the comparisons of the more- and the less-adjusted. It is also supported by the informal statements secured in the interviews. For example, the following excerpt from the case of a divorced woman shows that she felt that her husband was too easily influenced by his family: [34]

"My husband and I are sorta thinking of going back together. His folks were just about the whole cause of our trouble. They didn't like me, and told lies on top of lies about us. They even said I tried to commit suicide. He was too easily influenced by them. I guess I am too easily influenced by others too. We are alike in this way.

"My husband, when we were living together, wanted to be around his folks all the time. After our divorce, he changed and stayed by himself away from them. He wants me to come back and maybe I will. I still love him. He has our two little children, and we may go back together for their sakes too."

Table 32 shows that on *self-rating,* there were two significant differences between married and divorced for men, but none for women. Married men felt that they were only "a little" influenced by others, whereas a larger per cent of divorced

[33] Significant chi squares were: self-ratings of married and divorced men, 19.8; ratings of mate by married and divorced men, 72.6; ratings of mate by married and divorced women, 80.5; ratings of mate by more and less adjusted married men, 16.0; ratings of mate by more and less adjusted married women, 15.8.
[34] Case No. 199.

than married men thought of themselves as being rather easily
influenced by others.

TABLE 32

*Easily Influenced by Others: Per Cent of Happily-Married
and Divorced, with Critical Ratios of the Difference
of Per Cents*

	Ratings on Self					
	Men			Women		
	Married N = 157	Divorced N = 139	CR	Married N = 155	Divorced N = 175	CR
Markedly	1.9	7.2		5.8	7.4	
Considerably	5.1	15.8	3.1	7.1	11.4	
Somewhat	22.3	22.3		20.0	17.8	
A little	42.0	24.5	3.2	30.3	33.7	
Not at all	28.7	30.2		36.8	29.7	
	100.0	100.0		100.0	100.0	
	Ratings on Mate					
Markedly	2.6	26.6	5.9	6.5	33.3	5.9
Considerably	10.3	30.2	4.3	8.5	30.4	4.9
Somewhat	21.9	18.7		14.4	8.3	
A little	42.6	13.7	5.5	33.3	15.5	3.7
Not at all	22.6	10.8	2.7	37.3	12.5	5.2
	100.0	100.0		100.0	100.0	

In the comparison of self-ratings of persons with high and
low adjustment scores, differences were found for married
men, married women, and divorced men. A larger per cent of
the more adjusted married men said they were "a little" *and*
"not at all" influenced by others,[35] with the less-adjusted saying they were "considerably" influenced by others.[36] The more
adjusted married women reported more frequently not being
influenced at all,[37] whereas a larger per cent of the less-adjusted

35 Per cents: 75.8 and 60.8, CR 2.0.
36 Per cents: 13.7 and 3.1, CR 2.7.
37 Per cents: 43.2 and 21.6, CR 2.7.

rated themselves "somewhat" *and* "a little" influenced.[38] Divorced men with high marital-adjustment scores had a larger per cent with self-ratings of "somewhat" *and* "a little" influenced by others,[39] with the less-adjusted more frequently rating themselves as "markedly" influenced by others.[40]

Ratings of mate by happily married men and women were decidedly different from those of divorced men and women. The happily-married rated their mates as only "a little" *and* "not at all" influenced by others much more frequently than did the divorced. Ratings of "markedly" *and* "considerably" influenced by others were given by 6 in 10 divorced men and women as compared with only 1 in 7 of the happily-married. Also, each of these four ratings differentiated between the happily-married and the divorced.

In the comparison of ratings of mate by persons in the more- and the less-adjusted of the given groups, no differences were found for divorced men or divorced women. However, a decidedly larger per cent of the more adjusted married men rated mates in the lower three categories, "somewhat," "a little," *and* "not at all"; [41] the less-adjusted reported more frequently that their mates were "considerably" influenced by others.[42] For married women, very significant differences were also found, but the differences were but one category apart: a larger per cent of the more-adjusted reported mates to be "not at all" influenced,[43] and the less-adjusted reported mates to be "a little" influenced by others.[44]

The data of the informal interviews emphasizes the tendency of persons who are maladjusted in marriage to blame their marital difficulties on the fact that the mate is greatly influenced by relatives, friends, and acquaintances. Divorced

[38] Per cents: 68.6 and 45.6, CR 2.8.
[39] Per cents: 51.9 and 37.1, CR 2.0.
[40] Per cents: 11.2 and 2.5, CR 2.2.
[41] Per cents: 92.0 and 70.0, CR 3.8.
[42] Per cents: 26.0 and 5.6, CR 3.8.
[43] Per cents: 45.9 and 18.0, CR 3.4.
[44] Per cents: 54.0 and 25.4, CR 3.6.

men and women frequently charged that the marriage would not have broken up if their mates had not accepted the suggestions and advice of outsiders.

ADAPTABILITY

Adaptability is similar in meaning to adjustment and accommodation and designates the ability to adjust to others with a minimum of friction. It appears that some persons are highly adaptable and others relatively unadaptable in their relations with others. It also appears that adaptability is related to marital adjustment in so far as it is indicated by "giving in" in arguments, by not dominating others, by slowness in getting angry, and by quickness in getting over anger.

"Giving in" in Arguments. Stubbornness, as indicated by not yielding in an argument, is associated with marital maladjustment, and adaptability, as indicated by readily yielding, is associated with marital adjustment. The evidence indicates that ratings on this personality trait not only separate happily married men and women from divorced men and women, but also, the more- from the less-adjusted of the married and of the divorced.[45]

The following is from an interview with a husband of a happily married couple, whose average combined marital adjustment score was among the less-adjusted—72.5 per cent of the happily married couples had scores above that of this couple. The excerpt from his case history shows that, from the viewpoint of the husband, the wife was extremely stubborn, and that the husband, himself, was not very adaptable. From the interview it appeared that he would not hesitate to talk to his wife in the same way that he talked to the interviewer about her and the marriage situation: [46]

[45] Significant chi squares: self-ratings of married and divorced men, 18.7; self-ratings of more and less adjusted married men, 12.5; ratings of mate by married and divorced men, 50.9; by women 53.4; ratings of mate by more and less adjusted divorced men, 25.4.

[46] Case no. 131.

"I am not sure I would marry again if the same conditions were present which have been present in this one. I often feel that I would be more free if I were single.

"My wife is awful stubborn, and if she sets her head to do something, she'll do it in spite of hell and high water. Now I'm not saying that she isn't a good woman, for she is. But then she can get on a feller's nerves sometimes, especially with her religion. She takes every word of the Bible and lives up to it. For that matter, I believe in the Bible too, but what I don't like is the way some people on "the hill" can go down to that Pentecostal church and swear to God they are righteous, and yet they would steal the slop from a pig if they could. When I go to church, I get my mind on the people, and off the Lord, so why the hell should I go. My wife don't like it 'cause I swear, but that's an old, old habit. She don't like it 'cause I use tobacco, and says that's another reason I won't get to heaven, but I think that a lot of people who think they are going to heaven won't get there.

"A single life is an empty life, and a married life is too full. So what the hell can you do but get married and find it out."

Table 33 shows that divorced and married men gave significantly different *self-ratings* on the degree to which they "gave in" in arguments. Divorced men were found more frequently in the "considerably" and "not at all" categories than were the married, who reported more frequently that they yielded "a little." While the same general pattern was present in the ratings of married and divorced women, the only difference which was close to being statistically significant was in the category of "markedly" *and* "considerably," with the divorced having the higher per cent.

In addition to distinguishing between married and divorced persons, self-ratings on "giving in" in arguments also differentiated between the more- and the less-adjusted of married men and divorced men. The more adjusted married men more often than the less-adjusted reported themselves as giving in "considerably" *and* "somewhat." [47] By contrast, the less-

47 Per cents: 60.5 and 32.6, CR 3.2.

TABLE 33

*"Giving in" in Arguments: Per Cent of Happily-Married
and Divorced, with Critical Ratios of the Difference
of Per Cents*

	Men			Women		
	Married N = 151	Divorced N = 139	CR	Married N = 151	Divorced N = 169	CR
	Ratings on Self					
Markedly	13.2	11.5		11.2	13.6 ⎫	1.9
Considerably	17.2	27.4	2.1	23.2	31.4 ⎭	
Somewhat	36.4	33.8		38.4	29.0	
A little	30.5	15.8	3.0	21.9	16.6	
Not at all	2.7	11.5	3.0	5.3	9.4	
	100.0	100.0		100.0	100.0	
	Ratings on Mate					
Markedly	17.4	7.9	2.4	10.9	6.7 ⎫	2.5
Considerably	19.5	12.2		19.7	11.6 ⎭	
Somewhat	36.3	24.5	2.2	42.9	15.9	5.3
A little	24.8	23.0		19.0	34.1	3.0
Not at all	2.0	32.4	6.9	7.5	31.7	5.3
	100.0	100.0		100.0	100.0	

adjusted had a significantly larger per cent in the categories of "a little" *and* "not at all." [48] Differences also were found between the more and less adjusted divorced men, though not as great as those found for married men. Here, only one significant difference was found, namely, that the more-adjusted had a larger per cent who gave in "somewhat" in arguments. [49]

Table 33 also shows that *ratings of mate* by married persons differed significantly from ratings by divorced persons. About a third of divorced men and women felt that their mates did not yield in an argument at all, whereas only a few married

[48] Per cents: "a little," 45.7 and 22.6, CR 3.0; "a little" *and* "not at all," 50.0 and 25.0, CR 3.1.
[49] Per cents: 39.0 and 23.9, CR 2.1.

men and women gave this rating. Another third of divorced women reported that their mates yielded in arguments only "a little," and this was significantly larger than the per cent of married women who gave this rating to their mates. Happily married men and women reported much more frequently than did divorced that their mates "gave in" in arguments "markedly," "considerably," and "somewhat."

Separating the married and divorced into the more- and the less-adjusted, differences were found on ratings of mate for only one group—divorced men. Half of the less-adjusted and only one seventh of the more-adjusted reported that their mates did not "give in" in arguments at all.[50] The more-adjusted had a significantly larger per cent who rated mates as "considerably," "somewhat," and "a little" inclined to "give in" in arguments.[51]

A general pattern of response, though not always statistically significant, was evident in self-ratings on conceding in arguments. Happily married and more adjusted persons placed themselves in middle categories, with the divorced and less-adjusted rating themselves at either extreme of the continuum. This might mean that stubbornness, as indicated by not conceding in arguments at all, or spinelessness, as indicated by readily "giving in," is unfavorably associated with marital adjustment.

Another hypothesis, however, is supported by the ratings of the mate on this personality trait, namely, that the degree of adaptability is associated with the degree of marital adjustment. Married men and women and the more-adjusted rated their mates as much more willing to "give in" in an argument than did divorced men and women and the less-adjusted. Inasmuch as arguments and difficulties are indices of marital maladjustment, it is consistent that divorced persons and the less-adjusted reported that their mates were unwilling to yield

---

[50] Per cents: 50.5 and 15.9, CR 4.8.
[51] Per cents: "considerably," 18.3 and 7.9, CR 2.0; "somewhat," 31.7 and 14.6, CR 2.7; "considerably," "somewhat," and "a little," 75.6 and 41.6, CR 4.5.

in arguments, and that the happily-married and the more-adjusted rated their spouses as adjustable in an argument.

Dominating: Pressing Opinions and Ideas on Others. The table below shows that the degree of marital adjustment is associated with the degree to which one considers the mate to

TABLE 34

*Dominating—Pressing Opinions and Ideas on Others:
Per Cent of Happily-Married and Divorced, with
Critical Ratios of the Difference of Per Cents*

	Men			Women		
	Married N = 151	Divorced N = 139	CR	Married N = 151	Divorced N = 168	CR
Ratings on Self						
Markedly	9.3	10.8		6.0	7.7	
Considerably	19.2	12.9		4.6	10.1	
Somewhat	18.5	26.6		21.9	17.3	
A little	28.5	25.2		27.8	31.0	
Not at all	24.5	24.5		39.7	33.9	
	100.0	100.0		100.0	100.0	
Ratings on Mate						
Markedly	6.8	23.7	4.0	3.3	26.2	5.7
Considerably	14.2	25.2	2.4	10.0	16.7	
Somewhat	20.9	18.0		22.7	17.3 }	2.1
A little	23.6	15.1		23.3	17.3 }	
Not at all	34.5	18.0	3.6	40.7	22.5	3.5
	100.0	100.0		100.0	100.0	

be dominating.[52] This emphasis on judgments on the mate's tendency to dominate is due to the fact that no differences were found on *self-ratings,* either between married and divorced men or women, as shown in the table, or between the more- and less-adjusted of the given groups.

[52] Significant chi squares: ratings of mate by married and divorced men, 28.8; by women, 40.4; ratings of mate by more and less adjusted divorced men, 9.8.

The table shows that divorced men and women *rated their spouses* as much more dominating than did the happily-married. Ratings on mate in the two top categories of "markedly" *and* "considerably" were given by about 50 per cent of divorced men and by only 20 per cent of the married; the corresponding per cents for women were about 40 for the divorced and 10 for the married. Ratings on mate in the two least dominating categories of "a little" *and* "not at all" were given by about 60 per cent of married men and by about 30 per cent of the divorced; the corresponding per cents for women were about 60 and 40, respectively. When only the top and the bottom categories, "markedly" and "not at all," are considered, there is no question that happily married men and women were inclined to rate their mates as much less dominating than were the divorced.

Splitting the groups on the basis of adjustment scores into the more- and the less-adjusted, it was found that the same general pattern on ratings of the mate described above, though not so pronounced, also applied within three of the four groups: divorced men, married men, and married women. The less adjusted divorced men had a larger per cent who rated their mates as "markedly" *and* "considerably" dominating,[53] whereas the more-adjusted reported more frequently "a little" *and* "not at all." [54] The less adjusted married men had a larger per cent stating their mates were "somewhat" dominating.[55] For married women, the differences were but one category apart: a larger per cent of the less-adjusted rated their mates "a little" dominating,[56] while the more-adjusted rated their mates more frequently as "not at all" dominating.[57]

The following excerpt is from the case history of a husband of a happily married couple, whose marital-adjustment score

[53] Per cents: "markedly," 31.9 and 16.2, CR 2.4; "markedly" *and* "considerably," 49.4 and 40.0, CR 2.5.

[54] Per cents: "a little," 18.7 and 7.7, CR 2.1; "a little" *and* "not at all," 41.2 and 22.0, CR 2.7.

[55] Per cents: 34.0 and 16.1, CR 2.6.

[56] Per cents: 37.3 and 21.8, CR 2.1.

[57] Per cents: 43.7 and 25.5, CR 2.2.

was among the upper 15 per cent of the scores of married couples. This couple had known each other since childhood and had been engaged five years. While the wife listed the "kindness, consideration, free-heartedness, attention, and politeness" of her husband as things which satisfied her most about her marriage, the husband stressed the lack of domination as the thing which satisfied him most. In the questionnaire the wife checked both herself and her husband as "not at all" dominating, while the husband checked both as only "a little" dominating: [58]

"My wife and I both like living with her mother, and before her father died, with her folks. I think it is because we never poke our noses in each other's business. If we are out late, or if I do anything without my wife, my mother-in-law never asks any questions. Or, if we go down-town or out of town and do not ask her to go along, she never gets her feelings hurt. That also works with my wife and myself. I think that a dominating person is about the worst person to be around. But neither of us tries to dominate the other. I have a horse, and sometimes after getting through work, I go out to my horse. While my wife does not enjoy such things, she appreciates my interest. I do the same with the things which she enjoys. I think of my days as my own, but I spend the evenings with her, if she has nothing to do."

In contrast with the above happily married couple is the following description of dominating behavior toward a former husband by a divorced woman, who, in the questionnaire, rated herself as "somewhat" dominating and her husband as "considerably" dominating: [59]

"I was always very sickly at home, so I always had my own way. My mother ruled my dad, and I ruled my brothers. Naturally, I always had the idea that I was boss over all men. Where I work, the boys take orders from me.

"I have always been boss in my family. I ruled my husband, even

[58] Case no. 122.
[59] Case no. 91.

after he began to drink (giving her head an emphatic nod). Believe me, you've got to call their bluff if you get along with a drunk. One time he told me, when drunk, that he was going to 'beat up' on me and the kid. There was an ax behind him, and I picked that up and I said, 'If you lay a hand on me or that boy, I'll strike this ax right in your back and split your head right open.' I'm amiable and good and easy to get along with until I get mad, and then you'd better look out."

What is the interpretation of the tendency of the maritally adjusted persons to rate their mates as much less dominating than the maladjusted? One hypothesis is that the adjusted engage in democratic and equalitarian practices to a greater extent than the maladjusted. Equalitarian practices imply that there will be little domination of one spouse by the other. This hypothesis is to some extent supported by the fact that there was no significant difference between the self-ratings and mate-ratings of either happily married men or happily married women, whereas there were very significant differences between the self-ratings and mate-ratings of both divorced men and women.[60]

Another hypothesis which, in part, explains the tendency of the divorced to rate their mates as much more dominating than the happily-married rated their mates, is that difficulties in the marriage occurred and the divorced blamed their mates for the difficulties, feeling that if the mates had been less dominating and more democratic the difficulties might not have developed.

Speed of Getting Angry. Men and women experiencing marital adjustment give significantly different responses from those experiencing maladjustment on the speed with which they and their mates get angry. Table 35 indicates that the adjusted give ratings toward the bottom of the scale on this trait and the maladjusted toward the top. In general, the

[60] Chi squares: married men, 5.0; married women, 4.8; divorced men, 18.8; divorced women, 29.8.

slower the speed of getting angry, the greater the chances of marital adjustment.[61]

TABLE 35

Getting Angry Easily: Per Cent of Happily-Married and Divorced, with Critical Ratios of the Difference of Per Cents

	Ratings on Self					
	Men			Women		
	Married N = 156	Divorced N = 138	CR	Married N = 151	Divorced N = 170	CR
Markedly	9.6	18.1	2.1	12.6	14.1	
Considerably	11.5	17.4		9.3	15.3	
Somewhat	23.7	21.0		27.8	13.5	3.2
A little	41.1	21.0	3.7	35.8	37.1	
Not at all	14.1	22.5	1.9	14.5	20.0	
	100.0	100.0		100.0	100.0	
	Ratings on Mate					
Markedly	8.5	39.4	6.2	7.4	39.0	6.6
Considerably	13.7	25.5	2.5	12.8	21.5	2.0
Somewhat	27.5	14.6	2.7	23.6	12.8	2.5
A little	37.9	13.2	4.8	37.3	15.1	4.6
Not at all	12.4	7.3		18.9	11.6	
	100.0	100.0		100.0	100.0	

The table shows that on *self-ratings* the happily-married reported a slower speed of getting angry than did the divorced. The specific categories in which significant differences in per cents were found were: "somewhat," with more married women than divorced; "a little," with more married men than divorced; and "markedly," with divorced men having the larger per cent.

[61] Significant chi squares: self-ratings of married and divorced men, 17.9; of women, 11.8; ratings of mate of married and divorced men, 59.4; of women, 59.1; self-ratings of more and less adjusted married men, 18.6; ratings of mate of more and less adjusted divorced men, 12.1; of divorced women, 10.7.

Self-ratings on the speed of getting angry differentiated between the more and less adjusted married men and women; they did not differentiate between the more and the less adjusted divorced men and women. A significantly larger per cent of both married men and women having higher adjustment scores rated themselves as slower in getting angry than those with lower adjustment scores.[62]

Divorced men and women *rated their mates* as getting angry much more easily than did happily married men and women. About two thirds of divorced men and women rated their mates in the two top categories of "considerably" *and* "markedly," whereas less than a fourth of the married gave these ratings. The happily-married more frequently than the divorced rated the quickness with which their mates got angry as only "a little" *and* "not at all."

The more adjusted, as compared with the less adjusted married men, divorced men, and divorced women, rated their mates as relatively slow in getting angry. Married men with high scores more frequently reported "not at all" *and* "a little," [63] with those having lower scores reporting "considerably." [64] Divorced men with high scores gave the category of "a little" more frequently,[65] with those having lower scores reporting "markedly." [66] Divorced women with high scores reported "somewhat" *and* "a little" more frequently,[67] and those with lower scores reported the speed with which their mates got angry as "markedly." [68]

The above supports the conclusion that those who are adjusted in marriage get angry much less quickly than those who

[62] Per cents for men: "not at all," 18.0 and 5.9, CR 2.1; "a little," 44.3 and 25.5, CR 2.3; "a little" *and* "not at all," 62.3 and 31.4, CR 3.7; "considerably," 25.5 and 7.4, CR 3.3. For women: "a little," 39.3 and 21.6, CR 2.2; "markedly" *and* "considerably," 35.3 and 17.3, CR 2.6.

[63] Per cents: 54.4 and 38.0, CR 2.0.

[64] Per cents: 24.0 and 9.8, CR 2.5.

[65] Per cents: 18.3 and 5.6, CR 2.6.

[66] Per cents: 51.7 and 30.5, CR 2.8.

[67] Per cents: "somewhat," 18.7 and 8.1, CR 2.3; "somewhat" *and* "a little," 37.4 and 17.8, CR 3.1.

[68] Per cents: 47.1 and 30.0, CR 2.4.

are maladjusted. In American culture the expectation is that
marital and family relationships will be characterized by
friendliness and affection, rather than by quarreling and expressions of anger. While family members may make allow-
ances for a father, mother, or child who gets angry quickly, in
the long run the frequent expression of anger toward a spouse
or children is likely to create hostility and to interfere with
marital and family adjustment.

Getting over Anger Quickly. The speed with which a person gets over anger is correlated with the degree of marital
adjustment. One who is quick in getting over anger is a better
risk in marriage than one who is slow.[69]

Table 36 shows that on *self-ratings* a larger per cent of married than divorced men rated themselves in the three middle categories—"considerably," "somewhat," *and* "a little."
A larger per cent of married women rated themselves in the
middle category, "somewhat," whereas divorced women rated
themselves in the combined category of "a little" *and* "not at
all." While about two thirds of men and women of both the
married and divorced groups rated themselves "markedly"
and "considerably" quick in getting over anger, a slightly
higher, although statistically insignificant, per cent of divorced than married men and women gave the response
"markedly." The tendency of the divorced was to rate themselves at either end of the continuum, by putting themselves
in a very favorable light or by admitting that they did not get
over anger quickly.

The more- and the less-adjusted of the given groups, with
one exception, did not vary in self-ratings on speed of getting
over anger. The exception was that the more adjusted divorced
men rated themselves in the "somewhat" *and* "a little" category more frequently than did the less-adjusted.[70]

[69] Significant chi squares: self-ratings of married and divorced women, 16.2;
ratings of mate by married and divorced men, 22.2; by women, 29.4; ratings of
mate by more and less adjusted divorced women, 16.5.

[70] Per cents: 30.5 and 16.5, CR 2.2.

TABLE 36

*Getting Over Anger Quickly: Per Cent of Happily-
Married and Divorced, with Critical Ratios of the
Difference of Per Cents*

	Ratings on Self					
	Men			Women		
	Married N = 155	Divorced N = 142	CR	Married N = 151	Divorced N = 171	CR
Markedly	32.9	39.4		37.1	41.5	
Considerably	32.2	27.5 ⎫		26.5	25.7	
Somewhat	15.5	12.7 ⎬ 2.0		19.2	5.9	3.7
A little	14.2	10.6 ⎭		10.6	14.0 ⎫ 2.1	
Not at all	5.2	9.8		6.6	12.9 ⎭	
	100.0	100.0		100.0	100.0	
	Ratings on Mate					
Markedly	32.7	21.4	2.2	34.5	20.1	2.9
Considerably	36.6	29.3		32.4	22.0	2.1
Somewhat	19.0	15.0		16.9	15.9	
A little	8.4	20.7	3.0	13.5	26.2	2.8
Not at all	3.3	13.6	3.2	2.7	15.8	3.9
	100.0	100.0		100.0	100.0	

In *ratings of mate* on speed of getting over anger, married
men and women gave decidedly higher ratings than did the
divorced. In the two top categories of getting over anger
quickly, "markedly" *and* "considerably," there were 7 in 10
married to 5 in 10 divorced men, and more than 6 in 10 married women to 4 in 10 divorced. Divorced men and women
gave each of the two bottom categories, "a little" and "not at
all," as the speed with which their mates got over anger, much
more frequently than did the married. This tendency of the
divorced to give the mate a low rating is shown in the following excerpt from the life-history document of a divorced
woman: [71]

[71] Case no. 338.

"He was awful 'bout my friends and the same way about the kids, grouchy as an old bear, and the older he got the worse he got. He wouldn't let the girls have any girl friends, let alone having boys around. He was so grouchy when he was around the house, he got on my nerves right smart. When he once got a grouchy spell on, it took him a long time to get over it.

Ratings of mate on speed of getting over anger by persons whose marital-adjustment scores were in the more and the less adjusted groups, although not different for either married men or women, did differentiate between the more and the less adjusted divorced men and divorced women. A larger per cent of the more adjusted divorced men rated their mates in the upper three categories,[72] and a larger per cent of the less-adjusted in the lower two categories.[73] A larger per cent of more adjusted divorced women rated their mates as "markedly" quick in getting over anger,[74] and the less-adjusted more frequently reported "a little" *and* "not at all." [75]

The above indicates that one who is relatively quick in getting over anger is a better matrimonial risk than one who is relatively slow. The rapidity with which one gets over anger is an index of the speed with which certain problems or difficulties of marriage will be solved. Not only may anger itself create marital difficulties, but in so far as anger is associated with any marital difficulty, slowness in getting over it constitutes an obstacle in bringing about the solution of the problem, or in achieving reconciliation.

SUMMARY

The summary of this chapter will be included in that of the next chapter. Here, two general conclusions will be presented: First, marital adjustment appears to be associated with direc-

[72] Per cents: 75.6 and 55.5, CR 2.8.
[73] Per cents: 44.5 and 24.4, CR 2.8.
[74] Per cents: 32.0 and 12.5, CR 3.3.
[75] Per cents: 52.5 and 28.0, CR 3.4.

torial ability, as measured by the ratings of happily married and divorced persons on self and on mate, with reference to acceptance of responsibility, strictness in dealing with children, leadership, ability to make decisions readily, determination, and not being easily influenced by others. Second, marital adjustment is associated with adaptability, as measured by "giving in" in arguments, not being dominating, slowness in getting angry, and quickness in getting over anger.

This association between a general tendency of adaptability and marital adjustment is similar to one of the general conclusions of Terman and Oden.[76] They found a correlation between the marital adjustment of a sample of 567 of Terman's "genius" couples and ratings on general adjustment given by field workers. Husbands rated as satisfactory in general adjustment had a mean marital-adjustment score significantly higher than those who were judged to be somewhat or seriously maladjusted.[77] Burgess and Wallin suggest that the successful adjustment in marriage of some of their couples who got low adjustment scores in engagement may have been due to a general personality pattern of adaptability of one or both members of these couples.[78] On the basis of the conclusions of other studies and the findings of the present study it appears that one's adjustment in marriage is determined, in part, by a general personality pattern of adaptability.

[76] Lewis M. Terman and Melita H. Oden, *The Gifted Child Grows Up: Twenty-five Years' Follow-up of a Superior Group,* Stanford, Stanford University Press, 1947, pp. 246, 262–63.

[77] *Ibid.,* p. 246. CR 2.3.

[78] Ernest W. Burgess and Paul Wallin, *op. cit.* See chap. on "Adaptability."

10

PERSONALITY TRAITS (II)

AFFECTIONATENESS and sociability are two general types of behavior which are valued highly in a husband or in a wife. This is the general conclusion of the present chapter, which continues the analysis of specific personality traits.

AFFECTIONATENESS

Affection is defined as an inner feeling of warm regard or settled good will toward a person. It is a disposition to love, to be fond of, or to be strongly attached to a person. While it exists with or without its observable demonstration, there is the expectation that not only will spouses and family members be affectionate toward one another, but that they will demonstrate to some extent this affection. In general, persons are inclined to be affectionate toward those with whom they are intimately associated; also, they desire an expression of affection toward themselves. Two personality traits—affection and demonstration of affection—are discussed below.

The lack of affection and the failure to demonstrate affection are described in the following excerpt from the case history of a divorced woman, who in the questionnaire rated herself as "somewhat" affectionate and demonstrative, while rating her former husband as "a little" affectionate and "not at all" demonstrative: [1]

[1] Case no. 24.

"In my first marriage, we got along pretty well for the first three or four years. However, we quit being affectionate toward each other. I would go up to him and try to love him, but he would push me away; so I quit it. As far as sex was concerned, he may have been dissatisfied. I think I was too cold, and then he would be grouchy. It got so that I would talk to him, and he would not say a word. He just acted like he did not hear me.

"The final thing which led to my leaving him was that he slapped me in public. We had been with some friends to a tavern, and he had drunk a little too much. I shook him a little and tried to get him to come home with me. Some of his friends kidded him and told him he was a hen-pecked husband. So he got up and came over to where I was and slapped me on each ear. He was sorry afterwards, but I left him anyway."

Presence of Affection. The presence or lack of affection is associated with the presence or lack of marital adjustment.[2] Well adjusted persons think of their mates as "considerably" or "markedly" affectionate, while those experiencing marital maladjustment tend to think of their mates as "a little" or "not at all" affectionate.

On *self-ratings* the general pattern was for the happily-married and the more-adjusted to have a higher per cent who rated themselves in the upper categories of affection, and for the divorced and less-adjusted to be in the lower categories. Table 37 shows that happily married and divorced men and women did not differ on the selected level of significance, that is, with a critical ratio of 2.0. However, the self-rating of "markedly" *and* "considerably" by men was almost statistically significant.

In the comparison of the more- and less-adjusted, only divorced men differed significantly: the more-adjusted rated themselves as "somewhat" *and* "considerably" affectionate,[3]

[2] Significant chi squares: self-ratings of more and less adjusted divorced men, 9.9; ratings of mate by married and divorced men, 42.9; by women, 39.9; ratings of mate by more and less adjusted divorced men, 19.4; by married women, 7.5, 3 degrees of freedom.
[3] Per cents: 75.3 and 55.4, CR 2.7.

and the less-adjusted had a larger per cent in "a little" *and* "not at all" affectionate.[4]

TABLE 37

Affectionateness: Per Cent of Happily-Married and Divorced, with Critical Ratios of the Difference of Per Cents

	Men			Women		
	Married N = 152	Divorced N = 140	CR	Married N = 150	Divorced N = 171	CR
Ratings on Self						
Markedly	37.5	27.1	1.9	42.0	33.9	
Considerably	36.2	36.4		30.0	39.2	
Somewhat	23.0	28.6		21.3	17.0	
A little	2.6	6.5		6.7	8.1	
Not at all	0.7	1.4		0.0	1.8	
	100.0	100.0		100.0	100.0	
Ratings on Mate						
Markedly	40.0	18.7	4.0	42.7	19.9	4.4
Considerably	39.3	25.9	2.4	34.7	31.3	
Somewhat	14.7	27.3	2.6	18.0	21.1	
A little	5.3	18.7	3.5	4.6	19.3	4.0
Not at all	0.7	9.4	3.5	0.0	8.4	3.6
	100.0	100.0		100.0	100.0	

The table shows that happily married and more adjusted persons *rated their mates* as much more affectionate than did the divorced and the less-adjusted. The rating of "markedly" affectionate was given mates by about 4 in 10 married men and women as compared with about 2 in 10 divorced men and women. "Considerably" affectionate was given by a larger per cent of married than divorced men. A larger per cent of divorced than married men was in each of the three lowest ratings, "somewhat," "a little," and "not at all"; for women this was true for only the two lowest ratings. When the two lowest

4 Per cents: 14.2 and 3.7, CR 2.4.

ratings were combined, the excess of divorced over married was very great for both men and women.

Ratings of mates by the more- and by the less-adjusted were significantly different only for married women and for divorced men. A larger per cent of married women with higher scores rated their mates as "markedly" *and* "considerably" affectionate,[5] while those with lower scores more frequently gave ratings of "somewhat." [6] Divorced men with higher adjustment scores tended to rate their mates as "markedly" *and* "considerably" affectionate,[7] while those with lower scores had a larger per cent who rated mates as "a little" *and* "not at all" affectionate.[8]

In American culture, affectionate behavior is supposed to be associated with happiness in marriage. When a marriage is adjusted, it is likely that the spouses will not only be affectionate, but will judge each other generously, while the reverse may be true for the maladjusted. So the actual extent of affection of the adjusted and the maladjusted may be more or less than the ratings of the mate indicate. Nevertheless, the rating one gives the mate on affection is a predictive item in marital adjustment.

Demonstration of Affection. Demonstration of affection, particularly the value a person places on its expression in his mate, is significantly related to marital adjustment.[9] The evidence gives a rather consistent picture of happily married and more adjusted men and women satisfying their mate's desire for demonstration of affection to a greater extent than the divorced and less-adjusted.

Table 38 shows that on *self-ratings* a larger per cent of married than divorced men checked themselves in one of the

[5] Per cents: 83.2 and 64.0, CR 2.7.
[6] Per cents: 30.0 and 13.4, CR 2.6.
[7] Per cents: 56.8 and 37.3, CR 2.6.
[8] Per cents: 41.8 and 16.0, CR 3.7; "not at all," 20.9 and 1.2, CR 4.0.
[9] Significant chi squares: ratings of mate by married and divorced men, 12.3; rating of mate by more and less adjusted divorced men, 12.2.

upper three categories, "markedly," "considerably," *and* "somewhat." It is interesting to note that a larger per cent of divorced than married women rated themselves in the upper two categories.

TABLE 38

Demonstrativeness: Per Cent of Happily-Married and Divorced, with Critical Ratios of the Differences of Per Cents

| | Ratings on Self | | | | | |
| | Men | | | Women | | |
	Married N = 152	Divorced N = 138	CR	Married N = 151	Divorced N = 168	CR
Markedly	23.7	22.5 ⎫		17.9	27.4 ⎫	
Considerably	24.4	20.3 ⎬ 2.1		21.2	25.6 ⎭	2.5
Somewhat	26.3	20.3 ⎭		23.8	17.3	
A little	13.8	18.1		23.8	19.0	
Not at all	11.8	18.8		13.3	10.7	
	100.0	100.0		100.0	100.0	

	Ratings on Mate					
Markedly	22.9	24.1		18.2	15.2	
Considerably	25.5	22.6		23.7	20.6	
Somewhat	28.1	14.6	2.8	25.0	16.3	1.9
A little	15.7	22.6		20.3	30.9 ⎫	
Not at all	7.8	16.1	2.2	12.8	17.0 ⎭	2.7
	100.0	100.0		100.0	100.0	

Divorced men and women with lower adjustment scores had a larger per cent who rated themselves as "markedly" *and* "considerably" demonstrative than those with higher adjustment scores, the difference being statistically significant, however, only in the case of men.[10]

On *ratings of mate,* a larger per cent of married men and women than divorced reported "somewhat"; a larger per cent

[10] Per cents: 50.0 and 38.8, CR 2.1.

of divorced than married men "not at all"; and a larger per cent of divorced than married women "not at all" *and* "a little." However, the dividing point was the upper three categories for the married as against the lower two for the divorced.

In comparing the ratings of mate by the more- and by the less-adjusted, differences were found for divorced men and for divorced women. The more adjusted divorced men rated their mates as "considerably" *and* "somewhat" demonstrative more often than did the less-adjusted,[11] who rated their mates as being "a little" *and* "not at all" demonstrative.[12] Divorced women with higher adjustment scores rated their mates "considerably" *and* "markedly" demonstrative more frequently than those with lower scores,[13] who in turn rated their mates more frequently as "not at all" demonstrative.[14]

The importance of demonstration of affection for marital adjustment is suggested by a comparison of the men and women of the divorced and of the married samples. In the divorced group, women were more demonstrative than men, as measured by both self-ratings and by ratings of mate, though the size of the difference was just below the selected level of significance.[15] In the married group there were no statistically significant differences, although "markedly" *and* "considerably" demonstrative was given by a larger per cent of men than women, and men rated their mates more demonstrative than women rated themselves.[16]

Thus, future research may show that women in maladjusted marriages are more demonstrative than men, and that the lack of demonstration of affection by men is one of the factors associated with maladjusted marriages. Among the happily-married, men may be more demonstrative than women and

11 Per cents: 43.8 and 25.0, CR 2.6; "somewhat," 18.8 and 8.0, CR 2.6.
12 Per cents: 49.9 and 30.0, CR 2.5; "not at all," 23.9 and 7.5, CR 2.9.
13 Per cents: 40.8 and 25.9, CR 2.2.
14 Per cents: 22.5 and 10.5, CR 2.1.
15 Per cents on self-ratings of "markedly" *and* "considerably": 53.0 and 42.8, CR only 1.8; on judgments by mate, 46.7 and 35.8, CR only 1.9.
16 Per cents on self-ratings: 48.0 and 39.1, CR only 1.6; on ratings by mate, 48.4 and 41.9, CR only 1.1.

may be more generous in thinking that their mates are demonstrative.

SOCIABILITY

Sociability is the disposition to unite with others for companionship. It is the inclination toward conviviality, fellowship, or association with others, and is the opposite of seclusiveness and social isolation. The four personality traits which are used as indices of sociability are: being sociable in that one makes friends easily, likes belonging to organizations, cares what people say and think, and having a sense of humor. Happily married and divorced men and women gave themselves and their mates ratings on these traits, as they did for the other personality traits.

Making Friends Easily. A high degree of sociability is associated with marital adjustment, and a low degree of marital maladjustment.[17] This is shown in the next chapter in the analysis of the number of friends that happily married and divorced persons had before marriage, after marriage, and in common during marriage. The personality trait of being sociable also differentiated between the happily-married and the divorced. In the informal statements made in the interviews, the divorced often complained about the unsociable nature of their mates. This is illustrated in the following excerpt from the case of a divorced husband: [18]

"I always liked a nice home. My mother was a wonderful housekeeper and homemaker. She was a teacher, and so was my father, and I was used to a good home in which friends were always welcome. My wife never kept a nice place at all. She wasn't a good cook, did not like to clean things up, and did not take good care of the children, although all she had to do was to keep house. She just wasn't a homemaker. I'm sociable and like people. I was never

17 Significant chi squares: ratings of mate by married and divorced men, 17.9; by women, 20.8; ratings of mate by more and by less adjusted divorced men, 22.8; by divorced women, 12.2.

18 Case no. 814.

free to bring people home or to have my friends there when I wanted to. She might not say anything, but she showed she didn't want anyone around, and made it very uncomfortable when any of them came. I was very dissatisfied with the way she did."

Table 39 shows that *self-judgments* on being sociable were not very discriminating between the married and the divorced. This was also true for the more- and less-adjusted.

T A B L E   3 9

Sociability—Makes Friends Easily: Per Cent of Happily-Married and Divorced, with Critical Ratios of the Difference of Per Cents

	Ratings on Self					
	Men			Women		
	Married N = 158	Divorced N = 141	CR	Married N = 156	Divorced N = 176	CR
Markedly	42.4	38.3		39.1	34.1	
Considerably	27.8	40.4	2.3	30.8	39.8	
Somewhat	20.9	15.6		19.2	19.3	
A little	6.4	5.0		9.0	6.2	
Not at all	2.5	0.7		1.9	0.6	
	100.0	100.0		100.0	100.0	
	Ratings on Mate					
Markedly	42.6	27.0	2.8	49.0	27.6	4.0
Considerably	34.8	29.9		30.7	30.6	
Somewhat	16.1	24.1		13.1	21.8	2.1
A little	5.2	11.7	2.0	5.9	14.1	2.4
Not at all	1.3	7.3	2.6	1.3	5.9	2.2
	100.0	100.0		100.0	100.0	

There was only one significant difference between married and divorced: a larger per cent of divorced than married men rated themselves as "considerably" sociable. Divorced men and women with higher adjustment scores, as compared with those with lower scores, had a larger per cent who reported themselves as "somewhat" sociable.[19]

Happily married men and women *rated their mates* as "markedly" sociable to a much greater extent than did the divorced. Significantly larger per cents of divorced than married men and women gave ratings in each of the two lowest categories. If "somewhat," "a little," *and* "not at all," are combined into a single category, there is no question that divorced men and women gave this rating of sociability to their mates more frequently than did the married.[20]

Ratings of mate by the more-adjusted, as compared with the less-adjusted, were different for married men, divorced men, and divorced women. In all three the pattern was the same: the more-adjusted rated their mates as significantly more sociable than did the less-adjusted. The categories in which there was a significantly larger per cent of the more-adjusted than of the less-adjusted were, for married men, "markedly" *and* "considerably," [21] and for divorced men and women, "markedly," "considerably," *and* "somewhat." [22]

The data on self-ratings and rating of mate support the conclusion that sociability, or ease in making friends, is an important factor in marital adjustment and that an unsociable person, as judged by the mate, is a poor risk in marriage. The fact that ratings of mate on sociability discriminated between the happily-married and the divorced and between the more- and less-adjusted seems to mean that a person places a high value on sociability in a spouse. It also probably means that persons faced with marital difficulties tend to find defects in

19 Per cents for men: 17.5 and 7.7, CR 2.0. For women: 25.9 and 14.6, CR 2.0; "considerably" *and* "somewhat" also significant, 67.9 and 52.0, CR 2.3.

20 For men, CR 3.7; "a little" *and* "not at all" also significant, CR 3.3. For women, CR 4.2; "a little" *and* "not at all" also significant, CR 3.3.

21 Per cents: 81.3 and 64.7, CR 2.3.

22 Per cents for men: 93.7 and 65.1, CR 4.5. For women: 88.6 and 69.0, CR 3.2. While this means that less adjusted divorced men and women rated their mates more frequently as "a little" *and* "not at all" sociable, a significantly larger per cent of the less-adjusted was in both "a little" and "not at all"; for men, "a little," 17.4 and 6.3, CR 2.2; "not at all," 17.4 and 0.0, CR 3.9; for women, "a little," 22.8 and 10.1, CR 2.3; "not at all," 8.1 and 1.3, CR 2.1.

the mate, such as a lack of sociability, on which to blame the marital difficulties.

Enjoyment in Belonging to Organizations. Marital adjustment has been found to be associated with sociability, as measured by the ease with which one makes friends. Enjoyment in belonging to organizations is another index of sociability. The degree to which one likes to belong to organizations is related to the degree of marital adjustment.[23]

Table 40 shows that neither married nor divorced *rated their interest* in belonging to organizations very high—only a third or less rating it as "markedly" *and* "considerably." However, a significantly larger per cent of married than divorced women rated themselves as "somewhat" interested, whereas a larger per cent of divorced than married women rated themselves as "not at all" interested in belonging to organizations.

The comparison of the more- and less-adjusted on self-ratings revealed differences for divorced men. The more-adjusted rated themselves as "somewhat" *and* "a little" interested more frequently than did the less-adjusted,[24] who more often rated themselves as "markedly" *and* "considerably" interested.[25]

Table 40 shows that both married men and women gave significantly higher ratings *on their mates'* interest in belonging to organizations than did divorced men and women. In the category "not at all," the per cent of divorced men was larger than that of the married, and when "a little" was combined with "not at all," the difference became even more pronounced. Thus, a larger per cent of married than divorced men were in the upper three categories. For women, about half of the divorced, as compared with about a quarter of the married, said their mates were "not at all" interested in or-

[23] Significant chi squares: self-ratings by married and divorced women, 9.4; ratings of mate by married and divorced men, 11.7; by women, 15.1.
[24] Per cents: 48.7 and 31.5, CR 2.3.
[25] Per cents: 45.7 and 29.5, CR 2.2.

TABLE 40

Likes Belonging to Organizations: Per Cent of Happily-Married and Divorced, with Critical Ratios of the Difference of Per Cents

	Men			Women		
	Married N = 157	Divorced N = 139	CR	Married N = 151	Divorced N = 171	CR
	Ratings on Self					
Markedly	17.2	16.5		13.3	9.4	
Considerably	16.6	18.7		13.9	18.1	
Somewhat	20.4	25.2		24.5	14.6	2.2
A little	21.0	18.7		24.5	22.8	
Not at all	24.8	20.9		23.8	35.1	2.2
	100.0	100.0		100.0	100.0	
	Ratings on Mate					
Markedly	13.2	8.7		10.7	6.8 ⎱	2.2
Considerably	15.8	15.8		15.3	9.3 ⎰	
Somewhat	25.7	12.9	2.8	18.7	15.4 ⎱	2.0
A little	17.7	21.6		29.3	21.6 ⎰	
Not at all	27.6	41.0	2.4	26.0	46.9	3.8
	100.0	100.0		100.0	100.0	

ganizations. The per cent of married was larger than the divorced in the combined category of "markedly" *and* "considerably" and also in the combined category of "somewhat" *and* "a little."

On ratings of mate by the more- and by the less-adjusted, differences were found for married women and divorced men, with the latter having by far the greater differences. The one difference for married women was that a larger per cent of the less- than of the more-adjusted rated their mates as "a little" interested in organizations.[26] For divorced men, the statement that their mate was "not at all" interested in belonging to organizations was given by about half of the less-

[26] Per cents: 40.0 and 24.4, CR 2.0.

adjusted and by about a third of the more-adjusted.[27] By contrast, a larger per cent of the more-adjusted rated their mates as "considerably," "somewhat," *and* "a little" interested in organizations.[28]

These results further support the conclusion that sociability is an important factor in marital adjustment. Moreover, belonging to an organization is an index of conventionality,[29] for, on the whole, organizations not only tend to attract persons whose behavior is conventional, but they put pressure on such persons to continue following the mores of the community. This is particularly true of a small community, like that from which the subjects of the present study were drawn. Also it is particularly true of certain organizations, such as the church, which was the primary organization to which these people belonged, if they were connected with any organiza tion.

Cares What People Say and Think. Marital adjustment is associated with sensitivity to what people say and think about one's behavior.[30]

Table 41 shows that, on *self-ratings,* the pattern of response of men and of women was very similar. A larger per cent of married than divorced men and women indicated that they cared "somewhat" *and* "a little" about what people say and think. Divorced persons tended to rate themselves either at the top or at the bottom of the rating scale.

Self-ratings of persons with higher adjustment scores were significantly different from those with lower scores in three of the four groups: happily married men, divorced men, and divorced women. Less adjusted married men rated themselves as caring "considerably" what people say and think more fre-

[27] Per cents: 53.8 and 35.5, CR 2.4.
[28] Per cents: 54.4 and 35.2, CR 2.5; "somewhat," 17.7 and 6.6, CR 2.2; "somewhat" *and* "a little," 39.2 and 22.0, CR 2.4.
[29] See p. 237.
[30] Significant chi squares: ratings of mate by married and divorced women, 24.2.

quently than did the more-adjusted.[31] More adjusted divorced men rated themselves "somewhat," [32] and more adjusted divorced women rated themselves "considerably" [33] more frequently than did the less-adjusted.

TABLE 41

Cares What People Say and Think: Per Cent of Happily-Married and Divorced, with Critical Ratios of the Difference of Per Cents

	Ratings on Self					
	Men			Women		
	Married $N = 156$	Divorced $N = 142$	CR	Married $N = 157$	Divorced $N = 174$	CR
Markedly	14.7	22.5		29.3	30.5	
Considerably	21.8	21.1		22.3	29.9	
Somewhat	21.2	15.5 ⎫	2.0	19.7	13.8 ⎫	2.4
A little	15.4	10.6 ⎭		14.0	8.0 ⎭	
Not at all	26.9	30.3		14.7	17.8	
	100.0	100.0		100.0	100.0	

	Ratings on Mate					
Markedly	21.9	23.9		13.1	10.4	
Considerably	23.9	23.9		20.2	9.7	2.6
Somewhat	23.2	12.3	2.4	25.5	12.2	3.0
A little	12.3	15.3		15.7	23.2	
Not at all	18.7	24.6		25.5	44.5	3.5
	100.0	100.0		100.0	100.0	

On *ratings of mate,* sensitivity to what people say and think appears to be a more important value for women than for men. For men there was but one category in which the married and divorced differed significantly: a larger per cent of married rated their mates as caring "somewhat" about what people say and think. However, for women there were three

[31] Per cents: 31.4 and 15.7, CR 2.4.
[32] Per cents: 19.5 and 8.9, CR 2.0.
[33] Per cents: 39.2 and 25.2, CR 2.1.

categories in which the married and divorced differed significantly in ratings of their mates: a larger per cent of married
than divorced rated their mates "considerably" and also
"somewhat," while a larger per cent of divorced judged their
mates as "not at all" sensitive to what people say and think.
The dividing point between married and divorced women
was the upper three categories as against the lower two: ratings of "markedly," "considerably," *and* "somewhat" were
given by about 6 in 10 married to 3 in 10 divorced.[34]

A comparison of the more- and less-adjusted on ratings of
their mates indicated that three of the four groups differed
significantly: happily married men, divorced men, and divorced women. A larger per cent of more adjusted than of less
adjusted married men rated their mates as caring "a little"
and "not at all" what people say and think,[35] with the less-
adjusted having a larger per cent in the upper three categories.
More adjusted divorced men rated their mates "somewhat"
and "a little," [36] and more adjusted divorced women rated
their mates "considerably" *and* "somewhat" [37] more frequently than did the less-adjusted.

The above analysis of the questionnaire data does not show
a clear-cut relationship between marital adjustment and caring about what people say and think. On the whole, it appears
that the happily-married and the more-adjusted cared somewhat, but not too much, about the opinions of others, whereas
the divorced and the less-adjusted either did not care at all or
cared considerably.

The life-history materials secured in the informal interviews, however, revealed that there probably was an association between marital adjustment and community opinion and
pressure. These life-history documents show that sensitivity
to the thoughts and statements about oneself by parents, brothers and sisters, members of one's church, superiors in the in-

[34] CR 4.7.
[35] Per cents: 35.5 and 19.6, CR 2.1.
[36] Per cents: 38.3 and 18.0, CR 3.0; "somewhat," 19.8 and 9.0, CR 2.0.
[37] Per cents: 28.6 and 16.8, CR 2.0.

dustrial and business world, and others, was a potent factor in social control. In the small-city and rural environment in which the subjects of this study resided, the verbal statements and opinions of others often were important values to husbands and wives. This is shown in the responses of a happily married wife to questions on this item: [38]

When asked if she cared what people say and think, she replied, "Of course I do, don't you?" When asked if her mother cared about the opinions of others, she said, "I should say she did! That's the way she raised us, by what people would say. She always said, 'Them that lies down with dogs expects to get up with fleas.'" Later she came back to this question of her own accord: "You can't tell me there is anyone who doesn't care what people say about her. Wouldn't you rather have people say, 'There goes one of the nicest girls in town,' than to have them say, 'There goes a very bad girl'"?

The importance of extrafamilial attachments on family unity is illustrated by an incident in an interview which the author had with a happily married couple. A neighbor dropped in to see the couple, and on being briefly informed as to the reason for the interviewer's presence, "preached" a short sermon to the interviewer, to Sister Mary, and to Brother Ben: [39]

"Brother, belief in Jesus Christ and God the Father makes for happiness in home life. Isn't that right, Sister Mary? Now, if one is saved, happiness floods the home, and he just doesn't think of separating if a little sin comes into the life of the other. Now Brother Ben, here, used to sin a lot, used to drink quite a lot, but through Sister Mary's prayers and the prayers of our people at the church, he has been saved from his sin. Also, in our church we just don't believe in divorce. If God is in the house, people will get along all right."

The following is a part of the interpretation of the case, written by the author after the interview:

[38] Case no. 185.
[39] Case no. 100.

This case resembles others interviewed in that many happily married couples are highly religious as contrasted with the divorced group. Three factors appear to be involved: (1) Religion is an indication of conventional and conforming behavior. (2) It is significant that the friends of this couple were religious and that their religion is opposed to divorce. Consequently, the pressure and support of a circle of religious friends with their expectations that families will stay together, determined, in part, the unity of this family. (3) In many of these families in which religion is significant, the members engaged in praying together and reading the Bible together, and these serve as common activities, which psychologically unite the husband and wife. One of the functions of religion in these homes is to cause the couple to reinforce each other religiously and thereby create conforming attitudes with reference to the maintenance of the family.

The above analysis tends to emphasize the interdependence of factors associated with marital adjustment. Sensitivity to what people say and think is just one of these factors.

Sense of Humor. Adjustment in marriage is associated with a sense of humor in oneself and in one's mate, while maladjustment is associated with little or no sense of humor.[40] A sense of humor can sometimes be inferred from the actions of the family. For example, the author made the following record of the situation of an interview with a happily married couple in which a sense of humor in the parents was inferred from the behavior of the children: [41]

When we arrived we found that the husband was visiting his sister on an adjoining farm. So my assistant interviewed the wife while I played with their three children. The children were all exceptionally fine children. They were able to adjust well to each other and to me, a stranger. They had a good sense of humor and did

[40] Significant chi squares: self-ratings of married and divorced men, 8.9, with 3 degrees of freedom; ratings of mate by married and divorced men, 41.5; by women, 43.4; ratings of mate by the upper and lower half of divorced men, 15.5; by married women, 15.2.

[41] Case no. 113.

not quarrel among themselves, but tended to joke with one another. This is a reflection of the relationship within the home.

Examination of the answers on "sense of humor" in the questionnaire showed that the husband of the above case marked both himself and his wife as having to a "considerable" degree a sense of humor, while the wife marked herself "considerable" and her husband "markedly."

The husband of another happily married couple, when asked if he had any criticism or disillusionment about his marriage, replied: [42]

"I have none. Well, if I *must* say something, I will just have to say this: my wife doesn't bake enough pies. I can eat a pie in a single meal. I like them hot with butter on. Tell my wife that she baked six last week and that still wasn't enough." This was all said in a good-natured and good-humored way, and apparently was his way of praising her pies.

The evidence on sense of humor as presented in Table 42 shows that on *self-judgments,* married and divorced men differed significantly, but women did not. A larger per cent of married than divorced men thought of themselves as having a very good sense of humor, as indicated by the response "markedly." When the three lowest categories—"somewhat," "a little," *and* "not at all,"—were combined into a single category, significantly more divorced than married men rated themselves in this category. There were no significant differences in self-ratings of persons with higher and lower adjustment scores.

A person's *rating of his mate* on sense of humor, as is indicated in Table 42, is a much more effective means of distinguishing between the adjusted and the maladjusted in marriage than is one's self-rating. The proportion who rated this personality trait as "markedly" present in their spouses was, for married men, about 4 in 10 to 1 in 10 for the divorced, and,

[42] Case no. 22.

for married women, about 5 in 10 to 2 in 10 for the divorced. Divorced men and women rated their spouses as almost or entirely devoid of a sense of humor much more frequently than did the married.

TABLE 42

Sense of Humor: Per Cent of Happily-Married and Divorced, with Critical Ratios of the Difference of Per Cents

| | Ratings on Self | | | | | |
| | Men | | | Women | | |
	Married $N = 153$	Divorced $N = 139$	CR	Married $N = 152$	Divorced $N = 171$	CR
Markedly	45.8	32.4	2.3	36.2	28.1	
Considerably	36.6	38.1		36.2	40.9	
Somewhat	13.7	20.1		20.4	19.9	
A little	3.2	7.3	2.4	5.9	7.6	
Not at all	0.7	2.1		1.3	3.5	
	100.0	100.0		100.0	100.0	
	Ratings on Mate					
Markedly	39.1	13.2	4.9	47.3	21.2	4.9
Considerably	35.1	33.1		32.0	31.5	
Somewhat	20.5	25.7		16.0	18.8	
A little	4.6	22.8	4.6	4.0	15.8	3.5
Not at all	0.7	5.2	2.3	0.7	12.7	4.2
	100.0	100.0		100.0	100.0	

Mate-ratings on sense of humor, besides separating the happily-married and the divorced, also differentiated between the more- and the less-adjusted in three of the four groups, the exception being married men. Married women, with higher adjustment scores, more frequently rated their mates as "markedly," [43] whereas those with lower scores had a larger per

[43] Per cents: 55.5 and 32.0, CR 2.8.

cent in "somewhat," "a little," *and* "not at all." [44] The more adjusted divorced women had a larger per cent who rated their mates as possessing a sense of humor "markedly" *and* "considerably." [45] The more adjusted divorced men had a larger per cent who reported "considerably" *and* "markedly," [46] while the less-adjusted had a larger per cent who rated their mates as not having a sense of humor at all.[47]

Here again, happily married persons were inclined to see in their mates those qualities which are evaluated highly in the culture. Inasmuch as a good sense of humor is one of these, married persons credited their mates with a great sense of humor, while divorced persons were inclined to give an unfavorable description of their mates by reporting that they had little or no sense of humor.

Higher ratings of their mates by married than by divorced persons may be interpreted in at least three ways: First, the happily-married actually had a greater sense of humor than the divorced, and this in itself was important for marital adjustment. Second, although this trait in itself may not have been important for marital adjustment, it might have been indicative of significant underlying attitudes which were important. Third, the relationship between a sense of humor and marital adjustment might mean that certain situations which would be sources of irritation between the maladjusted would simply be considered humorous by adjusted spouses.

COMPARISON OF SELF- AND MATE-RATINGS

The hypothesis formulated at the beginning of the study was that happily married men and women would have a higher degree of agreement in their self- and mate-ratings than

[44] Per cents: "somewhat," 28.0 and 10.9, CR 2.8; "somewhat," "a little," *and* "not at all," 38.0 and 13.4, CR 3.6.
[45] Per cents: 62.3 and 45.7, CR 2.3.
[46] Per cents: "considerably," 43.0 and 25.3, CR 2.4; "markedly" *and* "considerably," 56.9 and 34.5, CR 2.9.
[47] Per cents: 13.8 and 1.3, CR 3.0.

would divorced men and women. This hypothesis proved to be correct, as measured by chi squares.

For happily married men there were no significant differences between ratings of self and of mate for any of the 16 personality traits; for happily married women there was only one. Even on this personality trait—cares what people say and think—the difference between self- and mate-ratings was much smaller than in the case of divorced women.[48] People expect women to be more concerned than men with what people say and think, and apparently both married and divorced women met this expectation.

On ratings of self and of mate, divorced men varied in 11 of the personality traits and divorced women varied in 14. In all cases the divorced rated themselves in a more favorable light than they did their mates. Divorced persons tended to place their mates in lower categories than themselves on personality traits culturally defined as desirable, such as assuming responsibility readily, having a sense of humor, being sociable, getting over anger quickly, being affectionate, and yielding in arguments.[49] On traits defined by the culture as undesirable, divorced persons tended to rate their mates in higher categories than themselves. This was particularly true for being easily influenced by others, getting angry easily, and dominating.[50]

Ratings on personality traits given their mates by the happily-married and the divorced probably were determined by three components: the mate's actual type of behavior, the person's affection or bitterness toward the mate, and the values of the person doing the rating. The data seem to indicate that the second and third component were particularly important. The close agreement between self- and mate-ratings of

[48] Chi square for married, 15.2; for divorced, 65.8. The per cents of married women rating self and mate in the upper categories were, respectively, 51.6 and 33.3, and for divorced, 60.4 and 20.1.

[49] Respective chi squares for men: 49.8, 25.3, 19.0, 13.2, 21.2, and 26.7. For women: 113.2, 17.2, 16.5, 27.2, 23.3, and 55.7.

[50] Respective chi squares for men: 39.2, 27.3, and 18.8. For women, 72.5, 41.4, and 29.8.

the happily-married probably indicates similarity of values, affection, and the unity of the spouses. The divergence of self- and mate-ratings by divorced persons probably indicates a lack of unity, bitterness toward the mate, and possibly a difference of values. It also indicates a desire on the part of the divorced to justify themselves as far as the divorce was concerned by making the behavior of the mate responsible for it.

PERSONALITY TRAITS OF PARENTS

Happily married and divorced persons not only rated themselves and their mates on the 16 personality traits, but also rated their fathers and mothers. A detailed analysis of these ratings will be found in Appendix 2. Here, only a summary statement will be given. Married and divorced men differed significantly in the ratings they gave their fathers on 9 of the traits and women on 8. In ratings of their mothers, happily married and divorced men differed in 10 of the traits and women in only 3. In general, the differences in ratings of parents were in the same direction as the differences in self-ratings and ratings of mate. Thus, to some extent, marital adjustment can be predicted from the ratings persons give their parents.

SUMMARY

The above conclusions from the self-ratings and ratings of mate on personality traits apply to the comparison of a happily married and a divorced group, to the comparison of the more and the less adjusted happily married men, happily married women, divorced men, and divorced women, and to the population from which the cases were drawn. While this should be emphasized, the conclusions will be extended to the general population in the following tentative statement: Marital adjustment is positively associated with certain personality traits, namely, the ready assumption of responsibility, strictness in dealing with children, leadership in the community, quickness in making decisions, expressions of determination, resistance to influence of relatives or friends, yielding in arguments quickly, not being dominating, slowness in getting angry, quickness in getting over anger, tendencies toward sociability, enjoyment in belonging to organizations, moderate concern with what people say and think, a sense of humor, affectionateness, and demonstration of affection. In more general terms, a person is a good marital risk if he is characterized by directorial ability, adaptability, affectionateness, and sociability.

Ratings of mate were more discriminating between happily married and divorced men and women than were self-ratings. This seems to indicate that divorced persons rated themselves in the direction of culturally acceptable behavior, thus decreasing the difference between them and the happily-married. On ratings of the mate, the happily-married tended to be generous, whereas the divorced tended to report that their mates were engaging in culturally unacceptable behavior. This tendency of the happily-married to rate their mates up, and of the divorced to rate their mates down, increased the difference between happily-married and divorced on mate-ratings.

The great difference between the ratings of self and of mate on the part of divorced persons probably indicates that the ratings do not give an actual picture of the personality traits of the persons concerned. If a divorced person rated himself as "getting angry easily," it might mean that the person had the feeling that "something must have been wrong with me, or the marriage would have lasted." On the other hand, the rating of the mate in culturally unacceptable categories may have been due to the accumulated bitterness of unsatisfying marriage relationships with the consequent blaming of the other for the difficulties of the marriage. The hypothesis of this interpretation is that fundamental tensions between a couple are symbolized in complaints against the spouse in a quite different area of behavior from that in which the original irritations arose.

Regardless of the meaning of the responses, the main conclusion from the viewpoint of prediction is that the responses about the personality traits of self and mate discriminated between the happily married and divorced men and women and between the more and the less adjusted happily married men, happily married women, divorced men, and divorced women. Consequently, these traits function as predictive items in forecasting marital adjustment.

11

GENERAL PERSONALITY PATTERNS

THE PRECEDING two chapters classified 16 specific personality traits under four general patterns of behavior—directorial ability, adaptability, affectionateness, and sociability—and dealt with these in terms of subjective ratings on a fivefold scale. The present chapter considers two general personality patterns—sociability and conventionality—and uses objective behavioral indices as measures of their relative presence or absence. Four indices of sociability were used in the previous chapter: making friends easily, enjoyment in belonging to organizations, being concerned with what people say and think, and having a sense of humor. In this chapter sociability is measured by the number of friends one had before marriage, after marriage, and in common during marriage. Conventionality is measured by the social acceptability of the place where the marriage was contracted, and by certain religious behavior. The general hypothesis was that highly sociable and conventional persons would be more prevalent in the happily married than in the divorced sample.

SOCIABILITY

Conclusions of Other Studies. Burgess and Cottrell used the number of friends before marriage as one index of a "social type" of personality. They found that the extent of friendship with both sexes is associated with marital adjustment.[1] A hus-

[1] Ernest W. Burgess and Leonard S. Cottrell, *Predicting Success or Failure in Marriage*, New York, Prentice-Hall, 1939, pp. 128–32, 395–97.

band with a few men friends and almost no women friends before marriage had the poorest chances of marital success, while
those with several or many men and women friends were in
the "good" adjustment group. A wife who had almost no men
or women friends before marriage was a "poor" matrimonial
risk, while those having many women friends and a few, several, or many men friends were in the "good" adjustment
group.

Kirkpatrick found that an excess or deficiency of women
friends on the part of the husband was unfavorable to marital
adjustment.[2]

Terman and Oden analyzed 567 of Terman "genius"
couples in terms of marital-adjustment scores secured in 1940.
They found that husbands who had rated low in 1922 in sociability, as measured by play interests, got a mean marital-
adjustment score which was significantly lower than husbands
who rated higher in sociability; wives of the low and high
sociability groups did not differ in their average marital-
adjustment scores.[3]

The evidence of our study supports the conclusion that sociability, as measured by the possession of friends before marriage, after marriage, and in common with the spouse during
marriage, is a positive factor in marital adjustment, and the
absence of sociability, as measured by the relative lack of
friends, is a negative factor. Happily married and divorced
persons gave ratings on the number of friends of themselves
and of their mates on a fourfold scale: almost none, a few,
several, and many.

Friends before Marriage. A sociable woman, as measured
by the number of both women and men friends, is a good marital risk. About 1 in 4 divorced women as compared to 1 in 7

2 Clifford Kirkpatrick, "Factors in Marital Adjustment," *American Journal of Sociology*, XLIII, 1937, p. 282.

3 Lewis M. Terman and Malita H. Oden, *The Gifted Child Grows Up: Twenty-five Years' Follow-up of a Superior Group*, Stanford, Stanford University Press, 1947, p. 246. CR 2.2.

married women reported "almost no" *and* "a few" women friends.[4] This, of course, means that more happily-married than divorced reported "several" *and* "many" women friends. Likewise, "almost no" men friends were reported more frequently by divorced than by married women,[5] with happily-married more frequently reporting "several" men friends before marriage.[6]

Marital adjustment was also associated with the judgment of the husband that the wife was a sociable person before marriage. Divorced men more frequently than married stated that their wives had "few" women friends before marriage, the ratio being 1 in 4 divorced to 1 in 10 married.[7] "Several" *and* "many" women friends of wives were reported by 9 in 10 happily married husbands as compared with 7 in 10 divorced.[8] Also, a larger per cent of happily married than divorced men reported their wives as having "several" *and* "many" men friends, though the difference was just below our level of significance.[9]

Sociability of a husband before marriage is not as essential to marital adjustment as is sociability of a wife. The number of a man's men friends, judged either by him or by his wife, was not at all related to marital adjustment. However, significant differences were found on the number of women friends, as judged by the wife. If a wife said her husband had "several" women friends before marriage, it was very favorable for marital adjustment.[10] On the other hand, if a wife indicated that her husband had "many" women friends before marriage, it was a very unfavorable factor.[11] This may mean that wives differentiated between sociability and promiscuity, identifying

[4] Per cents: 26.0 and 15.5, CR 2.1.
[5] Per cents: 19.6 and 7.9, CR 2.8.
[6] Per cents: 39.0 and 25.8, CR 2.3.
[7] Per cents: 25.3 and 11.9, CR 2.6.
[8] Per cents: 87.4 and 72.0, CR 2.9.
[9] Per cents: 61.8 and 48.6, CR only 1.9.
[10] Per cents: 50.0 and 29.5, CR 3.2.
[11] Per cents: 33.7 and 17.3, CR 3.0.

"several" women friends before marriage with sociability and "many" with promiscuity.

Friends after Marriage. The number of friends after marriage is even more highly associated with marital adjustment than the number before marriage. Wives who had sociable personalities, as measured by either their own or their husbands' judgments that they had "several" *and* "many" women friends, were good marital risks. The rating of the wife's women friends in the combined category of "several" *and* "many" was given about 9 in 10 married to 6 in 10 divorced wives and also husbands.[12] Happily married husbands were more generous in rating the number of the wife's women friends than were happily married wives in rating themselves: 52.6 per cent of the wives reported "several," while 49.7 per cent of husbands reported "many." Both of these per cents were significantly higher than the per cents of divorced wives rating themselves and of divorced husbands rating their wives.[13] Wives who were near the bottom of the sociability scale, as measured by their having "almost no" women friends as reported by themselves and by their husbands, were very likely to be in the divorced rather than in the happily married group.[14] Even if wives or their husbands reported the wife as having "a few" women friends, it was unfavorable for marital adjustment.[15]

What is the relationship between the number of male friends of the wife during marriage and her marital adjustment? The statement of the wife that she had "almost no" male friends was decidedly unfavorable to marital adjustment,[16] and it was somewhat unfavorable if the husband gave

12 Per cents for wives: 85.9 and 64.4, CR 5.1. For husbands: 89.0 and 61.1, CR 5.1.

13 Per cents for wives on "several": 52.6 and 34.7, CR 2.9. For husbands on "many": 49.7 and 26.0, CR 3.5.

14 Per cents for wives: 10.9 and 1.2, CR 3.6. For husbands: 10.4 and 0.6, CR 3.7.

15 Per cents for wives: 24.8 and 12.9, CR 2.5. For husbands: 28.6 and 10.4, CR 3.6.

16 Per cents: 41.4 and 16.0, CR 4.6.

this statement about the wife.[17] On the other hand, a higher per cent of happily married than divorced women reported "several" male friends,[18] and a decidedly greater per cent of married than divorced women reported "several" *and* "many" male friends: 56.2 as against 31.3.[19] Also, more of the happily married than of the divorced men reported that the wife had "many" male friends.[20] The discriminating value of this item, judgment by the husband of the number of the wife's male friends, was not increased materially by combining "several" and "many" into a single category.[21]

The number of friends of the husband during marriage is not as important for marital adjustment as is the number of friends of the wife. However, some differences for men were found. A somewhat larger per cent of divorced than of happily married women reported that their husbands had "a few" men friends,[22] and also "almost none." [23] A decidedly larger per cent of divorced than of married men's self-judgments, and also of wives' judgments of their mates, were in the combined category of "almost none" *and* "a few." [24] Of course, this means that a much larger per cent of happily married than divorced men and women reported the men friends of the husband as "several" *and* "many." [25]

The number of women friends of the husband, as given by him, is a fair index of the degree of marital adjustment. The husband who reported "almost no" women friends had the poorest chances for marital adjustment.[26] A larger per cent of happily married than divorced men gave ratings on women friends in the combined category of "several" *and* "many,"

17 Per cents: 17.6 and 8.6, CR 2.0.
18 Per cents: 34.6 and 19.2, CR 2.7.
19 CR 3.9.
20 Per cents: 32.7 and 18.9, CR 2.2.
21 Per cents: 64.2 and 47.3, CR 2.4.
22 Per cents: 21.2 and 8.6, CR 2.9.
23 Per cents: 6.1 and 1.3, CR 2.2.
24 Per cents for men: 26.0 and 12.8, CR 3.2. For women: 27.3 and 9.9, CR 3.7.
25 Per cents for men: 87.2 and 74.1, CR 3.2. For women: 90.1 and 72.7, CR 3.7.
26 Per cents: 19.5 and 9.5, CR 2.2.

though the difference was just below our level of significance.[27] There were no differences between the reports of married and divorced women on women friends of the husband during marriage.

Friends in Common during Marriage. Part of the differences between the happily-married and divorced in their report of the number of friends during marriage was due to the larger number of men and women friends that the happily married couples had in common. This was the impression received in the interviews, and evidence of this was secured from answers to the question on the number of common friends of husband and wife during marriage.

The number of friends a husband and wife have in common is highly associated with marital adjustment, particularly for women. A wife who reported that she had "almost no" friends in common with her husband was much more likely to be in the divorced than in the happily married group,[28] and, if she reported only "a few" friends in common with her husband, there was a fair probability that she would be in the divorced rather than in the married group.[29] Also, a larger per cent of divorced than married husbands reported "almost no" friends in common with the wife,[30] or reported only "a few." [31] In the combined category of "almost none" *and* "a few," there was a decidedly larger per cent of divorced men and women than happily-married.[32]

A wife who said that she had "many" friends in common with her husband appears to have placed a high value on sociability, and this was unquestionably associated with marital adjustment.[33] The same was true for husbands.[34] When "several"

[27] Per cents: 63.9 and 51.9, CR 1.8.
[28] Per cents: 11.9 and 0.0, CR 4.6.
[29] Per cents: 32.7 and 19.5, CR 2.4.
[30] Per cents: 7.8 and 1.2, CR 2.7.
[31] Per cents: 31.2 and 14.5, CR 3.1.
[32] Per cents for men: 39.0 and 15.7, CR 4.1. For women: 44.6 and 19.5, CR 4.6.
[33] Per cents: 39.1 and 23.8, CR 2.6.
[34] Per cents: 41.3 and 26.0, CR 2.3.

and "many" were combined into a single category, it became a very distinguishing predictive item for forecasting marital adjustment: respectively, 84.3 and 61.1 per cent of married and divorced men [35] and 80.5 and 54.5 per cent of married and divorced women reported this degree of friends in common during marriage.[36] This means, of course, that "a few" *and* "almost no" friends in common during marriage is associated with marital maladjustment.

The following excerpt from the life-history document of a divorced man illustrates the fact that, even though one is a sociable person, chances of success in marriage are reduced unless the husband and wife have mutual friends: [37]

"We got along quite well, and I enjoyed married life. In fact I think I will marry the girl I am now going with. The main trouble with my marriage was that my wife resented the amount of time I spent with my friends. These were boyhood chums. I used to play basketball and go out evenings with them. She always wanted to do something else. She did not want me to hang around with them. They were perfectly fine fellows, and I resented this attempt on her part to keep me away from them. One quarrel gradually led to another, and we finally separated. Her in-laws kept interfering, too, since she had been a little spoiled when she was a child. They took her side. Later on, when she had a child by another man, and we went through with the divorce, her folks agreed that I was in the right."

From the differences between happily married and divorced men and women on the number of friends before marriage, after marriage, and in common during marriage, it appears that the sociable person, as measured by the possession of "several" or "many" friends, is a good marital risk, and that the unsociable person, as measured by the possession of "almost no" or "a few" friends, is a poor marital risk. Also, the report of

[35] CR 4.1.
[36] CR 4.6.
[37] Case no. 689.

"several" *and* "many" mutual friends of the husband and wife increased the likelihood of adjustment in marriage.

CONVENTIONALITY

The analysis of our data shows that conventionality is a very significant predictive item for forecasting marital adjustment. It was measured by considering the place where the marriage was contracted, affiliation with a church, age when attendance at Sunday school was terminated, and regularity of church attendance. What are the findings of other studies on these and related items?

Conclusions of Other Studies. Terman secured ratings on the type of religious training on a fivefold scale: very strict, strict, considerable, little, and none. He decided not to include this item in his marital-prediction scale and indicated that it had little or no correlation with marital happiness. In fact, he says that, if religious training ever was a factor in marital happiness, it appears no longer to exert such an influence.[38] Yet his data showed that certain types of religious training and the degree of marital happiness were associated on our level of significance, that is, there would be only 5 chances or less in 100 that the differences would be due to chance. Men reporting "considerable" religious training had significantly higher happiness scores than those reporting "little" *and* "none." [39] A comparison of those with high and those with low happiness scores revealed that (1) men reporting "considerable" religious training had a significantly larger per cent in the high group; [40] (2) men reporting "little" *and* "none" had a significantly larger per cent in the low group; [41] (3) women reporting "very strict" had a significantly higher per cent in the low

[38] Lewis M. Terman, *et al., Psychological Factors in Marital Happiness,* New York, McGraw-Hill, 1938, pp. 264, 369–70. See pp. 230–31 for data on CRs.

[39] CR 2.1.

[40] CR 2.0.

[41] CR 2.0.

happiness group; [42] and (4) women reporting "strict" *and* "considerable" had a significantly larger per cent in the high group. [43]

Burgess and Cottrell present Sunday school and church attendance, where the marriage took place, and type of official performing the ceremony as some of the indices of a certain "social type" of personality. They report that all of these items showed a positive relationship with marital adjustment. [44] Both husbands and wives who never went to Sunday school or stopped going after they were 10 years of age had a markedly lower per cent of successful marriages, as measured by adjustment scores, and a higher per cent of unsuccessful marriages, than those who went until they were 19 years of age or older. Husbands who, before marriage, never attended church were the poorest matrimonial risks, and those who attended two, three, or four times a month were the best. Wives who never attended church before marriage were the poorest risks, and those who attended four or more times a month were the best. Those married in a church or parsonage were better matrimonial risks than those married at home or elsewhere. Persons married by a minister, priest, or rabbi were decidedly more successful than those married by a civil servant, which in most cases would be a justice of the peace.

Burgess and Cottrell feel that these items probably are not in and of themselves significant for marital adjustment, but rather reveal sentiments and attitudes which are the underlying important factors. Our thesis is that they reveal a general conventional pattern of behavior.

In the present study, some of the items used as measures of conventionality are also indices of sociability. The social contacts of many persons in the population from which the samples were drawn were restricted almost exclusively to Sunday school and church attendance.

[42] CR 2.2.
[43] CR 2.7.
[44] *Op. cit.,* pp. 122–26, 392–94.

Place of Marriage. The question on this item probably should have been divided into two parts: who performed the ceremony, and where the couple was married. While it was phrased as follows, it actually gave the two kinds of information:

Where married: at home _____; at church _____; by judge _____; at minister's home _____; by justice of the peace _____; elsewhere _____.

Being married by a justice of the peace is not preferred in our culture and is unquestionably associated with maladjustment in marriage. Table 43 shows that more than 1 in 4 divorced men and women were married by a justice of the peace as compared with 1 in 8 happily married men and women.[45]

TABLE 43

Per Cent of Happily-Married and Divorced Married in a Given Place or by a Given Person

Person or Place	Men		Women	
	Married N = 173	Divorced N = 161	Married N = 171	Divorced N = 183
At home	27.7	15.5	29.2	14.8
At church	12.7	9.3	11.1	8.2
By judge	1.2	2.6	1.2	0.5
At minister's home . . .	38.7	39.1	40.4	46.5
By justice of peace . . .	13.3	29.2	11.7	27.3
Elsewhere	6.4	4.3	6.4	2.7
	100.0	100.0	100.0	100.0

Marriage at home, at church, or at a minister's home is preferred and is associated with marital success: the respective per cents of happily-married and divorced who reported one of these places were for men 79.1 and 63.9, and for women 80.7 and 69.5.[46]

[45] CR for men: 3.6. For women: 3.7.
[46] CR for men: 3.1. For women: 2.4.

Attendance at Sunday School. The later the age at which attendance at Sunday school is terminated, the greater the chances of marital success. Table 44 gives the per cents of married and divorced men and women for given ages at which they stopped going to Sunday school. It will be observed that about the same per cents of happily-married and divorced reported that they either never went or had stopped at the age of 10 or under. Beginning with the age period 11–14, there was a larger per cent of divorced than happily-married who reported they had stopped going to Sunday school. From a positive viewpoint, the per cents of happily married and divorced men who were attending at the time of *and* during marriage were, respectively, 43.6 and 18.4,[47] and for married and divorced women, 56.3 and 35.9.[48]

T A B L E 44

Per Cent of Happily-Married and Divorced Who Attended Sunday School at Given Ages

Age When Attended	Men		Women	
	Married N = 163	Divorced N = 157	Married N = 165	Divorced N = 181
Never went	11.7	7.6	3.0	5.5
Stopped at 10 years and under	4.9	10.8	2.4	3.3
Stopped at 11–14 years	10.4	22.3	11.5	17.7
Stopped at 15–18 years	18.4	26.8	19.4	29.3
Stopped at 19–25 years	11.0	14.0	7.3	8.3
Attended at time of marriage	12.3	2.6	12.7	14.9
Attended during marriage	31.3	15.9	43.7	21.0
	100.0	100.0	100.0	100.0

Affiliation with a Church. Being a member of a church is probably a mark of a conventional, sociable person, and is highly associated with marital adjustment. Not belonging to a church is a highly predictive item for marital maladjustment.

[47] CR for attendance at the time of marriage, 3.3; for during marriage, 3.2.
[48] CR for during marriage, 3.8.

Divorced men and women as compared with married not only belonged to a church much less frequently at the time of marriage, but continued to be unaffiliated with a church. The per cents of divorced and married men who did not belong to a church at marriage were, respectively, 42.2 and 17.7,[49] and at the time of interviewing, 41.0 and 21.8.[50] For women, the per cents of divorced and married unaffiliated at marriage were, respectively, 20.0 and 5.3,[51] and at the time of interviewing, 25.9 and 13.3.[52]

Data on affiliation with a church were also analyzed in terms of the differential proportion of married and divorced couples in the following four categories: one spouse was a member of a church and the other not a member, both were not members of a church, spouses were members of different churches, and both were members of the same church. A decidedly larger per cent of divorced men and women than married reported that one mate belonged to a church and the other did not,[53] or that both were not church members.[54] A larger per cent, though not statistically significant, of divorced than married reported belonging to different churches.[55] On the other hand, about 6 in 10 married to 3 in 10 divorced reported that the husband and wife belonged to the same church.[56]

Frequency of Church Attendance. Frequent attendance at church is positively correlated with the probability of marital adjustment. Tables 45 and 46 give the per cent of married and divorced men and women for given frequencies of attending church during the first and during the last half of marriage and the critical ratios of the difference of per cents. They show that the happily-married attended church much more fre-

[49] CR 3.5.
[50] CR 3.8.
[51] CR 3.3.
[52] CR 3.0.
[53] Per cents for men: 23.7 and 13.5, CR 2.3. For women: 26.2 and 15.8, CR 2.4.
[54] Per cents for men: 26.3 and 11.7, CR 3.3. For women: 23.0 and 12.1, CR 2.7.
[55] Per cents for men: 21.2 and 16.0. For women: 20.8 and 14.5.
[56] Per cents for men: 58.9 and 28.8, CR 5.4. For women: 57.8 and 30.1, CR 5.2.

quently than did the divorced. They also show that the significance of church attendance for both men and women was at the extremes: "never going to church" was without question associated with marital maladjustment, and "going four or more times a month" was unquestionably associated with marital adjustment.

TABLE 45

Regularity of Church Attendance of the Happily-Married and Divorced during the First Half of Marriage, by Per Cent, with Critical Ratios of the Difference of Per Cents

Monthly Attendance	Men			Women		
	Married N = 165	Divorced N = 162	CR	Married N = 167	Divorced N = 186	CR
None	17.6	34.0	3.4	12.0	30.1	4.1
Once or less	28.5	35.1		30.5	27.9	
2 or 3 times	23.0	12.3	2.5	13.8	13.4	
4 or more times	30.9	18.6	2.6	43.7	28.6	3.0
	100.0	100.0		100.0	100.0	

TABLE 46

Regularity of Church Attendance of the Happily-Married and Divorced during Last Half of Marriage, by Per Cent, with Critical Ratios of the Difference of Per Cents

Monthly Attendance	Men			Women		
	Married N = 163	Divorced N = 160	CR	Married N = 166	Divorced N = 182	CR
None	18.4	46.9	5.5	12.7	37.9	5.4
Once or less	28.2	28.1		29.5	27.4	
2 or 3 times	19.6	14.3		16.2	15.5	
4 or more times	33.8	10.7	5.0	41.6	19.2	4.6
	100.0	100.0		100.0	100.0	

The tables show that not only was "never going to church" for both men and women a highly negative factor in marital adjustment, and "going frequently" a highly positive factor, but that, whereas married men and women reported about the same frequency of attendance for the first and the last half of marriage, divorced men and women reported a decline in frequency in the last half of marriage.

The importance given to religion and church attendance by happily married couples is shown in the following short excerpts from the life-history documents of happily married cases. The first is simply a statement on frequency of church attendance and on the church as a common interest: [57]

"We always go to church together. A while ago we went at least twice on Sunday and to prayer-meeting during the week. We're not going as much as we used to."

The next case shows the value attached to religion by a couple who had been married 47 years and had become so interdependent and so well adjusted to each other that they behaved almost identically with reference to all situations: [58]

"Now, if you carry one thing away from this home, I want you to carry this. To be happy, a man and wife has to love each other and they have to be saved and practice the Christian life. These two things are the most important things in making a success in marriage."

The scheme of values of a happily married couple is indicated by the following list of things which they gave as necessary for the success of a marriage: [59]

1. Have a religion and live up to it. If a man and wife really live their religion and read their Bible, they will not let troubles bother them, and will get along. We do not believe in divorce,

[57] Case no. 150.
[58] Case no. 7.
[59] Case no. 90.

for our religion is against it. Moreover, we do not even think of it, for we get along so well.

2. The man or woman should not try to be the whole boss. They should work things out together.

3. Keep away from dance halls and beer joints; they will break up a home faster than anything else. If one goes to dance halls, the wife or husband may think that the other is dancing too much or too close to someone. If one goes to a beer joint, a person may get tight and be too fresh with another person.

4. A woman should keep the house clean and have the meals ready when the husband comes home from work.

5. A man should come in from work happy and stay home with the wife and not go running around.

The above list, which was given by this particular happily married couple, could be duplicated by excerpts from many other case histories. They are conventional values and emphasize the point that the factors discussed in this section, such as where the marriage took place, age at which attendance at Sunday school was terminated, affiliation with a church, regularity of church attendance, and the like, are not in and of themselves important for marital success. Our interpretation is that they are indices of basic tendencies of conventionality, sociability, and stability.

SUMMARY

Sociability, as measured by the number of friends, and conventionality, as measured by religious practices, are positively associated with marital adjustment. The positive associations of specific items and marital adjustment are summarized as follows, and in all cases the associations apply to the reports of both men and women unless otherwise indicated:

1. The wife having several or many men and women friends before marriage.

2. The husband having several, but not many, women friends before marriage, as judged by the wife.

3. Having several or many men and women friends after marriage.

4. Having several or many men and women friends in common during marriage.

5. Not being married by a justice of the peace.

6. Being married at home, at church, or at a minister's home.

7. Attending Sunday school at the time of marriage and during marriage.

8. Being a member of a church at the time of marriage and during marriage.

9. Going to church four or more times a month.

12

THE COMPANIONSHIP FAMILY

Persons entering marriage for the first time, as well as those who have been previously married, hope to find a companion in the mate. Companionship involves intimacy, sympathetic understanding, common interests, mutual respect on the basis of equality, and democratic relationships.[1] Some persons find their wish satisfied; some adjust to the absence of companionship because the marriage may satisfy other cherished values; others maintain formal family relationships and secure companionship on the outside; still others separate themselves from the situation in which their wish for companionship is not being satisfied.

The companionship family has been presented by some writers as the ideal toward which families should strive for happiness in marriage.[2] However, little or no evidence has been presented by previous studies to support the hypothesis that a high degree of companionship within the family is associated with a high degree of marital adjustment, and a low degree of companionship with marital maladjustment.

The present study included several items in the questionnaire which in a general way are related to the association between the companionship family and marital adjustment, and the informal interviews which accompanied the filling out of

[1] For a discussion of the companionship family see Ernest W. Burgess and Harvey J. Locke, *The Family: From Institution to Companionship*, New York, American Book Co., 1950, especially pp. 437, 518.
[2] Paul H. Landis, *Your Marriage and Family Living*, New York, McGraw-Hill, 1946, pp. 329–30.

the questionnaires gave additional information. It is not suggested that the following discussion provides an adequate test of the hypothesis that the companionship family is correlated with marital adjustment. It does present, however, some evidence to support the hypothesis, and it emphasizes the advisability of making a systematic study in order to test further the conclusion that companionship relations are conducive to adjustment in marriage.

INTIMACY OF COMMUNICATION

Intimate, friendly, and prolonged communication between a husband and a wife tends to weld them together, whereas a decided decline in this type of communication tends to break up existing attachments. This conclusion was supported, in part, by items in the questionnaire, but was supported to a much greater extent by the case materials secured in the interviews.

Presence of Face-to-face Communication. Communication in face-to-face association was present in almost all of the happily married homes, but was not infrequently absent in the homes of couples who later became divorced. In the interviews it was found that happily married couples communicated with each other by glances and inflections which had a particular meaning to them, and that communication was as much by tone of voice and manner of speaking as by the words which were spoken. The unity existing between a husband and wife was shown in the tendency of each spouse to reaffirm what the other said, the taking over and completing of a sentence which the other had begun without the feeling on the part of either that there had been an interruption, and the tendency to talk about the activities of the self, of the mate, or of the family in terms of "we" rather than "I."

The following remarks by a happily married woman, about talking intimately with her son and husband, illustrate the type of communication which existed between the members of a large proportion of happily married couples: [3]

"Two years ago my son got syphilis, and I did not know it until this fall. I asked him why he had not told me, and he said he was afraid we would turn him out. I told him, 'I am the same mother I was before it happened, and you are my son. Whatever you do, you are still my son.' That was such a load off his mind, and it seems that I can talk to him now the way I used to. I told my husband when you came the other day that I wanted to tell you about this, and yet I didn't want to. For you are the only one that I have ever talked to about it. I didn't want to tell you in front of my husband, but we both agreed that I should talk to you about it."

Loss of Unity through Decline in Communication. A decided reduction of intimate communication between a husband and wife generally results in a decrease in family unity. This does not mean, of course, simply a decline in the number of words spoken, for a glance or a caress may convey more meaning than a large number of words. It refers primarily to less face-to-face communication, resulting from the husband and wife having different work schedules or living away from each other. Under such conditions, it is extremely difficult to maintain companionship relations and relatively easy for misunderstandings to develop. Continuous communication is apparently necessary for the maintenance of emotional attachments.

In the first of the two following excerpts from divorced cases, the husband and wife both worked and had different schedules: [4]

"The real difficulty in our marriage was that I worked as a telephone operator from 2:30 to 10:00 P. M., while my husband worked from 8:00 A. M. to 5:00 P. M. He generally had gone to work by the time I woke up, and was asleep when I got home from work. We had a great deal in common during the first of our

[3] Case no. 14.
[4] Case no. 602.

marriage. We both felt that our marriage was extremely happy, and that our personalities fit together. But, little by little, we lost contact with each other. I felt a little disturbed when we finally separated, but not much. I did not want the divorce, even though he had been paying attention to other women. I felt that if we stayed together, we could get back to the intimacy which had been present at first."

The second case is of a husband and wife who had a long period of separation during the early months of marriage: [5]

Wife. "You know, you do not have all the questions in this questionnaire. The most important one in our case is left out. We were separated for the first months of our marriage. I think that was where I made my mistake. I should have gone along with him, when he had to go to another city. Another thing in our marriage was selfishness; he was always trying to do things for his own advancement without much thought of me."

Husband. "The main difficulty in our marriage was that my wife got to be an habitual drunkard. She worked at a place where the owner drank, and insisted on all his assistants also drinking.

"I have a lot of ambition, and she never seemed interested in my future. She thought it was foolish to spend so much time in my work and making contacts. I want to increase my economic and social standing, but she would be satisfied with a little home and what we are now making.

"I had to be away from home almost as soon as we were married. I was away about 14 months during the first year and a half. I would come back once in a while, but my work kept me in another place.

"I never was much of a man to work at making the family go. I thought that marriage would work out all right if we just went along. I guess I made a mistake, for if I had worked at it, it might have gone better."

Sympathetic Understanding. Sympathetic understanding means the ability to share the feelings, activities, and values

[5] Case no. 841.

of another to such an extent that one reacts to these from the viewpoint of the other. This ability to play the role of the other and to react accordingly was present in a considerable proportion of the happily married couples and seems to have been almost completely absent in the divorced group. The following brief excerpts from happily maried cases show two ways in which sympathetic understanding is expressed—suffering with the suffering of a loved one, and pretending to enjoy something in order not to hurt the feelings of other members of the family: [6]

"My wife's illness is one of the dissatisfactions of our marriage. Her illness does not make me love her less. I just hate to see her in that condition."

A wife reported, "I am interested in music and my husband is also. I think we both enjoy music very much." But the husband reported, "My interest in music is not very great. I pretend to enjoy it because my wife wants me to enjoy good music."

"Yesterday was my birthday and I got a lot of things. If my wife or one of the children gives me something I do not really like, I pretend to like it, for I don't want to hurt their feelings."

The above conclusions on family unity through face-to-face communication, the loss of unity through a decline in communication, and the function of sympathetic understanding in marital adjustment, are very tentative in that they are based on impressions derived from life-history documents secured in the informal interviews. The remainder of this section on the relationship between intimacy of communication and marital adjustment is based on the statistical analysis of items in the questionnaire.

Frequency of Kissing. In American culture frequency of kissing is considered one measure of intimacy of association. In the present study, the hypothesis was that there would be

[6] Respective case numbers: 157, 64, and 203.

more intimacy of association between the happily married than between divorced spouses, as measured by the following question on frequency of kissing: [7]

Do you kiss your mate: every day _____; now and then _____; almost never _____.

A far larger per cent of happily-married than divorced kissed each other "every day." This frequently was reported by three fourths of the happily married men and women as contrasted with less than half of the divorced.[8] While the divorced had a significantly larger per cent than the married who reported "now and then," [9] they also had a decidedly larger per cent than the married in the "almost never" category. For men, kissing "almost never" was reported by 1 in 5 divorced to 1 in 20 married; [10] for women it was 1 in 5 divorced to 1 in 60 married.[11]

Thus, there is some evidence from the questionnaires that companionship was more prevalent between spouses who were adjusted in marriage than between spouses who were maladjusted. This is the interpretation in so far as the frequency of kissing is an index of intimacy of association and in so far as the latter is a component of the companionship family.

Talking Things over Together. Another question which tends to measure intimacy of association and companionship is the degree to which family members talk things over. It had the following form: [12]

[7] This question, developed first by Burgess and Cottrell, was in the marital-adjustment test. The analysis is of the total sample, excluding the forced marriages of the divorced sample. Ernest W. Burgess and Leonard S. Cottrell, *Predicting Success or Failure in Marriage,* New York, Prentice-Hall, 1939, pp. 53–54.

[8] Per cents for men: 76.2 and 43.1, CR 6.7. For women: 77.7 and 48.5, CR 6.1.

[9] Per cents for men: 35.4 and 19.5, CR 3.5. For women: 30.3 and 20.7, CR 2.2.

[10] Per cents: 21.5 and 4.3, CR 5.0.

[11] Per cents: 21.2 and 1.6, CR 6.0.

[12] This is a modification of a question used by Burgess and Cottrell: "Do you confide in your husband (wife)? almost never ____; rarely ____; in most things ____; in everything ____." *Op. cit.,* p. 53.

During marriage have you, in general, talked things over with your mate: almost never _____; now and then _____; almost always _____; always _____.

Happily married men and women talked things over together much more frequently than did the divorced. "Always" talked things over was reported by about 6 in 10 happily-married to less than 3 in 10 divorced.[13] "Almost never" talked things over was reported by about 1 per cent of happily married men and women, by about 10 per cent of divorced men, and by about 20 per cent of divorced women.[14] Combining "almost always" *and* "always" into a single category, the respective per cents of happily married and divorced men were 90.8 and 59.0,[15] and of women 96.4 and 54.8.[16]

Women tend to place a higher value on talking things over than do men. This is implied by the higher contingency correlation between the way happily married and divorced women answered the question than the contingency correlation between the men's answers.[17] Moreover, divorced women reported much more frequently than divorced men that they and their spouses "almost never" talked things over together; the respective per cents were 20.4 and 9.0.[18] This appreciation by women of talking things over between the mates is also emphasized by the significantly larger per cent of happily married women than men reporting "almost always" *and* "always": the respective per cents were 96.4 and 90.8.[19]

Thus, companionship, as measured by the frequency the husband and wife talked things over together, was much more prevalent among the happily-married than among the divorced. Of course, it should be remembered that the answers of the divorced were secured after the divorce, and that part

[13] Per cents for men: 55.6 and 25.0, CR 6.3. For women: 59.7 and 26.1, CR 7.0.
[14] Per cents for men: 1.5 and 9.0, CR 3.3. For women: 0.5 and 20.4, CR 5.3.
[15] CR 7.4.
[16] CR 9.7.
[17] For women: .47. For men: .39.
[18] CR 3.4.
[19] CR 2.3.

of their responses may have been due to the divorce situation
and not to the situation in the marriage itself.

Engaging in Outside Interests Together. The following
question, like the two preceding ones, was used in the marital-
adjustment test: [20]

Do you and your mate engage in outside interests together: all of
them _____; some of them _____; very few of them _____; none
of them _____.

It was used first by Burgess and Cottrell, and they included it
to test the hypothesis that affectionate and intimate companionship is basic to marital adjustment.[21] Their hypothesis was
supported in that the way persons answered this question was
correlated with the way they answered the marital-happiness
question.

In the present study, joint participation in all outside interests was reported by a decidedly larger per cent of happily
married than of divorced persons.[22] For the combined category of "all" *and* "some" of the activities together, the per
cents of happily-married and divorced for men were, respectively 92.8 and 67.0,[23] and for women, 91.3 and 49.2.[24] A somewhat larger per cent of divorced than happily married men,
and a decidedly larger per cent of divorced than happily married women reported that they engaged in "no" activity together.[25]

Women who are maladjusted in marriage place a higher
value on engaging in outside interests with their mates than
do maladjusted men. At least this is implied in the comparison
of the per cent of divorced women and men who reported engaging in "very few" *and* "no" outside activities together: 50.8

---

[20] See pp. 48–52. The total samples of married and divorced were used for
this question, excluding only the forced marriages of the divorced sample.
[21] *Op. cit.*, p. 52.
[22] Per cents for men: 47.2 and 23.3, CR 4.0. For women: 51.5 and 21.0, CR 5.4.
[23] CR 5.9.
[24] CR 8.5.
[25] Per cents for men: 6.8 and 2.1, CR 2.1. For women: 14.5 and 1.5, CR 4.6.

and 33.0 per cent, respectively.[26] Happily married women and men did not differ significantly in reporting "very few" *and* "no" outside activities together: 8.7 and 7.2 per cents, respectively. This possibly means that companionship, as measured by engaging in outside interests together, is valued more by women than by men, and that happily married women had had this value satisfied in their marriages, whereas divorced women had not.

The wife of the following divorced case was interested in activities outside the home to a much greater extent than the husband. Both indicated that there were serious difficulties in amusement interests, in sex relations, and in affectional expressions. The divorced wife had a great deal of affection for her husband, saying, "I would go to hell with him if he asked me to." The husband describes the different interests of himself and his first wife and the similarity of interests in his present marriage: [27]

"I was only 19 when we married, and my wife was 18. I had a job and wanted a home. Soon after marriage, I found that my wife was of a different nature than myself. She was speedy and quick, wanted to run around, whereas I was slower and liked to be at home. For instance, she wanted me to go to dances, whereas I would prefer to stay at home. I knew something about her general tendencies. I told her that if we went to dances, it might break up our home. But after a while, I consented to learn to dance. We had other difficulties, such as unsatisfying sex relations and constant bickering, but I think I would have put up with these if she hadn't gotten interested in another man. She went out with this man for a period of two years. When I found that they were having sex relations, I sued for divorce. After thinking it over, I decided it would be better for the children to have her sue for it.

"My present wife is of a different nature. She seems to like the same things I do. She has no interest in running around and she divorced her husband because he was more of a gadabout than she. We are very happy together."

26 CR 2.7.
27 Case no. 671.

EQUALITY OF HUSBAND AND WIFE

In the sections which follow references are made to the equality of the husband and the wife in the enjoyment of certain activities, and to equality in taking the lead. Here attention will be given to two items which were specifically oriented to feelings of equality. The first question was whether a husband or wife felt superior, inferior, or equal to his mate, and the second concerned the comparable intellectual ability of the husband and the wife.

Feelings of Equality toward Mate. Kelly, in his study of 76 couples who were given a marital-adjustment test and who rated themselves and their mates on 36 personality traits, found that a high degree of marital compatibility is associated with the willingness of the husband and wife to admit the superiority of the mate, or, in other words, to assume a general attitude of humbleness.[28]

The hypothesis of the present study was that the happily-married would think of themselves as neither superior nor inferior to their mates, whereas a larger per cent of divorced than of happily-married would think of themselves as superior to their mates. This hypothesis was only partly supported.

For men, although a larger per cent of happily-married than divorced checked "equal," 67.6 to 58.9, the difference was not clearly significant,[29] but to the question whether one had a "feeling of superiority over the mate," a significantly larger per cent of divorced than happily married men gave an affirmative reply.[30] This means, of course, that the happily-married, more often than the divorced, reported themselves as either equal or inferior to their mates.

For women, differences between the married and divorced

---

[28] E. Lowell Kelly, "Marital Compatibility as Related to Personality Traits of Husbands and Wives as Rated by Self and Spouse," *Journal of Social Psychology*, XIII, 1941, pp. 193–98.

[29] CR 1.6.

[30] Per cents: 35.6 and 19.7, CR 2.6.

were decidedly significant. Three fourths of the happily married women as compared to one half of the divorced reported self and mate as equal,[31] and 4 in 10 divorced to 1 in 10 married rated themselves superior to the mate.[32]

Thus, marital adjustment seems to be associated with rating oneself as equal to the mate or rating oneself inferior.

Intelligence of Self and Mate. The second question dealing with the equality of the husband and the wife was on intelligence, and was phrased as follows:

Do you think that your intelligence as compared with that of mate is: more _____; less _____; equal _____.

A significantly larger per cent of both divorced men and women than married considered themselves as more intelligent than their mates.[33] By contrast, a rating of oneself and one's mate as equal in intelligence was given by a significantly larger per cent of both happily married men and women than of divorced.[34]

Thus, marital adjustment appears to be associated with attitudes of equality between husband and wife. It will be remembered that at the beginning of the chapter equality was given as a component of the companionship family.

SHARED OR INDIVIDUAL ENJOYMENT OF ACTIVITIES

Another question on the association between companionship within the family and marital adjustment had the following specific hypotheses: mutual enjoyment of certain culturally approved activities is related to marital adjustment; mutual enjoyment of certain culturally disapproved activities is associated with marital maladjustment; and marital mal-

[31] Per cents: 75.6 and 52.6, CR 3.8.
[32] Per cents: 41.2 and 11.5, CR 5.5.
[33] Per cents for men: 28.9 and 14.2, CR 2.7. For women: 30.3 and 7.7, CR 4.9.
[34] Per cents for men: 77.5 and 60.5, CR 2.7. For women: 78.6 and 61.6, CR 3.0.

adjustment is associated with individual enjoyment of, toler-
ance of, indifference to, and open conflict over activities.

Each person was asked to indicate his feeling, and how he
thought his mate felt, on each of 12 activities by checking one
of five possible answers for himself and one for his mate:
"enjoyed very much," "enjoyed," "indifferent," "tolerated
in mate," and "open conflict." The following were the 12
activities in the order in which they were listed: reading,
playing cards, gambling, drinking, dancing, movies, parties,
church, listening to the radio, music, politics, and sports. The
answers were coded so that one could analyze whether *both* or
just one of the mates had a given feeling about an activity.

Mutual Enjoyment of Activities. Marital adjustment is associated with the mutual enjoyment of certain activities, while
maladjustment is associated with the mutual enjoyment of
others. Evidence to this effect was secured by comparing the
degree of mutual enjoyment by happily married and divorced
men and women for the various activities. Enjoyment was defined as "enjoyed" *and* "enjoyed very much."

Table 47 shows that a significantly larger per cent of both
happily married men and women than divorced reported mutual enjoyment of 5 activities: church, reading, radio, sports,
and music. In addition more married than divorced men reported mutual enjoyment of politics, and more married than
divorced women reported mutual enjoyment of parties. The
table shows that drinking and dancing were reported as mutually enjoyable by a significantly larger per cent of both divorced men and women than of the happily-married. Also,
mutual enjoyment of card playing was reported by a significantly larger per cent of divorced than of happily married
women. No significant differences were found on mutual enjoyment of gambling and movies.

The activities on which mutual enjoyment was associated
with marital adjustment were essentially either those in the
home or those which are subjected to considerable social con-

trol. By contrast, drinking and dancing, which were associated with marital maladjustment, are generally outside the home and provide situations where association and flirting with persons of the opposite sex are possible.

TABLE 47

Per Cent of Happily-Married and Divorced Reporting the Mutual Enjoyment of Given Activities, with Critical Ratios of the Difference of Per Cents

Activities	Men			Women		
	Married	Divorced	CR	Married	Divorced	CR
Church	77.2	37.8	7.2	76.6	31.4	8.3
Reading	71.3	48.1	4.3	73.1	44.9	5.2
Radio	89.2	72.4	3.9	90.4	77.6	3.2
Sports	50.3	33.3	3.1	57.5	37.8	3.5
Music	85.0	75.0	2.3	92.2	74.4	4.2
Politics	19.8	13.5	2.0	15.6	15.4	
Parties	54.5	50.6		59.9	41.0	3.4
Drinking	6.0	23.1	4.4	7.2	15.4	2.3
Dancing	26.9	37.8	2.1	24.0	39.1	2.9
Cards	39.5	39.1		38.3	51.3	2.4
Gambling	1.2	3.2		2.4	1.9	
Movies	65.9	69.2		69.5	74.4	

Individualism. Individualistic behavior, as indicated by only one spouse reporting the enjoyment of various activities, is definitely associated with marital maladjustment. In none of the 12 activities was there a larger per cent of happily-married than divorced who reported that they alone or mate alone enjoyed the activity.

For men there were 9 activities in which a significantly larger per cent of divorced than married reported that they alone enjoyed the activity: church, reading, radio, sports, music, parties, drinking, dancing, and playing cards.[35] Also,

[35] The respective per cents: 9.6 and 0.0, CR 4.1; 24.4 and 10.2, CR 3.4; 9.0 and 3.0, CR 2.3; 34.6 and 20.4, CR 2.9; 9.6 and 3.6, CR 2.2; 5.8 and 1.2, CR 2.3; 19.9 and 10.2, CR 2.4; 9.0 and 1.8, CR 2.9; 20.5 and 7.8, CR 3.3.

there were 4 activities in which a larger per cent of divorced than married men reported that mate alone enjoyed the activity: parties, drinking, dancing, and movies.[36]

For women there were 8 activities in which a significantly larger per cent of divorced than married reported they alone enjoyed the activity: church, reading, radio, sports, music, politics, dancing, and movies.[37] Also, there were 6 in which divorced more frequently than married reported that the mate alone enjoyed the activity: reading, parties, drinking, dancing, playing cards, and gambling.[38] Certain of these activities showing individualistic behavior are particularly interesting. "Going to church enjoyed by self alone" was reported by 5 in 10 divorced to 1 in 10 married, and "reading by self alone" by 4 in 10 divorced to 1 in 10 married. "Drinking enjoyed by mate alone" was reported by over 5 in 10 divorced to 1 in 10 married, and "gambling enjoyed by mate alone" by 4 in 10 divorced to 1 in 10 married.

Thus, there is empirical evidence that individualistic, behavior is associated with family disorganization. This is true even though the activity enjoyed by only one mate is culturally acceptable, such as going to church, reading, listening to the radio, or appreciating music. Granted that there are a few mutually enjoyable activities, such as drinking and dancing, which are unfavorably associated with marital adjustment, on the whole, the common or shared enjoyment of activities is highly associated with marital adjustment, and individualistic behavior is highly associated with marital maladjustment.

Toleration of Activities. Persons were asked if they tolerated the participation of the mate in the various activities listed above, or whether the mate tolerated their participation in

36 The respective per cents: 11.5 and 4.2, CR 2.5; 8.3 and 0.6, CR 3.4; 23.1 and 5.4, CR 4.6; 11.5 and 5.4, CR 2.0.

37 The respective per cents: 46.2 and 9.0, CR 7.5; 38.5 and 12.0, CR 5.5; 11.5 and 3.0, CR 3.0; 15.4 and 3.0, CR 3.9; 21.8 and 0.6, CR 6.1; 6.4 and 1.2, CR 2.5; 19.2 and 8.4, CR 2.8; 15.4 and 5.4, CR 3.5.

38 The respective per cents: 14.7 and 7.2, CR 2.2; 7.7 and 0.6, CR 3.3; 55.8 and 10.2, CR 8.8; 8.3 and 3.0, CR 2.1; 22.4 and 9.0, CR 3.3; 40.4 and 9.6, CR 6.4.

these activities. In all cases where a significant difference between the per cents of happily-married and divorced was found, the divorced had the larger per cent who showed toleration. This was true for both men and women.

A larger per cent of divorced than married men reported they tolerated the following activities by their wives: church, drinking, dancing, cards, politics, and parties.[39] The activities which men reported their wives tolerated in them were: church, reading, sports, music, and listening to the radio.[40] For women, a larger per cent of divorced than married reported they tolerated their husbands going to parties,[41] and reported husbands tolerated church and music for them.[42]

The per cents were in all cases very small. However, inasmuch as significant differences were found, the conclusion is that toleration of individualistic behavior in the mate is not conducive to marital adjustment, but is associated with marital maladjustment.

Indifference. Indifference toward the 12 activities listed was reported much more frequently by the divorced than by the happily-married. This was true particularly for indifference on the part of "self alone" or "mate alone." In no activity did a significantly larger per cent of married than divorced men or women report indifference of "self alone" or "mate alone." By contrast, a significantly larger per cent of divorced than married men reported "self alone" as indifferent toward dancing,[43] and "mate alone" as indifferent toward dancing, reading, church, cards, and parties.[44] For women, a significantly larger per cent of divorced than married reported "self

[39] The respective per cents: 2.6 and 0.0, CR 2.1; 5.8 and 0.0, CR 3.2; 6.4 and 0.6, CR 2.9; 5.8 and 0.6, CR 2.7; 3.8 and 0.0, CR 2.6; 4.5 and 0.0, CR 2.8.
[40] The respective per cents: 3.2 and 0.0, CR 2.4; 7.7 and 1.2, CR 2.9; 8.3 and 1.2, CR 3.0; 3.2 and 0.0, CR 2.4; 5.1 and 1.2, CR 2.0.
[41] Per cents: 3.2 and 0.0, CR 2.4.
[42] The respective per cents: 7.1 and 0.6, CR 3.1; 3.2 and 0.0, CR 2.4.
[43] Per cents: 18.6 and 4.8, CR 3.9.
[44] The respective per cents: 5.8 and 1.2, CR 2.3; 16.7 and 9.0, CR 2.1; 5.8 and 0.0, CR 3.2; 16.7 and 4.8, CR 3.5; 4.5 and 0.6, CR 2.3.

alone" as indifferent toward drinking, parties, reading, cards, and gambling,[45] and "mate alone" as indifferent toward church, reading, radio, music, and dancing.[46]

Indifference on the part of *both* self and mate was reported by a significantly larger per cent of happily married than divorced men on drinking, dancing, cards, and movies,[47] and by more happily married than divorced women on drinking.[48] More divorced than happily married men reported both self and mate were indifferent toward church and listening to the radio,[49] and for women, this was true for church, parties, sports, and music.[50]

Thus, it appears that not only individualistic behavior, but also indifference toward certain activities on the part of one or the other of the mates, is associated with marital maladjustment. This is true particularly for indifference toward culturally approved activities. On the other hand, indifference toward some activities, particularly those which are outside the home and those which are culturally disapproved, is associated with marital adjustment.

Conflict over Activities. Each person was also asked if there was open conflict between himself and his mate over any of the 12 activities. Conflict over drinking, reading, sports, and parties was reported by a larger per cent of divorced men;[51] conflict over drinking was reported by one fourth of the divorced and by one seventh of the married. For women, the activities where conflict was reported by a larger per cent of

45 The respective per cents: 18.6 and 4.2, CR 4.1; 5.1 and 0.6, CR 2.4; 12.2 and 6.0, CR 1.94; 14.7 and 3.6, CR 3.5; 15.4 and 3.6, CR 3.7.

46 The respective per cents: 35.3 and 7.8, CR 6.1; 28.8 and 9.0, CR 4.6; 8.3 and 3.0, CR 2.1; 14.7 and 0.6, CR 4.8; 16.7 and 6.0, CR 3.1.

47 The respective per cents: 46.1 and 30.1, CR 3.0; 45.5 and 23.7, CR 4.1; 36.5 and 23.7, CR 2.5; 16.8 and 7.1, CR 2.7.

48 Per cents: 37.1 and 25.0, CR 2.3.

49 The respective per cents: 37.8 and 10.2, CR 5.8; 8.3 and 2.4, CR 2.4.

50 The respective per cents: 28.2 and 13.2, CR 3.3; 44.9 and 24.0, CR 4.0; 32.1 and 22.2, CR 2.0; 10.3 and 4.2, CR 2.1.

51 The respective per cents: 24.4 and 15.0, CR 2.1; 3.2 and 0.0, CR 2.4; 5.1 and 0.6, CR 2.4; 6.4 and 1.8, CR 2.1.

divorced than married were: going to church, drinking, and of sports; [52] drinking as a source of conflict was reported by one half of the divorced and by one fifth of the married.

The wife in the following case gives drinking as the major difficulty in her marriage. The interpretation was written by the author at the time of the interview: [53]

Wife. "The main difficulty in our marriage was his drinking. I hate the smell of drink. It makes me sick to my stomach, and when he began to get drunk and stay drunk, I got so that I thought I could not stand it. He drank a little before we were married, but not to excess. It was after our child was born that he got to drinking more. The men around where we lived drank a good deal. After each spell, he would tell me how sorry he was and that he would never touch a drop again. But he couldn't keep his promises.

"We never separated before the divorce. He kept staying here. But we were sleeping in different rooms. I applied for the divorce in November and did not get it until May of this year. I think he thought I would not go through with it. I kept hoping that he would quit drinking. When he found I had got the divorce, he went outside and cursed so that all the neighbors could hear him. He then took his things and moved out.

"I still think a lot of him. I would do anything for him. But I don't think I would live with him again, for I would be afraid he would keep on drinking. He has not drunk for the last two months. It may be because they would fire him from his job, or it may be because of me, or because of our little girl."

Husband. "My wife's goddam family is the root of our trouble. We were married when I was 38 and she was about ten years younger. We lived by ourselves for a few years, and then one of her old uncles wanted someone to come and stay with him. Other relatives wouldn't do it, so we moved in. Just living there was bad, for there was no freedom in living with Uncle John. What was worse was that her damn father and sisters would come in and eat off us.

[52] The respective per cents: 9.6 and 0.0, CR 4.1; 47.4 and 19.8, CR 5.3; 2.6 and 0.0, CR 2.1.
[53] Case no. 890.

"Another thing was that people as old as us and with as much difference in age have more trouble in developing likes for the same things.

"She is a fine woman. In fact, today she helped me paper two rooms of my shack. She washes my clothes even though we are divorced."

Interpretation. The husband and wife agree fairly well in their answers to the questions. My impression is that she would be considered superior to him, and she so considers herself, but this was not a major point in her mind. My judgment is that they had divergent interests, that difficulty arose when they moved in with Uncle John, and also that their work schedules did not fit together. The man married for companionship and a home, and found neither during the last part of his marriage. His excessive drinking might be traced to this.

DEMOCRATIC AND INDIVIDUALISTIC BEHAVIOR

Democratic behavior has been listed as one of the components of the companionship family. The question designed to test the extent of democratic behavior was on who took the lead in different types of situations. Happily married and divorced persons were asked whether the lead was taken by the wife more than the husband, by the husband more than the wife, or by both about equally. Seven kinds of situations were listed: making family decisions, disciplining the children, handling family money, affectionate behavior, religious behavior, recreation, and meeting people.

Equality in Taking the Lead. Democratic relationships, as measured by reported equality in taking the lead, was decidedly more prevalent among happily married than divorced couples. Table 48 shows that in six of the seven items more than half of the married men and women reported that husband and wife were equal in taking the lead, whereas this was

TABLE 48

Per Cent of Happily-Married and Divorced Reporting Democratic Relationships in Given Situations, with Critical Ratios of the Difference of Per Cents

Situation	Men			Women		
	Married	Divorced	CR	Married	Divorced	CR
1. Making Family Decisions						
Own family	62.3	35.9	3.2	66.9	36.3	4.7
Your parents	28.8	40.7		31.6	31.0	
Mate's parents	30.8	27.5		25.6	11.9	2.2
2. Disciplining the Children						
Own family	55.2	40.4		58.3	22.0	4.8
Your parents	33.1	33.3		31.3	36.1	
Mate's parents	34.7	19.6	1.9	35.5	19.0	2.3
3. Handling Money						
Own family	50.9	38.1		58.1	34.8	3.7
Your parents	30.8	25.4		30.3	32.9	
Mate's parents	27.6	25.0		28.6	11.7	2.7
4. Affectionate Behavior						
Own family	59.9	41.0	2.5	59.0	33.3	3.7
Your parents	43.5	58.0		39.8	50.0	
Mate's parents	50.9	38.2		44.1	37.8	
5. Religious Behavior						
Own family	52.9	38.9		59.7	25.0	5.0
Your parents	37.9	51.9		41.7	42.5	
Mate's parents	37.9	41.3		37.2	23.9	
6. Recreation						
Own family	57.6	42.6	2.0	54.2	36.4	2.7
Your parents	33.3	60.4	3.2	42.0	43.0	
Mate's parents	37.0	38.9		32.0	29.2	
7. Meeting people						
Own family	40.4	32.3		42.6	33.7	
Your parents	35.6	41.4		30.9	35.7	
Mate's parents	38.7	33.3		32.2	25.8	

reported much less frequently by divorced men and women. In all items, less than 40 per cent of divorced women reported democratic relations, and this was true for divorced men in four of the seven items. The differences between married and divorced women were much greater than between married and divorced men.

In addition to the ratings by men and women on which one took the lead in their own families, ratings by them were secured for "own mother and father" and "mate's mother and father." Table 48 shows that happily married men and women rated democratic relationships between themselves higher than such relationships between either their own parents or the parents of the mate, with both of the latter being rated about the same. By contrast, divorced men and women tended to rate democratic relations between themselves and their mates lower than those between their own parents and higher than those between parents of mate. Thus, the tendency for the divorced was to rate their parents highest, themselves and their mates next, and their mates' parents lowest in democratic relationships.

Lead Taken by One Spouse More than the Other. As was indicated in the preceding section, individualistic behavior was decidedly more prevalent among the divorced than among the happily-married. In three of the seven items presented in Table 48, a significantly larger per cent of divorced than of married men reported that the husband took the lead: in disciplining the children, in religious behavior, and in meeting people.[54] On wives taking the lead, as judged by the men, the married and the divorced did not differ in any of the seven types of situations.

A larger per cent of divorced than of married women reported that either the husband alone or the wife alone made decisions [55] and disciplined the children.[56] In affection [57] and

[54] Per cents: discipline, 25.5 and 13.6 CR only 1.9; religion, 25.9 and 8.9, CR 3.2; meeting people, 38.7 and 25.5, CR only 1.9.

in religion,[58] a larger per cent of divorced than married women reported the wife took the lead, whereas in handling money [59] and in recreation,[60] a larger per cent of divorced than married women reported that the husband took the lead. Thus, more individualistic behavior was reported by divorced than by married persons.

Comparison of the Reports of Husbands with Those of Wives. A comparison was made of the reports of happily married men with those of happily married women, and the same was done for the divorced. It revealed that there were significant differences in two of the seven situations for both the married and the divorced.

Happily married men and women differed on which one made family decisions and on who took the lead in affectionate behavior. On the item, makes family decisions, a larger per cent of men than women reported that the husband took the lead.[61] On affectionate behavior, the husbands and wives were each inclined to think that the other took the lead. Thus, a significantly larger per cent of husbands reported that the wife took the lead than the per cent of wives who reported that they took the lead,[62] and a larger per cent of wives reported that the husband took the lead than the per cent of husbands who reported that they took the lead.[63]

Divorced men and women differed on who took the lead in disciplining the children and in religious behavior. A larger per cent of women than men reported that the wife took the lead in disciplining the children,[64] while more men than

[55] Per cents: men alone, 41.8 and 20.5, CR 3.6; women alone, 22.0 and 12.7, CR 2.0.

[56] Per cents: men alone, 20.6 and 6.7, CR 2.8; women alone, 57.4 and 35.0, CR 3.0.

[57] Per cents: 33.3 and 10.8, CR 4.3.

[58] Per cents: 71.1 and 33.1, CR 5.4.

[59] Per cents: 48.3 and 25.0, CR 3.8.

[60] Per cents: 44.3 and 31.6, CR 2.0.

[61] Per cents: 30.5 and 20.5, CR 2.1.

[62] Per cents: 20.4 and 10.8, CR 2.2.

[63] Per cents: 31.2 and 19.7, CR 2.3.

[64] Per cents: 57.4 and 34.0, CR 2.5.

women felt that this was done about equally.[65] On religion, a larger per cent of women than men reported that the wife took the lead,[66] with more men than women reporting that the husband took the lead.[67]

The above analysis emphasizes the value attached by many persons, particularly women, to democratic behavior in the family. The happily-married tended to feel that equality between husband and wife was present in their marriages, while the divorced felt that it was relatively absent.

This type of question could be used to help predict before marriage the likelihood of adjustment in marriage. Persons contemplating marriage could be asked whether they felt that the wife more than the husband, the husband more than the wife, or both husband and wife about equally should or would take the lead in different kinds of situations. Those who received democratic ratings would be given higher weights on the question than those who received individualistic ratings. This question could then be combined with other predictive items into a marital-prediction test.

SUMMARY

The present study indicates that there is an association between certain aspects of the companionship family and marital adjustment. Marital adjustment is positively associated with the following components of the companionship family:

1. Intimacy of association, as indicated by frequent kissing, by always, or almost always, talking things over, and by joint participation in all, or almost all, outside activities and interests.

2. Equality, as indicated by the judgments of husband and wife that the mates are equal, and by their rating the intelligence of the mates as equal.

65 Per cents: 40.4 and 22.0, CR 2.1.
66 Per cents: 71.1 and 35.2, CR 4.1.
67 Per cents: 25.9 and 3.9, CR 3.7.

3. Shared enjoyment of certain activities, as indicated by the husband and wife mutually enjoying culturally approved activities, especially those within the home.

4. Democratic relationships within the family, as indicated by both husband and wife taking the lead to about the same extent in making family decisions, in disciplining the children, in handling money, in affectionate behavior, in religious activities, and in recreation.

13

ECONOMIC FACTORS

IT IS commonly believed that economic factors are of primary importance in marital adjustment. At the beginning of the present study, the author was of the opinion that marital adjustment is correlated with economic security and with such economic items as the type of work done by the parents and by the person, the social status of that work, the degree of mobility entailed by the work, regularity of income, amount of income, whether or not the person had savings, and the gainful employment of the wife. Some of these views began to be questioned as the study progressed, for it was found that some persons were recommending families as happily married who were living under very unfavorable economic conditions, as judged by common sense. Interviews with some happily married couples were being held in one-, two-, or three-room "shacks" in the most deteriorated areas of the city. They had incomes which were very low, engaged in work with a status near the bottom of socially valued occupations, and had no savings.

The following excerpt from the life-history document of a happily married husband is an example of this extremely low economic level of a good many happily married couples: [1]

"There were several of us in our family. We got along all right for poor folks. I never went to school and my father and mother never went that I know of, 'cause there weren't any schools much then. My wife and I had a large family—twelve children altogether, so

[1] Case no. 154.

we haven't had much extra money. We're just poor folks—always have been. We haven't anything now—not a cent. But we get along pretty well for poor folks."

This chapter will review the findings of other studies, and then present the conclusions of the present study on the relationship between marital adjustment and occupations, economic level, employment of the husband, and employment of the wife.

CONCLUSIONS OF OTHER STUDIES

Negative Findings. Terman found no correlation between either occupational status, or income, and marital happiness, although he found that the unhappily-married were inclined to blame their troubles on insufficient income as well as on other things.[2] Bernard reported a zero correlation between marital happiness and income.[3] Kirkpatrick found no association between marital happiness and the occupational status of fathers.[4]

Positive Correlations. Evidence on a relationship between marital adjustment and (1) control by the community over the occupation, and (2) low mobility of the occupation was collected by Lang.[5] He secured the specific occupations of 17,533 men whose marital adjustment was estimated by friends and acquaintances on a five fold happiness scale: very unhappy, unhappy, average, happy, and very happy. Those occupations with high community control, such as minister, college profes-

---

[2] Lewis M. Terman, *et. al., Psychological Factors in Marital Happiness,* New York, McGraw-Hill, 1938, pp. 167–71.

[3] Jessie Bernard, "Factors in the Distribution of Success in Marriage," *American Journal of Sociology,* 1934, XL, p. 51.

[4] Clifford Kirkpatrick, "Factors in Marital Adjustment," *American Journal of Sociology,* 1937, XLIII, p. 278.

[5] Richard Lang, *The Rating of Happiness in Marriage,* unpublished M. A. thesis, University of Chicago, 1932. For a discussion of Lang's study, see Ernest W. Burgess and Leonard S. Cottrell, *Predicting Success or Failure in Marriage.* New York, Prentice-Hall, 1939, pp. 139–46.

sor, athletic coach, high school teacher, and educational ad-
ministrator were in the upper quartile of happiness ratings.
In the lowest quartile there were those whose occupations entailed considerable mobility and little community control,
such as laborer, traveling salesman, truck driver, railroad
worker, carpenter, mechanic, plumber, and real-estate salesman. However, the distribution of occupations according to
marital-happiness ratings gave no clear-cut relationship between marital adjustment and community control or lack of
mobility.

Burgess and Cottrell found that, although marital adjustment was correlated with specific economic items, the importance of the economic item was negligible when other factors
were held constant. Marital adjustment was positively associated with the following specific items: [6] (1) an occupation with
high status, (2) an occupation with little mobility and high
community control, (3) wife's gainful employment before
marriage, (4) stability as measured by regularity of employment before marriage, and (5) economic security, as measured
by a moderate monthly income coupled with some savings at
the time of marriage. However, when the factors of psycho-
genic traits, cultural impress, social type, and response patterns were held constant, the association of the economic
factor with marital adjustment decreased to practically zero.
This last finding led them to conclude that economic items
which were found to be correlated with marital adjustment
were almost entirely the effect of other variables.

TYPE OF OCCUPATION

This section considers the degree to which marital adjustment
in the present study was related to the type of occupation engaged in by the fathers of happily married and divorced persons, to the type of occupation of men and women at the time
of marriage, and to the type of occupation of men and women

[6] *Op. cit.,* pp. 136–58.

during marriage. The classification of specific jobs into the following 11 occupational types was made on the basis of the classification used by the Bureau of the Census of the United States: [7]

1. Professional and semiprofessional workers.
2. Farmers and farm managers.
3. Proprietors, managers, and officials, except farm.
4. Clerical and sales.
5. Craftsmen and foremen.
6. Operatives.
7. Domestic service.
8. Protective service.
9. Service workers, except domestic and protective.
10. Farm laborers and foremen.
11. Laborers, except farm.

Occupation of Father. There were no significant differences in the occupational classifications to which the fathers of married and divorced men and women belonged. About 40 per cent of the fathers of both the married and the divorced engaged in farming, and a little over a third engaged in semiskilled and unskilled labor. The other two most prevalent occupations were professional and semiprofessional, and proprietors of own business.

Occupations of Men at Marriage. There were no significant differences in occupations of married and divorced men at marriage. The five most prevalent occupations for married and divorced were: unskilled, skilled, clerical and sales, farming, and professional and semiprofessional.[8] These five occupations account for 86.2 per cent of married and 86.3 per cent of divorced men's occupations at marriage.

[7] Bureau of the Census, United States Department of Commerce, *Alphabetical Index of Occupations and Industries, Sixteenth Census of the United States, 1940*, Washington, United States Printing Office.

[8] The respective per cents of married and divorced for the five occupations: 32.5 and 31.5; 16.6 and 19.2; 13.9 and 13.7; 11.9 and 17.8; and 11.3 and 4.1.

Occupations of Women at Marriage. There was a significantly larger per cent of divorced than married women in the
general occupation classification of service workers excluding domestic workers.[9] This occupational category includes
waitresses, beauticians, cooks, cleaning women, and practical
nurses. A larger per cent, although not definitely significant, of
married than divorced were in professional or semiprofessional
work.[10] There were no significant differences in the other
three most prevalent occupations: clerical and sales, domestic
service, and unskilled work.[11] These five occupations account
for about 95 per cent of married and divorced women's occupational activities at the time of marriage.

Occupations of Men during Marriage. Married and divorced men's occupations during marriage were concentrated
in unskilled activities. This category included factory workers,
men working on the railroads, miners, truck drivers, and fill-,
ing-station attendants. Approximately 4 in 10 married men
and 5 in 10 divorced were in this one occupational category.[12]
Approximately 87 per cent of married and 83 per cent of divorced men were engaged in this and in the next four largest
occupational categories: skilled, professional and semiprofessional, clerical and sales, and farmers.[13]

The professional and semiprofessional occupational category included a significantly larger per cent of married than of
divorced men.[14] This, in part, was due to the operation of two
selective factors: First, those recommending happily married
persons tended to give the names of persons who were in the
public eye—ministers, doctors, and teachers; second, since
professional persons are in the public eye, there is some evi-

[9] Per cents: 21.7 and 7.8, CR 2.4.

[10] Per cents: 23.6 and 10.9, CR 1.8.

[11] Per cent of married and divorced for these three occupations: 36.3 and
43.5; 12.7 and 15.2; and 12.7 and 6.5.

[12] Per cents: 38.9 and 48.8; CR only 1.8.

[13] The respective per cents of married and divorced: 14.7 and 11.8; 14.6 and
3.9; 12.1 and 9.2; and 6.4 and 9.2.

[14] CR 3.2.

dence that social pressures restrict their marital difficulties to the family circle rather than letting them become public knowledge through divorce. Of all gainfully employed men in Indiana in 1940, the per cent engaging in professional and semiprofessional occupations was 5.2; the married sample with 14.6 per cent was overrepresented, and the divorced sample with 3.9 per cent included a slightly lower per cent than that of the general population.

Occupations of Women during Marriage. About 90 per cent of married and divorced women who worked during marriage were in five occupational categories: clerical and sales, professional and semiprofessional, unskilled, service workers except domestic, and domestic service.[15]

A significantly larger per cent of married than of divorced women were in the occupational categories of professional and semiprofessional,[16] and in clerical and sales.[17] There was a significantly larger per cent of divorced than of married women in domestic service.[18] This might be an indication that the divorced were from a lower economic level than the married. Also, it is known that a considerable period of separation precedes divorce, and during this period domestic service is one of the occupations in which women, whose educational level is that of the general population, can find employment. Moreover, happily married women probably tended to avoid domestic service, either on the wife's volition or through the suggestion of her husband. Some evidence of this is that a significantly larger per cent of married women were working in domestic service at the time of marriage than were doing so during marriage.[19]

Thus, the occupations of the happily married and divorced

15 Respective per cents of married and divorced for these five occupations: 53.0 and 37.9; 16.7 and 6.9; 12.1 and 6.9; 9.1 and 20.7; 3.0 and 23.0.
16 CR 1.9.
17 CR 2.4.
18 CR 3.0.
19 Per cents: 12.7 and 3.0, CR 2.0.

men and women were similar to those of the general population of the area in which the study was made, and with minor
exceptions the happily-married and divorced were not significantly different. The analysis of occupations has shown that
the sample of the present study is much more representative of the general population than the samples of other
studies.

ECONOMIC LEVEL

The economic level of a family is intimately related to its economic security. The general hypothesis was that the divorced
would be on a lower economic level during marriage than that
of the married and, thus, have less security. It will be recalled
that the divorced and the married were rather evenly distributed over the city and the county.[20] Therefore, if the hypothesis were supported, it would mean that, in this particular
area, economic level fluctuated independently from residence.
Economic level was measured by: the level of rent and of home
ownership, the presence or absence of life insurance, the possession or lack of savings, the presence or absence of certain utilities, the degree to which given things were owned, the extent
of borrowing on credit, the adequacy of income to meet the
needs of the family, and the efficiency of home management.

In addition to measuring the economic security of families,
the above items will again help to describe the population
from which the samples were drawn.

Rent and Home Ownership. The question on the amount
of rent and home ownership was phrased as follows:

During marriage the average rent per month was: $_____.
If you owned your home, the value of the home was: $_____.

A significantly larger per cent of divorced men and women
than of married reported that they rented, rather than owned,

[20] See map on p. 16.

their homes. The per cents who reported renting a home were as follows: [21]

Married men	61.5
Married women	66.1
Divorced men	76.8
Divorced women	82.3

Of those who rented, about two thirds of both the happily-married and the divorced reported rent of $20 a month or less as the average during marriage, and over three fourths reported $30 a month or less.[22]

Of those who owned their home, a significantly larger per cent of happily married men and women than divorced reported that the home had a value of over $2,500, which, of course, means that the divorced lived in less expensive houses. This class of homes was reported by about 6 in 10 happily-married to 4 in 10 divorced.[23]

Life Insurance. The economic level and security of a family is measured, in part, by the possession or lack of life insurance. According to this index, divorced persons had decidedly less security than the married during marriage and at the time of the interview.[24] The following was the question on insurance:

During marriage has either mate carried life insurance: yes _____; no _____. Is life insurance carried *at present:* yes _____; no _____.

A larger per cent of both divorced men and women than of married reported that the family had no life insurance during marriage, the ratio being 1 in 5 divorced to 1 in 12 married.[25] No insurance at the time of the interview also was reported by

---

[21] CR for men: 3.0. For women: 3.5.

[22] Per cents for $20 or less: men, 66.2 and 66.7; women, 70.3 and 67.6. For $30 or less: men, 81.3 and 90.5, CR 2.1; women, 86.8 and 90.3. It should be remembered that a dollar in 1940 went a lot further than a dollar today.

[23] Per cents for men: 60.5 and 41.7, CR 2.1. For women: 59.2 and 41.9, CR 1.9.

[24] For the divorced, the question was phrased "at the time of the divorce."

[25] Per cents for men: 19.5 and 7.6, CR 2.7. For women: 23.2 and 8.5, CR 3.3.

a significantly larger per cent of both divorced men and women than of married, the ratio being about 1 in 3 to 1 in 10.[26]

Savings. Information was secured on savings at the time of marriage and accumulated savings during marriage. Subjects were asked to indicate the amount of savings by checking one of four categories: none, $200 or less, $200 to $1,000, and over $1,000.

A significantly larger per cent of happily married than of divorced couples had savings at the time of marriage and accumulated savings during marriage. Joint savings at the time of marriage of $200 to $1,000 *and* over $1,000 were reported by a larger per cent of married men and women than of divorced.[27] A larger per cent of divorced than of married men and women reported no savings at the time of marriage, although the difference for men was just below significance.[28]

Accumulated savings at the time of divorce or at the time of interviewing the married couples, differed greatly between the two groups. The category "none" was checked by slightly over half of the divorced men and by about three fourths of the divorced women, as compared with about 20 per cent of the happily married men and women.[29] A greater proportion of married than of divorced men listed their savings as over $1,000,[30] and a greater proportion of married than of divorced women checked each category other than "none." [31]

A comparison of the men and women of the happily married group and the men and women of the divorced group revealed no significant differences in their statements on savings at marriage, but did reveal significant differences on accumulated savings. A larger per cent of married men than

[26] Per cents for men: 31.9 and 9.5, CR 4.2. For women: 36.8 and 10.1, CR 5.2.
[27] Per cents for men: 32.4 and 21.6, CR 2.2. For women: 25.3 and 15.6, CR 2.3.
[28] Per cents for men: 51.2 and 41.0, CR only 1.9. For women: 61.1 and 48.8, CR 2.4.
[29] Per cents for men: 55.5 and 19.6, CR 6.7. For women: 73.6 and 22.6, CR 9.4.
[30] Per cents: 46.4 and 18.5, CR 5.4.
[31] Per cents: $200 or less, 22.6 and 9.6, CR 3.3; $200 to $1,000, 20.7 and 6.2, CR 4.0; over $1,000, 34.1 and 10.7, CR 5.2.

women indicated savings of over $1,000; [32] a larger per cent of divorced men than women was in the combined category of $200 or less *and* $200 to $1,000, and also over $1,000; [33] and a larger per cent of divorced women than men reported no accumulated savings at all.[34] The fact that more savings were reported by both married and divorced men than by the women may mean that men are more accurate, or possibly that they placed a higher value on savings than did women. However, the very much larger per cent of divorced women than men who said there were no accumulated savings at the time of divorce—73.6 as against 55.5—reflected the derogatory attitudes of divorced women toward their husbands' economic efforts.

Irrespective of the above differences between the statements of men and women, it is apparent that happily married and divorced couples differed in the reported amount of savings at the time of marriage and of accumulated savings during marriage. This may mean that economic security is associated with marital adjustment.

Utilities and Other Home "Necessities." Table 49 gives the list of utilities and other home necessities included in the questionnaire and the per cent of the happily-married and the divorced who checked each of them. The question was whether they had had these items at any time during the marriage.

The table shows that almost all of the happily-married and divorced had had electric lights, about 8 in 10 had had running water in the house, and about 6 in 10 had had a house with a bathroom. The other four items were owned by the happily-married more frequently than by the divorced.

"Taking a newspaper" was reported by practically 100 per cent of the happily-married as compared with less than half of the divorced. Having a telephone was reported by about

[32] Per cents: 46.4 and 34.1, CR 2.3.
[33] Per cents: less than $200 to $1,000, 26.0 and 15.8, CR 2.3; over $1,000, 18.5 and 10.7, CR 2.0.
[34] Per cents: 73.6 and 55.5, CR 3.5.

two thirds of the happily-married and by about a fourth of the divorced. A larger per cent of happily married men and women than divorced indicated that during marriage they had had an indoor toilet and a furnace.

TABLE 49

Per Cent of Happily-Married and Divorced Who during Marriage Had Certain Utilities and Other Home "Necessities," with Critical Ratios of the Difference of Per Cents

Item	Men			Women		
	Married N = 168	Divorced N = 153	CR	Married N = 165	Divorced N = 160	CR
Furnace	58.9	47.7	2.0	61.8	47.5	2.6
Bathroom	63.1	58.8		63.0	59.4	
Indoor toilet	42.3	24.8	3.3	58.2	35.6	4.1
Running water	80.4	81.0		82.4	80.0	
Electric lights	97.0	94.1		96.4	96.9	
Telephone	66.1	24.8	7.4	69.1	27.5	7.5
Newspaper	97.6	45.8	10.4	97.6	48.1	10.1

It is interesting that a significantly larger per cent of both married and divorced women than men reported an indoor toilet.[35] This seems to indicate that women placed a higher value on modern plumbing than men did, and tended to claim having had it during marriage.

Items Owned by the Family. Table 50 lists the following eight items, and the per cents of the happily-married and divorced who reported they owned them: home, car, radio, electric refrigerator, piano, electric washer, victrola, and furniture. No differences were found between the married and the divorced on the ownership of a car, victrola, or furniture. Ownership of a car was reported by about 85 per cent of both happily married and divorced persons, and ownership of furniture by about 95 per cent of both groups.

[35] CR for married: 3.3. For divorced: 2.1.

However, on other items considered "essential" to home-making—a home, an electric refrigerator, an electric washer, and a radio—both happily married men and women reported ownership more frequently than did the divorced. On one item—a piano—happily married women, but not men, reported ownership more frequently than did the divorced.

TABLE 50

Per Cent of Happily-Married and Divorced Who during Marriage Owned Certain Things, with Critical Ratios of the Difference of Per Cents

Item	Men			Women		
	Married	Divorced	CR	Married	Divorced	CR
1. A home	60.1	41.9	3.3	60.7	38.0	4.2
2. A car	85.5	83.1		84.5	85.4	
3. A radio	93.6	73.8	4.0	95.8	74.3	5.5
4. An electric refrigerator	71.1	31.9	7.2	72.0	29.2	7.9
5. A piano	34.1	27.5		34.5	24.6	2.0
6. An electric washer	74.0	46.9	5.1	75.6	40.4	6.6
7. A victrola	38.2	40.6		41.7	35.7	
8. Furniture	98.8	95.6		97.6	91.2	

Various explanations may account for the more frequent reporting of ownership of items by the happily-married than by the divorced. The happily-married may have had more economic stability than the divorced, and this allowed them to buy more items for home-making. Another explanation is that these items may be indices of the values of the two groups, with the happily-married more frequently than the divorced preferring home ownership, an electric refrigerator with the more satisfying meals which it provides, an electric washing machine, relieving the wife of some of the hard work of keeping the family clean, and other items. A third possible explanation is that the failure of the divorced to buy items to the same extent as the married may be an index of the marital maladjustment preceding divorce. Persons experiencing marital maladjustment may hesitate to assume ownership of items for the family, if there is a chance that the family will break up.

Borrowing on Credit. Credit is almost a prerequisite to the satisfaction of some of the needs and desires of a person or family. It can be measured by determining whether or not money has been borrowed. Borrowing money one or more times during marriage was reported much more frequently by the married than by the divorced, the ratio being about 8 in 10 married to 6 in 10 divorced.[36] About the same ratio was found when the happily-married and the divorced were matched for the number of years married by restricting the analysis to those married 20 years or less.[37] Apparently the married had better credit, and used this credit more often to purchase desired things for the family.

Adequacy of Income. Marital adjustment is related to the degree to which persons feel that the total income meets the economic needs of the family. On a four fold scale—very adequate, adequate, inadequate, and very inadequate—the married rated their incomes toward the upper end of the scale and the divorced toward the lower. This was true for both men and women.

In the top category, "very adequate" income, no statistically significant differences were found. However, the rating "adequate" was given by a decidedly larger per cent of married men and women than divorced.[38] A larger per cent of divorced than married women gave ratings in each of the two lowest categories—"inadequate" and "very inadequate," [39] but a significant difference between divorced and married men was secured only when these were combined.[40]

[36] Per cents for men: 81.4 and 59.4, CR 3.5. For women: 80.9 and 59.5, CR 3.6.
[37] Per cents for men: 80.2 and 60.0, CR 2.8. For women: 80.4 and 60.9, CR 2.7.
[38] Per cents for men: 57.1 and 36.0, CR 3.0. For women: 65.7 and 44.4, CR 3.4.
[39] Per cents: "inadequate," 24.2 and 13.9, CR 2.1; "very inadequate," 12.1 and 1.2, CR 3.8; "inadequate" *and* "very inadequate," 36.3 and 15.1, CR 4.2.
[40] Per cents: 26.7 and 15.3, CR 2.1.

On adequacy of income, the ratings of men differed from those of women, particularly for the divorced. A larger per cent of married men than women gave the rating "very adequate," but this difference was below the selected level of significance.[41] This highest rating was given by a significantly larger per cent of divorced men than women.[42] The higher rating by men was in harmony with the cultural expectation that husbands will earn enough income to support their families adequately. The fact that divorced women gave significantly lower ratings on adequacy of income than divorced men is again an illustration of the negative evaluations given to the mate's behavior on the part of divorced persons.

The life-history documents reveal some of the attitudes of happily married and divorced persons on the adequacy of the income to meet the needs of the family. Many of the subjects in the present sample, as has been indicated above, were from a somewhat low economic level. However, even though the income was extremely limited, the happily-married secured satisfaction by cooperating in meeting the minimum needs of the family. This is shown in the following excerpt from the case of a happily married husband: [43]

"I don't believe in a man bringing his pay check home and handing it over to a woman, and I don't believe in him keeping it and spending it all by himself. After we pay our bills, we put what money we have left together, and, if I need a few cents to spend for tobacco or something, I take a little bit with me to work. If the wife wants something, she goes and gets it. But there have been many times, since I only get paid every two weeks, that after we got our bills paid, we only had ten or fifteen cents left. Then we'd go buy us a Pepsi-Cola apiece. If we had a few cents more, we would go to the show."

This cooperative democratic handling of the money is in radical contrast to the feeling on the part of many divorced hus-

[41] Per cents: 27.6 and 19.3, CR only 1.7.
[42] Per cents: 37.3 and 19.2, CR 2.7.
[43] Case no. 132.

bands and wives that the other spouse did not cooperate even to the extent of meeting the minimum needs of the family. Also, divorced husbands and wives often differed in what they considered the minimum needs of the family. This conflict over adequacy of income is illustrated in the following excerpt from the case of a divorced husband: [44]

"Sure I loved her. I was making good money, and we was gone about all the time. Our whole trouble was over money. Finally, I was making enough money. Not enough to keep her the way she had been kept, and she told me so. It made me mad, and I said, 'If that's the way you feel, you can just leave,' and she did. She just told me I wasn't making enough to support her the way she was used to being supported, so she got out. We agreed every other way. Got along swell. We both liked to gad about, and were gone every Sunday."

Efficiency of Home Management. The economic level of a family depends to some extent on the efficiency of home management. Inasmuch as the wife is primarily responsible for managing the affairs of the home, the following question was asked:

As far as managing the affairs of the home is concerned do you feel that the wife has been: very satisfactory _____; satisfactory _____; unsatisfactory _____; very unsatisfactory _____.

A significantly larger per cent of married than divorced men rated their wives "very satisfactory," [45] with a larger per cent of divorced than married in each of the other three categories.[46] A significantly larger per cent of divorced than married women rated themselves "unsatisfactory" *and* "very unsatisfactory." [47]

Happily married men were generous in rating their wives as

[44] Case no. 2.
[45] Per cents: 80.6 and 35.1, CR 7.0.
[46] Per cents: "satisfactory," 35.1 and 18.8, CR 2.8; "unsatisfactory," 15.6 and 0.0, CR 5.3; "very unsatisfactory," 14.3 and 0.6, CR 4.6.
[47] Per cents: 16.1 and 2.7, CR 3.7.

compared with the way the wives rated themselves, the respective per cents in the top category of "very satisfactory" being 80.6 and 44.5.[48] A significantly larger per cent of divorced men than women, 14.3 and 4.6, respectively, rated the wife "unsatisfactory" in managing the affairs of the home.[49]

From the data above it appears that from the point of view of both the husband and the wife, divorced women were less efficient in managing the home than were the married.

The above supports the hypothesis that the divorced were on a lower economic level and had less security than the happily-married, for the divorced had less home ownership, paid lower rents, had less life insurance and savings, had fewer utilities and other home necessities, had less credit, and wives were less efficient as home managers.

EMPLOYMENT OF HUSBAND

The conventional expectation in the United States is that the husband will be the chief breadwinner, and that he will be regular in his employment, stay on the same job, and provide for the needs of his family. This section indicates the extent to which the married and the divorced were alike or differed on these items.

Regularity of Employment. The happily-married and the divorced were asked to indicate the regularity of employment of the chief breadwinner during the first and last half of the marriage. They were given four possible choices: irregularly employed, always employed but continually changing jobs, regularly employed in seasonal work, and regularly employed the year around.

Regular employment of the chief breadwinner the year around was reported by about three fourths of happily married men, divorced men, and happily married women, but by

48 CR 6.7.
49 CR 2.2.

less than two thirds of divorced women. This was true for both the first and the last half of the marriage.[50] This means that, while happily married and divorced men did not differ in this category of "regular the year around," a significantly smaller per cent of divorced than of married women reported the chief breadwinner to be regular the year around in employment.[51] It also means that, while married men and women were in substantial agreement on the regularity of employment of the breadwinner, divorced men and women disagreed. Divorced women indicated that employment was irregular more often than did the men,[52] and divorced men more often than divorced women reported their employment to have been regular.[53] This discrepancy between divorced men and women in reporting on the regularity of employment may have been due to the husband's desire to conform to the social role of being a good provider, on the one hand, and on the other, to the wife's tendency to cast the blame for marital difficulties on the husband.

In the area in which the study was made, certain industries were seasonal. Therefore, in addition to "regular the year around," the category "regularly employed in seasonal work" was included. For the first half of the marriage, a significantly larger per cent of married than divorced men and women reported that employment was regular, but in seasonal work.[54] Likewise, for the last half of the marriage, a larger per cent of married than divorced men and women reported regular employment in seasonal work,[55] although in the case of women the difference was below the selected level of significance.

Regularity of employment probably was more frequent among the happily-married than among the divorced. How-

[50] Respective per cents for first half of marriage: 74.9, 80.4, 72.7, and 62.6. For last half of marriage: 75.8, 72.3, 78.4, and 63.6.
[51] CR for first half, 2.0; for last half, 3.0.
[52] Per cents for the first half: 26.4 and 10.4, CR 3.8. For second half: 27.3 and 15.7, CR 2.6.
[53] CR for first half, 3.6; for last half, only 1.7.
[54] Per cents for men: 9.0 and 3.1, CR 2.2. For women: 8.5 and 3.3, CR 2.1.
[55] Per cents for men: 9.7 and 3.8, CR 2.1. For women: 9.3 and 4.5, CR only 1.8.

ever, the statement that the chief breadwinner, or husband, was irregularly employed may have been simply an index of the maladjustment in the marriage.

Happily married women not only reported that the husband was regularly employed, but often took pride in and identified themselves with the work of the husband. This is shown in the following excerpt from the case of a happily married woman who talked more about her husband than about herself, and who, when asked a question which referred to her alone, invariably answered it in the plural: [56]

"We have been married thirty-three years. Perhaps you think that my husband acts a little queerly, but that is because he is blind in one eye from an accident last summer.

"He is the chief sawyer in the mill, and he knows a lot of important people in town. He always has had long periods of working with the same company, and has never been unemployed any time during our marriage.

"If you want to know anything about Johnny, just ask Mr. _____ or Mr. _____." (Both of the men she mentioned were well known in the city.) "He knows so many people; why, everyone calls to him when he goes down the street."

Longest Period of Employment. When the married and divorced groups were approximately matched for the number of years married by excluding those married over 20 years, no differences on the longest period of employment were found between married and divorced men, either for the first or the last half of the marriage. For married and divorced women, a larger per cent of married than divorced reported that the chief breadwinner had had a period of employment of over two years for both the first and the last half of the marriage.[57]

Husband's Efforts to Provide. The attitude of divorced women toward their former mates is revealed in the striking

[56] Case no. 185.
[57] Per cents for first half: 77.1 and 59.9, CR 2.7. For last half: 73.9 and 60.9, CR 2.1.

differences between their evaluations of the husband's efforts to provide for the needs of the family and divorced men's evaluations of their own efforts to provide,[58] in contrast with the evaluations by happily married men and women of the husband's efforts. Whereas half of the divorced men rated their efforts "very satisfactory," only a fifth of the divorced women gave this rating. Over 93 per cent of the divorced men, and only 48 per cent of the divorced women gave ratings of "satisfactory" or "very satisfactory." By contrast, practically all of the married men and women rated the efforts of the husband "satisfactory" or "very satisfactory," with a decidedly larger per cent of women than men giving the top rating, "very satisfactory." [59]

Thus, although no differences were found between the ratings by married and divorced men, decided differences were present between the ratings given by women. Three fourths of the married women rated the husband's efforts "very satisfactory," whereas, as was noted above, only a fifth of the divorced gave this rating.[60] While there was only one per cent of the married women who rated the husband's efforts as "unsatisfactory" or "very unsatisfactory," 50 per cent of the divorced women gave these ratings.[61]

Some of the low ratings by divorced women of the husband's efforts to provide for the needs of the family undoubtedly were due to their rationalizing this as one cause of the divorce. However, divorced women prior to the divorce may have felt that the husband's efforts to provide were unsatisfactory; if so, the low rating might have been symptomatic of difficulties in marital relationships.

The wife in the following divorced case had different standards for the economic needs of the family from those of her

[58] Per cents: "very satisfactory," 50.0 and 21.6, CR 3.9; "satisfactory," 43.1 and 26.8, CR 2.2; "unsatisfactory," 4.2 and 28.9, CR 4.0; "very unsatisfactory," 2.8 and 22.7, CR 3.5.

[59] Per cents: 77.8 and 56.7, CR 4.0.

[60] Per cents: 77.8 and 21.6, CR 9.0.

[61] Per cents: "unsatisfactory," 28.8 and 0.6, CR 7.1; "very unsatisfactory," 22.7 and 0.6, CR 6.2.

husband. From the statements of the wife and the husband, it is evident that the feeling of the wife that the husband was not sufficiently concerned with providing for the needs of the family was only one factor in the disruption of this family: [62]

Wife. "My family was very poor, and so maybe I want security more than some. My parents, and also my brother, objected most strongly to my marrying this man. I wish I had seen things as clearly as my brother did." (This elderly woman is living with this brother and is keeping house for him.)

"I left Peter because in fits of anger he used to beat me. He never was kind to me, and we did not have much in common. While I used to work steadily to get things to eat and to clothe the children, he used to spend his money freely, and we could never agree on how the money should be spent. He was always too independent, and never considerate of me."

Husband. (This man is a farmer and owns a considerable amount of land.) "The first inkling I had that there was a great difference between us was when my wife left me, leaving a note that she was going to divorce me and go and live with her brother. Of course, we had occasional unimportant quarrels before that. The reason she gave for divorcing me was that her brother wanted her to become his housekeeper and said that at his death he would will her his entire estate of about $10,000. She felt that she would have more security by doing this.

"Her family has always been poor, and thus she has always had a very strong desire to have a good deal of money, and she was always a willing worker. Since my family has been quite well off, I did not share her intense desire for money. Consequently, though we did not argue over it much, it was a source of disagreement between us.

"It may seem strange to you, but my former wife, my present wife, and myself are all good friends. My present wife is an entirely different kind of person from my former wife. My present wife and I are very much alike, so I am happy. Probably my former wife is happy living with her brother in town. So we all get along together just fine."

[62] Case no. 688.

Happily married and divorced men, as well as happily married women, agreed in reporting the conformity of the husband to the conventional pattern of regularity of work, relatively long periods of employment on the same job, and provision for the needs of the family. Divorced women, however, gave decidedly lower ratings on these points to their husbands than the divorced men gave themselves. The assumption is that a derogatory attitude of women toward the employment of the husband is a predictive item of maladjustment.

EMPLOYMENT OF WIFE

Did the happily-married and divorced differ in the proportion of wives who worked outside the home? Was marital adjustment affected by the employment of the wife? What was the attitude of husbands toward the wife working? These three questions will be considered in the following paragraphs.

Extent of Employment of the Wife. The question on employment was asked for the first and last half of marriage, and was phrased as follows:

Who in the family worked outside the home for money: wife _____; husband _____; both _____.

Table 51 gives the per cent of happily married and divorced men and women for the first and last half of the marriage who reported that the wife was gainfully employed. The per cents refer to the husband and wife both working, for only a negligible per cent reported that the wife alone worked. The table shows that, in the first half of the marriage, about the same per cents of divorced and married men reported that the wife was gainfully employed, whereas in the last half, a larger per cent of divorced than married reported that the wife worked. This difference, however, was not statistically significant.[63] For women, a larger per cent of divorced than married

[63] CR 1.4.

reported that in the first half and also the last half of marriage the wife was gainfully employed.[64]

TABLE 51

Per Cent of Happily-Married and Divorced Who Reported Wife Gainfully Employed, for First and Last Half of Marriage

	First Half	Last Half
Married men	28.8	25.8
Divorced men	26.5	34.0
Married women	29.1	29.8
Divorced women	40.2	41.4

A comparison of answers given by married men and women revealed no differences for either half of the marriage. A similar comparison for divorced men and women showed that, for the first half of the marriage, there was a significantly larger per cent of divorced men than women who reported the conventional pattern of the husband alone working,[65] whereas more divorced women than men reported that both worked.[66] For the last half of the marriage, the pattern was the same, but the difference was not statistically significant.

In general, the answers of the happily-married and the divorced to this question gave little support to the conclusion that marital adjustment is associated with the husband being the sole support of the family. It appears that the difference between married and divorced women may have been due, in part, to the tendency of divorced wives to rate their former husbands down.

Marital-Adjustment Scores. The lack of importance attached to the husband's being the sole worker outside of the home is in agreement with a study of the relationship be-

---

[64] CR for the first half, 2.2.; for last half, 2.2.
[65] Per cents: 73.5 and 59.8, CR 2.7.
[66] Per cents: 39.1 and 25.9, CR 2.6.

tween the employment of the wife and marital adjustment made by the author and Muriel Mackeprang.[67] In this analysis there were two investigations: the first compared certain cases of the present study; the second undertook the specific problem of analyzing the relationship between full-time employment of the wife and marital adjustment. In the latter study, the cases were from a highly educated group in metropolitan Los Angeles.[68]

In the comparison of the divorced and happily married groups, those cases were selected which met the following qualifications: (1) interviews had been secured from both husband and wife; (2) subjects had no prior marriages, and pregnancy was not the reason for marriage; (3) data were given on the last half of marriage; (4) employment of the chief breadwinner was regular and had lasted for one year or longer; and (5) husband and wife both worked, or husband alone worked. The fifth qualification gave an experimental group with the wife working and a control group with the wife not working. The resulting samples were as follows: 44 happily married couples of which both husband and wife worked, 110 happily married couples of which wife did not work, 34 divorced couples of which the husband and wife worked, and 68 divorced couples of which the wife did not work.

In both the happily married and divorced groups, the marital adjustment of working wives was compared with that of wives who did not work. A similar comparison was made for the husbands of the two groups of wives.[69]

No significant differences were found in this study for either wives or husbands. The respective mean adjustment scores of happily married wives who worked and those who did not

[67] Harvey J. Locke and Muriel Mackeprang, "Marital Adjustment and the Employed Wife," *American Journal of Sociology*, LIV, 1949, pp. 536–38.

[68] Muriel Mackeprang, "A Comparison of the Marital Adjustment of Couples in Which the Wives Are Employed Full Time outside the Home with Couples in Which Wives Are Full-Time Homemakers," unpublished M.A. thesis, University of Southern California, 1949.

[69] Marital-adjustment scores computed on the basis of the Burgess-Cottrell question and weights, which gave a maximum score of 194.

were 167.8 and 164.1; [70] of happily married husbands of working and nonworking wives, 168.2 and 168.7; [71] of divorced
wives who worked and those who did not work, 105.8 and
111.3; [72] and of divorced husbands of working and nonworking
wives, 109.8 and 110.8.[73] In none of these comparisons was the
difference between mean marital-adjustment scores statistically significant.

The fact that questions were not primarily concerned with
the effect on marital adjustment of the wife's working constitutes a serious limitation of these findings. For instance, if
there had been specific information concerning the regularity
or the length of employment of the wife as well as that of the
chief breadwinner, and also if the length of employment had
been related to the length of marriage, the findings might have
been different. In spite of these and other limitations, the fact
that no relationship is shown between the wife's working and
marital adjustment supports one of the hypotheses in the
Locke-Mackeprang study.

In this study the junior author's hypothesis was that there
would be no significant difference in marital adjustment of
either the wives or their husbands. The senior author, on the
other hand, entertained the hypothesis that marital adjustment of gainfully employed wives would be significantly
higher than that of homemaking wives, while husbands of the
employed wives would be significantly lower in marital adjustment than husbands of homemaking wives.

Questionnaires were secured from 41 employed wives and
their husbands and 51 homemaking wives and their husbands.[74] Cases of employed wives were obtained through
the cooperation of the American Association of University

[70] CR 0.6.
[71] CR 0.1.
[72] CR 1.0.
[73] CR 0.1.
[74] In addition, certain questionnaires were secured from only one spouse: 8
employed wives, 5 husbands of employed wives, 3 homemaking wives, and 2
husbands of homemaking wives. With few exceptions, findings are based upon
information from couples only.

Women, Business and Professional Women's clubs, Women
Lawyers' Club, Women's Medical Society, and through the
efforts of students and other individuals in Los Angeles. Lists
of homemaking wives were secured from persons in the above-
mentioned organizations and from other individuals.

The employed and homemaking samples were matched for
college or professional training of wife, residence in Los Angeles, and full-time employment or homemaking. Both husbands and wives were roughly matched for age, education,
length of time married, and husband's income.[75] On these
items, no significant differences between the experimental and
control groups of wives or of husbands were found. In the two
groups the husbands' occupations were also essentially alike.

The questionnaires contained fifty items worded similarly
for the employed and the homemaking samples. The items
fell into three general categories: social characteristics of the
samples, marital-prediction factors, and marital-adjustment
items. The latter consisted of certain questions used previously
in the marital-adjustment studies of Burgess and Cottrell, of
Terman, and of the present study.[76] Two ways of constructing a marital-adjustment test were used: (1) sixteen Burgess-
Cottrell questions and weights alone,[77] where the maximum
score was 167 points, and (2) these questions plus additional
items from Terman and the present study. The Burgess-
Cottrell-Terman-Locke test added two questions from Terman: contemplation of separation or divorce, and a self-rating
marital-happiness item. Five questions were taken from the
present study: conflict with reference to twenty-two specified
items, getting on each other's nerves around the house, amount
of time spent together, sex satisfaction, and frequency of intercourse during marriage. The maximum score on this test was
235 points.

[75] CRs between husbands and between wives, respectively: age, 0.7 and 0.8;
education, 0.7 and 0.9. CR of length of time married, 1.4; husband's income, 0.2.
[76] Ernest W. Burgess and Leonard S. Cottrell, *op. cit.*, pp. 64–65; Lewis M.
Terman *et al., op. cit.*, p. 58; for questions of the present study, see pp. 48–52.
[77] Items omitted from the Burgess-Cottrell test were the following: Nos. 3, 7,
8, 19, 21–27, *op. cit.*, pp. 64–65.

On the Burgess-Cottrell test the respective mean scores of gainfully employed wives and homemaking wives, 139.5 and 142.8, were not significantly different.[78] The difference between mean scores for husbands of employed wives and husbands of homemaking wives, 137.8 and 136.4, also was not statistically significant.[79]

For the Burgess-Cottrell-Terman-Locke test the mean score of employed wives was 193.6, and 196.5 for homemaking wives. These were not significantly different. The mean score for husbands of employed wives was 191.4, and 189.7 for husbands of homemaking wives. Again the difference between the mean scores was not statistically significant.[80]

The above data seem to indicate that for the population studied there were no significant differences between the marital adjustment of employed and homemaking wives or their husbands.

An additional question which arose in the course of the study was whether the marital adjustment of husbands and their wives in each group differed significantly. Rearranging the mean marital adjustment scores given above for the Burgess-Cottrell test, the respective scores for employed wives and their husbands were 139.5 and 137.8, with the difference being insignificant.[81] The respective mean scores for homemaking wives and their husbands were 142.8 and 136.4. This difference of 6.4 points is not significant on the level adopted for this study, for there are 10 chances in 100 that it is due to chance.[82] However, it suggests the hypothesis that husbands of homemaking wives are less adjusted in marriage than their spouses, whereas employed wives and their husbands are about equal in marital adjustment.

Certain limitations of this study may have been responsible for the failure to find significant differences between the mari-

[78] CR 0.8.
[79] CR 0.3.
[80] CR for wives: 0.4. For husbands: 0.2.
[81] CR 0.4.
[82] CR only 1.6.

tal adjustment of employed wives and homemaking wives or
between the marital adjustment of their husbands: (1) the
samples may have been too small to reveal differences; (2) inasmuch as both groups in this study were college graduates or
equivalent, a selective factor for high marital adjustment may
have been functioning in the choice of the samples, for previous studies have indicated a positive correlation between
high marital adjustment and high educational level; (3) subjects were taken who were engaging in homemaking or employment at the time the questionnaires were filled out, without considering the long-time aspects in marriage of employment or homemaking; and (4) the most serious limitation of
this study was that these groups were not matched for certain
variables.

Significant differences were found between the groups for
number of children, sociability, and living with in-laws. Couples with the wife engaged in homemaking, as compared
with full-time employment, had a decidedly larger percentage
with children—84.1 to 36.5.[83] On the whole, the homemaking
wives and their husbands were more sociable, as measured by
the number of their friends, than were the employed group.[84]
Also a larger percentage of couples with the wife engaging
in homemaking lived with in-laws than did couples of which
the wife was employed.[85] If these variables had been matched,
differences in marital adjustment between the employed and
homemaking groups might have been found.

The available data, however, support the hypothesis that
employment of the wife is not associated with her marital adjustment or with her husband's marital adjustment. This hypothesis should be subjected to further investigation, with a
more careful matching of variables and with the use of larger

[83] CR 4.7.
[84] Per cents of homemaking and employed wives with "many" friends of
same sex during marriage: 66.7 and 43.9, CR 2.2; before marriage, 76.5 and 60.9,
CR 1.6. Per cents of husbands of homemaking and employed wives having
"several" friends of same sex during marriage: 31.4 and 21.9, CR 2.1; before
marriage, 41.2 and 24.3, CR 1.7.
[85] Per cents of homemaking and employed: 15.6 and 2.4, CR 2.1.

and more representative samples. This is particularly needed, for not infrequently divorced men, like the two who made the following statements, report that the working of the wife was the primary factor in the divorce: [86]

"The first ten years of our marriage, my wife and me got along fine. I earned good money and managed it right. Then I lost my job and couldn't get another, and she got out and made money. She got independent. She wanted to run everything, and she was no manager at all. If she wanted anything, she would run up town and charge it.

"She would go to work and the kids would go to school, and I would be all alone. She wanted me to stay right at home, cook the meals, and do all the work. She would call up home to see if I was there. She wanted to boss everything.

"I did go out with some girls, and she told me she had had intercourse with an insurance man, but I doubt it. But he was around a lot and awful friendly. I think she told me she was with him to make me jealous. She might have at that. I admitted I had been with a girl."

The second man, likewise, reported that he and his wife were happy until she started to work, at which time she became too independent: [87]

"If she had not started to work, I think we would have been living together today. But after she got her job, she was independent, and all our troubles really began then. If she got sore about anything, she would go out and not cook our meals.

"After our divorce, I thought I could not stand being separated from her. Of course, I was also away from our son. I would go over to their place Sunday mornings to see him, but I also wanted to see her."

Husband's Attitude toward Wife's Working. Divorced and married men differed greatly in their answers to the question: "If the wife worked during marriage, did the husband

[86] Case no. 795.
[87] Case no. 335.

approve or disapprove?" A significantly larger per cent of divorced than married men disapproved,[88] as in the cases given above. This means, of course, that a significantly larger per cent of the married than of the divorced approved the wife's working. This, like other favorable reactions to the behavior of the spouse by the married, may mean that those adjusted in marriage tend to approve, in general, the behavior of the spouse. It may mean also that those who are maritally adjusted are considerate of the reaction of the spouse, and if the husband disapproves, the happily married wife does not work, or if the wife wants to work, the happily married husband is agreeable to her doing so. This is revealed in the following excerpt from the case of a happily married husband: [89]

"The only thing I would like to have my wife do, other than that which she is now doing, is to quit work. She has worked for nine years, and I think she would feel better if she quit. But I am good natured about it. She is getting a little nervous, and I do not let it bother me. I understand the reason. She is a good woman and a good wife."

Divorced men and women differed significantly in their answers to the question of the approval or disapproval by the husband if his wife worked, whereas happily married men and women did not differ. A larger per cent of divorced women than men said that the husband approved the wife's working.[90] This seems to indicate that wives of maritally-maladjusted couples either did not admit the grievances of the husband, or communication between the maritally maladjusted was so inadequate that the reaction of the spouse was not known.

SUMMARY

Of the economic items which were found to be unrelated to marital adjustment or maladjustment, three were of partic-

[88] Per cents: 63.6 and 40.0, CR 2.3.
[89] Case no. 203.
[90] Per cents: 73.2 and 36.4, CR 3.4.

ular interest: occupations of fathers, occupations of men at the time of marriage, and the gainful employment of the wife outside the home.

The present study found that many happily married men and women lived on incomes and in homes which, from a common-sense point of view, would make marital adjustment difficult if not impossible. Nevertheless, the economic items associated with marital adjustment that are listed below support, in part, the original hypothesis that economic security would be more prevalent among the happily-married than among the divorced. The items which are positively associated with marital adjustment apply to both men and women, except where noted:

1. The wife not being a "service worker" at the time of marriage.

2. Professional or semiprofessional positions during marriage. Also, for women, clerical and sales work.

3. The wife not being engaged in "domestic" work during marriage.

4. Good houses, as measured by higher than average rents, higher than average values if house was owned, having modern plumbing, and having a furnace.

5. Economic security, as measured by having life insurance and some savings.

6. Sociability, as measured by having a telephone.

7. Wide interests, as measured by taking a newspaper.

8. Interest in homemaking, as measured by ownership of such things as a home, an electric refrigerator, an electric washer, and a radio.

9. Regularity of employment of the husband.

10. The feeling by women that the husband's efforts to provide were satisfactory or very satisfactory.

11. Wife efficient in managing the home.

12. The feeling that the income of the family was adequate to meet the needs of the family.

13. The husband's approval of the wife's working.

14

ADJUSTMENT IN SUBSEQUENT MARRIAGES

THE POPULAR view is that neither divorced persons nor those who have experienced bereavement are good risks in a subsequent marriage. In the case of bereaved persons, the view is that such persons tend to idealize the behavior of the first mate to such an extent that it is difficult to be satisfied with a new mate in a second marriage. In the case of divorced persons, it is assumed that personality defects or other characteristics were involved in the maladjustment of the former marriage, and that these may operate in a second marriage so that adjustment is difficult if not impossible. This popular view is more or less accepted by divorced persons and verbalized by them. It was expressed as follows by a divorced woman who had remarried and was experiencing unhappiness in her second marriage: [1]

"After two unhappy marriages, it looks like there must be something wrong with me, but Lord knows, I've tried to do my best to make a good home. I certainly hate to go through all that divorce business again, but I don't know— I just can't stand this."

The present study, while not specifically oriented toward the study of persons in subsequent marriages, collected data which give some evidence on the probable marital adjustment of bereaved and divorced persons in subsequent marriages. Specifically the analysis in this chapter attempts to formulate tentative hypotheses regarding three questions: What

[1] Case no. 378.

298

is the likelihood that bereaved persons will make a good adjustment in a remarriage? Do divorced persons constitute good or bad risks in subsequent marriages? Are there any differences between divorced and bereaved persons in their adjustment in a subsequent marriage?

ADJUSTMENT OF BEREAVED PERSONS WHO HAVE REMARRIED

The hypothesis at the beginning of the study was that bereaved persons do not make as good a risk in a subsequent marriage as do remarried divorced persons, and that they are not as adjusted as persons who have been married only once. It was felt that the surviving member of a marriage would remember the good qualities of the deceased, and that the new mate would suffer in comparison. By contrast, it was thought that a divorced person would remember the things he did not like about his former mate, and that the new mate, consequently, would have an advantage. The analysis did not support the original hypothesis that marriages of bereaved persons who remarry will be maladjusted.

In the happily married group there were 21 persons who had had a prior marriage which had been terminated by the death of the mate. The mean marital-adjustment score [2] of these 21 persons was 169.7 as compared with 166.8 for those happily married persons who had been married only once, and 159.1 for those happily married cases, in which the prior marriage had been terminated by divorce. Although bereaved persons had higher mean scores than the other two groups, the differences were not statistically significant. However, the size of the difference between the mean score of the bereaved who had remarried and of the divorced who had remarried, 10 points, gave a critical ratio of 1.3, or 82 chances in 100 that the difference was real. If the size of these two groups had been

[2] The Burgess-Cottrell marital-adjustment test was used in computing the adjustment scores. See p. 53 for the effects of using their questions.

larger, it is possible that the bereaved persons would have had a significantly higher mean score than those with a prior divorce.

On the basis of our present data, however, the original hypothesis seems to have been disproved. The present hypothesis is that bereaved persons are equally as good risks in subsequent marriages as are persons who have been married only once, and may be better risks than remarried divorced persons.

If this hypothesis is supported by later studies, how can the higher marital-adjustment scores of bereaved persons, as compared with those of remarried divorced persons, be explained? For one thing, it is likely that remarried bereaved persons are highly adaptable or they probably would not have entered into a subsequent marriage. If they are more adaptable, then they may adjust themselves to the exigencies of the marital state more easily than the remarried divorced persons who did not adjust themselves to the exigencies of their former marriages. It is presumably more difficult for bereaved than for divorced persons to adjust to a second marriage, and possibly only a highly selected segment of the bereaved, the most adaptable, enter into a second marriage.

Information from the life-history documents secured in the informal interviews supports, to some extent, the statistical and the interpretative analysis given above. This is illustrated in the following excerpt from the case of a man whose former mate had died. His first marriage had been a happy one, but he was able to adapt very successfully to his second marriage. The author, after his interview with this man, made the following notation: "This man is very happy in his home, and with the companionship he finds in his present wife. He is a vigorous man, who is very sociable, and it is not difficult for him to adapt to people.[3]

"We get along just fine. We never quarrel. We talk things over all the time. My first wife was prettier than this one. But this one

[3] Case no. 95.

makes up for it in her good disposition and her willingness to work together with me. She may be too 'saving' at times. I tell her she is 'almost stingy.' Both of my wives have been very 'saving.' I turn over my checks to her, and she pays the bills. She is not very well, and I help her around the house to lighten the load. Of course, she does not help me in the yard. That is my job.

"I think one reason we get along so well is that we are very nearly of the same age. We sympathize with each other. The man across the street has remarried and has a wife 20 years younger than himself. How can they sympathize with each other's desires and activities? He goes out with her a lot now, but in a few years he won't want to do it, and she may want to go out as much as ever. In our case, we adjust to each other. My wife likes movies, but I don't care for them, and she said, 'I don't like them well enough to go alone and would rather stay home with you.' That is the way it is with us. I will give up some things for her. We like the same things."

A systematic study is needed of the marital adjustment of bereaved persons who enter into a second marriage. A careful analysis could determine whether or not the hypothesis presented above is correct, namely, that bereaved persons who remarry are more adaptable than those who do not remarry. Also, such a study could determine the specific conditions under which bereaved persons adjust or do not adjust in a subsequent marriage.

DIVORCED PERSONS IN SUBSEQUENT MARRIAGES

The evidence which is available at the present time, while not conclusive, indicates that divorced women are as likely to be as adjusted in a subsequent marriage as women who have been married only once. This is the conclusion from the data of the present study as well as from another study conducted by William Klausner and the author.[4] The evidence of the

---

[4] Harvey J. Locke and William J. Klausner, "Marital Adjustment of Divorced Persons in Subsequent Marriages," *Sociology and Social Research*, XXXIII, 1948, pp. 97–101. This was a pilot study and has been expanded into a major study which is now in process.

latter study indicates that divorced men probably are not as good marital risks as men married only once.

The Evidence from the Present Study. Of those couples who were recommended by an outsider as the most happily married known to him, 17 husbands or wives had had a prior marriage which had been terminated by divorce. On the basis of this small sample, there were no significant differences between the mean marital-adjustment score of the divorced and that of the remainder of the married sample.

One hundred and forty six persons in the divorced sample who had married again gave information on the happiness of their present marriages.[5] Table 52 shows that nearly half rated their present marriage "very happy," about one third rated it "happy," and only 1 in 10 rated it "unhappy" *and* "very unhappy." Thus, 76.7 per cent of these cases rated their subsequent marriages as "happy" *and* "very happy," which compares rather favorably with the 93.6 per cent of the happily married persons who gave these two highest ratings.

TABLE 52

Ratings of Marital Happiness of Present Marriages by Persons Whose Prior Marriage Had Ended in Divorce *

Happiness Rating	Number	Per Cent
Very happy	65	44.5
Happy	47	32.2
Average	18	12.3
Unhappy	7	4.8
Very unhappy	9	6.2
	146	100.0

* This sample was composed of 83 men and 63 women.

Inasmuch as the married were the *most happily married* known to people in the community, it is to be assumed that a larger per cent of this group would rate their marriages in the

[5] About 1 in 10 of the total divorced sample had been divorced more than once. See p. 24.

two top categories than would the remarried divorced group, which was essentially a sample from the general population. The conclusion that divorced persons in the sample of the present study constitute fairly good risks in subsequent marriages seems warranted.

The above, of course, is a statistical analysis of data included in the questionnaires. As has been indicated many times in previous sections of the book, there are always persons who vary from the general pattern. There are those who are happier than most of the remarried divorced group, and there are those who are less happy. The following two excerpts were chosen to illustrate these two extremes of adjustment and maladjustment of divorced persons in subsequent marriages. In the first case, a divorced man, although still somewhat attached to his first wife and still willing to point out some of her good qualities, found in his remarriage some of the satisfactions which were lacking in the first union: [6]

"Since our divorce, I have seen my first wife a couple of times. Once I caught up with her before I knew who she was and said, 'Hello, Mom,' and she smiled very nice at me and was very pleasant. I think we could have made up at that time.

"My present wife is everything my first wife was not. She enjoys sex and has a better personality. She is cheerful, and my first wife was sort of nagging. However, she is not as intelligent nor anywhere near as good a housekeeper as was my first wife.

"My divorce and remarriage were a shock to me. Being a Christian, I got to thinking that it was wrong to be divorced and remarried. Then a minister pointed out the scripture saying, 'What God hath joined together let no man put asunder.' This minister pointed out that God didn't put my first wife and me together because we were not Christians when we were married, and that helped me a great deal, for I did not commit adultery in marrying the second time."

The second case is by a woman who has been married twice and is interested in marrying again. It describes the factors in the break-up of her first marriage, the apparently good adjust-

[6] Case no. 907.

ment of her first husband in his new marriage, and her unsatisfying relationships with her second husband: [7]

"I began working soon after my first marriage, and I think that was
my fatal mistake. At any rate, he was very irresponsible and appeared to be lazy.

"He became attracted to another woman, which was a final thing
leading to my application for divorce, but there were a lot of
other things which preceded it. I take part of the blame. He says
that I nagged, and I imagine that I did, but my biggest fault was
in assuming the financial burden of supporting the family. Since
his remarriage, he has gotten a good job and apparently is making
good.

"My second husband and I would have gotten along together
were it not for his jealousy of my son. It got so I could hardly put
my arm around my son without this man being jealous. I guess also
he knew that I still thought of my first husband, so we broke up.

"I'd like to get married again, but if I do it will be for keeps.
What kind of a husband do you think I ought to have? I got acquainted with a man last summer who said he was separated from
his wife. He came down here a lot. He liked my boy and he liked
me. I told him that I wasn't going to break up any other man's
home. My home had been broken up by another woman. But he
telephoned a few times, and Christmas he sent me fourteen beautiful roses. He has asked me not to marry for six months, saying that
he thinks he will be divorced from his wife by then. I don't like to
look forward to old age alone."

To the author's question, "If you had your life to live over again,
what would you do?" the woman's 14-year old son interrupted
with this statement for her:

"I'd do what I have done."

The mother said, "Now son, you know you have told me that you
wish your dad and I had not separated."

The son replied, "Yes, I have said that, and I spend my summers
with my dad and like him very much, particularly when we are
alone. I feel that my step-mother doesn't like his giving me things.
I like her and I like her parents. They have a little boy four years
old, and I like this brother of mine."

[7] Case no. 909.

The data from the questionnaires of those happily-married who had had a prior marriage ending in divorce, from those divorced persons who were remarried, and also from the life-history documents, indicate that divorced persons, on the whole, are happy and adjusted in second marriages. This was the basis of the following hypothesis: There is no significant difference in the degree of marital adjustment of divorced persons in subsequent marriages and the adjustment of persons married only once.

The Evidence from the Locke-Klausner Study. A study by the author and Klausner was designed to test this hypothesis. Two groups were secured: one of 47 persons who had been divorced and had entered into subsequent marriages, and the other of 64 persons who had been married only once. The cases were obtained through members of sociology courses, who distributed questionnaires to persons of their acquaintance. The sample was drawn from the Los Angeles metropolitan area.

Only two restrictions were imposed in gathering the data. The student was asked to secure only those marriages which had been in existence for not less than one nor more than fifteen years and to try to obtain persons from each group. This admittedly crude attempt to obtain somewhat homogeneous groups in terms of length of marriage worked rather well: only 4 per cent of the marriages which were secured were of less than one year's duration, and only 4 per cent exceeded 15 years of marriage.

The social characteristics of the remarried divorced and the married-only-once groups were fairly comparable in religious faith,[8] educational attainment, level of yearly income, and na-

---

[8] Both the groups were predominantly Protestant, 60 and 61 per cent, respectively, while 14.9 per cent and 11 per cent were Catholic. Four per cent of the remarried divorced group and 6 per cent of the married-only-once group were Jewish, and about one fifth of both groups claimed to have no church affiliation. The median for years of education of the remarried divorced group was 13.4 and the median for the married-only-once sample was 14.3 years. A yearly family income of less than $3,000 was obtained by 48.7 per cent of the

tionality. The sex distribution was fairly equal; males constituted 44.7 per cent and 48.4 per cent, respectively, of the two groups.

In considering the significance of the findings given below, certain limitations of the study should be kept in mind: the smallness of the samples, the more or less incidental matching of the experimental and the control group, the unrepresentative character of the samples as indicated by their high educational level, the exclusion of divorced persons where remarriage had not occurred, and the inclusion of persons who had more than one prior marriage. Moreover, a total of 350 questionnaires were distributed, and of these 127, or 36.3 per cent, were returned.[9] This one-third return raises the question whether the results would have differed had all questionnaires been returned.

The following analysis is based on the marital-adjustment test of Burgess and Cottrell and their weights. It will be remembered that the maximum score of this test was 194 points.[10]

---

remarried group and by 54.8 per cent of the married-only-once. The respective per cents of the remarried-divorced and the married-only-once who were American born of American-born parents were 61.7 and 70.3. About 1 in 25 and 1 in 10, respectively, were foreign born.

[9] Of these, 16 were not utilized for the following reasons: (1) Eleven were completed by colored persons and were not used because of the small number represented. (2) One divorced remarried person returned a completed questionnaire, but answered all questions on the basis of his first marriage. (3) Two divorced persons returned questionnaires, but they had not remarried. And (4) two persons returned questionnaires which were short one page of the marital-adjustment scale.

[10] As no attempt was made to obtain the cases of both husband and wife, it was necessary to decide whether to include as separate cases the few husbands and their wives where both sides of the marriage were secured. The question arising from these instances was: Would the inclusion of such cases distort the findings derived from the total group represented? Specifically, would the fact that there were fourteen marriages in the married-only-once group in which the scores of both partners were secured tend toward duplication or "stacking," thus influencing the total adjustment picture of that group?

A test was made to see if this was true. Mean marital-adjustment scores were worked out for three groups: (1) the remarried-divorced; (2) the married-only-once, including all cases as separate individuals, even though the cases of the spouse were included; and (3) the married-only-once, including only one side of the 14 cases where questionnaires were secured from both mates. The

Three types of comparisons were made: (1) the total married-only-once men and women with the total remarried divorced group, (2) the married-only-once women with the remarried divorced women and a like comparison of the men, and (3) the men with the women of the corresponding group.

In the first study, the author combined into a single group the men and women from his happily married sample who had had a prior marriage ending in divorce and compared these men and women with the total remaining men and women of his happily married sample. A similar procedure was followed in the second study by a comparison of the combined scores of men and women in the two groups. The results indicated that the remarried divorced group achieved as high a degree of adjustment in the present marriages as those persons who were married only once. The respective mean scores were 149 and 151.

It was then decided to make an additional comparison of these two groups in terms of the three general categories "poor," "fair," and "good" marital adjustment used by Burgess and Cottrell.[11] In this comparison, scores ranging from 20 to 120 indicated "poor" marital adjustment, from 120 to 159 "fair" adjustment, and from 160 to 194 points "good" adjustment. The distribution of the scores of the two groups in these three categories was quite similar. The remarried divorced and the married-only-once group had 44.7 per cent and 50.0 per cent, respectively, in the "good" adjustment category; 38.3 and 39.1 per cent in the "fair"; and 17.0 and 10.9 in the "poor" marital-adjustment category.

The second type of comparison was by sex. When the marital-adjustment scores of remarried divorced women were

divorced, the married-only-once with all cases, and the married-only-once unpaired cases did not differ significantly in their mean adjustment scores, the respective means being 149, 151, and 154.5. Consequently, it was concluded that all cases could be utilized for further comparisons, treating the marriage partners, in instances where they were couples, as individuals, and including them in the respective groups.

11 Ernest W. Burgess and Leonard S. Cottrell, *Predicting Success or Failure in Marriage*, New York, Prentice-Hall, 1939.

compared with those of the women married only once, the means of the marital-adjustment scores of the two groups were, respectively, 157 and 151 points, and this difference was not statistically significant.[12]

Thus far the data verified the original hypothesis. However, the hypothesis was not supported when the scores of remarried divorced men were compared with the scores of men who had been married only once. The average adjustment score of those men who had had prior marriages terminated by divorce was 138 as compared with 159 for men married only once. This difference of 21 points in the means of the two groups is statistically significant. While there is some chance, of course, that the difference was due to chance, it probably represents a real difference.[13]

If divorced women are good risks in a subsequent marriage, and divorced men are poor risks as compared with persons married only once, then one would expect a difference between the degree of marital adjustment of divorced men and women who have entered into a subsequent marriage, or a difference between the marital adjustment of men and women in the married-only-once group. This question initiated the third comparison. It was found that the adjustment scores of the married-only-once men and women did not differ significantly.[14]

The comparison of the remarried divorced men and the remarried divorced women revealed a 19-point difference, the respective scores being 138 and 157, and the difference was just below the level of significance established for the study.[15] While this difference is slightly below the 5-per cent level of significance, the suggestion is that a statistically significant difference might be found if the sample were larger. The tentative conclusion is that divorced men are less adjusted in subsequent marriages than divorced women.

12 CR only 0.8.
13 CR 2.3.
14 The respective means: 159 and 151, CR only 1.3.
15 CR only 1.9.

SUMMARY

From the above analysis of bereaved persons who entered a subsequent marriage and remarried divorced persons, the following tentative conclusions can be drawn:

1. Bereaved persons make as good an adjustment in subsequent marriages as the adjustment of persons who have been married only once, and better than that of divorced persons who enter into subsequent marriages.

2. Remarried divorced women are as well adjusted in their present marriages as women who remain married to their first mates.

3. Remarried divorced men are less adjusted in their present marriages than those men who have been married only once.

15

CONCLUSIONS AND PROBLEMS FOR RESEARCH

FAMILY counselors, social workers, ministers, and others, who are faced with the necessity of assisting people with their family problems, are constantly impressed with the lack of available knowledge on many of the problems which are brought to them. Such persons may go to the literature on the family, only to find that much of that which has been and is being written on the family consists of *opinions* on why some families get along very successfully, while other families are having almost insurmountable difficulties which often lead to separation or divorce. Those who are attempting to assist people may find the knowledge which is summarized in this final chapter of the present study particularly valuable, even though it must be used with great caution. Here an effort is made to bring together the various conclusions of several studies, including those of the present study.

The present chapter attempts to answer the following specific questions: To what extent can one predict from data secured during engagement the likelihood that an engagement will terminate in marriage and that those who marry will be successful in their marriages? To what extent can one predict at a given time in marriage the likelihood that the marriage will later be broken by separation or divorce or remain unbroken? Are the predictive factors associated with marital adjustment, which have been derived from one study of a particular group, applicable to other groups? What predictive items has the present study found to be associated with marital adjustment? What are the items on which the happily married and the divorced group did not differ? To what extent do the various studies of marital adjustment agree or disagree on the items which are associated with marital adjustment? What are the general conclusions of the present study and how are these related to problems for future research?

LONGITUDINAL STUDIES OF MARITAL ADJUSTMENT

To what extent can adjustment tests taken by couples at a given time predict the probability of their adjustment at a later time? Some persons insist that the prediction of marital adjustment is not feasible because it does not predict the adjustment of the *individual marriage*.[1] Such persons are obviously not trained in scientific procedures, for anyone who has even an elementary knowledge of scientific prediction in any area of behavior realizes that prediction is always in an *actuarial* frame of reference. Like life insurance, prediction of marital adjustment is concerned with probabilities. Persons engaged in research on the prediction of marital adjustment claim no more than this.[2] Studies have demonstrated the feasibility of investigating engaged couples or married couples at a given time and, from the data secured, predicting the likelihood of marital adjustment at a later time.

Most persons who have made studies of marital adjustment have secured information about a group of adjusted and maladjusted marriages and have assumed that those items which differentiated between the two groups would be predictive factors in marital adjustment. This was the assumption of

[1] Albert Ellis, "The Value of Marriage Prediction Tests," *American Sociological Review*, XIII, 1948, pp. 710–18.

[2] For a criticism of this point of view of Ellis and others see Lewis M. Terman and Paul Wallin, "The Validity of Marriage Prediction and Marital Adjustment Tests," *American Sociological Review*, XIV, 1949, pp. 497–504.

Terman,[3] of Burgess and Cottrell,[4] and of the author of the present study. Three longitudinal studies have secured evidence which indicates the probable validity of this assumption.

Predicting Divorce and Permanence of Marriage. Terman in 1940 gave a marital-adjustment or happiness test, a prediction or marital-"aptitude" test, and a sex-adjustment test to 643 married persons of his "genius" subjects and their spouses. Two follow-up studies were made: one five years after the tests were given,[5] and the other after eight years.[6] During these years some of the couples had become divorced; hence, a comparison could be made between broken and unbroken marriages in terms of test scores secured in 1940. Analysis of the two reports shows that "for each of the three tests, prediction of marital success or failure was better *eight* years after the tests were given than *five* years after."[7] The discussion will be confined to the analysis of broken and unbroken marriages eight years after the 1940 tests were administered.

Marital-adjustment and sex-adjustment test scores were available on 52 husbands and wives from broken marriages and 591 husbands and wives from unbroken marriages. Marital-prediction scores were available on 52 husbands and 51 wives from broken marriages and 580 husbands and wives of unbroken marriages.

The maximum marital-adjustment score was 100 points. Table 53 shows that the mean or average adjustment scores for

[3] Lewis M. Terman *et al., Psychological Factors in Marital Happiness,* New York, McGraw-Hill, 1938.

[4] Ernest W. Burgess and Leonard S. Cottrell, *Predicting Success or Failure in Marriage,* New York, Prentice-Hall, 1939.

[5] Lewis M. Terman and Melita H. Oden, *The Gifted Child Grows up: Twenty-five Years' Follow-up of a Superior Group,* Stanford, Stanford University Press, 1947, chap. 19.

[6] Lewis M. Terman and Paul Wallin, *op. cit.* Also, Lewis M. Terman, "Prediction Data: Predicting Marriage Failure from Test Scores," *Marriage and Family Living,* XII, 1950, pp. 51–54.

[7] Lewis M. Terman, "Prediction Data: Predicting Marriage Failure from Test Scores," *Marriage and Family Living,* XII, 1950, pp. 51–54, footnote on p. 53.

broken and unbroken marriages were, respectively, 49.8 and 63.8 for husbands and 48.7 and 66.7 for wives. The size of the critical ratios indicates that the 1940 marital-adjustment test significantly differentiated between those who remained married in 1948 and those who by that time had been either divorced or separated.

TABLE 53

Mean Adjustment, Prediction, and Sex-Adjustment Scores of Broken and Unbroken Marriages, with Critical Ratios of the Differences of the Mean Scores *

Tests	Means		CR	Biserial Correlations
	Broken Marriages	Unbroken Marriages		
I. Adjustment				
Husbands	49.8	63.8	4.4	.35
Wives	48.7	66.7	5.8	.46
II. Prediction				
Husbands	82.4	91.5	3.8	.25
Wives	69.2	80.0	5.3	.41
III. Sex				
Husbands	12.8	15.0	3.1	.28
Wives	17.4	20.8	3.7	.33
IV. Adjustment + Sex				
Husbands	62.3	79.0	4.5	.38
Wives	66.3	87.5	5.5	.48
V. Adjustment + Prediction				
Husbands	132.2	155.3	5.1	.36
Wives	118.2	146.9	6.4	.52
VI. Adjustment + Prediction + Sex				
Husbands	144.7	170.3	4.9	.37
Wives	134.9	167.5	6.2	.54

* Data from Lewis M. Terman, "Prediction Data: Predicting Marriage Failure from Test Scores," *Marriage and Family Living,* XII, 1950, p. 52.

The marital-prediction test had a maximum score of 155 for men and 117 for women. The respective means of the prediction scores of broken and unbroken marriages of men were 82.4 and 91.5, and for women 69.2 and 80.0. Again the size of the critical ratios indicates that the marital-prediction test administered in 1940 separated broken from unbroken marriages eight years later.

The maximum score for the sex-adjustment test was 22 for men and 30 for women. The mean scores of men of broken and unbroken marriages were, respectively, 12.8 and 15.0, and for women, 17.4 and 20.8. Here, likewise, the critical ratios were large, indicating that the average sex-adjustment score of men and women in unbroken marriages was higher in 1940 than in marriages which ended in divorce or separation within the next eight years.

Table 53 gives the results of combining the scores of the three tests in various ways: adjustment + sex, adjustment + prediction, and adjustment + prediction + sex. Such combinations were more predictive than was the score of any one test alone. This is shown by the increased size of the critical ratios and the larger biserial correlations when the tests were combined.

The evidence from this study of broken and unbroken marriages of "genius" subjects supports the conclusion that tests at a given time can predict the probability of marital adjustment at a later time. Terman tentatively concludes that the marital-adjustment test and the marital-prediction test each predict marital success or failure about as well as scholastic-aptitude tests predict college grades.[8]

Most of the items used by Terman in the 1940 tests had been used in his earlier study of the psychological factors in marital happiness. The fact that these items predicted the marital adjustment of a new group of persons eight years after the tests were administered tends to support the assumption that items which differentiate between a given adjusted and maladjusted

[8] *Ibid.*, p. 53.

married group can be used to predict the adjustment of certain groups of persons other than those in the original investigation.

Predicting Marital Adjustment from Adjustment in Engagement. The first attempt to predict marital adjustment from adjustment in engagement was that of Kelly.[9] Using questions identical to those used by Terman in his original study, he secured personality and background data on 300 couples before marriage, and then two years after marriage he secured marital-adjustment data from 82 of these. The marital-prediction scores computed from the premarital data worked fairly well in indicating the likelihood of marital adjustment of couples two years after marriage. The correlation between marital-prediction scores and marital-adjustment scores was .50 for husbands and .56 for wives.[10]

Thus, Kelly's study indicates the feasibility of predicting at a given time the likelihood of marital adjustment at a later time. The results of his study, also, tend to support the use of predictive items derived from one study in the prediction of marital adjustment in a new group of persons.

Burgess and Wallin have gone far beyond the original efforts of Kelly to predict marital adjustment from data secured in the engagement period. They secured data from 1,000 engaged couples, and in 1944 made a report on 505 of these couples who had been married three or four years and on whom marital information had been obtained.[11] Their more extended analysis will be published in the near future.[12] In their initial report they indicated that scores of adjustment in

[9] E. Lowell Kelly, "Concerning the Validity of Terman's Weights for Predicting Marital Happiness," *Psychological Bulletin*, XXXVI, 1939, pp. 202–203.

[10] These correlations were adjusted for the extremely low range of happiness scores of his sample.

[11] Ernest W. Burgess and Paul Wallin, "Predicting Adjustment in Marriage from Adjustment in Engagement," *American Journal of Sociology*, XLIX, 1944, pp. 324–30.

[12] Ernest W. Burgess and Paul Wallin, *Engagement and Marriage*, New York, Harcourt Brace and Co., to be published in 1951.

engagement predict (1) the likelihood that the engagement will not be broken but will eventuate in marriage, and (2) the chances of adjustment after three years of marriage.

Engagement-adjustment scores were significantly different for the 123 couples who had broken their engagements and the remaining 877 whose engagements had not been broken. A larger proportion of both men and women who had broken their engagements, as compared with those whose engagements were not broken, had low engagement-adjustment scores. The per cents of men of broken and unbroken engagements, whose engagement adjustment scores were 119 or less, were, respectively, 14.6 and 5.7.[13] For women, the corresponding per cents were 17.1 and 5.8.[14] Scores of 160 or more were secured by 28.5 per cent of men and 21.9 per cent of women of broken engagements as compared with 38.3 per cent of men and 39.7 per cent of women in unbroken engagements.[15] Also, the mean adjustment scores of broken and unbroken engagements for men were, respectively, 146.4 and 153.1, and for women, 144.2 and 153.2.[16] All of the differences were significant on a level considerably above the minimum selected for the present study. Burgess and Wallin conclude that differences in engagement-adjustment scores of broken and unbroken engagements differentiate with appreciable accuracy between the extremes of adjustment in engagement.

The Burgess-Wallin study also shows that it is possible to predict adjustment in marriage from adjustment in engagement. For 505 of their engaged couples who had married and on whom information as to their marital adjustment had been secured, they found a positive association between engagement-adjustment scores and marital-adjustment scores. The correlation for men was .43, and for women, .41.

By 1949 Burgess and Wallin had marital-adjustment data on almost 700 couples of the original engaged group. Wallin

13 CR 2.7.
14 CR 4.3.
15 CR for men: 2.2. For women: 3.3.
16 CR for men: 3.3. For women: 4.5.

reports that most of the items associated with high marital-success scores were also associated with high engagement-adjustment scores.[17]

The study of Burgess and Wallin, like the studies of Terman and Kelly, presents evidence that adjustment can be predicted from data secured at an earlier period in the association. Also, like the other two studies, they used items in their study which had proved significant in the original investigation of Burgess and Cottrell. This is additional support for the assumption that items which differentiate between marital adjustment and maladjustment of one sample can be used to predict the marital adjustment of another group.

It is neither claimed nor assumed that the marital-prediction items presented below are applicable to all groups in the United States, not to mention groups in other cultures. The studies reviewed above, however, do imply that marital-prediction items have greater generality of application than to the population from which they are derived.

MARITAL-PREDICTION ITEMS

Significant differences between the happily-married and the divorced, presented in the preceding chapters, are summarized in Table 54. The weights opposite the answers of each question give a clear‚picture of the degree to which happily married and divorced men and women differed on the various items.

The method of weighting was the same as that described in the chapter on measuring marital adjustment.[18] If the happily-married and divorced did not differ significantly in the per cent who gave a given answer to a question, then a weight of 4 points was assigned that answer or category. If a significantly larger per cent of happily-married than divorced responded in a given category, then a weight of 5 or more points was given,

---

[17] Lewis M. Terman and Paul Wallin, *op. cit.*, p. 501.
[18] See pp. 46–47.

with the greater the difference the higher the weight. If the divorced had a larger per cent than the married, then a weight of 3 or less points was assigned, with the greater the difference the lower the weight. For example, in the first item persons were asked to check "mate paid attention to (became familiar with) another person," if this item represented a serious difficulty in their marriage. The following per cents of married and divorced men checked or did not check this item, and, inasmuch as a much larger per cent of divorced than married checked it, a weight of 1 point was given for "checked" and a weight of 7 points for "not checked."

	Married	Divorced	Weight
Checked	2.7	65.9	1
Not checked	97.3	34.1	7

The main thing to keep in mind for the correct interpretation of the items in the table is that a weight of 4 points for a response means that the happily-married and the divorced did not differ significantly on that response; that a weight of 5 or more points means that the happily-married had a significantly larger per cent; and that a weight of 3 or less points means that the divorced had a significantly larger per cent.

The list of items does not include some on which the happily-married and divorced differed. In the two chapters on personality traits it was shown that ratings of mate were much more differentiating than were self-ratings. Therefore, self-ratings are omitted here. In the discussion of the companionship family, differences between the happily-married and divorced were presented on democratic relationships, not only between themselves and their mates, but between their own parents and between the parents of their mates. The latter are omitted, for it was felt that they measured essentially the same things as democratic relationships between self and mate. Also, all of the marital-adjustment items are omitted, for they are summarized in the chapter on measuring marital adjustment.

The present list includes 137 items for men and 140 for women.

The items, taken together, give a wide range of scores, extending on each side of that which would have been secured if the happily-married and divorced had answered the questions in very much the same way. If there were no significant differences between the happily married and divorced men and women, the total scores for men would be 4 times the 137 items or 548 points, and for women, 4 times the 140 items or 560 points. Actually, the maximum score for men was 693 and the minimum 389, with a difference of 304 points. For women the maximum score was 721 and the minimum 381, with a difference of 340 points.

The items are classified under the chapter titles in which they were discussed previously.

TABLE 54

Significant Marital-Prediction Items, with Assigned Weights for the Various Categories

Items	Weights for Men	Weights for Women
MARITAL DISAGREEMENTS AND CONFLICTS		
Check any of the following if they represent serious difficulties in your marriage.		
1. Mate paid attention (became familiar with) another person:		
Checked	1	1
Not checked	7	7
2. Lack of mutual affection (no longer in love):		
Checked	1	1
Not checked	7	7
3. Adultery:		
Checked	1	1
Not checked	7	7

Items	Weights for Men	Weights for Women
4. Unsatisfying sex relations:		
Checked	2	2
Not checked	6	6
5. Venereal disease:		
Checked	4	3
Not checked	4	5
6. Desire to have children:		
Checked	3	5
Not checked	5	3
7. Difficulties over money:		
Checked	3	3
Not checked	5	5
8. Nonsupport:		
Checked	2	1
Not checked	6	7
9. Desertion:		
Checked	2	2
Not checked	6	6
10. Drunkenness:		
Checked	2	1
Not checked	6	7
11. Gambling:		
Checked	3	2
Not checked	5	6
12. Mate sent to jail:		
Checked	3	2
Not checked	5	6
13. Do not have mutual friends:		
Checked	3	3
Not checked	5	5
14. Selfishness and lack of cooperation:		
Checked	3	3
Not checked	5	5
15. Interference of in-laws:		
Checked	2	4
Not checked	6	4
16. Ill health:		
Checked	3	4
Not checked	5	4

Items	Weights for Men	Weights for Women
17. Constant bickering:		
Checked	2	2
Not checked	6	6

Indicate feelings during periods of difficulty between you and mate.

18. Lonely:		
Very	2	3
Somewhat	4	4
A little	4	5
Not at all	5	5
19. Miserable:		
Very	3	3
Somewhat	4	4
A little	4	4
Not at all	5	5
20. Irritated:		
Very	2	3
Somewhat	4	4
A little	5	5
Not at all	5	5
21. Angry:		
Very	2	3
Somewhat	4	4
A little	5	5
Not at all	5	4
22. Insecure:		
Very	3	2
Somewhat	3	3
A little	5	5
Not at all	5	6
23. Worried:		
Very	2	2
Somewhat	4	4
A little	5	5
Not at all	5	5
24. Hurt:		
Very	3	3

Items	Weights for Men	Weights for Women
Somewhat	4	5
A little	5	5
Not at all	5	4
25. Inferior:		
Very	3	4
Somewhat	4	3
A little	5	4
Not at all	4	5
26. Self-confident:		
Very	3	4
Somewhat	4	3
A little	4	4
Not at all	5	5
27. Critical of mate:		
Very	2	2
Somewhat	4	4
A little	4	5
Not at all	5	5

COURTSHIP AND ENGAGEMENT

Items	Weights for Men	Weights for Women
28. Met mate at the home of a friend:		
Yes	3	3
No	5	5
29. Met mate at a dance hall:		
Yes	4	3
No	4	5
30. Length of acquaintance:		
12 months or less	4	3
13 through 24 months	4	4
Over 24 months	4	5
31. Length of engagement:		
Less than a month	3	3
One to five months	4	3
Six to eleven months	4	4
Twelve months and over	5	5
32. Conflict with mate before marriage:		
None	5	5
A little	5	5

Items	W	M
Moderate	3	
A good deal	2	
Very great	2	
33. Affection for mate before marriage:		
None	2	3
A little	2	3
Moderate	2	3
A good deal	4	4
Very great	6	5

Check which of the following were reasons for marrying.

	W	M
34. Love:		
Yes	6	6
No	2	2
35. To have a home:		
Yes	5	5
No	3	3
36. Common interests:		
Yes	5	5
No	3	3
37. To have children:		
Yes	5	5
No	3	3
38. To satisfy sex interests:		
Yes	5	6
No	3	2
39. Economic security:		
Yes	4	5
No	4	3
40. To escape from own family:		
Yes	4	3
No	4	5
41. Age at the time of marriage—		
For men:		
Under 21	3	..
21–23	4	..
24–29	5	..

Items	Weights for Men	Weights for Women
30 and over	4	..
For women:		
Under 18	..	3
18–20	..	4
21–29	..	5
30 and over	..	4
42. Comparative ages of husband and wife:		
About equal	5	5
Three to ten years difference	3	3

PARENTAL INFLUENCES ON MARITAL ADJUSTMENT

43. Happiness of your childhood:		
Very happy	4	5
Happy	4	5
Average	4	4
Unhappy	4	3
Very unhappy	4	3
44. Conflict between you and father before marriage:		
None	3	3
A little	5	5
Moderate	4	4
A good deal	4	4
Very great	4	4
45. Conflict between you and mother before marriage:		
None	4	4
A little	4	5
Moderate	5	4
A good deal	3	3
Very great	3	3
46. Discipline in your parental home:		
Never had own way	3	3
Usually had own way	5	5
Always had own way	3	4
47. Happiness of parents' marriage:		
Very happy	5	4
Happy	4	4
Average	3	4
Unhappy	4	4
Very unhappy	4	4

Items	Weights for Men	Weights for Women
48. Attitude of your parents toward mate before marriage:		
Approval	5	6
Disapproval	3	2
Indifference	3	3
Did not know mate	4	4
49. During marriage did you and mate live with wife's parents:		
Yes	3	3
No	5	5
50. During marriage did you and mate live with husband's parents:		
Yes	4	3
No	4	5
51. Your attitude toward living with in-laws:		
Disliked	3	3
Did not mind	4	5
Enjoyed	5	4

SEXUAL BEHAVIOR

Items	Weights for Men	Weights for Women
52. Number of persons you had intercourse with before marriage:		
None	5	4
One	4	4
A few	3	4
Many	3	4
53. Your judgment on premarital relations of spouse with others:		
Believed spouse had	3	4
Knew spouse had	2	3
Suspected spouse had	3	3
Did not believe, know, or suspect . . .	5	5
54. Mate's judgment on your premarital intercourse with others:		
Believed you had	3	4
Knew you had	3	4
Suspected you had	4	4
Did not believe, know, or suspect	5	4

Items	Weights for Men	Weights for Women
55. Mate over-modest and shy toward sex:		
Very much	3	3
A good deal	3	3
Some	5	5
Very little	5	5
Not at all	4	4
56. Strength of your sex interest as compared with that of mate:		
Very much greater	3	3
Much greater	4	3
About the same	5	5
Much less intense	3	4
Very much less intense	3	3
57. Birth control methods were used:		
Yes	4	5
No	4	3
58. Fear of pregnancy made sex less enjoyable:		
Yes	3	3
No	5	5
59. Refused sex when mate desired it:		
Frequently	4	3
Sometimes	3	4
Rarely	5	5
Never	4	3
60. Desired intercourse with someone other than mate:		
Very frequently	4	3
Frequently	3	3
Sometimes	3	3
Rarely	4	4
Never	5	5
61. Number of persons other than mate with whom you had intercourse during marriage:		
None	5	4
One	4	4
A few	2	4
Many	2	4
62. Your judgment on mate's intercourse with others during marriage:		
Believed mate had	3	3

Items	Weights for Men	Weights for Women
Knew mate had	2	2
Suspected mate had	2	2
Did not believe, know, or suspect	7	7
63. Mate's judgment on your intercourse with others during marriage:		
Believed you had	3	4
Knew you had	2	4
Suspected you had	2	2
Did not believe, know, or suspect	6	5
64. Was mate jealous of you:		
Yes	2	2
No	6	6

CHILDREN AND MARITAL ADJUSTMENT

65. Where children were present, mate desired them:		
Yes	5	6
No	3	2
66. Where children were absent, you desired them:		
Yes	5	5
No	3	3
67. Where children were absent, mate desired them:		
Yes	6	6
No	2	2

PERSONALITY TRAITS: RATING ON MATE

68. Assumes responsibility readily:		
Markedly	5	6
Considerably	5	5
Somewhat	4	3
A little	3	3
Not at all	2	2
69. Strict with children:		
Markedly	4	4
Considerably	5	4
Somewhat	4	5
A little	4	4
Not at all	2	3
70. Leader in the community:		
Markedly	5	5

Items	Weights for Men	Weights for Women
Considerably	5	5
Somewhat	5	5
A little	4	4
Not at all	3	3
71. Able to make decisions readily:		
Markedly	4	5
Considerably	5	5
Somewhat	4	4
A little	3	3
Not at all	3	3
72. Determined:		
Markedly	4	4
Considerably	4	4
Somewhat	4	4
A little	3	3
Not at all	3	3
73. Easily influenced by others:		
Markedly	2	2
Considerably	3	3
Somewhat	4	4
A little	5	5
Not at all	5	5
74. "Gives in" in arguments:		
Markedly	5	5
Considerably	5	5
Somewhat	5	5
A little	4	3
Not at all	2	2
75. Dominating—presses opinions and ideas on others:		
Markedly	3	2
Considerably	3	3
Somewhat	4	4
A little	4	4
Not at all	5	5
76. Gets angry easily:		
Markedly	2	2
Considerably	3	3
Somewhat	5	5

Items	Weights for Men	Weights for Women
A little	5	5
Not at all	5	5
77. Gets over anger quickly:		
Markedly	5	5
Considerably	5	5
Somewhat	4	4
A little	3	3
Not at all	3	3
78. Affectionate:		
Markedly	5	5
Considerably	5	4
Somewhat	3	4
A little	3	3
Not at all	2	2
79. Demonstrative:		
Markedly	4	4
Considerably	4	4
Somewhat	5	5
A little	3	3
Not at all	3	3
80. Sociable—makes friends easily:		
Markedly	5	5
Considerably	4	4
Somewhat	4	3
A little	3	3
Not at all	3	3
81. Likes belonging to organizations:		
Markedly	4	5
Considerably	4	5
Somewhat	5	4
A little	4	4
Not at all	3	3
82. Cares what people say and think:		
Markedly	4	4
Considerably	4	5
Somewhat	5	5
A little	4	3
Not at all	4	3

Items	Weights for Men	Weights for Women
83. Has sense of humor:		
Markedly	5	5
Considerably	4	4
Somewhat	4	4
A little	2	3
Not at all	2	2

GENERAL PERSONALITY PATTERNS

Items	Weights for Men	Weights for Women
84. Number of your friends of the same sex before marriage:		
Almost none	4	3
A few	4	3
Several	4	5
Many	4	5
85. Number of your friends of the opposite sex before marriage:		
Almost none	4	3
A few	4	4
Several	4	5
Many	4	4
86. Number of mate's friends of the same sex before marriage:		
Almost none	3	4
A few	3	4
Several	5	4
Many	5	4
87. Number of mate's friends of the opposite sex before marriage:		
Almost none	3	4
A few	3	4
Several	5	5
Many	5	3
88. Number of your friends of the same sex after marriage:		
Almost none	3	3
A few	3	3
Several	5	5
Many	5	5

Items	Weights for Men	Weights for Women
89. Number of your friends of the opposite sex after marriage:		
Almost none	3	3
A few	5	3
Several	5	5
Many	5	5
90. Number of mate's friends of the same sex after marriage:		
Almost none	3	3
A few	3	3
Several	5	5
Many	5	5
91. Number of mate's friends of the opposite sex after marriage:		
Almost none	3	4
A few	3	4
Several	5	4
Many	5	4
92. Number of friends in common with mate during marriage:		
Almost none	3	2
A few	3	3
Several	5	5
Many	5	5
93. Where married:		
At home	5	5
At church	4	4
By judge	4	4
At minister's home	4	4
By justice of the peace	3	3
94. Age at which stopped going to Sunday school:		
Never went	4	4
10 years or younger	4	4
11–14	3	4
15–18	3	3
19–25	4	4
Still going at marriage	5	4
Went during marriage	5	5

Items	Weights for Men	Weights for Women
95. Church affiliation of you and your mate at the time of marriage:		
Only one spouse a member	3	3
Neither belonged to a church	3	3
Both belonged to same church	5	5
Both belonged to different churches . . .	4	4
96. Frequency of monthly church attendance during first half of marriage:		
No times	3	3
Once or less	4	4
2 or 3 times	5	4
4 or more times	5	5
97. Frequency of monthly church attendance during last half of marriage:		
No times	3	3
Once or less	4	4
2 or 3 times	4	4
4 or more times	5	5

THE COMPANIONSHIP FAMILY

98. Feelings of equality toward mate:		
Superior	3	2
Inferior	5	5
Equal	4	5
99. Your intelligence as compared with that of mate:		
More	3	3
Less	4	4
Equal	5	5

Check only one answer for each of the following activities.

100. Church:		
You and mate both enjoyed	6	6
You only enjoyed	3	2
Mate only enjoyed	4	4
Both were indifferent	3	3
Open conflict	4	3

Items	Weights for Men	Weights for Women
101. Reading:		
You and mate both enjoyed	5	5
You only enjoyed	2	3
Mate only enjoyed	3	4
Both were indifferent	4	4
Open conflict	4	4
102. Radio:		
You and mate both enjoyed	5	5
You only enjoyed	3	3
Mate only enjoyed	4	4
Both were indifferent	3	4
Open conflict	4	4
103. Sports:		
You and mate both enjoyed	5	5
You only enjoyed	3	3
Mate only enjoyed	4	4
Both were indifferent	4	3
Open conflict	3	4
104. Music:		
You and mate both enjoyed	5	5
You only enjoyed	3	2
Mate only enjoyed	4	4
Both were indifferent	4	3
Open conflict	4	4
105. Parties:		
You and mate both enjoyed	4	5
You only enjoyed	3	4
Mate only enjoyed	3	3
Both were indifferent	4	3
Open conflict	3	4
106. Drinking:		
You and mate both enjoyed	3	3
You only enjoyed	3	4
Mate only enjoyed	3	2
Both were indifferent	5	5
Open conflict	3	3
107. Dancing:		
You and mate both enjoyed	3	3
You only enjoyed	3	3

Items	Weights for Men	Weights for Women
Mate only enjoyed	3	3
Both were indifferent	5	4
Open conflict	4	4
108. Cards:		
You and mate both enjoyed	4	4
You only enjoyed	3	4
Mate only enjoyed	4	3
Both were indifferent	5	4
Open conflict	4	4
109. Gambling:		
You and mate both enjoyed	4	4
You only enjoyed	4	4
Mate only enjoyed	4	2
Both were indifferent	4	4
Open conflict	4	4
110. Who took the lead in making family decisions:		
Wife	3	3
Husband	4	3
Both about equally	5	5
111. Who took the lead in disciplining the children:		
Wife	4	3
Husband	3	3
Both about equally	5	5
112. Who took the lead in handling family money:		
Wife	4	4
Husband	4	3
Both about equally	4	5
113. Who took the lead in affectionate behavior:		
Wife	3	3
Husband	3	4
Both about equally	5	5
114. Who took the lead in religious behavior:		
Wife	4	3
Husband	3	4
Both about equally	5	5
115. Who took the lead in recreational behavior:		
Wife	4	4
Husband	3	3
Both about equally	5	5

Items	Weights for Men	Weights for Women

ECONOMIC FACTORS •

116. At marriage wife, if employed, was in a service occupation, such as waitress, beautician, or cook:

Yes		3
No		5

117. At marriage wife, if employed, was in professional or semiprofessional work:

Yes		5
No		3

118. During marriage husband engaged in professional or semiprofessional work:

Yes	5	. .
No	3	. .

119. During marriage wife, if employed, engaged in professional work or clerical and sales:

Yes		5
No		3

120. During marriage wife, if employed, engaged in domestic service:

Yes		2
No		6

121. You rented a house during marriage:

Yes	3	3
No	5	5

122. If owned a house during marriage, it had a value of $2,500 or more (in 1940 dollars):

Yes	5	5
No	3	3

123. Life insurance was carried by one or more members of the family:

Yes	5	5
No	3	3

124. The family had some savings at the time of marriage:

$200 or more	5	5
Less than $200	3	3

125. Savings were accumulated during marriage:

Some	5	6
None	3	2

Items	Weights for Men	Weights for Women

Indicate whether or not you had the following during marriage.

126. Furnace:

Yes	5	5
No	3	3

127. Indoor toilet:

Yes	5	5
No	3	3

128. Telephone:

Yes	6	6
No	2	2

129. Newspaper:

Yes	7	7
No	1	1

Indicate whether or not the family owned the following.

130. A home:

Yes	5	5
No	3	3

131. A radio:

Yes	5	5
No	3	3

132. An electric refrigerator:

Yes	6	6
No	2	2

133. An electric washer:

Yes	5	5
No	3	3

134. During marriage the family borrowed money:

Yes	5	5
No	3	3

135. Adequacy of total income of the family to meet family needs:

Very adequate	4	4
Adequate	5	5
Inadequate	3	3

Items	Weights for Men	Weights for Women
Very inadequate	3	2
136. Efficiency of the wife in managing the affairs of the home:		
Very satisfactory	6	6
Satisfactory	3	6
Unsatisfactory	2	2
Very unsatisfactory	2	2
137. Statement on the regularity of employment of husband during marriage:		
Was regular	4	5
Was not regular	4	3
138. Husband had a relatively long period of employment (over two years):		
Yes	4	5
No	4	3
139. Husband's efforts to provide for the needs of the family were:		
Very satisfactory	4	6
Satisfactory	4	4
Unsatisfactory	4	2
Very unsatisfactory	4	2
140. If wife worked, the husband:		
Approved	5	4
Disapproved	3	4
141. Your education was:		
1–8 years (grade school)	4	4
9–12 years (high school)	4	4
13–16 years (college)	4	5
graduate work	5	5

NONDIFFERENTIATING ITEMS

The failure to find significant differences between adjusted and maladjusted marriages is fully as important as is the discovery of differences. In the present study there were several items which did not discriminate between the happily-married and the divorced, either for men or for women. Below is a list of the items in which the per cents of happily married and divorced men and women did not differ on the level of significance selected for the study:

1. American or foreign birth.

2. State in which born.

3. Rural or urban environment during childhood or adolescence.

4. Being an only, the youngest, or the oldest child.

5. Degree of mobility, as measured by the number of states lived in before or after marriage.

6. Level of education of parents.

7. Different amusement interests as a serious marital difficulty.

8. Differences in religion as a serious marital difficulty.

9. Frequency of seeing each other during courtship.

10. Degree of affection before one's marriage for mother or for father.

11. Conflict between mother and father before one's marriage.

12. Proximity of one's own family to the home of the mate's parents.

13. Reported premarital intercourse with future spouse.

14. The absence or presence of children in the family.

15. The average number of children in the family.

16. Type of occupation engaged in by one's father.

17. The marital status of the parents at the time of a person's marriage.

18. The state of health of a person before marriage and also during marriage.

There were no differences on the following two items. However, here the comparison was not between the happily-married and the divorced. The first item concerns a comparison *within* the happily married group and *within* the divorced group. The second compares families in which the wife was employed with those in which she was a homemaker.

1. Marital adjustment of those born during, before, or after the depression.

2. Marital adjustment of employed wives and homemaking wives, and, also, the marital adjustment of their husbands.

INDEPENDENT CRITERIA OF ADJUSTMENT AND OF PREDICTION

Theoretically the marital-prediction test is used to tell what is going to happen, and the marital-adjustment test to see if that which was predicted really happened. The prediction criterion and the adjustment criterion should be as independent from each other as possible, for, if they are composed of similar questions, they might be measuring approximately the same thing. Under such conditions one would expect that the degree of adjustment as measured by the adjustment test would be about the same as that which was predicted by the marital-prediction test. In the present study the weights in the marital-prediction test given above were determined by the same statistical procedure as were the weights in the marital-adjustment test. In other words, weights were assigned to answers in terms of the degree of difference between the happily-married and divorced responses to the possible answers of a question. This means, of course, that there would be a high correlation between the marital-prediction and the marital-adjustment scores.

The general procedure used to solve the problem of the prediction and the adjustment test measuring the same thing has been to construct the marital-adjustment test from indices of marital satisfaction or agreement and marital dissatisfaction or disagreement. By contrast, the marital-prediction test has been constructed from other indices which are logically different, such as the length of engagement, degree of sociability, degree of adaptability, and the like. This was the method used in the Burgess-Cottrell study and Terman's study of psychological factors in marital happiness.

There are other criteria for determining marital adjustment and maladjustment than those which have been most commonly used. Kirkpatrick used "well adjusted" and "poorly adjusted" as judged by an outsider.[19] Terman in his study of "genius" couples used unbroken and broken marriages.[20] The present study used "happiness in marriage as judged by an outsider" and divorce. Such indices of marital adjustment and maladjustment allow one to include the marital-adjustment items in the prediction test if one so desires. It will be remembered that Terman found that the combination of prediction and adjustment items into a single test was more discriminating between broken and unbroken marriages than was either test by itself.

THE FINDINGS OF DIFFERENT STUDIES

What items have the different marital-prediction studies found to be associated with marital adjustment? To what extent are the items supported by more than one study? Also, to what extent are items that are found positively associated with marital adjustment by one or more studies, found to be unrelated to adjustment by other studies? Table 55 has been constructed to answer such questions as these.[21]

In considering the findings reported in Table 55 it should be remembered that some of the studies used different criteria of marital adjustment, selected different prediction items, phrased the questions differently, and provided different possible answers to given questions. It should also be remembered that the samples of the various studies were drawn from differ-

[19] Clifford Kirkpatrick, "Factors in Marital Adjustment," *American Journal of Sociology*, XLIII, 1937, pp. 270–83.

[20] Lewis M. Terman, "Prediction Data: Predicting Marriage Failure from Test Scores," *Marriage and Family Living*, XII, 1950, pp. 51–54. Also, Lewis M. Terman and Melita H. Oden, *op. cit.*, chap. 19.

[21] Two tabulations in this general type have been made previously. One, prepared in 1939, is in Ernest W. Burgess and Leonard S. Cottrell, *op. cit.*, pp. 357–59. The other, published in 1947, is in Clifford Kirkpatrick, *What Science Says About Happiness in Marriage*, Minneapolis, Burgess Publishing Co., pp. 11–45.

ent sections of the country and from different socio-economic groups.

An analysis of the table reveals that 82 items have been found to be associated with marital adjustment. It will be noted that some of the items of the present study have been summarized under more general items. Of the 82 items, 51, or 62 per cent, were found favorable to marital adjustment by more than one study. There are 19 items where no relationship was discovered by one or more studies, although a positive relationship had been discovered by one or more other studies.

This apparent disagreement on whether or not an item is favorable to marital adjustment may be due, in part, to the differences outlined above, or may be due, partly, to the statistical level of significance selected for inclusion of an item in the table. The general rule was to include an item as favorable to marital adjustment if a critical ratio of 2.0 was reported between adjusted and maladjusted marriages on the item. However, there are always 5 chances in 100 that an item with a critical ratio of 2.0 may be unrelated to marital adjustment and be due to chance, or that an item with a critical ratio of somewhat less than 2.0 may be significant.

It will be noted that the findings of several investigators are presented in the second column of the table. The name or names of the investigators who reported given findings are inserted under these items. The third column includes two studies—one by Terman and the other by Terman and Oden. Unless otherwise indicated, the item is reported in Terman's initial study of the psychological factors in marital happiness. The fourth column is limited to the conclusions of Burgess and Cottrell from their study of predicting success or failure in marriage. The last column includes the specific findings of the present study. Appendix 3 includes the specific references of the various reports, along with the date of the study, the area where it was made, the size of the sample, and the criteria used in selecting adjusted and maladjusted families.

A Comparison of Findings of Marital-prediction Studies: Items Favorable
to Adjustment in Marriage, and Items Having No Relationship

(H, husband; W, wife; if H or W not given, then it is for both)

Items	Studies by Bernard, Davis, Hamilton, Hart, Kelly, Kirkpatrick, Landis and Landis, Schroeder, and Winch	Terman's Study, 792 Couples; Terman and Oden, 567 Couples	Study of Burgess and Cottrell, 526 Individuals	This Study, 929 Individuals, of Whom 802 Were Husbands and Their Wives
Acquaintance	. . . . .	Extremely well acquainted.	2 or more years.	W, over 2 years.
Activities, enjoyment of	Self and mate enjoy engaging in activities together. (Kirkpatrick)	. . . . .	. . . . .	Self and mate both enjoy church, reading, listening to radio, sports, music, but do not enjoy or are indifferent to drinking, dancing, and cards.
Adaptability	. . . . .	Rated by outsider as satisfactory in general adjustment. (Terman and Oden)	. . . . .	Adaptable personality.

Affection toward mate before marriage	.	.	.	Very great.
Age at marriage	H, 24 and over. W, 20 and over. (Hart) H, 25 and over. (Davis)	W, 20 and over.	H, 22 to 30. W, 19 and over.	H, 24 to 29. W, 21 to 29.
Age difference	H, 0 to 10 years older. W, 0 to 5 years younger. (Bernard)	.	H, older by 1 to 3 years, or same age as W.	About the same age.
Attachment, to father	.	Good deal or very close.	H, very close.	No relationship.
Attachment, to mother	.	Good deal or very close.	Very close.	No relationship.
Attachment, prefer one parent to other	W, absence of greater intimacy with one parent. (Kirkpatrick)	W, absence of markedly greater attachment.		.
Attachment, to siblings	.	No relationship. (Terman and Oden)	H, none. W, none or to younger brother.	.
Babies, learned origin of at age		W, 12 to 16 years.		.

343

(H, husband; W, wife; if H or W not given, then it is for both)

Items	Studies by Bernard, Davis, Hamilton, Hart, Kelly, Kirkpatrick, Landis and Landis, Schroeder, and Winch	Terman's Study, 792 Couples; Terman and Oden, 567 Couples	Study of Burgess and Cottrell, 526 Individuals	This Study, 929 Individuals, of Whom 802 Were Husbands and Their Wives
Birth control methods	No relationship on the use of contraceptives. (Davis)	Trust in contraceptives; no relationship to methods of contraception.	. . .	W, are used.
Brothers or sisters	W, has brothers. (Hamilton)	No relationship to presence of opposite sex siblings. (Terman and Oden)	H, 2 or more siblings.	. . .
Children, presence of	No relationship. (Hamilton) (Bernard) (Landis and Landis)	No relationship.	None or one.	No relationship.
Children, desire for	. . .	. . .	No children, but desired by both. One or more children, and desired by both.	No children, but mate desires. One or more children, and desired by both.

Church, attendance	3 or more times a month. (Schroeder)	· · · · ·	H, 2 or more times a month. W, 4 times a month.	H, 2 or more times a month. W, 4 or more times a month.
Church, membership in	Church member. (Schroeder)	· · · · ·	Church affiliation.	Both belong to same church.
Conflict, with father	· · · · ·	None or very little.	None.	A little.
Conflict, with mother	· · · · ·	H, none. W, none or very little.	H, little or none.	H, moderate. W, a little.
Conflict, with mate before marriage	· · · · ·	· · · · ·	· · · · ·	None or very little.
Conflict over certain activities	· · · · ·	No complaints about behavior of spouse or about the marriage.	Nothing which annoys about mate or the marriage.	No conflict over: mate pays attention to another, lack of mutual affection, adultery, sex relations, money, nonsupport, desertion, drunkenness, gambling, mate sent to jail, friends, selfishness and lack of cooperation, constant bickering. H, no conflict over in-laws. W, no conflict over venereal disease.

(H, husband; W, wife; if H or W not given, then it is for both)

Items	Studies by Bernard, Davis, Hamilton, Hart, Kelly, Kirkpatrick, Landis and Landis, Schroeder, and Winch	Terman's Study, 792 Couples; Terman and Oden, 567 Couples	Study of Burgess and Cottrell, 526 Individuals	This Study, 929 Individuals, of Whom 802 Were Husbands and Their Wives
Courtship, length of	. . .	. . .	3 or more years.	. . .
Discipline in parental home	. . .	Firm but not harsh. No, rare, or occasional punishment.	. . .	Usually has own way.
Economic, efforts of husband	. . .	. . .	. . .	W, very satisfactory.
Economic level	Home owned. (Schroeder)	. . .	Home owned.	Do not rent but own home; have life insurance; own home utilities or necessities; have established credit.
Education	Beyond high school. (Schroeder) Equal. (Hamilton)	Beyond high school.	H, college graduate, or professional. W, college, postgraduate, or professional.	H, graduate work. W, beyond high school. No relationship to level of education of parents.

Employment, length of			H, average of 15 months.	W, reports husband had a job of over 2 years.
Employment, regularity of			Regular.	W, reports husband was regularly employed.
Employment, of wife	W, employed. (Davis)		W, regularly employed before marriage.	No relationship to wife's employment during marriage. H, approves wife working.
Engagement, length of		H, 6 months or longer. W, 3 months or longer.	9 months or longer.	A year or longer.
Equality of husband and wife	Thinks mate superior. (Kelly) H, nonpatriarchal attitude of husband Husband and wife about equally favorable toward "feminism." (Kirkpatrick)			H, inferior to mate. W, inferior to mate or equal. Both take the lead about equally in certain activities.
Family background, level			Superior.	
Family background, similarity			Similar.	

347

(H, husband; W, wife; if H or W not given, then it is for both)

Items	Studies by Bernard, Davis, Hamilton, Hart, Kelly, Kirkpatrick, Landis and Landis, Schroeder, and Winch	Terman's Study, 792 Couples; Terman and Oden, 567 Couples	Study of Burgess and Cottrell, 526 Individuals	This Study, 929 Individuals, of Whom 802 Were Husbands and Their Wives
Fear of pregnancy	.	No relationship.	.	Does not make sex less enjoyable.
Feelings during periods of difficulty	.	.	.	Not at all or a little lonely, miserable, irritated, angry, insecure, worried, hurt, inferior, critical of mate.
Friends, men before marriage	.	.	H, several or many. W, a few, several, or many.	H, wife had several or many. W, self had several.
Friends, men after marriage	.	.	.	Several or many.

	(Kirkpatrick) / (Schroeder) / (Davis) / (Bernard)			
Friends, women before marriage	H, no excess of women friends before marriage. (Kirkpatrick)	H, large number.	H, several or many. W, many.	H, wife had several or many. W, self had several or many; husband had several, but not many.
Friends, women after marriage	. . . .	. . . .	. . . .	H, self has a few or more; wife has several or many. W, self has several or many.
Friends, in common during marriage	. . . .	. . . .	. . . .	Several or many.
Happiness of childhood	. . . .	Above average and extremely happy.	. . . .	Above average.
Happiness of parents' marriage, rated by subject	H, happy. (Schroeder)	Happy and very happy.	H, very happy.	H, very happy.
Health	W, healthy. (Davis)	. . . .	H, healthy.	No relationship.
Home management	. . . .	. . . .	. . . .	Very satisfactory.
Homosexuality	. . . .	H, no homosexual desires.	. . . .	. . . .
Income	No relationship. (Bernard)	No complaint that income insufficient. No relationship to amount.	Moderate.	Reported as adequate for needs of the family.

(H, husband; W, wife; if H or W not given, then it is for both)

Items	Studies by Bernard, Davis, Hamilton, Hart, Kelly, Kirkpatrick, Landis and Landis, Schroeder, and Winch	Terman's Study, 792 Couples; Terman and Oden, 567 Couples	Study of Burgess and Cottrell, 526 Individuals	This Study, 929 Individuals, of Whom 802 Were Husbands and Their Wives
In-laws, attitude toward living with	.	.	.	H, enjoys. W, does not mind.
In-laws, lived with during marriage	.	.	No relationship.	Did not live with wife's parents. W, did not live with husband's parents.
Jealousy	.	.	.	Mate does not show it.
Marriage, reasons for	.	.	.	Love, to have a home, common interests, to have children, to satisfy sex interests. W, economic security and not to escape own family.

Marital status of parents	Not divorced or separated.	. . . .	. . . . .	No relationship.
Married by	Minister or priest. (Schroeder)	. . . .	Minister, priest, or rabbi.	Minister or priest.
Married, place of	. . . .	. . . .	At church or parsonage.	At home.
Meeting place, first	. . . .	Other than "pick-up" or private or public recreation.	. . . .	Other than "home of a friend" or dance hall.
Membership in organizations	. . . .	. . . .	3 or more.	. . . .
Mental ability	. . . .	H, does not feel much superior. W, husband not inferior. (Terman) No relationship to childhood I.Q. (Terman and Oden)	. . . .	Mates feel equal.
Mother of husband, attractiveness as rated by husband	. . . .	H, average or above.	. . . .	. . . .

(H, husband; W, wife; if H or W not given, then it is for both)

Items	Studies by Bernard, Davis, Hamilton, Hart, Kelly, Kirkpatrick, Landis and Landis, Schroeder, and Winch	Terman's Study, 792 Couples; Terman and Oden, 567 Couples	Study of Burgess and Cottrell, 526 Individuals	This Study, 929 Individuals, of Whom 802 Were Husbands and Their Wives
Occupation	. . .	No relationship.	H, certain occupations. W, teaching, or same or similar to what she wants.	W, at marriage, if employed, in service, professional, or semiprofessional; during marriage, in professional or semiprofessional; not domestic service.
Order of birth	. . .	W, not only child. (Terman) No relationship. (Terman and Oden)	H, not only child; if only child, or youngest child, not married to only or youngest.	No relationship.
Parents' approval of the marriage	. . .	. . .	Approved by both.	Approved by both.

"Petting" (or "spooning")	W, none. (Davis)	W, never. (Terman) No relationship. (Terman and Oden)	No relationship.	.
Personality "traits"	Not having an over-reactive touchiness or a sense of inferiority. (Winch)	.	.	Mate assumes responsibility readily, strict in dealing with children, leadership in the community, quick in making decisions, expresses determination, not easily influenced by others, "gives in" in arguments quickly, not dominating, slow in getting angry, quick in getting over anger, tendencies toward sociability, enjoyment in belonging to organizations, somewhat concerned with what people say and think, sense of humor, affectionateness, and demonstration of affection.

(H, husband; W, wife; if H or W not given, then it is for both)

Items	Studies by Bernard, Davis, Hamilton, Hart Kelly, Kirkpatrick, Landis and Landis, Schroeder, and Winch	Terman's Study, 792 Couples; Terman and Oden, 567 Couples	Study of Burgess and Cottrell, 526 Individuals	This Study, 929 Individuals, of Whom 802 Were Husbands and Their Wives
Physical type of husband	. . . .	W, has no, some, or close resemblance to wife's father.	. . . .	. . . .
Physical type of wife	H, resembles husband's mother. (Hamilton)	H, has no or some resemblance to husband's mother.	. . . .	. . . .
Rearing, rural or urban	Country or small town. (Schroeder)	No relationship. (Terman and Oden)	Reared in the country.	No relationship.
Religious home training	. . . .	H, considerable. W, strict and considerable. (Terman) No relationship. (Terman and Oden)	. . . .	. . . .

354

Savings			H, has some.	Some at time of and during marriage.
Sex, desire to be of the opposite sex		W, never desires.		
Sex, frequency of intercourse during marriage	Less than once a day at the beginning of marriage. (Davis)	Ratio of actual frequency to preferred frequency is close to unity. (Terman) (Terman and Oden)		
Sex, intercourse during marriage	Report never committed adultery. Desires no extramarital relations. (Hamilton)	Infrequent refusal. Infrequent desire for extramarital intercourse. (Terman) No relationship. (Terman and Oden)		Rarely refuses mate. Never desires with another. Never has with another. Do not know, believe, or suspect mate. Mate does not know, believe, or suspect me.
Sex instruction	W, some. (Davis) From mother or books. (Schroeder)	H, more than inadequate. (Terman) No relationship. (Terman and Oden)	Adequate knowledge and skill in sexual activity. (nonstatistical conclusion)	

(H, husband; W, wife; if H or W not given, then it is for both)

Items	Studies by Bernard, Davis, Hamilton, Hart, Kelly, Kirkpatrick, Landis and Landis, Schroeder, and Winch	Terman's Study, 792 Couples; Terman and Oden, 567 Couples	Study of Burgess and Cottrell, 526 Individuals	This Study, 929 Individuals, of Whom 802 Were Husbands and Their Wives
Sex, pleasure and satisfaction	Pleasure at the beginning and throughout marriage. (Davis) No complaints about sexual adequacy of mate. (Hamilton)	W, pleasure at first intercourse. H, indifference, or interest and pleasant anticipation. High degree of satisfaction in intercourse. No sexual complaints.	. . . .	H, very enjoyable with wife. W, enjoyable or very enjoyable with husband.
Sex, premarital	W, none. (Davis) (Hamilton)	H, none or only with future spouse. W, none.	. . . .	H, none. Do not believe, know, or suspect mate had. H, wife does not know, believe, or suspect.
Sex, prudishness or modesty	. . . .	Husband does not think of mate as over-modest or prudish.	. . . .	Very little or some modesty and shyness in matters of sex.

Characteristic				
Sex, orgasm	In at least 20 per cent of copulations. (Hamilton)	Adequate capacity for orgasm. (Terman) (Terman and Oden) No relationship to multiple orgasms. (Terman)	·	·
Sex, responses of parents to child's early curiosity	·	Frank and encouraging.	·	·
Sex, sources of information	·	Parents and teachers.	·	·
Sex shock	·	W, none during years 10 to 15. (Terman) No relationship. (Terman and Oden)	·	·
Sex, strength of interest or desire	W, not married to a man with low sex desire. (Hamilton) W, about the same intensity. (Davis)	Equality or near equality.	·	Equality or near equality.
Sleeping arrangement	·	Not in different rooms.	·	·
Sociability	·	Rated by an outsider as sociable. (Terman and Oden)	Sociable personality.	Sociable personality.
Sunday school attendance	Beyond 18 years. (Schroeder)	·	Beyond 18 years.	H, beyond 10 years. W, beyond 14 years.

GENERAL CONCLUSIONS

Science holds as one of its tenets the view that the conclusions of any study must be verified by repetitions of the experiment. This subjection of the conclusions of a study to continued investigation is particularly needed in the social sciences. The following conclusions from the present study, while presented in the form of rather dogmatic statements concerning the relationship between given behavior or situations and marital adjustment, are to be viewed as hypotheses for future research.

1. Marital adjustment ranges along a continuum from very great to very little adjustment. Happiness in marriage, as judged by an outsider, represents adjustment, and divorce represents maladjustment.

2. The alienation process is generally a slow cumulation of conflicts and disagreements, accompanied by the psychological withdrawal of one or both spouses. If the course of the alienation process is far advanced, the spouses tend to express derogatory attitudes toward each other, tend to have many complaints about the mate and the marriage, and tend to exaggerate the deficiencies of the mate and the marriage.

3. The development of binding ties of affection, common interests and activities, similar attitudes and values, along with respect for the individuality of the partner, begins prior to the marriage ceremony and continues afterwards. Consequently, the experiences during the period of courtship and engagement are likely to be potent forces making for or against the success of a marriage. The longer the courtship the greater the probability that the uniting process will be well advanced prior to marriage and will continue after the ceremony.

4. Marital adjustment involves adaptation not only to the mate, but also to the mate's parents. The type of home atmosphere, revealed by such things as the degree of happiness in childhood and the happiness of the marriage of the parents, determines, in part, the *readiness* of a person to make the necessary adjustments to the behavior of others in the marriage

situation. Some emancipation from the parental home prior to, as well as after, marriage increases the chances that one will be able to adjust to the behavior of the mate and of the in-laws.

5. Sexual relations in marriage are to be considered in terms of conflict, or lack of conflict, between the behavior of the individual and cultural values. They are also to be considered as an intimate form of communication. When there is a wide difference between the sexual behavior of a person and the cultural expectations relative to sex, such as the expectation that intercourse will be confined to the marriage relationship, the conflict will be reflected in the relationships between the spouses. Sexual intercourse, when coupled with affection, satisfaction, and enjoyment of the sex act, is one of the most subtle and potent forms of communication between the persons involved, and tends to weld them together.

6. There is no relationship between the presence or absence of children, or the size of the family, and marital adjustment. There is, however, an association between marital adjustment and those personality characteristics which are reflected in a desire for children.

7. Marital adjustment is associated with directorial ability, as measured by the ready acceptance of responsibility, strictness in dealing with children, leadership, the ability to make decisions readily, determination, and not being too easily influenced by others.

8. Marital adjustment is associated with a general personality pattern of adaptability. It can be measured by such traits as yielding in arguments, not being dominating, slowness in getting angry, and quickness in getting over anger.

9. The capacity to give and receive affection, as measured by replies to questions on affectionateness and demonstration of affection, is associated with success in marriage.

10. Sociability, or the tendency to join with others for companionship, is highly associated with marital adjustment. It can be measured by such personality traits—as rated by oneself or by the mate—as sociability, enjoyment of belonging to

organizations, some concern with what people say and think, and a sense of humor. It also can be measured by the number of friends of the husband or wife before marriage, after marriage, and in common during marriage.

It is to be expected that future investigators will construct more adequate measures of directorial ability, adaptability, affectionateness, and sociability than those used in the present study.

11. Conventionality is highly associated with marital adjustment. It can be measured by such things as having the marriage ceremony performed by a minister or priest, attendance at Sunday school up to a certain age, and affiliation with, and attendance at, church.

12. The companionship family, defined as having intimate communication, sympathetic understanding, common interests, mutual respect on the basis of equality, democratic behavior, and shared rather than individualistic behavior, is highly associated with marital adjustment.

13. Certain economic factors, such as economic security and stability, certain values associated with homemaking, appreciation of the efforts of the husband to provide for the needs of the family, appreciation of the work of the wife in homemaking, and other variables related to economic factors, are associated with marital adjustment.

14. The gainful employment of the wife outside the home is not associated with marital adjustment or maladjustment. On the other hand, the approval by the husband of the wife's working is associated with marital adjustment.

15. Bereaved persons and divorced women make as satisfactory an adjustment in subsequent marriages as the adjustment of persons who have been married only once.

RESEARCH PROBLEMS

The contributions of present research demonstrate the feasibility of increasing our knowledge of marital adjustment or maladjustment by designing more refined methods of research and by concentrating on more crucial and significant problems. The following are illustrations of procedures which are necessary if more adequate knowledge is to be attained.[22] Detailed investigations should be made of such general conclusions or hypotheses as those listed above. For example, an association between marital adjustment and the general personality trait of adaptability is one of the conclusions of the present study, of the study of "genius" subjects by Terman,[23] and of the Burgess-Wallin study of engagement and marriage.[24] However, no adequate test of adaptability has been devised, nor is it known under what conditions it operates. Burgess and Wallin report that certain couples with low prediction scores in the engagement period were later found to be well adjusted in marriage. Their explanation was that one or both members of a couple were so adaptable that they were able to meet and successfully solve difficult problems as they developed in the marriage.[25] Such general conclusions should be verified by detailed investigations and carefully designed tests.

Attention should be given to those combinations of personality characteristics of husbands and wives which are associated with marital adjustment. The general practice has been simply to calculate the relationship between marital adjustment and given personality traits of husbands and of wives. An exception was the study by Winch, who found certain combi-

[22] Suggestions for research will be found at the end of each chapter in Ernest W. Burgess and Harvey J. Locke, *The Family*, New York, American Book Co., 1950, particularly pp. 446–49, 477–79. Also, Ernest W. Burgess, "The Family and Sociological Research," *Social Forces*, XXVI, 1947, pp. 1–6; Meyer F. Nimkoff, "Trends in Family Research," *American Journal of Sociology*, LIII, 1948, pp. 477–82. The Social Science Research Council will publish in the near future a research bulletin which seeks to identify the main directions which family research has had in the past, and to suggest what appear to be the important emphases which should characterize research in the immediate future.
[23] Lewis M. Terman and Melita H. Oden, *op. cit.*, p. 246.
[24] Ernest W. Burgess and Paul Wallin, *op. cit.* See chapter on "Adaptability."
[25] Ernest W. Burgess, "The Family in a Changing Society," *American Journal of Sociology*, LIII, 1948, p. 420.

nations of neurotic and nonneurotic personalities to be favorable, and others unfavorable, to marital adjustment.[26]

Studies should be made of *family* success as contrasted with *marital* success. Family interaction includes not only relations between the husband and wife, but between parents and children, brothers and sisters, and sometimes between family members and in-laws. It is assumed that criteria of family integration or disintegration would be different from criteria of marital adjustment. The problem is to devise tests of family success and to discover the predictive items associated with scores on such tests.

Efforts should be made to get the Bureau of the Census to collect more adequate data on marriage and the family, and then such data should be utilized in studies of marital adjustment. For example, Ogburn, even with the inadequate data collected by the Census, found that the ratio of husbands with wives absent or divorced to husbands living with wives was twice as high where husbands had not finished the elementary schools as where they were college graduates.[27]

Studies should be made of the similarities and the differences in marital adjustment and prediction factors in the many economic, ethnic, and racial groups; for different lengths of marriage; in different religious faiths; and in various sections of the country, in subcultures of a city,[28] and in different countries or nations.[29]

26 Robert F. Winch, *The Relationship between the Neurotic Tendency and the Adjustment in Engagement,* unpublished M.A. thesis, University of Chicago. His findings are summarized in Ernest W. Burgess and Harvey J. Locke, *op. cit.,* pp. 465–66.

27 William F. Ogburn, "Education, Income, and Family Unity," *American Journal of Sociology,* LIII, 1948, pp. 474–76.

28 Two studies in process are investigating certain differences in marital adjustment in the subcultures of Los Angeles: James Peterson, *The Relation of Objective and Subjective Factors to Adjustment and Maladjustment in Marriage;* Robert Williamson, *Economic Factors in Marital Adjustment.*

29 Two studies of this nature are in process: Georg Karlsson, *Communication and Adaptability as Related to Marital Adjustment in Swedish Marriages;* and Harvey J. Locke, *Do Marital Adjustment and Prediction Items Found Significant in Previous Studies Differentiate Between Happy and Unhappy Marriages in Sweden?*

Follow-up studies should be made to test the degree to which predictions of marital adjustment are verified. Longitudinal studies, which are carefully planned, adequately financed, and carried on over the life cycles of the subjects, probably would give clues to the causative as well as to the associative factors in marital adjustment.

Cooperative studies in various areas of behavior by teams of social scientists are now in progress at various universities. Such an approach should be directed to problems of marital adjustment. Teams of investigators, composed of persons trained in biology, psychiatry, psychology, anthropology, and sociology, should plan and carry through research in success or failure in marriage. This will be the basis on which much of the research of the future will be organized and integrated.

The development of such research programs and procedures as those outlined above would result in the growth of a body of knowledge on the associative and possibly on the causative factors of marital adjustment. It is to be expected that this will be done in the not too distant future. When it is done, a relatively exact science of predicting marital adjustment will be built on the foundation which has already been established.

MARRIAGE AND DIVORCE QUESTIONNAIRE *

WE ARE TRYING to learn more about factors which make for happy and unhappy marriages. To do this we need the cooperation and assistance of two groups of people: those whose marriage have ended in divorce and those whose marriages are happy.

We are hoping to get 400 divorced persons and 400 nondivorced persons to help us in this study. You can help us a great deal by filling out the following questions as frankly and as carefully as possible.

Experience has shown that some people hesitate to answer personal questions if they have to reveal their identity. Therefore, we do not ask for names. Moreover, all questions can be answered by checks (√), numbers (1905), or letters (YS). This method safeguards your identity.

In some questions information is asked about both you and your mate. Use a circle (O) to indicate the information about yourself and a cross (X) to indicate the information about your mate. If information about both you and your mate is the same, put the (O) and the (X) on the same blank or answer.

Please answer all questions. If you cannot give the exact answer to a question, answer the best you can. If you have had more than one marriage, *give information only on your present marriage.*

---

* The questionnaire for the divorced group was identical with this one which was given to the married, except for the adaptation of language, such as the use of the past tense and the use of "former mate" in place of "mate."

1. Year of birth _____. Male _____. Female _____. White _____. Colored _____.
2. Number of times married _____; number of divorces _____.
   Year of first marriage _____;
      if ending in divorce_____, death _____, what year _____.
   Year of second marriage _____;
      if ending in divorce _____, death _____, what year _____.
   Year of third marriage _____;
      if ending in divorce _____, death _____, what year _____.
   Year of fourth marriage _____;
      if ending in divorce _____, death _____, what year _____.
3. Total number of divorces among your brothers, sisters, parents, aunts, and uncles: _____.
4. Number of your brothers and sisters: _____. Were you the oldest child: yes _____; no _____. Were you the youngest child: yes _____; no _____.
5. Number of brothers and sisters of your mate: _____. Was your mate the oldest child: yes _____; no _____. Was your mate the youngest child: yes _____; no _____.
6. Put an (O) in the blank which indicates your nationality and an (X) to indicate the nationality of your mate:
   American born of American-born parents _____.
   Foreign born of foreign-born parents _____.
   American born of foreign-born parents _____.
7. Put an (O) to indicate the state of your health and an (X) to indicate that of your mate:
   a. *Before marriage:* very sickly _____; sickly _____; average health _____; healthy _____; very healthy _____.
   b. *During marriage:* very sickly _____; sickly _____; average health _____; healthy _____; very healthy _____.
8. Put an (O) after the highest school grade which you completed and an (X) after the highest school grade which your mate completed:
   0 __ 1 __ 2 __ 3 __ 4 __ 5 __ 6 __ 7 __ 8 __;
   Grades
   1 __ 2 __ 3 __ 4 __; 1 __ 2 __ 3 __ 4 __;
   High School   College
   1 __ 2 __ 3 __ 4 __.
   Graduate

9. Put an (O) after the highest grade which your mother completed and an (X) after the highest grade which your father completed:

   0 __ 1 __ 2 __ 3 __ 4 __ 5 __ 6 __ 7 __ 8 __;
   Grades

   1 __ 2 __ 3 __ 4 __; 1 __ 2 __ 3 __ 4 __;
   High School   College

   1 __ 2 __ 3 __ 4 __.
   Graduate

10. Put an (O) to indicate marital status of your parents *at time of your marriage* and an (X) to indicate the marital status of your mate's parents: married (both living) _____; separated _____; divorced _____; both dead _____; one dead _____.

11. If your mother died before your marriage, how long before: years _____; months _____; days _____. If father: years _____; months _____; days _____.

12. Do you feel that in your parental home you: never had your own way about anything _____; usually had your own way _____; had your own way about everything _____.

13. Indicate the amount of conflict and affection which was present between the following persons *before your marriage:*

Degree of Conflict and Affection	Conflict				Affection		
	Father and Mother	You and Father	You and Mother	You and Your Mate	You and Father	You and Mother	You and Your Mate
None							
Very little							
Moderate							
A good deal							
Very great							

14. My childhood on the whole was: very happy _____; happy _____; about averagely happy _____; unhappy _____; very unhappy _____.

15. *Before marriage* was the attitude of your parents toward your

mate one of: approval _____; indifference _____; disapproval _____; did not know him _____.

16. *During the last half of your marriage,* did you and your mate ever live with:

    a. Husband's parents: yes _____; no _____. If so, how long: years _____; months _____; days _____.

    b. Wife's parents: yes _____; no _____. If so, how long: years _____; months _____; days _____.

17. If at any time during marriage you lived with your parents or your mate's parents:

    a. Did you dislike this: very much _____; some _____; did not mind it _____; enjoyed it _____; enjoyed it very much _____.

    Did you reveal this feeling to your mate: yes _____; no _____.

    b. Did your mate dislike this: very much _____; some _____; did not mind it _____; enjoyed it _____; enjoyed it very much _____.

    Did your mate reveal this feeling to you: yes _____; no _____.

18. How far do you and your mate live from husband's parents: miles _____; blocks _____. From wife's parents: miles _____; blocks _____.

19. Put an (O) for your parents and an (X) for your mate's parents to indicate whether you and your mate and the parents lived in the same: neighborhood _____; city or town _____; county _____; state _____; or different states _____.

20. Number of times a year you and your mate see: husband's parents _____; wife's parents _____. Number of times you see: your parents _____; mate sees his parents _____.

21. Put an (O) for yourself and an (X) for your mate to show the number of friends of the *same* sex *before marriage:* almost none _____; a few _____; several _____; many _____.

22. Put an (O) for yourself and an (X) for your mate to show the number of friends of the *opposite* sex *before marriage:* almost none _____; a few _____; several _____; many _____.

23. Check the place where you met mate:

    Home of a friend _____.   At business _____.

    Home of a relative _____.   At school _____.

At church _____.   Dance hall, skating rink, carni-
"Pick-up" _____.   val, or the like _____.
During travel _____.   Other place _____.
Neighborhood _____.

24. The length of time you knew your mate before marriage was:
    Less than 1 month _____.   2 years _____.
    3 months _____.   3 years _____.
    6 months _____.   5 years _____.
    9 months _____.   5 to 10 years _____.
    1 year _____.   Since childhood _____.

25. The length of time between your engagement and your mar-
    riage was:
    Less than 1 month _____.   1 year _____.
    3 months _____.   2 years _____.
    6 months _____.   3 years _____.
    9 months _____.   over 3 years _____.

26. Where married: at home _____; at church _____; by judge
    _____; at minister's home _____; by justice of the peace
    _____; elsewhere _____.

27. Check all the following reasons why you think you married
    your mate:
    Common interests _____.   To escape your own family
    To please parents _____.   _____.
    Love _____.   To take care of children _____.
    Loneliness _____.   Due to intoxication _____.
    Economic security _____.   To be looked up to by friends
    Pregnancy _____.   _____.
    To have a home _____.   To satisfy sex desires _____.
    To have children _____.

28. Underline *the two things* in the above list which you think
    were the most important reasons why you married your mate.

29. Number of children during: your first marriage _____; sec-
    ond marriage _____; third marriage _____; fourth marriage
    _____.

30. Did husband want the child or the children of present mar-
    riage: yes _____; no _____. Did wife want the child or the
    children: yes _____; no _____. If no children, does husband
    want children: yes _____; no _____. Does wife: yes _____;
    no _____.

31. Put an (O) in the blank to show the church to which you belong and put an (X) in the blank to show the church to which your mate belongs:

Nazarene _____.	Assembly of God _____.
Baptist _____.	Trinity Episcopal _____.
Methodist _____.	United Brethren _____.
Presbyterian _____.	Jewish _____.
Lutheran _____.	First Spiritualist _____.
Quaker _____.	Seventh Day Adventist _____.
Christian _____.	Salvation Army _____.
Church of Christ _____.	Catholic _____.
Christian Scientist _____.	Pentecostal _____.
Church of God _____.	Some other church _____.
Evangelical _____.	Do not belong _____.

32. Underline the church to which you belonged *at the time of marriage.*

33. *During the first half of your marriage,* regularity of church attendance:

a. *Of yourself* was: none _____; less than once a month _____; once a month _____; twice _____; three times _____; four times _____; more than four times _____.

b. *Of mate* was: none _____; less than once a month _____; once a month _____; twice _____; three times _____; four times _____; more than four times _____.

34. *During the last half of your marriage,* regularity of church attendance:

a. *Of yourself* was: none _____; less than once a month _____; once a month _____; twice _____; three times _____; four times _____; more than four times _____.

b. *Of mate* was: none _____; less than once a month _____; once a month _____; twice _____; three times _____; four times _____; more than four times _____.

35. Put an (O) to indicate the age at which you stopped going to Sunday school or other religious school and an (X) for your mate: never went _____; 10 years or younger _____; 11–14 years _____; 15–18 years _____; 19–25 years _____; still going at time of marriage _____; went during marriage _____.

36. Indicate the state in which you, your mate, your father, and

your mother were born by placing in the blank opposite the
state a:

       Y for the state in which you were born.
       S for your mate's birthplace.
       F for your father's birthplace.
       M for your mother's birthplace.

A foreign country _____.	Montana _____.
Alabama _____.	Nebraska _____.
Arizona _____.	Nevada _____.
Arkansas _____.	New Hampshire _____.
California _____.	New Jersey _____.
Colorado _____.	New Mexico _____.
Connecticut _____.	New York _____.
Delaware _____.	North Carolina _____.
District of Columbia _____.	North Dakota _____.
Florida _____.	Ohio _____.
Georgia _____.	Oklahoma _____.
Idaho _____.	Oregon _____.
Illinois _____.	Pennsylvania _____.
Indiana _____.	Rhode Island _____.
Iowa _____.	South Carolina _____.
Kansas _____.	South Dakota _____.
Kentucky _____.	Tennessee _____.
Louisiana _____.	Texas _____.
Maine _____.	Utah _____.
Maryland _____.	Vermont _____.
Massachusetts _____.	Virginia _____.
Michigan _____.	Washington _____.
Minnesota _____.	West Virginia _____.
Mississippi _____.	Wisconsin _____.
Missouri _____.	Wyoming _____.

37. Underline all the states in the above list in which you lived
for *six months* or more during your life *up to your marriage.*
38. Put a (√) in front of the states in which you lived for six
months or more *during marriage.*
39. Size of community in which you lived: at time of marriage
_____; at present time _____.
40. Number of towns lived in during marriage: _____; number
of counties _____.

41. *During the first half of your marriage,* did you live for the most part in a place of: 500 population or under _____; 500 to 1,000 population _____; 1,000 to 2,500 population _____; 2,500 population or over _____.

42. *During the last half of your marriage,* did you live for the most part in a place of: 500 population or under _____; 500 to 1,000 population _____; 1,000 to 2,500 population _____; 2,500 population or over _____.

43. Put an (O) for yourself and an (X) for your mate to indicate where childhood and adolescence were mainly spent: place of 2,500 and over _____; 2,500 and under _____; open country _____.

44. How frequently did you see mate during courtship: once a month _____; twice a month _____; once a week _____; twice a week _____; almost every day _____.

45. Total number of different houses in which you have lived during your marriage: _____.

46. Occupation of your father: _____. Mate's father: _____. Your occupation at time of marriage: _____.

47. Your occupations during marriage: _____

_____

48. Put an (O) for *your parents'* and an (X) for *your mate's parents':*
    a. Economic status: comfortable _____; meager _____; poor _____; very wealthy _____; wealthy _____; well-to-do _____.
    b. Social class: upper _____; middle _____; lower _____.

49. If wife worked during marriage, did husband: approve _____; disapprove _____.

50. Number of different jobs (not including housework) held *during marriage:* by wife _____; by husband _____. Number of changes of jobs due to advancement of husband: _____. Number of changes not due to advancement _____.

51. *During the first half of your marriage:*
    a. Who in the family worked outside the home for money: wife _____; husband _____; both _____.
    b. The chief breadwinner was: irregularly employed _____; always employed but continually changing jobs _____;

regularly employed in seasonal work _____; regularly employed the year around _____.

   c. The longest period of employment of the chief breadwinner was: 3 months or less _____; 6 months to 1 year _____; 1 to 2 years _____; over 2 years _____.

   d. Did the chief breadwinner of the family have an extended period of unemployment of: 3 to 6 months _____; 6 months to 1 year _____; 1 to 2 years _____; 2 years _____; over 5 years _____.

52. *During the last half of your marriage:*

   a. Who in the family worked outside the home for money: wife _____; husband _____; both _____.

   b. Has the chief breadwinner of the family been: irregularly employed _____; always employed but continually changing jobs _____; regularly employed in seasonal work _____; regularly employed the year around _____.

   c. The longest period of employment of the chief breadwinner has been: 3 months or less _____; 6 months to 1 year _____; 1 to 2 years _____; 2 years _____; over 5 years _____.

   d. The chief breadwinner of the family has had an extended period of unemployment of: 3 to 6 months _____; 6 months to 1 year _____; 1 to 2 years _____; over 2 years _____.

53. The combined savings of both husband and wife:

   a. At time of marriage was: none _____; $200 or less _____; $200 to $1,000 _____; over $1,000 _____.

   b. At present time is: none _____; $200 or less _____; $200 to $1,000 _____; over $1,000 _____.

54. *During marriage* has either mate carried life insurance: yes _____; no _____. Size of policy $_____. Is insurance carried *at present:* yes _____; no _____. Size of policy $_____.

55. The average income per month *during the first half* of your marriage was: husband $_____; wife $_____. *During the last half:* husband $_____; wife $_____.

56. On the whole do you feel that the total income has met the economic needs of the family: very adequately _____; adequately _____; inadequately _____; very inadequately _____.

57. *During marriage* the average rent *per month* has been: $_____.

   If you own your home, the value of the home is: $_____.

58. Number of times borrowed money during marriage: _____. Amount borrowed: $_____.

59. As far as managing the affairs of the home is concerned do you feel that the wife has been: very satisfactory _____; satisfactory _____; unsatisfactory _____; very unsatisfactory _____.

60. Do you feel that the husband's *efforts* to provide for the economic needs of the family have been: very satisfactory _____; satisfactory _____; unsatisfactory _____; very unsatisfactory _____.

61. *During marriage,* have you:

Owned	Had
home _____.	furnace _____.
car _____.	bathroom _____.
radio _____.	indoor toilet _____.
electric refrigerator _____.	running water _____.
piano _____.	electric lights _____.
electric washer _____.	telephone _____.
victrola _____.	newspaper _____.
furniture _____.	

62. Put an (X) in front of those things in the above list which you bought on payments.

63. Have you ever wished you had not married: frequently _____; occasionally _____; rarely _____; never _____.

64. If you had your life to live over again, do you think you would: marry the same person _____; marry a different person _____; not marry at all _____.

65. Do you and your mate engage in outside interests together: all of them _____; some of them _____; very few of them _____; none of them _____.

66. Put an (O) for yourself and an (X) for your mate to indicate the number of friends *during marriage:*

   a. Of the *same sex:* almost none _____; a few _____; several _____; many _____.

   b. Of the *opposite sex:* almost none _____; a few _____; several _____; many _____.

67. The number of friends you and your mate have in common: almost none_____; a few_____; several_____; many_____.
68. In leisure time husband prefers to be: "on the go" _____; to stay at home _____.
    Wife prefers to be: "on the go"_____; to stay at home_____.
69. During marriage have you, in general, talked things over with your mate: almost never _____; now and then _____; almost always _____; always _____.
70. Do you kiss your mate: every day _____; now and then _____; almost never _____. If so, do you kiss: as a matter of duty _____; or because of real affection _____.
71. In the following chart there is a list of five degrees of happiness in marriage. Please put a check (√) in the column opposite the degree of happiness which you think best characterizes the following marriages:

Degrees of Happiness in Marriage	Parents' Marriage		Present Marriage		Last Former Marriage	
	Your Parents' Marriage	Mate's Parents' Marriage	How You Feel About Your Marriage	Your Mate's Feeling About His Marriage to You	How You Felt About This Marriage	Your Mate's Feeling About This Marriage
Very Happy						
Happy						
Average						
Unhappy						
Very Unhappy						

72. Put an (O) to show your feeling and an (X) to show the feeling of your mate toward the following *during your marriage.* Place an (O) and an (X) opposite every item:

Activities	Enjoy Very Much	Enjoy	In- different	Tolerate It in Mate	Open Conflict
Reading					
Playing Cards					
Gambling					
Drinking					
Dancing					
Movies					
Parties					
Church					
Listening to Radio					
Music					
Politics					
Sports					

73. In the following chart there is a list of activities in which the husband or wife may take the lead, that is, one is more dominant than the other. We want information on three married couples: you and your mate; your mother and father; and your mate's mother and father. Indicate in the proper space whether the husband or the wife tends to take the lead. If in a given activity both the husband and wife are about equal, put a check (√) for both:

Activities	Your Marriage		Your Parents' Marriage		Mate's Parents' Marriage	
	Wife Takes Lead	Husband Takes Lead	Mother Takes Lead	Father Takes Lead	Mate's Mother Takes Lead	Mate's Father Takes Lead
Making family decisions						
Disciplining children						
Handling family money						
Affectionate behavior						
Religious behavior						
Recreation behavior						
Meeting people						

74. Do you think that your intelligence as compared to that of your mate is: more _____; less _____; equal _____.

75. Do you feel that in comparison to your mate you are: superior _____; inferior _____; equal _____.

76. Please answer the following questions as truthfully as you can for yourself *at the present time.* They represent our way of becoming acquainted with you. In front of each question you will find: Yes No ? Cross out the correct answer for each question. Try to answer by *Yes* or *No* if it is possible. If you are entirely unable to give even a tentative *Yes* or *No,* cross out the question mark.

   Yes No ? Do you feel lonesome even when you are with other people?

   Yes No ? Are you usually even-tempered and happy in your outlook on life?

Yes No ? Do you often feel just miserable?

Yes No ? Does some particularly useless thought keep coming into your mind to bother you?

Yes No ? Are you usually in good spirits?

Yes No ? Do you often experience periods of loneliness?

Yes No ? Are you in general self-confident about your abilities?

77. Give approximate degree of your feelings *during periods of difficulty* between you and your mate:

Feelings	Very	Somewhat	A little	Not at all
Lonely				
Miserable				
Irritated				
Angry				
Insecure				
Worried				
Hurt				
Inferior				
Self-confident				
Critical of mate				

78. Check any of the following things which you think have caused *serious* difficulties in your marriage:

1. Mate's attempt to control my spending money _____.

2. Other difficulties over money _____.

3. Religious differences
_____.

4. Different amusement interests _____.
5. Lack of mutual friends _____.
6. Constant bickering _____.
7. Interference of in-laws _____.
8. Lack of mutual affection (no longer in love) _____.
9. Unsatisfying sex relations _____.
10. Selfishness and lack of cooperation _____.
11. Adultery _____.

12. Desire to have children _____.
13. Sterility of husband _____.
14. Sterility of wife _____.
15. Venereal disease _____.
16. Mate paid attention (became familiar with) to another person _____.
17. Desertion _____.
18. Nonsupport _____.
19. Drunkenness _____.
20. Gambling _____.
21. Ill health_____.
22. Mate sent to jail _____.
23. Cruelty to step-children _____.
24. Other reasons _____.

79. Underline *the two things* in the above list which you think have caused the greatest conflict in your marriage.

80. What things annoy and dissatisfy you most about your marriage: _____
_____
_____.

81. What things does your mate do that you don't like: _____
_____
_____

82. What things in your marriage satisfy you most: _____
_____
_____.

83. State approximate extent of agreement or disagreement between you and your mate on the following items. The examples should be considered as *only one of many topics* which come under each point.
Please place a check opposite every item:

Check One Column For Each Item Below	Always Agree	Almost Always Agree	Occasionally Disagree	Frequently Disagree	Almost Always Disagree	Always Disagree
1. Handling family finances (Example: Instalment buying)						
2. Matters of recreation (Going to dances)						
3. Religious matters (Different religious beliefs)						
4. Demonstrations of affection (Frequency of kissing)						
5. Friends (Dislike of mate's friends)						
6. Intimate relations (Sex relations)						
7. Do you get on each other's nerves around the house?						
8. Ways of dealing with in-laws						
9. The amount of time that should be spent together						
10. Table manners						
11. Conventionality (Right, good, or proper conduct)						
12. Aims, goals, and things believed to be important in life						

84. When disagreements have arisen, they usually have resulted in: husband giving in _____; wife giving in _____; agreement by mutual give and take _____; neither giving in _____.

85. *During your present marriage* how many times have you left your mate because of conflict: _____. How many times has your mate left you: _____. How long was the longest time of such a separation: years _____; months _____; days _____.

86. Do you feel that your mate is overly jealous about your talking, dancing, or other kinds of association with those of the opposite sex: yes _____; no _____.
    Do you resent this: yes _____; no _____.

87. Have either you or your mate talked over with a third party (minister, lawyer, friend, in-laws, etc.) the difficulties arising in your marriage: yes _____; no _____.

88. Have you ever wanted a divorce: yes _____; no _____. Thought about a divorce: yes _____; no _____. Talked over with your mate the advisability of a divorce: yes _____; no _____. Has your mate ever wanted a divorce: yes _____; no _____.

89. Have you ever filed suit for divorce: yes _____; no _____. Has your mate: yes _____; no _____.

90. Do you seriously think that your marriage will *probably* end in divorce: yes _____; no _____. If so, how long from now: years _____; months _____.

91. Do you think that there is a *possibility* that your marriage will end in divorce: yes _____; no _____.

The following questions are on sexual intimacies. It is generally agreed that personal sex relations are very important in adjustment or maladjustment in marriage. We are hoping that, inasmuch as your identity will remain unknown, you will have no hesitation in answering these questions. However, if you do have any hesitation in answering any one of them honestly and accurately, please leave the space blank.

92. Do you feel that your mate is over-modest and shy in attitudes toward sex: very much _____; a good deal _____; some _____; very little _____; not at all _____.

93. Have birth control methods been used: yes _____; no _____.

94. Does fear of having children make sex intercourse less enjoyable: yes _____; no _____.

95. Does your mate believe _____, know _____, suspect _____ that you had sex intercourse with others *before marriage:*

yes _____; no _____. Did you tell your mate: yes _____; no _____.

96. Do you believe _____, know _____, suspect _____ that your mate had sex intercourse with others before marriage: yes _____; no _____. Did your mate tell you: yes _____; no _____.

97. *Before marriage,* with how many persons did you have sex intercourse: none _____; one _____; a few _____; many _____.

98. Did you have sex intercourse with your mate *before marriage:* yes _____; no _____.

99. Do you believe _____, know _____, suspect _____ that your mate has had sexual intercourse with some other person *during your marriage:* yes _____; no _____. Did your mate tell you: yes _____; no _____.

100. Does your mate believe _____, know _____, suspect _____ that you have had sex intercourse with some other person *during your marriage:* yes _____; no _____. Did you tell your mate: yes _____; no _____.

101. *During marriage,* have you desired sex intercourse with someone other than your mate: very frequently _____; frequently _____; sometimes _____; rarely _____; never _____.

102. *During marriage,* with how many persons other than your mate have you had sex intercourse: none _____; one _____; a few _____; many _____.

103. What is the degree of your sex satisfaction with your mate: very enjoyable _____; enjoyable _____; tolerated _____; disgusting _____; very disgusting _____.

104. What do you think is the degree of sex satisfaction which your mate has with you: very enjoyable _____; enjoyable _____; tolerated _____; disgusting _____; very disgusting _____.

105. Have you ever refused sex intercourse when your mate desired it: frequently _____; sometimes _____; rarely _____; never _____.

106. Has the average number of times of intercourse per month from the time of marriage until the present: increased greatly _____; increased _____; remained the same _____; decreased some _____; decreased greatly _____; ceased entirely _____.

107. Do you feel that the strength of your sex interest, as compared with that of your mate, is: very much greater _____; much greater _____; about the same _____; much less intense _____; very much less _____.

108. Compare on the scale which follows the personality traits of your parents, your mate and yourself, marking *F* for father, *M* for mother, *S* for your mate, and *Y* for yourself. If two or more have the same degree of a trait, place the letters *F, M, S,* or *Y* in the same blank:

Traits	Ratings on Traits				
	Has the trait markedly	Has the trait considerably	Has the trait somewhat	Has the trait a little	Hasn't the trait at all
Able to make decisions readily					
Assumes responsibility readily					
Is a leader in the community					
Dominating, presses his opinions and ideas on others					
Sociable, makes friends easily					
Determined					
Strict with children					
Affectionate					
Demonstrative, "makes over" people he thinks a lot of					
"Gives in" in arguments					

Traits	Has the trait markedly	Has the trait considerably	Has the trait somewhat	Has the trait a little	Hasn't the trait at all
Has sense of humor					
Gets angry easily					
Gets over anger quickly					
Cares what people say and think					
Likes belonging to organizations					
Easily influenced by others					

APPENDIX 2

PERSONALITY TRAITS OF PARENTS

THE DIFFERENTIAL RATINGS given fathers and mothers on personality traits by happily married and divorced men and women are outlined below. The data are analyzed in terms of chi squares and critical ratios. Chi squares, given in the footnotes, indicate whether or not the ratings of the happily-married and divorced for a given personality trait have significantly different distributions in the five categories—markedly, considerably, somewhat, a little, and not at all. Critical ratios indicate whether or not the happily-married and divorced differ significantly in per cents for any given category. A plus sign is used to denote that the happily-married had the larger per cent, and a minus to show that the per cent was larger for the divorced. As in other parts of the book, only critical ratios of 2.0 or more are included, which gives only 5 chances or less in 100 that the difference could have been due to chance.

The 16 personality traits are given below in the order in which they were presented at the beginning of Chapter 9. First, differences will be presented for the personality traits of fathers as rated by happily married and divorced men and by happily married and divorced women:

1. *Assumes responsibility readily.*
    Women: markedly, +2.1; considerably, —2.3.
2. *Easily influenced by others.*[1]
    Men: somewhat *and* a little, +2.4; markedly *and* considererably, —2.3.
    Women: markedly, +2.2; somewhat, a little *and* not at all, —2.1.

[1] Chi square for men: 8.1, 3 degrees of freedom.

384

3. *Gets angry easily.*[2]
   Men: somewhat *and* a little, +2.8; not at all, −2.4.
   Women: considerably *and* somewhat, +2.4.
4. *Gives in in arguments.*
   Men: not at all, −2.3.
   Women: markedly *and* considerably, −2.3.
5. *Is a leader in the community.*[3]
   Men: not at all, −2.0.
   Women: markedly, +2.4; not at all, −2.4.
6. *Has sense of humor.*
   Men: markedly *and* considerably, +2.3.
7. *Dominating.*
   Men: considerably, +2.3.
8. *Affectionate.* No differences.
9. *Gets over anger quickly.* No differences.
10. *Sociable.*[4]
    Women: considerably, −2.5.
11. *Able to make decisions readily.*[5]
    Women: markedly, +3.3; a little *and* not at all, −3.2.
12. *Strict with children.* No differences.
13. *Likes belonging to organizations.* No differences.
14. *Cares what people say and think.*
    Men: somewhat, +2.0; markedly *and* considerably, −2.0.
    Women: somewhat *and* a little, +2.5; markedly *and* considerably, −2.1.
15. *Demonstrative.*
    Men: somewhat, +2.3; not at all, −2.1; a little *and* not at all, −2.4.
16. *Determined.*[6]
    Men: markedly *and* considerably, +2.7.

The following are the differences between happily-married and divorced ratings of mother:

1. *Assumes responsibility readily.* No differences.

[2] Chi square for men: 9.7.
[3] Chi square for women: 11.3.
[4] Chi square for women: 8.0, 3 degrees of freedom.
[5] Chi square for women: 12.7.
[6] Chi square for men: 8.8, 3 degrees of freedom.

2. *Easily influenced by others.*[7]
      Men: a little, +3.2; not at all, −2.5.
3. *Gets angry easily.*[8]
      Men: somewhat, +2.3; somewhat *and* a little, +3.0; not at
      all, −2.7.
4. *Gives in in arguments.* No differences.
5. *Is a leader in the community.*[9]
      Women: Somewhat, +3.0; not at all, −3.7.
6. *Has sense of humor.*
      Men: a little *and* not at all, −2.0.
7. *Dominating.* No differences.
8. *Affectionate.* No differences.
9. *Gets over anger quickly.*
      Men: somewhat *and* a little, +2.1.
      Women: somewhat, +2.1; not at all, −2.9.
10. *Sociable.*
      Men: somewhat, +2.2; somewhat, a little, *and* not at all,
      +2.3; considerably, −2.1.
11. *Able to make decisions readily.*
      Men: a little *and* not at all, −2.3.
12. *Strict with children.*
      Men: not at all, −2.7.
13. *Likes belonging to organizations.*
      Men: somewhat *and* a little, +2.4.
14. *Cares what people say and think.*
      Men: markedly *and* considerably, −2.3.
      Women: markedly *and* considerably, −2.0; a little, +2.6; a
      little *and* somewhat, +2.5.
15. *Demonstrative.*[10]
      Men: markedly, considerably, *and* somewhat, +2.4; a little,
      −2.5.
16. *Determined.* No differences.

It is apparent from the above that the divorced, much more
frequently than the married, rated their fathers and mothers as

[7] Chi square for men: 14.2.
[8] Chi square for men: 12.9.
[9] Chi square for women: 16.7.
[10] Chi square for men: 10.2.

not possessing a given personality trait at all, or rated them in the two top categories. Thus, it would appear that, on the whole, it is favorable to marital adjustment if, on personality traits, a person rates his father and mother in the middle category of "somewhat," rather than on either extreme.

APPENDIX 3

RESEARCH INVESTIGATIONS (IN THE CHRONOLOGICAL
ORDER OF COLLECTING THE SAMPLES)

Author and Publication	Time When Sample Collected	Area of Study	Size of Sample	Criteria of Marital Adjustment
Katherine B. Davis, *Factors in the Sex Life of Twenty-two Hundred Women*, 1929.	1920–1921.	Various parts of the United States.	1,000 married women: 872 happy, 116 unhappy.	Answers to the question: "Is your married life a happy one? If not, why?"
Hornell Hart and Wilmer Shields, "Happiness in Relation to Age at Marriage," *Journal of Social Hygiene*, XII, 1926, pp. 403–407.	1924.	Philadelphia.	500 marriage-license applications, and 500 cases from the Court of Domestic Relations.	Marriage-license cases considered adjusted; cases from the Court of Domestic Relations considered maladjusted.
Gilbert V. Hamilton, *A Research in Marriage*, 1929.	1924–1926.	New York City.	100 men and 100 women, including 55 couples.	Score on a marital-satisfaction test, composed of 13 questions on satisfaction in marriage.

Reference	Date	Location	Sample	Measure
Jessie Bernard, "The Distribution of Success in Marriage," *American Journal of Sociology*, XXXIX, 1933, pp. 194–203. Also, "Factors in the Distribution of Success in Marriage," *Ibid.*, XL, 1934, pp. 49–60.	1931–1932.	St. Louis, Los Angeles, Seattle.	115 married men, and 137 married women.	Score on a true-false test of 100 terms or traits of a successful marriage.
Ernest W. Burgess and Leonard S. Cottrell, *Predicting Success or Failure in Marriage*, 1939.	1931–1933.	Chicago and vicinity.	526 individual marriages; 317 husbands, 153 wives, 30 couples, 15 assisted by an interviewer, and 11 unknown.	Score on a marital-adjustment test composed of 26 questions.
Lewis M. Terman *et al.*, *Psychological Factors in Marital Happiness*, 1938.	Dec. 1934–May 1935.	Three-fourths in and around Los Angeles, remainder in San Francisco.	792 couples.	Scores on a marital-happiness test composed of 9 general questions.[a]
Clifford Kirkpatrick, "Factors in Marital Adjustment," *American Journal of Sociology*, XLIII, 1937, pp. 270–83. Also, "A Methodological Analysis of Feminism in Relation to Marital Adjustment," *American Sociological Review*, IV, 1939, pp. 325–34.	1935–1936.	Minnesota and vicinity.	104 well adjusted and 70 poorly adjusted couples: relatives and friends of students.	Rated by students as "well" and "poorly" adjusted.

Author and Publication	Time When Sample Collected	Area of Study	Size of Sample	Criteria of Marital Adjustment
Clifford Kirkpatrick, "Community of Interest and the Measurement of Marital Adjustment," *The Family*, XVIII, 1937, pp. 133–37.	1935–1936.	Minnesota and vicinity.	284 individuals of whom 105 were couples; 58 well-adjusted and 47 poorly-adjusted; relatives and friends of students.	Rated by students as "well" and "poorly" adjusted.
Clarence W. Schroeder, *Divorce in a City of 100,000 Population*, 1939. Chapter 6.	1934–1938.	Peoria, Illinois.	410 divorced and 406 married. Of the 816 individuals, 473 were women.	"Divorced" for maladjusted; "married" for adjusted.
Edith Webb Williams, *Factors Associated with Adjustment in Rural Marriages*, Cornell University Library, 1938.	1938.	Rural New York and vicinity.	200 couples.	Score on the Burgess-Cottrell marital-adjustment test.
E. Lowell Kelly, "Concerning the Validity of Terman's Weights for Predicting Marital Happiness," *Psychological Bulletin*, XXXVI, 1939, pp. 202–203. Also, "Marital Compatibility as Related to Personality Traits of Husbands and Wives as Rated by Self and Spouse," *Journal of Social Psychology*, XIII, 1941, pp. 193–98.	1938–1939.	Connecticut.	82 couples from 300 engaged couples interviewed prior to marriage.	Score on the Terman marital-happiness test.

Robert F. Winch, "Personality Characteristics of Engaged and Married Couples," *American Journal of Sociology*, XLVI, 1941, pp. 686–97.	1940.	Chicago and vicinity.	The Burgess-Wallin sample of 1,000 engaged couples.	Score on the Burgess-Wallin engagement-adjustment test.
Judson T. Landis, "Length of Time Required to Achieve Adjustment in Marriage," *American Sociological Review*, XI, 1946, pp. 666–77.	About 1944.	Michigan and vicinity.	409 couples b who were parents and friends of college students.	Self-ratings on a fivefold happiness scale: very happy, happy, average, unhappy, and very unhappy; only 0.8 per cent in lowest two categories.
Lewis M. Terman and Melita H. Oden, *The Gifted Child Grows Up: Twenty-five Years' Follow up of a Superior Group*, 1947, chap. 19. Also, Lewis M. Terman, "Prediction Data: Predicting Marriage Failure from Test Scores," *Marriage and Family Living*, XII, 1950, pp. 51–54.	1940–1945 and 1940–1948.	California.	643 "genius" subjects and their spouses.	Score on a marital-happiness test composed of 15 questions; similar to Terman's original marital-happiness test.
Harvey J. Locke and William J. Klausner, "Marital Adjustment of Divorced Persons in Subsequent Marriages," *Sociology and Social Research*, XXXIII, 1948, pp. 97–101.	1939–1944 and 1947–1948.	Monroe County, Indiana, and Southern California.	Indiana: 146 persons divorced and married again; 17 happily-married with a prior divorce; 344 happily married persons married only once. California: 47 divorced and married again; 64 married-only-once.	Score on the Burgess-Cottrell marital-adjustment test.

Author and Publication	Time When Sample Collected	Area of Study	Size of Sample	Criteria of Marital Adjustment
Harvey J. Locke and Muriel Mackeprang, "Marital Adjustment and the Employed Wife," *American Journal of Sociology*, LIV, 1949, pp. 536–38.	1939–1944 and 1948–1949.	Monroe County, Indiana, and Los Angeles.	Indiana: 154 happily married couples—44, both worked; 110, wife did not work. 102 divorced couples—34 both worked; 68 wife did not work. California: 41 employed wives and their husbands; 51 home-making wives and their husbands.	Score on the Burgess-Cottrell marital-adjustment test. Also, score on the Burgess-Cottrell-Terman-Locke marital-adjustment test.
Ernest W. Burgess and Paul Wallin, "Predicting Adjustment in Marriage from Adjustment in Engagement," *American Journal of Sociology*, XLIX, 1944, pp. 324–30. Also, *Engagement and Marriage*, to be published in 1951.	1940–1944 and 1940–1950.	Chicago and vicinity.	1,000 engaged couples, nearly 700 of whom constituted the married sample.	Score on an engagement-adjustment test, and score on a test similar to the Burgess-Cottrell marital-adjustment test.

a Some of the questions were composed of subparts, but the parts were scored as a unit.

b Judson T. Landis and Mary G. Landis, *Building a Successful Marriage*, New York, Prentice-Hall, 1948, give additional data on this sample of 409 couples: see tables 9, 11, and 20; figures 32, 33, 49–52, 54, 55, 58, 63, and 65. For a study of 544 younger married couples, see tables 11, 18, and 21; figures 22, 56, 57, 59–61, 64 and 104.

INDEX

INDEX

ability to make decisions readily, 184-86, 227
acquaintance, length of premarital, 89-90, 105
  and marital adjustment, 88-91, 342
activities, enjoyment of, 255-62, 267, 342
  indifference about, 259-60
adaptability, 192-204, 342
  of bereaved who remarry, 300
  a problem for research, 361
adjustment in engagement, 315-16
adjustment in marriage
  and adaptability, 192-204, 226-28
  constructing test of, 45-52
  continuum of, 42-45, 358
  definition of, 45
  in different cultures, 362
  and economic factors, 268-97, 360
  and findings of different studies, 340-57
  follow-up studies of, 363
  independent criteria of, 339-40
  and longitudinal studies, 311-17
  mean scores of, 52-54
  measuring, 42-66, 68-71
  method of assigning weights, 46-47
  modification of test of, 61-65
  of persons with high and low scores compared, 38-39
  predicting, 312-17, 319-37

and sex behavior, 125-57, 359; see also sex
  test of, 45-52, 67, 389, 390, 391, 392
  validity of criteria, 52-57
  see also specific items
affection
  conflict over, 75-76
  definition of, 206
  toward mate before marriage, 97, 105, 343
  for parents before marriage, 109, 338
affiliation with a church, 239-40, 244
age
  difference of, 103-04, 105, 343
  equality of and marital adjustment, 103-04, 105
  optimum, for adjustment in marriage, 102, 105
  of subjects, 29
  at the time of marriage, 100-03, 343
  variables, 100-04
agreements and disagreements in marriage, 67-71
  as an index of adjustments, 85
alienation, typical process of marital, 71-73, 358
Amsterdam, 161
amusement, conflict over, 76, 79, 338
anger, 82-83, 199-204, 227, 385, 386

attachment
    between parents, 111-14
    parent-child, 107-11
    to parents before marriage, 108-
        10, 343
    to siblings, 343

babies, learn origin of, 343
Bernard, J., 14, 160, 269, 342-57,
    389
birth
    American or foreign, 338
    date of subject's, 31
    order of, 109, 352
birth place of subjects, 32-33, 338
birth control, use of, 142-43, 156,
    344
borrowing on credit, 280
Brink, T., van den, 161
Bureau of Census, 362
    occupational classification of,
        271
Burgess, E. W., 1, 3, 9-11, 13-14, 17,
    30, 31, 33, 34, 45, 47, 53, 55,
    56, 57-58, 59, 61, 71, 87, 89, 91,
    96, 100, 103, 108, 109, 112, 130,
    160, 167, 172, 173-74, 186, 205,
    229-30, 237, 245, 250, 252, 269,
    270, 290, 292-93, 299, 306, 307,
    312, 315-17, 339, 340, 342-57,
    361, 389, 390, 391, 392

Cahen, A., 164
California, 60, 391
car, ownership of, 278-79
cards, shared or individual enjoy-
    ment of, 256-58
caring what people say and think,
    217-21, 227
case studies, see life-history docu-
    ment
Census, Bureau of, 362
    occupational classification of,
        271
Chicago, 389, 391, 392

child, only, oldest, youngest, 109
childhood, happiness of, 107-08,
    123
childlessness, 162-63, 164, 170
children
    desire for, 167-69, 170, 344
    desire for and marital difficul-
        ties, 75, 76-77, 79
    and frequency of divorce, 159,
        161-65
    and marital adjustment, 158-70,
        359
    number of, 338
    presence of, 338, 344
    as a reason for marriage, 98-100
    reports of, on marital adjust-
        ment of parents, 60
    strictness with, 179-81, 227, 385,
        386
    who takes the lead in disciplin-
        ing, 262-66, 267
church
    affiliation with, 239-40, 244
    attendance at, 237, 240-43, 244,
        345
    married at, 237, 238, 244
    membership in, 345
    shared or individual enjoyment
        of, 256-58
common friends, 234-36, 244
communication
    decline of, and loss of unity, 247-
        48
    intimacy of, 246-53, 266
comparison
    of findings of different studies,
        342-57
    of marital adjustment of remar-
        ried divorced men and women,
        308
    of self- and mate-ratings on per-
        sonality traits, 225-26
companionship family, 245-67
    components of, 245
    definition of, 245
    and marital adjustment, 360
    weights assigned to items, 332-34

complaints
about one's marriage, 73-74
see also derogatory attitude
conclusions, general, 358-60
generality of, 40
and problems for research, 310-63
of other studies on economic factors, 269-70
of other studies on sex, 125-32
summary of, 310-63
conflict
over activities, 67-70, 260-62, 345
over affectional relationships, 75-76
on basic interests and activities, 67-70
over desire for children, 75, 76-77, 79
over disapproved behavior, 75, 77-78
over drunkenness, 75, 77-78
over economic questions, 75, 77
with father, 345
an index of maladjustment, 85
over individualistic behavior, 75-76, 78-79
over in-laws, 76, 79
lack of, on amusements, 76, 79
lack of, on religion, 76, 79
in marriage, 67-85
with mate before marriage, 345
with mother, 345
parent-child, 107-11
between parents, 111-14, 338
with parents before marriage, 108-10, 123
premarital with spouse, 96-97, 105
over sex, 75-76
over sterility, 75, 76-77
times left because of, 84
typical process of marital, 71-73
Connecticut, 390
contingency correlations of marital adjustment items, 62-65

continuum
of marital adjustment, 42-45, 54-55, 56-57, 66, 358
on personality traits, 172, 195, 202
control
community, over occupation, 269-70
social, over certain activities, 256-57
conventionality, 236-43, 244
agreement and disagreement on, 68-70
and marital adjustment, 221
belonging to organizations, 217
related to sociability, 237
cooperative research, 363
Cottrell, L. S., 3, 9-11, 13-14, 30, 31, 33, 34, 45, 47, 53, 55, 56, 57-58, 59, 61, 87, 89, 91, 96, 100, 103, 108, 109, 112, 130, 160, 167, 172, 173-74, 229-30, 237, 250, 252, 269, 270, 290, 292-93, 299, 306, 307, 312, 339, 340, 342-57, 389, 390, 391, 392
Court of Domestic Relations, 388
courtship
and engagement, 86-105
frequency of seeing mate during, 338
length of, 346
and marital adjustment, 86-105, 358
credit, as indicated by borrowing, 280
criteria
happily-married and divorced, 339-40
independent, of adjustment and prediction, 339-40
of marital adjustment, 45, 311, 358
validity of, 52-57
cross-sectional studies, 38

dancing, shared or individual enjoyment of, 256-58

Davis, K. B., 125-26, 342-57, 388
decisions
    ability to make readily, 184-86,
        227, 385, 386
    who took the lead in making
        family, 262-67
democratic and individualistic be-
    havior, 262-67
demonstration of affection, 209-12,
    227, 385, 386
derogatory attitude
    of divorced, 38-39, 65, 169, 175,
        179, 181, 191-92, 199, 214-15,
        224, 225-26, 227, 277, 281, 284,
        288, 289
    as an index of the degree of alien-
        ation, 358
desire for children, 167-69, 170
determination, 186-89, 227, 385,
    386
directorial ability, 175-92, 204-05
disagreements, 67-85
    as an index of maladjustment,
        85
discipline in parental home, 110-
    11, 123, 346
disciplining children, 262-66, 267
disorganization of family
    and decline of intimacy of com-
        munication, 246, 247-48
    and individualism, 258
divorced
    and dispersion after separation,
        34
    and distribution in city and
        county, 16-17
    and mean marital-adjustment
        score, 52-54
    method of securing names of,
        15
    mobility during marriage of, 34-
        35, 36
    nationality of, 30
    and reasons for not securing
        some mates, 22
    and remarriage of mates, 36
    see also specific items

drinking, shared or individual en-
    joyment of, 256-58
drunkenness, 75, 77-78

economic factors, 31-32, 286-97, 360
    conclusions of other studies on,
        269-70
    conflict over, 75, 77
    efforts of husband to provide,
        346
    weights assigned to, 335-37
economic
    level, 274-83, 346
    security, and economic level, 274-
        83, 297
    security, as a reason for marriage,
        98-99
    stability, 279
education
    and marital adjustment, 346,
        362
    of parents, 30, 338
    of subjects, 29-30
efficiency of home management,
    282-83, 297
electric lights in home, 277-78
Ellis, A., 311
employment
    comparison of men and women
        on regularity of, 284
    length of, 347
    longest period of, 285
    of husband, 283-88, 296-97, 347
    of wife, 270, 288-97, 347
    of wife, and marital adjustment,
        289-95, 339, 360
engagement
    adjustment in, and predicting
        broken engagement, 315-16
    adjustment in, and predicting
        marital adjustment, 315-17
    adjustment test, 391
    length of, 91-96, 105, 347
    and marital adjustment, 86-105,
        358
engaging in outside interests to-
    gether, 252-53, 266

equality
  of feelings toward mate, 254-55, 266, 347
  in taking the lead, 262-64, 267
escape own family, as a reason for marriage, 98-99
extramarital intercourse, 148-55, 156
  frequency of, 149-50, 156
  spouse's judgment on, 150-53, 156, 157

face-to-face communication, 249
family background, 347
family, the companionship, 245-67
family disorganization, 246-48, 258
family
  size of, 165-66, 170
  things owned by, 278-80, 297
family success as a problem for research, 362
fathers, ratings on personality traits of, 384-85
fear of pregnancy and sex enjoyment, 143-44, 156
feminism, 389
findings of different studies, 340-57
forced marriages
  age at time of, 101
  length of, 27
  length of engagement in, 92
  number of, 23-24
frequency of attendance at church, 240-44
frequency of kissing, 249-50, 266
friends
  agreement and disagreement on, in marriage, 68-70
  after marriage, 232-34, 244, 348-49
  before marriage, 230-32, 243, 348-49
  in common during marriage, 234-36, 244, 349
  making easily, as a personality trait, 212-15, 227, 385, 386
Freud, S., 106

furniture, ownership of, 278-79
furnace in home, 278

gambling, 256-58
general personality patterns, 229-44
  weights assigned to items, 330-32
Guilford, J. P., 46

Hamilton, G. V., 126-28, 159-60, 342-57, 388
handling money, 262-66, 267
happily-married
  and mean marital-adjustment score, 52-54
  and method of securing names, 15
  and mobility during marriage, 34-35, 36
  nationality of, 30
  and prediction items, 317-37
  and questionnaire used in the study, 364-83
  and reasons for marriage, 97-100
  see also specific items
happiness
  of childhood, 107-08, 123, 349
  marital test of, 312-14
  of parents' marriage, 112-13, 123, 349
Harriman, P. L., 172
Hart, H., 342-57, 388
Harter, A., 57, 60
Hill, R., 107, 160
home
  activities in, 256, 267
  efficiency of management of, 282-83, 297, 349
  married at, 238, 244
  ownership of, 274-75, 278-79, 297
  as a reason for marriage, 98-100
homosexuality, 349
humor, sense of, 221-24, 227, 385, 386
husband
  attitude of, toward wife working, 295-96, 297

husband (*continued*)
  efforts of, to provide, 285-87, 297
  employment of, 283-95, 297

ideal mate, conception of, 171
Illinois, 390
income, 349
  adequacy of, 280-82, 297
Indiana, 15, 29, 30, 32, 34-35, 41, 273, 391, 392
indifference about activities, 259-60
individualistic activities, 257-58
  conflict over, 75-76, 78-79
  and democratic behavior, 262-66, 267
  or shared enjoyment of activities, 255-62, 267
indoor toilet in home, 278
inferiority, feelings of, 254-55
influenced, easily, 189-92, 227, 384, 386
in-laws
  agreement and disagreement on, 68-70
  attitude toward living with, 119-24, 350
  conflict over, 76, 79
  frequency of living with, 119-20, 124, 350
  and marital adjustment, 358-59
  relationship with, 114-23
insecurity during marital difficulties, 82-83
insurance, life, 275-76, 297
intelligence, 255, 266
intercourse
  extramarital, 148-55, 156-57
  in marriage, 139-48, 155
  premarital with spouse, 133-34, 137, 156, 338
  refusal of, and degree of sex interest, 146-48, 156
  reported frequency of an understatement, 133-35, 155
interest in sex, 141-42, 156

interests
  common, as a reason for marriage, 98-100
  conflict on, in marriage, 67-70
  engaging in outside interests together, 252-53, 266
interviews, 18-21
  by different persons, 37
  of husband and wife separately, 19
  problem of standardizing, 18, 21
  on sex items, 132
  setting of, 19-21
intimacy of communication, 246-53, 266
investigations, 388-92
Iowa, 107

Jacobson, P., 161-65
jealousy, 153-55, 157, 350
justice of the peace, married by, 237, 238, 244

Karlsson, G., 362
Kelly, E. L., 254, 315, 317, 342-57, 390
Kentucky, 32-33
Kinsey, A. C., 13, 129
Keyserling, Count H., 67
Kirkpatrick, C., 230, 269, 340, 342-57, 389, 390
kissing, frequency of, 249-50, 266
Klausmer, W. J., 301, 305-08, 391

Landis, J. T., 128, 160-61, 342-57, 391, 392
Landis, M. G., 128, 160-61, 342-57, 392
Landis, P. H., 245
Lang, R., 269-70
leadership
  characteristic of, 184
  comparison of spouses' reports on, 265-66
  equality in, 262-64, 267
  personality trait of, 181-84, 227, 385, 386

less-adjusted
  definition of, 174
  of happily-married and divorced,
    171-72, 173-74
life-history document
  the problem of securing coopera-
    tion, 19-21
  recording, 18
  see also specific topics
life insurance, 275-76, 297
limitations
  of this study, 35-41
  of study of adjustment of di-
    vorced in subsequent mar-
    riages, 306
  of study of marital adjustment
    of employed wives, 291, 293-
    94
Locke, H. J., 71, 245, 290-95, 301,
    305-08, 361, 362-63, 391, 392
loneliness
  as a reason for marriage, 98, 99
  during marital difficulties, 82-83
longitudinal studies of marital ad-
    justment, 311-17
longitudinal study, not using it a
    limitation, 38
Los Angeles, 290, 292, 305, 389
loss of unity through decline in
    communication, 247-48
love as a reason for marriage, 98-99

Mackeprang, M., 289-95, 392
making friends easily, 212-15, 227
maladjustment, disagreement and
    conflicts an index of, 85
map of distribution of happily-
    married and divorced, 16
marital-aptitude test, 312-14
marital-happiness test, 312-14, 389,
    390, 391
marital-prediction items, 317-37
marital-satisfaction test, 388
marital status of parents, 338, 351
marriage, adjustment in, see ad-
    justment in marriage

marriage
  agreement on year of, 26-27
  broken, 312-15
  complaints about, 73-74
  date and length of, 25-29
  disagreements and conflicts in,
    67-85, 319-22
  general patterns of reasons for,
    98-99, 350
  happiness of remarried-divorced,
    302-03
  items to be used in a new test of
    adjustment of, 61-65
  length of prior, 24
  number of forced, 23-24
  place of, 238-44, 351
  predicting permanence of, 312-
    15
  unbroken, 312-15
married
  at home, 238, 244
  by whom, 351
married-more-than-once
  age of at time of first marriage,
    101
  length of engagement of, 92-93
  length of present marriage, 27
  length of previous marriage, 24
  size of sample, 24
married-only-once
  age at time of marriage, 101-02
  length of marriage, 27-28
  marital adjustment of, 299-300,
    309
Martin, C. E., 13, 129
mate-ratings on
  affection, 208-09
  being easily influenced, 190-91
  caring what people say and
    think, 218-19
  demonstration of affection, 209-
    12
  determination, 187-88
  dominating, 196-97
  giving in in arguments, 194-95
  leadership, 181-83

mate-ratings on (*continued*)
  liking to belong to organizations, 215-17
  making decisions readily, 184-85
  making friends easily, 212-15
  responsibility, 176-77
  sense of humor, 221-24
  speed of getting angry, 199-202
  speed of getting over anger, 203-04
  strictness with children, 179-81
measurement of adjustment in marriage, 42-66
meeting people, 262-66
meeting place, first, 351
mental ability, 351
method of weighting, 317-18
Michigan, 391
minister
  married by, 237, 244
  married at home of, 238, 244
Minnesota, 389, 390
mobility, 338
  of divorced, 34, 36
  and occupation, 269, 270
  of subjects during marriage, 34-35
money
  agreement and disagreement on, 68-70
  handling of, 262-66, 267
more-adjusted
  definition of, 174
  of happily-married and divorced, 171-72, 173-74
mother of husband
  attractiveness as rated by husband, 351
  ratings on personality traits of, 385-86
movies, shared or individual enjoyment of, 256-58
music, shared or individual enjoyment of, 256-58
mutual enjoyment of activities, 256-57, 267

nationality of subjects, 30
Netherlands, 161
newspaper taken by family, 277-78, 297
New York State, 390
New York City, 388
Nimkoff, M. F., 159, 361

objectives of family, agreement and disagreement on, 68-70
occupation
  of father, 271, 296-97, 338
  and marital adjustment, 352
  of men at marriage, 271
  of men during marriage, 272-73
  type of, 270-74
  of women at marriage, 272, 296-97
  of women during marriage, 273-74, 297
Oden, M. H., 58, 205, 230, 312-15, 342-57, 361, 391
Ogburn, W. F., 362
oldest child, 109
only child, 109
order of birth, 109, 338
organizations
  enjoyment in belonging to, 215-17, 227
  membership in, 351
ownership of home, 274-75, 297

parental influences
  on marital adjustment, 106-24, 358-59
  weights assigned to items, 324-25
parent-child attachments and conflicts, 107-11
parents
  approval or disapproval of spouse by, 118-19, 124, 352
  attachment or conflict between, 111-14
  living with, 119-20, 124
  happiness of marriage of, 112-13, 123

personality traits of, 226, 384-87
premarital attachment to, 108-10
premarital conflict with, 108-10,
123
see also in-laws
parties, shared or individual enjoyment of, 256-58
patterns, general, of personality,
229-44
Peoria, 390
personality
characteristics, combinations of,
as a problem for research, 361-
62
general patterns of, 229-44
patterns and marital adjustment,
359-60
personality traits, 353
ability to make decisions readily,
184-86, 227
affection, 207-09, 227
being easily influenced, 189-92,
227
caring what people say and
think, 217-21, 227
definition of, 172
demonstration of affection, 209-
12, 227
determination, 186-89, 227
dominating, 196-99, 227
giving in in arguments, 192-96,
227
of leadership, 181-84, 227
liking to belong to organizations,
215-17, 227
list of, 173
making friends easily, 212-15, 227
sense of humor, 221-24, 227
speed of getting over anger, 202-
04, 227
speed of getting angry, 199-202,
227
and marital adjustment, 359-60
of more- and less-adjusted, 171-
74
of parents, 226, 384-87

weights assigned to items, 327-30
Peterson, J., 362
petting, 353
Philadelphia, 388
physical type
of husband, 354
of wife, 354
piano, ownership of, 278-79
place of marriage, 238-44
politics, shared or individual enjoyment of, 256-58
Pomeroy, B., 13, 129
predicting
later marital adjustment from
earlier tests, 312-17
marital adjustment from adjustment in engagement, 315-17
prediction
independent criteria of marital,
339-40
of permanence of marriage, 312-
15
prediction items
findings of different studies, 340-
57
list of significant, 319-37
for marital adjustment, 317-37
prediction score, 319
pregnancy, fear of, 348
premarital
frequency of intercourse, 132-33,
156
intercourse with spouse, 133-34,
137, 156
judgment on, of spouse, 137-39,
155, 156
reported an understatement,
133-35, 155
variations of, by year of birth,
135-37, 155
presence of children, 162-65, 170
promiscuity, 231-32
propinquity of residence to that of
parents and in-laws, 122-23,
338
psychoanalysts, 106

Quensel, C., 162, 165
questionnaire
    construction of, 17-18
    items on marital-adjustment, 48-
        52
    items on marital-prediction, 319-
        37
    pretest of, 18
    used in the study, 364-83

radio
    ownership of, 278-79
    shared or individual enjoyment
        of, 256-58
ratings
    of personality traits of parents,
        384-87
    see also mate-ratings
reading, shared or individual en-
    joyment of, 256-58
recreation
    agreement and disagreement on,
        68-70
    who takes the lead in, 262-66, 267
refrigerator, ownership of, 278-79,
    297
refusals
    to cooperate, 22
    number of, 35-36
    reasons for, 36
refusing intercourse, 146-48, 156
regularity of employment
    comparison of reports of men
        and women, 284
    of husband, 283-85, 297
religion
    affiliation of subjects, 30-31
    agreement and disagreement on,
        68-70
    lack of conflict over, 76, 79
    and marital adjustment, 221, 338
    who takes the lead, 262-66, 267
    training in, 236-37, 354
religious practices, 237-43, 244
remarried, 299-303, 305-09
rent, 274-75, 297
representativeness of sample, 13-17

factors decreasing, 35-37
    on occupations, 273-74
research, 388-92
    cooperative, 363
    problems of, 360-63
residence
    distribution, of happily-married
        and divorced, 16-17
    and economic level, 274
    place of, 32-35
    propinquity to that of parents
        and in-laws, 122-23
responsibility, assuming readily,
    176-79, 227, 384, 385
role playing, 249, 284
running water in home, 277-78
rural-urban background, 354
    differences in proportion of
        childlessness, 164-65
    and marital adjustment, 338
    of subjects, 33, 338

sample
    cases secured by assistants, 37
    cases secured by author, 37
    composition of, 21-25, 40
    factors decreasing representative-
        ness of, 35-37
    method of securing names, 15-
        16, 36-37
    nature of, 13-41
    representative, 13-17, 29-32, 40
    size of, 21-25
    social characteristics of, 29-32
    and the use of volunteers, 13-14,
        17
San Francisco, 389
savings, 276-77, 297, 355
scholastic-aptitude tests, 314
Schroeder, C. W., 342-57, 390
scores
    comparison of marital adjust-
        ment of spouses, 57-60
    marital adjustment, for different
        sizes of families, 166
    mean of marital adjustment, 52-
        54

prediction, 319
Seattle, 389
security, economic, 274-83, 296-97
    as a reason for marriage, 98-99
self- and mate-ratings, comparison
    of, 225-26
self-ratings on
    affection, 207-08
    being easily influenced, 189-92
    caring what people say and
        think, 217-18
    demonstration of affection, 209-
        10, 212
    determination, 187-88
    dominating, 196
    friends after marriage, 232-34
    friends before marriage, 230-32
    giving in in arguments, 193-94
    leadership, 181-83
    liking to belong to organizations,
        215-16
    making decisions readily, 184-85
    making friends easily, 213-14
    responsibility, 176-77
    sense of humor, 222-23
    speed of getting over anger, 202-
        03
    speed of getting angry, 199-201
    strictness with children, 179-80
sense of humor, personality trait,
    221-24, 227
sex
    adjustment, test of, 312-14
    agreement and disagreement on,
        68-70
    conflict over, 75-76
    degree of interest, and frequency
        of refusing intercourse, 147-
        48, 156
    desire to be of the opposite, 355
    findings of different studies on,
        125-32
    instruction, 355, 357
    interviews on, 132
    and marital adjustment, 359
    in marriage, 139-48, 155, 355
    orgasm, 357

pleasure and satisfaction, 144-
    46, 155-56, 356
satisfaction of, as a reason for
    marriage, 98-100
shock, 357
spouse over-modest toward, 139-
    41, 155, 356
strength of interest or desire, 357
weights assigned to items, 325-
    27
shared or individual enjoyment of
    activities, 255-62, 267
Shields, W., 388
significant prediction items, 319-
    37
size of family, 161-65, 170
    and frequency of divorce, 161-63
    matched for years married, 165-
        66, 170
    unmatched for years married,
        165
social characteristics of sample, 29-
    32
Social Science Research Council,
    361
speed of getting angry, 199-202, 227
sports, shared or individual enjoy-
    ment of, 256-58
stability, economic, 279
sterility, conflict over, 75-77
St. Louis, 389
strictness with children, 179-81,
    227, 385, 386
studies, 340-57
    research, 388-92
subsequent marriages, adjustment
    in, 298-309
Sunday school attendance, 237, 239,
    244, 357
superiority, feelings of, 254-55
Sweden, 161, 165, 362
sympathetic understanding, 248-
    49

table manners, agreement and dis-
    agreement on, 68-70

talking things over together, 250-52, 266

telephone in home, 277-78, 297

Terman, L. M., 1-2, 13-14, 30, 31, 39, 47, 56, 57, 58, 61, 87, 89, 91, 100, 103, 107, 109, 110-11, 112, 130-31, 135, 136, 160, 205, 230, 236-37, 269, 292-93, 311, 312-15, 317, 339-41, 342-57, 361, 389, 390, 391, 392

test

  adjustment in engagement, 391

  marital-adjustment, 389, 390, 391, 392

  marital-adjustment, of present study, 47-52

  marital-aptitude, 312-14

  marital-happiness, 312-14, 389, 390, 391

  marital-satisfaction, 388

  method of assigning weights, 46-47

  modification of marital-adjustment, 61-65

  most differentiating items in marital-adjustment, 62-65

  sex-adjustment, 312-14

  scholastic-aptitude, 314

  true-false, of marital-adjustment, 389

Thompson, W. S., 37

time spent together, agreement and disagreement on, 68-70

toleration of activities, 258-59

traits, *see* personality traits

true-false test of marital adjustment, 389

utilities and other home necessities, 277-78

validity of marital-adjustment criteria, 52-57

values

  on adequacy of income of husband, 281

  of church attendance, 242

  clash of, in marriages ending in divorce, 66

  of conventionality, 242-43

  on democratic behavior, 266

  difference in, of divorced husbands and wives, 55-56

  on modern conveniences, 278

  on ownership of things for family, 279

  revealed in self- and mate-ratings on personality traits, 225-26

  on savings, 276-77

  on sociability, 234-35

  of women on engaging in outside interests together, 252-53

  of women in talking things over with husbands, 251

victrola, ownership of, 278-79

Wallace, K. M., 61

Wallin, P., 58, 172, 186, 205, 311, 312, 315-17, 361, 391, 392

Warren, H. C., 172

washing machine, ownership of, 278-79, 297

water, running, in home, 277-78

weights assigned to items on children, 327

  companionship family, 332-34

  courtship and engagement, 322-24

  disagreement and conflicts, 319-22

  economic factors, 335-37

  marital adjustment, 48-52

  parental influences and marital adjustment, 324-25

  personality traits, 327-30

  prediction, 319-37

  sex, 325-27

weights, methods of assigning, 46-47, 317-18

Whelpton, P. K., 37

wives

  employment of, 288-97

  employment of, comparison of

reports of men and women, 289
employment of, and marital-adjustment scores, 289-95
extent of employment of, 288-89
marital adjustment of nonworking, 289-95
husbands' attitude toward working, 295-97

Williams, E. W., 390
Williamson, R., 362
Winch, R. F., 342-57, 362, 391
worries during marital difficulties, 82-83

youngest child, 109

Zanten, J. H. van, 161-62